Teacher Key

See page 331 for Teacher Supplement.

Grammar and Composition I

FOURTH EDITION

James A. Chapman

A Teacher Edition of this text as well as a Tests/Quizzes book and Teacher Key are available. *Grammar and Composition I* is correlated with the English 7 Curriculum, which features a complete course of study in grammar, composition, literature, vocabulary, spelling, and poetry.

Grammar and Composition I

Fourth Edition

Staff Credits
Edition Editors: Heather Fulfer, Jean Spitsbergen, Brian Ashbaugh
Contributors: John DeKonty, Darrell Holley
Designer: Michelle Johnson
Layout Assistants: Heather Coop, Tyson Long, E. J. Burgos
Illustrator: Brian Jekel

A Beka Book, a Christian textbook ministry of Pensacola Christian College, is designed to meet the need for Christian textbooks and teaching aids. The purpose of this publishing ministry is to help Christian schools reach children and young people for the Lord and train them in the Christian way of life.

Acknowledgments

Sample from *Readers' Guide to Periodical Literature,* June 1998, Volume 98, no. 4, page 34, "Barter—Barbara's choice." Copyright ©1998 by the H. W. Wilson Company. Material reproduced with permission of the publisher.

Photos: Adobe/Eyewire: 153; Corel Corporation: cover, 39, 61, 79, 130, 143, 151, 222 except shuttle, 237; Corbis/Digital stock: 3, 11, 16, 19, 20, 43, 47, 83, 92, 105, 107, 112, 121, 127, 164, 175 (w/NASA & JPL), 194, 222 space shuttle, 235, 236, 272, 273, 274, 276, 277.

Cataloging Data
Chapman, James A.
Grammar and composition I / James A. Chapman—4th edition.
vi, 330p. : col. ill.; 28 cm.
Includes index.
I. English language—Grammar—1950. II. English language—Composition and exercises. III. A Beka Book, Inc.
Library of Congress: PE1112.C45 1999
Dewey System: 425

Table of Contents

Grammar Units

5 Nouns & Their Uses 80

6 Pronouns & Their Uses 106

7 Adjectives & Their Uses 122

8 Adverbs & Their Uses 152

9 Prepositions, Conjunctions, & Interjections 174

Composition* *Units*

*See also exercises in colored type throughout the book.

Part 1

Grammar

Grammar

Using Capitalization Rule 1

1 **Capitalize *proper nouns* and words formed from proper nouns.**

a. Capitalize names of *particular persons:* James Buchanan, J. P. Morgan, Dr. R. A. Torrey, Clarence Day, Jr.

b. Capitalize names of *particular places:*
- Continents—Africa, Australia, South America
- Countries—Chile, France, Zimbabwe, Korea
- Sections of the country—the South, the West, the Northeast (Do not capitalize these words when they refer only to a direction: west from Jacksonville, south of town, flying southeast.)
- States—Louisiana, South Carolina, Oklahoma, Maine
- Cities—Montgomery, Gettysburg, Lisbon, Lima
- Islands—Kodiak Island, Isle Royale, Isle of Man, Easter Island
- Bodies of water—Arabian Sea, Hudson River, Lake of the Woods
- Streets and highways—Lancaster Street, Camden Boulevard, Thurmond Avenue, Twenty-first Street (The second part of a hyphenated number is not capitalized.)
- Mountains—Mount Whitney, Ozark Mountains, Mount Rushmore
- Parks—Waterton Lakes National Park, Yosemite National Park, Granada Park

c. Capitalize names of *particular things:*
- Special organizations—Organization of American States, National Science Foundation, Boy Scouts of America, Congress
- Calendar items and special events—Veterans Day, Independence Day, National Cherry Festival, Dixie National Livestock Show, Friday, June (Do not capitalize the seasons: spring, summer, fall, winter.)
- Historical events and periods—Korean War, World War II, Battle of Waterloo, Age of Pericles, Hellenistic Age, Age of Exploration
- Nationalities, races, and religions—Native American(Indian), Welshman, Protestant, Baptist, Presbyterian
- Languages and particular courses—English, French, Portuguese, Greek, Speech 101, Typing II, Economics 302 (The number after the subject indicates that it is a particular course.)
- Brand names of business products—Oldsmobile sedan, Armour sausage, General Electric radio (Do not capitalize the common noun after the brand name.)
- Monuments, bridges, planets, documents, and any other particular things—Jefferson Memorial, Natural Bridges National Monument, Triborough Bridge, Saturn, Constitution of the United States, Hoover Dam, Bankhead Tunnel

d. Capitalize words referring to the *Deity* and *Holy Scripture:* Lord, Jehovah, Jesus Christ, the Old Testament, Galatians, His will (Do not capitalize the word *god* when referring to pagan deities.)

e. Capitalize words *formed from proper nouns:*
- Proper adjectives—Chinese, Italian, Alexandrian, Brazilian

  Note: Sometimes proper names and words formed from proper names lose their orginal meanings through frequent usage and are not capitalized: frankfurter, pasteurize, macadamia nut.
- Abbreviations of proper nouns—**AMA** (American Medical Association), **FTC** (Federal Trade Commission), **NRA**(National Rifle Association)

f. Capitalize a common noun or adjective only when it is a *part of a proper name:* Georgetown High School, Statue of Freedom, Holley Avenue; but a high school, a statue, an avenue.

Note: The phrase *Sunday school* is not a proper noun. Sunday is capitalized because it is a day of the week, but school is not capitalized.

UNIT 1

Exercise A Circle each letter that should be capitalized. (Rules 1a and 1b)

Example: Yesterday dr. fred osborne completed his tour of japan.

1. Yes, linda lived in barcelona, spain, on the shores of the mediterranean sea.
2. The nation of israel crossed the red sea on dry ground.
3. While in california, we stopped at the redwood national park.
4. Our outing will be held at the lakeview amusement park on thirty-ninth street.
5. The country of romania is southwest of russia and north of the balkan peninsula.
6. The north carolina Museum of Art has one of the finest art collections in the south.
7. The diomede islands lie in the bering strait between alaska and siberia.
8. When visiting dublin, ireland, you will want to see the monuments on o'connell street.
9. At the Geneva Conference, france granted independence to cambodia and laos.

Exercise B Four of the following sentences are correct. (1) Put *C* for each correct sentence. (2) For the other sentences circle each letter that should be capitalized. (Rule 1c)

_______ 1. We recently purchased a hewlett-packard computer.

_______ 2. My two favorite holidays are thanksgiving and christmas.

___C___ 3. In history class, we are studying the Battle of the Alamo.

_______ 4. The internal revenue service is an agency of the United States department of the treasury.

___C___ 5. The George Washington Bridge joins Fort Lee with New York City.

_______ 6. Glacier Bay National monument in Alaska can be reached only by airplane or boat.

_______ 7. The blue ridge parkway affords 469 miles of scenic beauty.

_______ 8. The New Jersey symphony orchestra performs in symphony hall.

___C___ 9. The Museum of the Confederacy in Richmond was the home of Jefferson Davis during the Civil War.

_______10. Last summer, we visited the chalmette national park near New Orleans.

_______11. The monroe doctrine is a document that prohibits any further European colonization on the American continents.

_______12. Jim knows how to say "hello" in french, spanish, and german.

_______13. President Lincoln issued the emancipation proclamation on january 1, 1863.

___C___14. Is that a Panasonic radio, or is it a Motorola?

_______15. Frank is a baptist and John is a methodist, but they are both christians.

Exercise C

Rewrite each of the following sentences, using capital letters correctly. (Rule 1d)

1. How may prophecies about christ are there in isaiah? How many prophecies about Christ are there in Isaiah?
2. O lord my god, in thee do I put my trust. O Lord my God, in Thee do I put my trust.
3. The everlasting god, the lord, the creator of the ends of the earth, fainteth not, neither is weary. The everlasting God, the Lord, the Creator of the ends of the earth, fainteth not, neither is weary.
4. The first book in the old testament is genesis; the first one in the new testament is matthew. The first book in the Old Testament is Genesis; the first one in the New Testament is Matthew.
5. Blessed is the nation whose god is the lord. Blessed is the nation whose God is the Lord.
6. Among the gods there is none like unto thee, O lord. Among the gods there is none like unto Thee, O Lord.
7. The lord god formed man of the dust of the ground. The Lord God formed man of the dust of the ground.
8. John the Baptist said, "Behold, the lamb of god." John the Baptist said, "Behold, the Lamb of God."
9. The book of obadiah in the bible contains only one chapter. The book of Obadiah in the Bible contains only one chapter.
10. Yea, lord, I believe that thou art the christ, the son of god. Yea, Lord, I believe that Thou art the Christ, the Son of God.

Exercise D

Cross out each incorrect small letter. Write a capital above it. (Rule 1e)

Example: I have eaten ~~c~~[C]hinese food as well as ~~i~~[I]talian food.

1. The ~~fbi~~[FBI] is an important crime-fighting organization.
2. The ~~n~~[N]orth ~~a~~[A]merican porcupine has quills that are barbed like fishhooks.
3. A spiny fish called the stickleback lives in ~~a~~[A]merican and ~~c~~[C]anadian waters.
4. Two labor unions, the ~~afl~~[AFL] and the ~~cio~~[CIO], merged in 1955.
5. The maned wolf of the ~~s~~[S]outh ~~a~~[A]merican plains has long, stiltlike legs.
6. Did you know that ~~a~~[A]ustralian sugar cane is in high demand because of its good quality?
7. The ~~ncaa~~[NCAA] establishes athletic standards and playing rules for its member schools.
8. The ~~a~~[A]ssyrian religion was closely related to the ~~s~~[S]umerian and ~~b~~[B]abylonian religions.
9. President Reagan supported the ~~sdi~~[SDI], a system of defending against ballistic missile attack.
10. Some ~~a~~[A]frican and ~~a~~[A]sian antelope have straight horns, four feet long.

Exercise E

Following are twenty-five expressions, each given in two versions. Suppose that each expression appeared within a sentence. Choose the expression that is correctly capitalized and write its letter *(A or B)* in the space at the left. In some cases neither version is correct. For these write *N* (for neither) in its space.

		A	B
B	1.	moved out west	moved out West
B	2.	on Cross street	on Cross Street
B	3.	the Golden age of Greece	the Golden Age of Greece
A	4.	a Bic pen	a Bic Pen
N	5.	on Twenty-Third Street	on Twenty-Third street
A	6.	a Christian school	a Christian School
B	7.	the planet jupiter	the planet Jupiter
A	8.	the Battle of Adrianople	the battle of Adrianople
A	9.	Grandfather Mountain	Grandfather mountain
N	10.	Neptune, God of the sea	neptune, god of the sea
N	11.	Death Valley national monument	Death Valley National monument
A	12.	a lesson in algebra	a lesson in Algebra
B	13.	a Baptist Church	a Baptist church
B	14.	Greenfield park	Greenfield Park
B	15.	fort Abercrombie	Fort Abercrombie
A	16.	math, English, History 101	Math, English, History 101
A	17.	Hudson's Bay Company	Hudson's Bay company
B	18.	a Southwest breeze	a southwest breeze
N	19.	Geography, Astronomy I, and botany	geography, Astronomy I, and Botany
A	20.	Kitt Peak National Observatory	Kitt Peak National observatory
B	21.	the Strawberry festival	the Strawberry Festival
A	22.	the John Day Highway	the John Day highway
B	23.	National Society For Medical Research	National Society for Medical Research
N	24.	Battle Of Tours	Battle of tours
A	25.	Wilson's bacon	Wilson's Bacon

Exercise F

Draw a line through each incorrect small letter. Write a capital above it.

C W N S
1. The civil war left deep wounds and hostilities between the north and the south.

N A A
2. Some historians suggest that the native americans migrated from asia.

W W U S M C P
3. During world war II, the united states marine corps did much of the fighting in the pacific.

S A P W
4. The spartans and the athenians fought during the peloponnesian war.

E S A
5. In 1588, the english fleet defeated the spanish armada.

W C
6. Mother received a westinghouse iron for christmas.

T M A
7. The holiday will be on the tuesday following the first monday in august.

B P E G
8. My older brother bill is taking biology, physics 401, english, and german.

A F S F
9. We saw alex cruising down fifty-second street in a ford convertible.

M M D
10. A new methodist church is being constructed on maple drive.

A P P B M
11. The athenians and the plataeans defeated the persians at the battle of marathon.

N P S D I
12. The national park service is a bureau of the department of the interior.

L G H
13. The lord god will wipe away the tears of his saints.

NRAO U S
14. The nrao is an observatory used by scientists in the united states.

M R B N D G D
15. The missouri river flows past bismarck, north dakota, to the site of garrison dam.

Exercise G

Write sentences using the following: (1) a country, (2) a section of the country, (3) a city, (4) an island, (5) a mountain, (6) a special organization, (7) a calendar item, (8) a brand name, (9) a word referring to the Deity, (10) a proper adjective.

1. Answers will vary. ______________________________
2. ______________________________
3. ______________________________
4. ______________________________
5. ______________________________
6. ______________________________
7. ______________________________
8. ______________________________
9. ______________________________
10. ______________________________

Using Capitalization Rules 2–6

2 Capitalize *titles of persons.*

a. **Capitalize titles when they are used *before a person's name,* as part of the name.**

President Roosevelt, Secretary of State Thomas Jefferson, Governor Henry, Mayor Holmes, King David, Captain Bligh, Dr. R. D. Byrd, Mrs. Jones

b. **Titles *following a name or used alone in place of a name* are not usually capitalized unless used in direct address.**

Thomas Jefferson, secretary of state; Patrick Henry, the governor of Virginia; Frank Holmes, the mayor; David, the king of Israel; the senator; the congressman; the pastor; the archbishop of Canterbury; "Good morning, Governor, Senator, Congressman, etc."

Exception: *President* is usually capitalized when it refers to the President of the United States of America.

Theodore Roosevelt, President of the United States; the President of the United States

c. **Capitalize *family-relationship words* when they are used *before a person's name* and when used *alone in place of the name.***

We visited Uncle Gene and Aunt Mary in Dallas, Texas.
What shall we buy Mother for Christmas?
Her father died at the age of ninety-two.
Several cousins have come to visit.
Yes, Dad, we will be glad to help.

Note: Do not capitalize these words when they are preceded by a possessive unless the title is considered part of the name.

my Uncle Raymond, my Aunt Irene (*Uncle* and *Aunt* are considered part of the name.)
my cousin Betty, his brother Bill (*Cousin* and *brother* are not part of the name.)

3 Capitalize the *titles of works.*

Capitalize the first and last words and all important words in the titles of *books, magazines, newspapers, poems, stories, plays,* and *works of art.* (Unimportant words are coordinating conjunctions, prepositions, and the articles *a, an,* and *the.*)

Far from the Madding Crowd (book)
"The Reaper and the Flowers" (poem)
Charioteer of Delphi (sculpture)

Exception: The article *the* is not capitalized before the title of a magazine or a newspaper when the title is written within a sentence.

the *Indianapolis Star* (newspaper)

4 Capitalize the *first word of every sentence* (including quoted sentences).

The steps of a good man are ordered by the Lord.
Plato once said, "No one has ever died an atheist."

5 Capitalize the pronoun *I* and the interjection *O.*

(The more common interjection *oh* is capitalized only when it stands at the beginning of a sentence. *Oh* is followed by a comma or an exclamation point, but *O* is never followed by punctuation.)

Do not I hate them, O Lord, that hate Thee?

6 Capitalize the *first word in every line of poetry,* whether or not the word begins a sentence.

With a slow and noiseless footstep
  Comes that messenger divine,
Takes the vacant chair beside me,
  Lays her gentle hand in mine.
—*Longfellow*

Using Capitalization Rules 2–6

Exercise A **Four of the following sentences are correct. (1) Write *C* before the number of each correct sentence. (2) For the other sentences underline each title that should be capitalized.** **(Rules 2a,b)**

_____ 1. When Cuban forces invaded the island of Grenada, president Reagan sent American troops to help defeat them.

__C__ 2. The attorney general is head of the Department of Justice.

__C__ 3. Jody is the secretary of our Sunday school class.

_____ 4. One of the most courageous pioneer women was mrs. Daniel Boone.

_____ 5. In the year that king Uzziah died, Isaiah saw a vision of God's glory.

__C__ 6. The Mayo Clinic was begun in 1889 by Dr. William Mayo and his two sons.

_____ 7. The "Big Three" during World War II were president Franklin D. Roosevelt, prime minister Winston Churchill, and general Joseph Stalin.

__C__ 8. Douglas MacArthur was one of America's greatest generals.

_____ 9. Well, mr. Green says that dr. Wimpole is the best doctor in town.

_____ 10. John Adams was the first president to live in the White House.

Exercise B **Draw a line through each incorrect small letter. Write a capital above it. Some of the sentences are correct.** **(Rule 2c)**

C 1. Her cousin Marge was a nurse during the Korean War.

2. Elaine's (U) uncle Herbert, who owns Skyline Bakery, taught her how to make lime pie.

3. Today, (G) grandfather Hodges said he will bequeath his gold watch to his grandson Chad.

4. My mother and my (A) aunt Eunice attended a family reunion in Savannah, Georgia.

5. Fred received a long letter from (A) aunt Emily.

6. We left (U) uncle Ned and (F) father to finish examining the old battleship.

7. Will you take us to the San Diego Zoo, (D) dad?

C 8. My father told me, "Always remember, that only what is done for Christ will last."

9. How many nephews and nieces does (U) uncle Phil have?

C 10. My brother Joel is the youngest of four brothers.

Exercise C Rewrite the following sentences, correcting all capitalization errors. (Rule 3)

UNIT 1

1. Some businessmen read the *wall street journal* during their lunch hour. Some businessmen read the Wall Street Journal during their lunch hour.
2. Edward Everett Hale's "the man without a country" is a touching story. Edward Everett Hale's "The Man without a Country" is a touching story.
3. The people in the painting *american gothic* by Grant Wood reminded Mary Ellen of her grandparents. The people in the painting American Gothic by Grant Wood reminded Mary Ellen of her grandparents.
4. Miss Moore's recitation of "the highwayman" was excellent. Miss Moore's recitation of "The Highwayman" was excellent.
5. The book *robinson crusoe* was written by Englishman Daniel Defoe. The book Robinson Crusoe was written by Englishman Daniel Defoe.
6. Thomas Gray took nine years to complete his famous poem "elegy written in a country churchyard." Thomas Gray took nine years to complete his famous poem "Elegy Written in a Country Churchyard."
7. Many high school students enjoy reading the magazine *car and driver.* Many high school students enjoy reading the magazine Car and Driver.
8. Poe's tale "the pit and the pendulum" is an eerie story of the Inquisition. Poe's tale "The Pit and the Pendulum" is an eerie story of the Inquisition.

Exercise D Draw a line under each word that should begin with a capital letter. (Rules 4, 5, 6)

1. thou art worthy, o Lord, to receive glory and honor and power.
2. angie said, "did you know that God considers rebellion to be as bad as witchcraft?"
3. the Lord is on my side; i will not fear. what can man do unto me?
4. psalm 51:10 says "create in me a clean heart, o God."
5. 'tis education forms the common mind:
just as the twig is bent the tree's inclined.
—*Alexander Pope*

Exercise A

This exercise covers all the capitalization rules you have studied. Draw a line through each incorrect small letter. Write a capital above it.

W B M
1. Cheyenne, wyoming, is northwest from biloxi, mississippi.

H S B
2. Charles haddon spurgeon was one of the best british preachers of all time.

B I S
3. The balearic islands lie off the eastern coast of spain.

J F K C P A E D S
4. The john f. kennedy center for the performing arts was designed by edward durel stone.

J P W DC
5. Thomas jefferson was the first president inaugurated in washington, d.c.

M B C C
6. Yes, mother gave me her old copy of *betty crocker's cookbook.*

G A A
7. The great awakening helped prepare the american colonists for independence.

C G N P K
8. The cumberland gap national park in kentucky is a beautiful place to spend a vacation.

E S B T S N Y C
9. The empire state building is on thirty-fourth street in new york city.

NASA
10. nasa directs all space shuttle missions for the United States.

M S J H T D
11. For many years, mrs. sarah j. hall worked to have thanksgiving day made a national celebration.

L A T
12. More than one million copies of the *los angeles times* are sold every day.

T O
13. The heavens shall praise thy wonders, o Lord.

D E J
14. In 1796, dr. edward jenner introduced a vaccine to prevent smallpox.

Exercise B

Write sentences illustrating the following capitalization rules.

Rule 2a. Answers will vary. ____________________

____

Rule 2b. ____________________

____

Rule 2c. ____________________

____

Rule 3. ____________________

____

Rule 5. ____________________

____

Exercise C Circle each letter that should be capitalized.

UNIT 1

1. We expect uncle tom and aunt alice to arrive tomorrow.
2. We studied about the elizabethan age in english literature.
3. Dad bought a new philco refrigerator for mom.
4. Michael burton, jr., and some friends are going to camp at greenwood state park beginning june 14.
5. Many native americans live in the state of arizona.
6. Did your brother david graduate from montrose high school?
7. The magna carta was signed by king john at runnymede, england.
8. The varnum family always goes to new england in the autumn.
9. I broke my davis tennis racket while we were up north at camp.
10. In thee, o lord, do i put my trust.

Exercise D Draw a line through each incorrect small letter. Write a capital above it.

F B F
1. Last night, father read us the story of brother francis, a traveling preacher in
M A
the middle ages.

AM F I O G M L G
2. The hymn "a mighty fortress is our god" was written by martin luther, a german reformer.

J C C A T
3. Believers in jesus christ were first called christians at antioch, a city in turkey.

NASA C C
4. The nasa space center at cape canaveral is frequently visited by foreign dignitaries.

B B P P B
5. John bunyan, a baptist preacher, wrote *pilgrim's progress* while he was in bedford jail.

E J W I
6. The early english reformer john wycliffe said, "i believe that in the end the truth will conquer."

C T A F E
7. We read in the *chicago tribune* that ambassador frank is touring many european countries.

O
8. One of my sister's favorite quotations is "oh, what a tangled web we weave when first we practice to deceive!"

DAR L P I D
9. The d.a.r. placed a wreath in lafayette park on independence day.

W W G D M A R
10. After world war II, general douglas macarthur wrote a book entitled *reminiscences.*

Grammar

Using End Marks

1 **A *declarative sentence* ends with a *period*.** (A declarative sentence is one that makes a statement.)

Fools make a mock at sin.

2 **An *imperative sentence* ends with a *period* or an *exclamation point*.** (An imperative sentence is one that gives a command or makes a request.)

Fret not thyself because of evildoers.
Give me liberty, or give me death!

3 **An *interrogative sentence* ends with a *question mark*.** (An interrogative sentence is one that asks a question.)

Whom have I in heaven but Thee?

4 **An *exclamatory sentence* ends with an *exclamation point*.** (An exclamatory sentence is one that shows sudden or strong feeling.)

How precious also are Thy thoughts unto me, O God!

5 **An *abbreviation* ends with a *period*.**

Mr. Mrs. Dr. B.S. Ph.D.

Exception: It is now general practice to omit periods for abbreviations of organizations.

AMA CIA NFL NSC RCA YMCA

Exercise A

Add periods, question marks, and exclamation points where they are needed in the following sentences.

1. I have not yet begun to fight! —*John Paul Jones*
2. Am I my brother's keeper?
3. Come unto Me, all ye that labor and are heavy laden.
4. How forcible are right words!
5. If the foundations be destroyed, what can the righteous do?
6. O Lord, our Lord, how excellent is Thy name in all the earth!
7. My God, My God, why hast Thou forsaken Me?
8. Speak, Lord, for Thy servant heareth.

Exercise B

Write sentences illustrating each of the five rules on this page.

1. Answers will vary. __________
2. __________
3. __________
4. __________
5. __________

Grammar

UNIT 2

Using Comma Rules 1–2

1 Use a *comma and a coordinating conjunction (and, but, or, nor, for, yet)* to join two simple sentences. (, and)

Many are called, **but** few are chosen. (two simple sentences—one on either side of the conjunction)

I have pursued mine enemies **and** overtaken them. (one simple sentence with a two-part verb—no comma needed)

2 Use a *single comma* to indicate that a word or words have been omitted, or to avoid a possible misreading. (,)

a. Use single commas to separate three or more *items in a series.*

My favorite pies are chocolate, lemon, and pecan. (words in a series)

The settlers roamed over hills, through valleys, and across swamps. (groups of words in a series)

(The single comma is placed after the word *chocolate* and after the word *hills* because the word *and* has been omitted. The single comma is placed after the word *lemon* and after the word *valleys* to avoid a possible misreading.)

Kansas **and** Nebraska **and** Iowa are Midwestern states. (No commas are needed in this series because no words are omitted between the words in the series.)

b. Use single commas to separate *two or more adjectives preceding a noun.* (Do not put a comma between the last adjective and the noun it modifies.)

Tall, slender pines can be used for making lumber. (The single comma is placed after the word *tall* because the word *and* has been omitted.)

If the last adjective is so closely related to the noun it modifies that the two words seem to form one expression, do not use the comma to separate that adjective from other adjectives.

We saw a red brick building. (No comma is used because the words *brick building* form one expression. You can usually determine if the comma is needed if you insert *and* between the adjectives. If the *and* sounds awkward, the comma is not needed. You may also reverse the adjectives, and if the adjectives sound awkward in the new position, the comma is not needed.)

We saw a red and brick building. (*and* sounds awkward—no comma needed)

We saw a brick red building. (adjectives reversed sound awkward—no comma needed)

c. Use a single comma any time *to avoid misreading.*

After eating Billy likes to take a nap. (There should be a comma after the word *eating* to avoid misreading.)

Exercise A

(1) Circle the coordinating conjunction in each of the following sentences. (2) If the coordinating conjunction joins two simple sentences, place a comma before the coordinating conjunction. (Rule 1)

1. Betty invited me to dinner, and I gratefully accepted her invitation.
2. The dress in the store window is beautiful, but the price is too high.
3. Danny likes basketball, but he does not enjoy football.
4. He had many difficulties to overcome, yet he did not give up.
5. The Lord is far from the wicked, but He heareth the prayer of the righteous.
6. We played and sang for almost an hour.

Exercise B

Place commas where needed in the following sentences. Some sentences may not require commas. (Rule 2a)

1. Students,parents,teachers,and visitors attended the school play.
2. The Lord is my rock and my fortress and my deliverer.
3. She walked through the doorway,down the hall,and into her classroom.
4. Protons,neutrons,and electrons are parts of the atom.
5. Tampa,Jacksonville,and Miami are large cities in the state of Florida.

Exercise C

Place commas where needed in the following sentences. Three sentences do not require commas. (Rule 2b)

1. Little Lady is a gentle riding horse.
2. The tired,sweaty runner maintained his pace.
3. I could not eat the dry,stale bread.
4. The new, shiny car glistened in the sunlight.
5. Yesterday was a dark,dreary day.
6. Some nations are held captive by harsh martial law.
7. Some European cities have crowded,narrow streets.
8. Our Western plains are often covered with long,red,shaggy grass.
9. Have you visited our modern lending library?
10. Many people in the United States live in warm,comfortable houses.

Exercise D

Commas are used correctly in the following sentences. Above each comma write the rule number that gives the reason for the comma. (Rule 1, 2a, 2b, or 2c)

1. A talebearer revealeth secrets,[1] but he that is of a faithful spirit concealeth the matter.
2. Holland,[2a] Belgium,[2a] and Luxembourg are often called the Low Countries.
3. Before leaving,[2c] your mother wants us to pray with her.
4. We will probably have hot,[2b] humid weather during July.
5. He is a very wealthy man,[1] but wealth cannot buy happiness.
6. When running,[2c] the cuckoo clock keeps excellent time.
7. Paul,[2a] Barnabas,[2a] and Mark traveled to Asia Minor.
8. Scraps of paper,[2a] paper clips,[2a] and thumb tacks lay scattered on his desk.
9. A dead fish can float downstream,[1] but it takes a live one to swim upstream.
10. What is that loud,[2b] irritating noise?

UNIT 2

Exercise E

Add commas where needed in the following sentences. Some sentences may not require commas. (Rules 1–2)

1. Resist the devil,and he will flee from you.
2. Roses and daffodils and tulips are beautiful flowers.
3. Louisiana,Mississippi,Alabama,and Florida are occasionally hit by hurricanes.
4. After running,Mark and Tom were exhausted.
5. There is true dignity in labor,and there is no true dignity without it.
6. How do you like that ceramic pepper shaker?
7. A gondola is a long,narrow canalboat used on the canals of Venice.
8. A man's heart deviseth his way,but the Lord directeth his steps.
9. An orchestra consists of strings,brass,woodwinds,and percussion.
10. We swept the floor,mopped it,and coated it with wax.
11. The food in this restaurant is good,but the prices are too high.
12. Look at the cracked,wrinkled paint on that old ship.
13. Wordsworth,Coleridge,and Southey are called the "Lake Poets."
14. The diamond cannot be polished without friction,nor can the man be perfected without trials.
15. Government cannot make good men,but good men can make good government.
16. A scorner seeketh wisdom and findeth it not.
17. We made a snowman,had a snowball fight, and made snow ice cream.
18. Weeping may endure for a night,but joy cometh in the morning.

Exercise F

Write two sentences for each of the rules on page 13.

Rule 1. Answers will vary.

____

Rule 2a. ______________________

____

Rule 2b. ______________________

____

Rule 2c. ______________________

____

Using Comma Rules 3–4

3 **Use a pair of commas to indicate a *nonessential element* in a sentence. (,---,)**

Mount Vernon, *the home of George Washington,* is located in Virginia. (The words *the home of George Washington* are nonessential to the meaning of the sentence. These words could be removed and the meaning of the sentence would be unchanged: Mount Vernon is located in Virginia.)

Note: The *pair of commas* is *one* mark of punctuation composed of two symbols, but these symbols are not to be thought of as two *single commas.* Also, if the nonessential elements come first or last in a sentence, you see only one half of the pair of commas.

a. Use a pair of commas to set off *nonessential appositives* and *appositive phrases.* An appositive is a word that follows a noun and explains or identifies that noun. An appositive phrase is an appositive plus its modifiers.

Joseph Henry, *an American physicist,* became famous for his discoveries in electromagnetism. (*Physicist* is the appositive, explaining Joseph Henry. *An* and *American* modify *physicist. An American physicist* is the appositive phrase.)

Note: If the appositive is short and closely connected to the noun it follows, omit the commas.

My sister *Joan* Pepin *the Short*

b. Use a pair of commas to set off words used in *direct address.*

The assistance you gave me, *Jill,* is greatly appreciated.

Rex, have you finished reading the entire Bible? (Here you see only one half of the pair of commas. The part before the word *Rex* is unnecessary.)

We missed you at church yesterday, *Gail.* (Here you see only one half of the pair of commas. The part after the word *Gail* is unnecessary.)

c. Use a pair of commas to set off the words *well, yes, no,* or *why* when they are nonessential. Remember, when these words come at the beginning of a sentence, you use only the second half of the pair of commas. The part before the word is unnecessary.

Well, how are you progressing in English class?

Yes, I will be glad to help.

d. Use a pair of commas to set off *parenthetical expressions* such as *of course, in fact, as a matter of fact, on the other hand, in my opinion,* and *in reality.*

Time wasted, *in fact,* can never be regained.

4 **Use a single comma to set off *introductory modifying phrases.*** (Do not use a comma after an introductory adverb phrase that comes immediately before the verb it modifies.)

In 1906, an earthquake destroyed the city of San Francisco. (short adverb phrase)

On a clear day in the Rockies, one can see for miles. (long adverb phrase)

In the center of the park stood a bronze statue of Paul Revere. (The introductory phrase comes immediately before the verb it modifies.)

Note: Sometimes good writers will omit the comma after a short introductory phrase if there is no possibility of a misreading, but in this book you should follow comma rule 4.

Using Comma Rules 3–4

Exercise A **(1) Decide whether the italicized appositives and appositive phrases are essential or nonessential. (2) If *nonessential,* write *N* in the blank and insert the commas. If *essential,* you need to do nothing.** (Rule 3a)

N 1. My oldest brother,*now a senior in college*,is preparing for the ministry.

N 2. Paris,*the capital of France*,is divided by the Seine River.

____ 3. His brother *Dave* is a missionary in Scotland.

N 4. Franz Schubert,*an Austrian composer*,was one of the greatest creators of fine songs.

____ 5. In 886, Alfred *the Great* defeated the Danes and forced them into the northeastern section of England.

N 6. Annie Oakley,*an American sharpshooter*,was an expert shot with a pistol, rifle, and shotgun.

N 7. Omaha,*the largest city in Nebraska*,has the world's largest cattle market.

____ 8. The American poet *Whitman* wrote a world-famous collection of poems.

Exercise B **Add commas where needed in the following sentences.** (Rule 3b)

1. Have you finished your history report yet,Rachel?
2. Hank,did you know that the North Star never rises or sets?
3. Your report,Kate,is due next week.
4. Scott,who was that man who was called the Swamp Fox?
5. Ten years have passed,Greg,since I last saw you.
6. Remember,my friend,when angry, count to ten before you speak.
7. Tim,what are some of the things for which you are especially grateful?
8. Ladies and gentlemen,we are standing on the brink of eternity.

Exercise C **Add commas where needed in the following sentences.** (Rules 3c and 3d)

1. Yes,I completed the assignment even though it was very difficult.
2. Charles,on the contrary,has good table manners.
3. Why,I did not know that his father was a doctor.
4. The President,of course,lives in Washington, D.C.
5. Some Latin American villages,in fact,do not have electricity or telephones.
6. By the way,the Library of Congress now contains over twenty-eight million books and pamphlets.
7. Well,as a matter of fact,the length of a bolt of lightning can exceed twenty miles.
8. Scientists,for instance,say that one stroke of lightning measures more than 15,000,000 volts.
9. No,I was not aware that flying lemurs can glide as far as 100 yards.
10. Good temper,in my opinion,is like a sunny day.

Exercise D Add commas where needed in the following sentences. Not all sentences require commas. (Rule 4)

1. On the first day of the week,many people go to church.
2. In the fear of the Lord is strong confidence.
3. In 1964,the strongest earthquake in American history shook Prince William Sound, Alaska.
4. On the kitchen counter was a list of chores for me to do.
5. On Wednesday,we heard that there would be thunderstorms in the afternoon.
6. After spending nearly twenty years in Kublai Khan's kingdom, Marco Polo returned home.
7. In 1793,missionary William Carey sailed for India from England.
8. During the 1800s,Japan began to trade with the Western world.

Exercise E Add commas where they are needed in the following sentences. (Rules 3–4)

1. No,Robert,I cannot play the guitar.
2. The idea was,in reality,a clever one,Charlie.
3. Well,Mrs. Olsen,your English teacher,told me that you made an *A*.
4. Did William the Conqueror invade England,Karen?
5. Honestly,I do not know what happened to your candy bar,Ryan.
6. Bob's sister Martha is,I believe,older than you are,Phil.
7. John Adams,the first Vice President,became the second President.
8. Safely aboard the rescue boat,we watched the ship sink.
9. Unfortunately,I have to move to another town,Cheri.
10. The orchestra played Beethoven's Ninth Symphony,one of his greatest works.
11. Yes,we will review capitalization next Tuesday,Kathy.
12. Fanny J. Crosby,the famous hymn writer,was blind from childhood.
13. The knock on the door,a very gentle tapping,was,in reality,very hard to hear.
14. The pistol that started the race was,of course,loaded with blanks.
15. Did Madame Curie,the discoverer of radium,receive the Nobel Prize for her work,Mrs. Finch?
16. He was,in fact,one of the signers of the Declaration of Independence.
17. With a drop of 1,612 feet,Ribbon Falls in Yosemite National Park is the tallest continuous waterfall in the United States.

Exercise F Write sentences illustrating the following rules from page 16.

Rule 3a. Answers will vary. ______

Rule 3b. ______

Rule 3c. ______

Rule 3d. ______

Rule 4. ______

Using Comma Rules 5–6

5 **Use commas to separate the parts of *dates and addresses* within sentences.** Use a comma after the last part if it does not end the sentence. (Do not use a comma between the month and the day or between the state and the ZIP code.)

John F. Kennedy was assassinated on November 22, 1963, in Dallas, Texas.
Our new address is 5243 North Spruce Street, Juniper, Colorado 62503.
We flew from Kansas City, Missouri, to Louisville, Kentucky, to visit my grandmother.

6 **Use a comma after the *salutation of a friendly letter.* Use a comma after the *closing of all letters.***

Dear John, Dear Uncle Andrew, Sincerely, Yours truly,

Exercise G **Add commas where needed in the following letter.** (Rules 1–6)

5627 St. John Street
Pensacola, Florida 32503
November 30, 1999

Dear Uncle John and Aunt Crissy,

I was so glad to see you when you were in town last week, and I miss you both very much. In fact, I have already asked my parents if we can visit you next summer.

How will you be celebrating Christmas this year? We will not be traveling. Instead, Grandmother will fly from Seattle, Washington, on December 20, 1999, to spend the holiday with us. We are, of course, looking forward to seeing her and to enjoying the hot, spicy apple cider that she always makes on Christmas Day. We also plan to attend the Christmas concert at our church, and Mother invited my friends Tammy, Joanna, and Sharon to go with us. We are really looking forward to this event. The living nativity scene, the highlight of the concert, is going to have real sheep in it this year!

During Christmas, my brother Chad and I will also give Grandmother a birthday gift since her birthday is on January 3. We made a new perch for her bird, a blue parakeet. Aunt Crissy, what would you like for your birthday?

Well, I should close now. I hope to hear from you soon.

With love,
Elizabeth

Reviewing Commas & End Marks

Exercise A Add commas and end marks where needed in the following sentences.

1. Dr.J.C.Meyers teaches biology,zoology,and chemistry.
2. I will,of course,be there as soon as possible.
3. How did you like the symphony's performance last night?
4. Yes,I will be glad to help in any way possible.
5. What a wonderful time we had on vacation!
6. Please wait in the office until Dr. Lincoln can see you.
7. Linda,have you finished typing your history report?
8. What a sight those snow-capped mountains are!
9. Study your vocabulary words daily.
10. Jean,what would you like for your birthday?

Exercise B Add commas where needed in the following sentences. Some sentences may not require commas.

1. Incidentally,Ruth,it was Wiley Post who first flew around the world alone.
2. Swimming and water skiing and canoeing are mostly summer activities.
3. Los Angeles,California,is,of course,one of the largest cities in America.
4. When he had batted,Bill went into the dugout.
5. The United States has a huge forest industry.
6. Wrath is cruel,and anger is outrageous.
7. No, I had not heard of Thaddeus Kosciusko,Fred.
8. I could,however,allow you to give your report on Friday.
9. Judge Roy Bean,a justice of the peace in West Texas,once fined a corpse $40 for carrying concealed weapons.
10. Dear Tom, Sincerely yours, Very truly yours,
11. In the bowl were oranges,apples,bananas,pears,and grapes.
12. Shakespeare's play *Romeo and Juliet* is a tragic love story.
13. Our family has toured the United States from Cape May,New Jersey,to Portland,Oregon.
14. Cold,damp weather is common in England.
15. The passenger ship *Queen Elizabeth II* leaves at 9:45 A.M.

Using Semicolons & Colons

The Semicolon

1 **Use a *semicolon* between independent clauses *if you do not use a comma and coordinating conjunction.*** (The coordinating conjunctions are *and, but, or, nor, for, yet.*)

A man becomes a Christian; he is not born one. —*Tertullian*

Nobody ever outgrows Scripture; the book widens and deepens with our years. —*Spurgeon*

2 **Use a *semicolon* between independent clauses joined by transitional words, such as *accordingly, consequently, for example, for instance, however, namely, nevertheless, that is, then, therefore, thus.*** (These words are not equivalent to coordinating conjunctions.)

The Bible teaches that God is a Spirit; thus we cannot see Him.

The Bible also teaches that God is a holy Being; that is, He is free from any sinful attributes or dispositions.

Note: These words are followed by a comma if they cause a distinct break in the flow of the sentence, but if the transitional word seems closely connected to the following clause (not requiring a pause when read), the comma may be omitted. The expressions *for example, for instance, that is, however,* and *namely* are always followed by a comma when they function as a connective.

3 **A *semicolon* may be necessary between independent clauses even with a coordinating conjunction *to make it obvious where the first clause ends.*** (This semicolon is usually needed when there are commas in the first clause or when the clauses are long.)

When a wicked man dieth, his expectation shall perish; and the hope of unjust men perisheth. (The semicolon is needed for a clearer distinction between the independent clauses.)

My brother enjoys playing football, but I prefer basketball, soccer, and sailing. (The distinction between the two clauses is clear and no semicolon is necessary.)

The Colon

1 **Use a *colon* before listed items introduced by such words as *as follows* or *the following.* Do not use a colon to introduce a list that is the complement of a verb or the object of a preposition.**

For our camping trip, we need: food, cooking equipment, sleeping bags, and a tent. (incorrect—colon separates the verb from its complement)

For our camping trip, we need the following: food, cooking equipment, sleeping bags, and a tent. (correct)

On our last vacation, we traveled through: Texas, Oklahoma, Kansas, and Nebraska. (incorrect—colon separates the preposition from its object)

On our last vacation, we traveled through the following states: Texas, Oklahoma, Kansas, and Nebraska. (correct)

2 **Use a *colon* between the *chapter and verse* of a Biblical reference.**

Titus 3:5 Ephesians 2:8 Romans 10:9

3 **Use a *colon* between the *hour and the minute* of a time reference.**

5:30 A.M. 6:00 P.M. 7:45 P.M.

4 **Use a *colon* after the *salutation of a business letter.***

Dear Mr. Stone: Dear Sir: Gentlemen:

Using Semicolons & Colons

Exercise A

Place semicolons where needed in the following sentences. **(Semicolon Rules 1–3)**

1. We are in the midst of hard times;nevertheless, brighter days are ahead.
2. Steve was not a born actor;he spent many hours practicing his lines.
3. For breakfast, I had scrambled eggs, bacon, and toast;and my brother had pancakes and sausage.
4. Napoleon of France had a very impressive army; nevertheless, he lost at Waterloo.
5. Jim wants to make the basketball team;thus he practices every night.
6. Envy seeks to elevate itself by degrading others;it detests the sounds of another's praise.
7. Help me, O Lord my God;O save me according to Thy mercy.
8. Pride is the offspring of ignorance;humility is the child of wisdom.
9. Exaggeration is but another name for falsehood;to exaggerate is to pass the bounds of truth.
10. Nothing can be more difficult than to speak lies;the wise, the rich, the great, the aged have all failed in their attempts.

Exercise B

Place colons where needed in the following sentences. **(Colon Rules 1–4)**

1. From the store, please bring the following:butter, milk, eggs, bread, and sugar.
2. Pastor Burton preached from Romans 8:30 and John 6:44.
3. Dr. Jones would like to see the following girls:Mary, Sue, and Robin.
4. The verses from Genesis 1:1 to Genesis 1:31 tell the story of creation.
5. Some indispensable requirements for success and happiness are as follows:meditating on God's Word, working hard, and doing right.
6. Proverbs 20:1 gives a warning concerning alcoholic beverages.
7. Before you start working, you need the following tools:a hammer, a saw, a plane, and several screwdrivers.
8. Jason presented a short devotional on Titus 3:5 at 10:00 P.M. last night.
9. When we went caroling, we sang the following songs:"Away in a Manger," "Silent Night," and "Hark! the Herald Angels Sing!"
10. Dear Sir: Gentlemen:

Exercise C

(1) Cross out any incorrect punctuation. (2) Add semicolons and colons where needed. (3) If a sentence is correct, write *C* before the number.

1. I have almost finished this painting;/however, I need the following items:/ one brush, two cloths, and a tube of red paint.
2. My pastor's favorite verse is 1 Peter 1:21;/consequently, he refers to it many times.
3. In our car, we can take Alan, Jim, and Paul;/and Larry can take Floyd and Oliver.
4. The bus was scheduled to arrive at 5:50 P.M.;/however, it still had not come at 6:05 P.M.

C 5. Foolishness is bound in the heart of a child, but the rod of correction shall drive it far from him.

6. Those who are contented with a little deserve much;those who deserve much are far more likely to be contented with a little.
7. Florence Nightingale was one of the greatest women of Victorian England;she founded the nursing profession as we know it today.

C 8. The heavens declare the glory of God, and the firmament showeth his handiwork.
9. Eric, Chris, and Doug like to camp out;but Tom, Phil, and Pete prefer to stay home.
10. Mr. Baskins would like to visit the Holy Land;however, finances will not permit him to go.

UNIT 2

Exercise D Add colons and semicolons where needed in the following sentences.

1. Columbus sailed away from Spain in 1492;two months later he discovered America.
2. He crossed the Atlantic Ocean in three small ships;it is a wonder that they made it.
3. The following men soon came to the Americas also:Balboa, Cortes, and De Soto.
4. In 1607, England gained interest in America;its first permanent colony was Jamestown.
5. In 1620, the Puritans almost starved to death in New England;nevertheless, they were determined to stay.
6. Squanto, an Indian, befriended the Pilgrims;he helped them grow more food so that they could survive the winter.
7. The leaders of the Pilgrim band wrote the *Mayflower Compact*;it was the first agreement for self-government in America.
8. At the first Thanksgiving, the following food was served:wild turkey, venison, succotash, fish, cranberries, and squash.
9. The Puritans were interested in education;thus they founded Harvard College in 1636.
10. The following men were great Puritan preachers:Cotton Mather, Jonathan Edwards, and Increase Mather.
11. A few of the original thirteen colonies were as follows:Delaware, Massachusetts, Virginia, and New Jersey.
12. Later, these colonies revolted against England;consequently, they gained their independence.

Exercise E Write one sentence for each of the rules on page 21 except Colon Rule 4.

1. Answers will vary.
2. ______
3. ______
4. ______
5. ______
6. ______

Grammar

Using Italics & Hyphens

1 **Underline (italicize) the titles of *books, magazines, newspapers, plays, works of art,* and the names of *ships, trains, aircraft,* and *spacecraft.*** (Underlining indicates those words that would be italicized if your sentences were set in type by a typesetter.)

Kidnapped is a classic book written by Robert Louis Stevenson.
I would like to have a subscription to the magazine American Ideals.
The sheet metal sculpture Red Petals stands $8^1/_2$ feet high.
Much Ado About Nothing is a comedy by William Shakespeare.
The General, a steam locomotive, became famous during the Civil War.

Note: The articles *a, an,* and *the* at the beginning of a title are italicized only when they are a part of the title.

Exception: The article *the* is not italicized before the title of a magazine or a newspaper, even if the article is actually a part of the title.

the Pensacola News-Journal

2 **Use a hyphen if you must *divide a word at the end of a line.***

a. **Do not divide a one-syllable word.** (*long,* not *lo-ng)*
b. **Divide only between syllables.** (*pen-guin,* not *peng-uin)*
c. **Do not divide after a single letter.** (*apex,* not *a-pex)*
d. **Do not carry over a two-letter syllable.** (*heron,* not *her-on)*
e. **Divide words with prefixes after the prefix.** (*anti-bacterial,* not *antibac-terial)*

3 **Use a hyphen in *compound numbers* from *twenty-one* through *ninety-nine.***

The missionary David Brainerd died at the age of *twenty-nine.*

4 **Use a hyphen in *fractions* used as *adjectives.***

A *two-thirds* majority is required to end debate on a matter. (*two-thirds* used as an adjective to modify *majority)*
One third of his crop was ruined by the frost. (*one third* used as a noun, not as an adjective)

Exercise A **Underline the words that should be in italics. (Rule 1)**

1. Oliver Twist is a book that describes the adventures of a poor orphan boy.
2. The American Magazine was the name of the first magazine to be published in America.
3. Claude Monet did the painting Water Lilies when he was almost blind.
4. My father-in-law prefers to read the Miami Herald instead of his local newspaper.
5. The Cheyenne is a small bronze sculpture that shows something of American life in the Far West.
6. The last issue of Science Digest contained an interesting article about the roadrunner.
7. An old fisherman's struggle with a giant marlin is described in the book The Old Man and the Sea.
8. The Pledge of Allegiance was first published in 1892 in the Youth's Companion magazine.
9. The book Gulliver's Travels was intended to make fun of men in high office.
10. The Guinness Book of World Records was first published in 1955.

Exercise B **Add hyphens where needed in the following sentences. Some sentences may not need hyphens.**

1. The dome of Hawaii's Mauna Loa volcano is seventy-five miles long.
2. The cookie recipe calls for only one third of the sugar that the cake recipe calls for.
3. Sunset Boulevard, a famous Los Angeles street, begins downtown and winds almost twenty-five miles through Los Angeles to the Pacific Ocean.
4. A two-thirds majority is required to consider a matter out of its scheduled order.
5. The Drake family lives on Fifty-second Street in Albany.
6. In 1967, Pennsylvania called its first constitutional convention in ninety-four years.
7. She spent two thirds of her allowance on candy.
8. Louisiana, the wettest state in the United States, has an annual rainfall of fifty-six inches.
9. A saguaro cactus nearly fifty-eight feet high was once found in the Maricopa Mountains of Arizona.
10. The Pacific Ocean contains almost one half of the earth's water.

Exercise C **Add hyphens where needed; underline words that should be in italics.**

1. You can find the article on page forty-one of <u>Outdoor Life</u>.
2. The oldest continuously published newspaper in Vermont is the <u>Rutland Herald</u>.
3. The steamship <u>United States</u> won the Blue Riband in 1952 with an average speed of about thirty-five knots.
4. <u>Reader's Digest</u> is a popular magazine in the United States.
5. Theodore Roosevelt, at the age of forty-two, was the youngest man ever to become President.
6. <u>Man Pointing</u> is a tall, skinny, bronze sculpture by Alberto Giacometti.
7. The Wright brothers' airplane, called <u>Flyer</u>, became the world's first successful airplane.
8. Ernest Hemingway's <u>For Whom the Bell Tolls</u> is a famous American novel.
9. <u>The Massacre of the Innocents</u> by Giovanni Pisano is an example of sculpture that ornamented pulpits in Italy during the 1200s.
10. Victoria, who ruled England for sixty-three years, spent over three fourths of her life as England's queen.

Exercise D **Write sentences illustrating each rule on page 24.**

1. Answers will vary. ____________________
2. ____________________

____

3. ____________________
4. ____________________

Using Quotation Marks Rules 1–5

1 **Use quotation marks to enclose the *exact words* of a speaker (a direct quotation). Do not use quotation marks for an indirect quotation, which is a rewording of the person's statement.**

Sir Edward Turner once said, "I have no secret of success but hard work." (direct quotation)

Sir Edward Turner once said that he had no secret of success but hard work. (indirect quotation)

2 **Capitalize the *first word* of a direct quotation. If the quotation is *interrupted by other words,* the second part should not begin with a capital letter unless the second part is the beginning of a new sentence or is a word that would be capitalized anyway.**

"The sluggard," saith the Lord, "**w**ill not plow by reason of the cold." (The word *will* is a continuation of the same sentence, not the beginning of a new sentence.)

"If you agree," said our class president, "**J**ohn is willing to act as chairman of the committee." (The word *John* is capitalized simply because it is a proper noun.)

"The Son abideth forever," Jesus said. "**I**f the Son therefore shall make you free, ye shall be free indeed." (The word *If* is capitalized because it begins a new sentence.)

3 **The exact words of a speaker should be *set off* from the rest of the sentence by using a comma, a question mark, or an exclamation point.**

"I really enjoy going to school**,**" said Glen.

"Do you realize the importance of using time wisely**?**" asked the instructor.

"Praise ye the Lord**!**" exclaimed the Psalmist.

4 ***Commas* and *periods* always go *inside* the closing quotation marks.**

5 ***Colons* and *semicolons* always go *outside* the closing quotation marks.**

The following students will sing "Amazing Grace"**:** Joy, Carol, and Renee.

Read Longfellow's poem "Paul Revere's Ride"**;** then write a summary of it.

Exercise

Place quotation marks where needed in the following sentences. **(Rules 1–5)** **Be sure to use correct capitalization.**

1. I believe it was Cicero who said, "Nothing is useful that is not honest."
2. "Gratitude is justly said to be the mother of most virtues," stated the sign on the wall.
3. "Towering genius disdains a beaten path," said Abraham Lincoln. "It seeks regions hitherto unexplored."
4. Yesterday Miss Ball held auditions for the school production of "A Christmas Carol"; today she will post the results.
5. My granddad used to say, "The wiser we are, the more we are aware of our ignorance."
6. During our family devotions this morning, Mom said, "He who has a high standard of living and thinking will certainly do better than he who has none at all."
7. The following seventh graders still have to recite the poem "IF": Alicia, Jane, Bobby, and Kyle.
8. "In the long run," remarked our Sunday school teacher, "character is better than money."

Using Quotation Marks Rules 6–10

6 ***Question marks*** **and** ***exclamation points*** **go** ***inside*** **the closing quotation marks when they apply to the quoted matter only. They go** ***outside*** **when they refer to the whole sentence.**

David said, "Is there not a cause**?**" (The question mark applies to the quoted words only.)

Who said, "Give me a man that we may fight together"**?** (The question mark applies to the whole sentence.)

Who said, "Who is this uncircumcised Philistine that he should defy the armies of the living God**?**" (A second question mark is not needed after the closing quotation mark.)

The women chanted, "Saul hath slain his thousands and David his ten thousands**!**" (The exclamation point applies to the quoted words only.)

7 **In quoting** ***more than one sentence,*** **use quotation marks only at the beginning and at the end of the whole quotation. Do not put quotation marks around each sentence.**

8 **In writing conversation, begin a new paragraph each time the speaker changes.**

Jesus said to the nobleman, "Except ye see signs and wonders, ye will not believe."

"Sir, come down ere my child die," he replied.

"Go thy way; thy son liveth," said the Lord.

9 **Use quotation marks to enclose titles of** ***short stories, short poems, songs, chapters, articles,*** **and other** ***parts*** **of books or magazines when used in a sentence.**

"The Gold Bug" "The Tide Rises, the Tide Falls" "Silent Night"

10 **Use single quotation marks for an element within a quotation that also requires quotation marks.**

"What poem begins with the line **'**Listen, my children**'**?" asked the teacher.

Exercise A

Rewrite the following sentences, placing quotation marks where needed. (Rule 6)

1. Who was it that said, Good laws make it easier to do right and harder to do wrong?

Who was it that said, "Good laws make it easier to do right and harder to do wrong"?

2. Oh, what a cruel tyrant is a bad habit! exclaimed the drug addict. "Oh, what a cruel tyrant is a bad habit!" exclaimed the drug addict.

3. Ought we ever to miss an opportunity to show kindness and attention to the aged? asked our pastor. "Ought we ever to miss an opportunity to show kindness and attention to the aged?" asked our pastor.

4. How he appreciated those words, Let not your heart be troubled! How he appreciated those words, "Let not your heart be troubled"!

Exercise B

Rewrite the following dialogue, supplying quotation marks and paragraphing correctly. (Rules 7, 8)

An author is known by his writings; a mother, by her daughter; a fool, by his words; and all men, by their companions, said Dad. We are creatures of imitation, and our habits are largely formed on the model of those with whom we regularly associate. Better be alone than in bad company. Jerry replied, Is that what the Bible means when it talks about evil communications corrupting good manners? Yes, evil qualities are catching as well as diseases, and the mind is perhaps more liable to infection than the body. Go with mean people, and you will think life is mean. Dad, I suppose that evil company is like tobacco smoke; one cannot be long in its presence without carrying away its smell. That's right, Jerry. If you wish to be respected, if you desire happiness and not misery, I advise you to associate with the intelligent and the good.

"An author is known by his writings; a mother, by her daughter; a fool, by his words; and all men, by their companions," said Dad. "We are creatures of imitation, and our habits are largely formed on the model of those with whom we regularly associate. Better be alone than in bad company."

Jerry replied, "Is that what the Bible means when it talks about evil communications corrupting good manners?"

"Yes, evil qualities are catching as well as diseases, and the mind is perhaps more liable to infection than the body. Go with mean people, and you will think life is mean."

"Dad, I suppose that evil company is like tobacco smoke; one cannot be long in its presence without carrying away its smell."

"That's right, Jerry. If you wish to be respected, if you desire happiness and not misery, I advise you to associate with the intelligent and the good."

Exercise C

Place quotation marks where needed in the following sentences. (Rules 9, 10)

1. Our class just finished reading a chapter entitled "Environment and Nutrition."
2. "Can you recall who wrote the poem 'Crossing the Bar'?" asked Alice.
3. The magazine that you borrowed contains an intriguing article called "The Role of the Code Breakers."
4. One of my favorite hymns is "How Firm a Foundation!"
5. "The Piece of String" is a short story written by Guy de Maupassant.
6. "Did you remember to say, 'May I help you?'" asked the manager.
7. "What misery accompanies those who do not know the Lord!" exclaimed the evangelist.
8. "Don't just stand there and say 'I don't know'!" shouted the sergeant.

Exercise D Place quotation marks where needed in the following sentences.

1. "Peace is such a precious jewel," said Matthew Henry, "that I would give anything for it but the truth."
2. Julia Ward Howe wrote "The Battle Hymn of the Republic" after hearing the popular song "John Brown's Body."
3. It is the good Christian who asks, "Should I do this?" It is the bad who asks, "Can I do this?"
4. A wise counselor said, "Never anticipate wealth from any other source than labor. He who waits for dead men's shoes may have to go a long time barefoot."
5. "What do you think of this statement: 'Truthfulness is a cornerstone in character; and if it is not firmly laid in youth, there will be ever after a weak spot in the foundation'?" asked Tammy.
6. In the pamphlet *The Everlasting Nation,* I just read an article entitled "Are the Jews God's Favorites?"
7. "Honesty is not only the first step toward greatness," declared the speaker. "It is greatness itself."
8. "What New Testament book says, 'Doth not even nature itself teach you that if a man have long hair, it is a shame unto him?'" asked Don.
9. "Oh, what a rich inheritance a spotless reputation leaves!" exclaimed the judge.
10. In that book are many short stories and poems, such as "The Man Who Would Be King" and "God That Madest All Things."

UNIT 2

Exercise E Change the following indirect quotations to direct quotations. Capitalize and punctuate them correctly.

1. Scott asked if I understood the chapter entitled "The Interaction of Atoms." Scott asked, "Do you understand the chapter entitled 'The Interaction of Atoms'?"
2. Jeff told his mother that he would be glad to wash the dishes since it was her birthday. Jeff told his mother, "I will be glad to wash the dishes since it is your birthday."
3. The general exclaimed that it was foolish to trust the Communists. The general exclaimed, "It's foolish to trust the Communists!"
4. Abraham Lincoln said that you could not help men permanently by doing for them what they could and should do for themselves. Abraham Lincoln said, "You cannot help men permanently by doing for them what they could and should do for themselves."

Grammar

G Using Apostrophes

1 **Use an apostrophe to form the *possessive case* of nouns.**

a. To form the possessive case of a *singular noun,* first write the *singular spelling* of the word. Then add an *apostrophe and s.* ('s)

a boy**'s** glove   a lion**'s** den   a cat**'s** paw   Charles**'s** theory

Exception: The following may be correctly written by adding the apostrophe only: (1) ancient proper names ending in *-es,* (2) the name *Jesus,* (3) such expressions as *for conscience' sake.*

Achilles' heel   Aristides' loyalty   Hippocrates' theory
Moses' leadership   Jesus' resurrection   for goodness' sake
for righteousness' sake   for conscience' sake

b. To form the possessive case of a *plural noun that does not end in s,* first write the *plural spelling* of the word. Then add an *apostrophe and s.* ('s)

the policemen**'s** fund   the children**'s** laughter

Note: Do not use an apostrophe to form the *plural* of a noun.
mowers sharpened (not mower's sharpened)

c. To form the possessive case of a *plural noun that ends in s,* first write the *plural spelling* of the word. Then add an *apostrophe.* (')

the boys**'** gloves   the horses**'** hoofs

2 **Use an apostrophe to show that letters have been *omitted* from a word. Such words are called contractions. Contractions are used only in informal writing or in conversation.**

didn't = did not   you're = you are   Mary's = Mary is   '77 = 1977

Several words require a slight change in spelling.

will not = won't   shall not = shan't   cannot = can't

Note: Possessive pronouns do *not* use apostrophes to show possession.
Whose comb is this? (*Whose* is a possessive pronoun.)
Who's going with us? *(Who's* is a contraction of *Who is.)*
Your speech was excellent. (*Your* is a possessive pronoun.)
You're improving every day. *(You're* is a contraction of *You are.)*

3 **Use an *apostrophe and s* to form the *plurals of letters, numbers, signs,* and *words used as words.***

*b***'s** and *c***'s**   *4***'s** and *5***'s**
= **'s** and – **'s**   &**'s** and *and***'s**

Note: The plurals of years written as numerals may be formed by adding *s* alone.
1730s   1900s

Exercise A

Form the possessive case for the following words. The first five are singular; the others are plural.

1. piano ___piano's___
2. clerk ___clerk's___
3. cross ___cross's___
4. roof ___roof's___
5. man ___man's___
6. deer ___deer's___
7. dishes ___dishes'___
8. men ___men's___
9. herons ___herons'___
10. mice ___mice's___

Exercise B Write the correct forms in the blanks.

	Singular	Singular Possessive	Plural	Plural Possessive
1.	fern	fern's	ferns	ferns'
2.	fox	fox's	foxes	foxes'
3.	pony	pony's	ponies	ponies'
4.	journey	journey's	journeys	journeys'
5.	knife	knife's	knives	knives'
6.	radio	radio's	radios	radios'
7.	child	child's	children	children's
8.	woman	woman's	women	women's
9.	goose	goose's	geese	geese's
10.	sheep	sheep's	sheep	sheep's

Exercise C Rewrite each of the following expressions in the possessive case.

Example: the ear of the horse the horse's ear

1. punishment of the thieves the thieves' punishment
2. fur of the rabbit the rabbit's fur
3. yoke of the oxen the oxen's yoke
4. the worth of a dime a dime's worth
5. the pay of two weeks two weeks' pay
6. eyes of the bats the bats' eyes
7. the lawn of Mr. Rees Mr. Rees's lawn
8. revolt of the Maccabees the Maccabees' revolt
9. choice of the people the people's choice
10. rewards of the victors the victors' rewards

Exercise D Write contractions for the following words.

1. we are we're
2. shall not shan't
3. you are you're
4. cannot can't
5. it is it's
6. is not isn't
7. who is who's
8. there is there's
9. will not won't
10. Bill is Bill's

Exercise E Cross out the incorrect word in parentheses.

1. Slander is a blight; (its, ~~it's~~) tongue is charged with poison.
2. Have you tended to the salvation of (your, ~~you're~~) immortal soul?
3. Albert Einstein was the man (whose, ~~who's~~) theory of relativity formed the basis for the release of atomic energy.
4. (~~Its~~, It's) time they recognized (their, ~~they're~~) responsibility.
5. (Yours, ~~Your's~~) is obviously the superior design.
6. (~~Whose~~, Who's) going to be the first to solve the problem?
7. (~~Your~~, You're) aware of the resources that are available, I hope.
8. (~~Theirs~~, There's) always time to do the things you want to do.
9. Is that fancy new lawnmower (yours, ~~your's~~)?
10. Yes, (~~their~~, they're) definitely interested in determining (~~whose~~, who's) most capable for the job.
11. Are you continually grateful for the liberty that is (ours, ~~our's~~)?
12. She asks for only that which is rightfully (hers, ~~her's~~).
13. Too many (cooks, ~~cook's~~) spoil the broth.
14. We can see that Satan has (his, ~~his'~~) demons well organized.
15. The trophy is (theirs, ~~their's~~) if they win this last game.

Exercise F Write sentences, using correctly the words listed below.

1. theirs Answers will vary.
2. it's
3. they're
4. you're
5. its
6. won't
7. whose
8. shan't
9. who's
10. your

Exercise G Rewrite each of the following expressions, correctly forming the plural of the italicized items.

1. all *a* and *b* all a's and b's
2. dot your *i* and cross your *t* dot your i's and cross your t's
3. too many *and* too many and's
4. their *ooh* and *ah* their ooh's and ah's
5. your *5* look like *S* your 5's look like S's
6. in the late *1900* in the late 1900s

Exercise H

The following sentences contain errors in the use of apostrophes. Cross out any incorrect words and rewrite them correctly. Supply apostrophes where needed.

1. Didn't Hattie Buell write the song "I'm a Child of the King"?
2. Penelope said, "I'll marry the man who's successful at stringing Ulysses' bow and shooting an arrow through twelve hollow ~~axhead's~~ axheads."
3. Little Rock is Arkansas's chief trading and transportation center.
4. Isn't it true that the Library of Congress owns America's largest collection of books printed before 1501?
5. In the early 1900s, most of the ~~Russian's~~ Russians were farmers.
6. One of Lenin's goals was to destroy all privately owned business.
7. Eli Whitney's ~~idea's~~ ideas contributed greatly to the Industrial Revolution.
8. The Smithsonian Institution, one of the world's finest institutes of research, is the fulfillment of James Smithson's desire to "increase knowledge among men."
9. Let's study Cyrus McCormick's inventions sometime.
10. It's a well-known fact that Alexander ~~Hamiltons'~~ Hamilton's ideas helped shape the financial system in our country.
11. Don't you know ~~whose~~ who's responsible for inventing the phonograph?
12. ~~You're~~ Your lives have been affected by the invention of the internal-combustion engine in more ways than ~~your~~ you're probably aware of.
13. There in ~~his'~~ his New Jersey factory, Thomas Edison's telegraph instruments were manufactured.
14. Phil's and Henry's posters are on Mr. Holley's desk. ~~Their~~ They're the best he's ever received.
15. Nathan's theme that he wrote in '98 is better than the one he wrote this year. He used too many *and*'s in his sentence structure this time.

Exercise I

Write sentences using the items listed.

1. singular possessive of *Maurice* Answers will vary.
   Maurice's
2. plural possessive of *man*
   men's
3. singular possessive of *goose*
   goose's
4. plural possessive of *thief*
   thieves'
5. *whose* must be used as a possessive
6. *its* must be used as a possessive

Exercise A **Add periods, question marks, and exclamation points wherever they are needed.**

1. Why are ye so fearful? How is it that ye have no faith?
2. Woe unto you, scribes and Pharisees, hypocrites!
3. Experience is a harsh school, but fools learn in no other.
4. Shall their unbelief make the faith of God without effect? God forbid. or !
5. Whoso sheddeth man's blood, by man shall his blood be shed.

Exercise B **Add all necessary punctuation for the following sentences.**

1. Venus, the brightest planet, lies under a thick blanket of clouds.
2. Yes, Peter, James, and John were disciples.
3. Have you read Walter Edmonds's short story entitled "Death of Red Peril"?
4. On September 2, 1945, World War II came to an end.
5. John, do you know when the Titanic sank?
6. In 1 Thess. 5:22, we read, "Abstain from all appearance of evil."
7. Keep thy heart with all diligence, for out of it are the issues of life.
8. Do you have my yellow lead pencil, Frank?
9. Henry Hudson's ship, the Half Moon, brought a crew of explorers to North America as early as 1609.
10. One of Julie's favorite paintings is Jan Vermeer's Young Woman with a Water Jug.
11. There are twenty-four states west of the Mississippi River, and there are twenty-six states east of the Mississippi.
12. For the experiment, we will need the following materials: a glass, a cup of salt, two iron nails, and some iodine.
13. When King Solomon had explored this world's wisdom, he related, "Then said I in my heart that this also is vanity."
14. Yes, as a matter of fact, I do need a few things from the store.
15. Truly my soul waiteth upon God; from Him cometh my salvation.
16. He opened the rock, and the waters gushed out; they ran in the dry places like a river.
17. To amend the Constitution, a three-fourths majority of the state legislatures must be obtained.
18. The Lord is with me as a mighty, terrible one; therefore, my persecutors shall stumble.
19. Fred Jones has taken up the hobby of numismatics; that is, he has become a coin collector.
20. Pontius Pilate, the Roman Empire's representative in Judea, asked, "What is truth?"

Reviewing Units 1–2

Exercise A Capitalization. Draw a line through each incorrect small letter. Write a capital above it.

1. in 1849, many people rushed to the west seeking gold.
2. president Ronald Reagan once served as governor of california.
3. have you read the book *gulliver's travels* by jonathan swift?
4. before general douglas macArthur left the philippine islands, he promised, "i shall return."
5. my bible teacher, mr. harper, is an expert in greek, hebrew, and latin.
6. during creation, god said, "let there be light."
7. as dan waited for dr. lee to arrive, he looked through *world* magazine.
8. faith high school is located at 5415 rawson lane.
9. if you were buying a new car, would you buy a chevrolet or a ford?
10. the fbi searched everywhere for the criminal and finally found him in the bahama islands.
11. it was king henry VIII who made thomas cranmer the archbishop of canterbury.
12. one of the best books that i have ever read is *ivanhoe* by sir walter scott.
13. anzac day celebrates the landing of new zealand and australian troops at gallipoli on april 25, 1915, during world war I.
14. the english poet percy bysshe shelley wrote the poem "ozymandias."

Exercise B Punctuation. Add punctuation where needed.

1. Yes, we left for Cody, Wyoming, at 3:20 on May 25, 1977.
2. "Wasn't it the Philippian jailer who said, 'What must I do to be saved?'" Diane asked.
3. Pete, you may leave for Dawn's party now; however, Jean and I will leave later.
4. The Prodigal Son, one of our Lord's parables, is in every way a perfect example of a short story.
5. This story in Luke 15:11–32 contains the following characters: a loving father, a wayward son, and an angry brother.
6. Congress, of course, can override the President's veto with a majority of two thirds.
7. The name Isaiah has two *a*'s and two *i*'s.
8. How unusual this novel is!
9. The Gulf Wind, a passenger train, was scheduled to begin service between New Orleans, Louisiana, and Jacksonville, Florida, on November 30, 1979.
10. "Heaven and earth shall pass away, but My words shall not pass away," said our Lord in Matthew 24:35.

Grammar

Recognizing Kinds of Sentences

There are four kinds of sentences classified according to their purpose.

1 **A *declarative sentence* makes a statement. It ends with a period.**

Kindness is like a calm and peaceful stream.

2 **An *imperative sentence* gives a command or makes a request. It ends with a period or an exclamation point.**

Attend to your own business, please. Stop that car!

The subject of an imperative sentence is the word *you,* understood but not expressed. The first sentence means: *You* attend to your own business, please. The second means: *You* stop that car!

3 **An *interrogative sentence* asks a question. It ends with a question mark.**

Are you memorizing these definitions?

4 **An *exclamatory sentence* shows sudden or strong feeling. It ends with an exclamation point.**

What grief a thoughtless act can bring!

Exercise A **(1) In the blank before each number, identify the kind of sentence. (2) Place the appropriate punctuation at the end of each sentence.**

declarative 1. God shall wipe away all tears from their eyes.

declarative 2. He cometh with clouds, and every eye shall see Him.

declarative or exclamatory 3. Behold, I come quickly. or !

imperative 4. Even so, come, Lord Jesus.

interrogative 5. Who is worthy to open the book?

interrogative 6. Who is a liar but he that denieth that Jesus is the Christ?

exclamatory 7. What desolations He hath made in the earth!

imperative 8. Grow in grace and in the knowledge of our Lord and Savior Jesus Christ.

exclamatory 9. How great a matter a little fire kindleth!

declarative 10. The face of the Lord is against them that do evil.

Exercise B **Write four sentences illustrating the four kinds of sentences. Punctuate each sentence correctly.**

1. (declarative) Answers will vary. __________
2. (imperative) __________
3. (interrogative) __________
4. (exclamatory) __________

Recognizing Subjects & Predicates

UNIT 3

1 **The *complete subject* of a sentence is that part about which something is said.** (complete subject = simple subject plus its modifiers)

The **fear** of the Lord is the beginning of wisdom.

2 **The *simple subject* is the main word or group of words in the complete subject.** (simple subject = complete subject minus its modifiers)

The **fear** of the Lord is the beginning of wisdom.

3 **The *complete predicate* of a sentence is the part that says something about the subject.** (complete predicate = simple predicate [verb] plus its modifiers and words that complete the verb)

The fear of the Lord **is** the beginning of wisdom.

4 **The *simple predicate (verb)* is the main word or group of words in the complete predicate.** (simple predicate [verb] = complete predicate minus its modifiers or words that complete the verb)

The fear of the Lord **is** the beginning of wisdom.

5 **A *verb phrase* is a main verb and its helping verbs.**

I *have put* my trust in the Lord.

To find the subject of a sentence, first find the verb. Then ask *who* or *what* before the verb. As you look for the subject, remember that the subject will never be in a prepositional phrase.

Everyone in the boat caught a fish. (*Who* or *what* caught? *Everyone* caught. *Everyone* is the subject. *Boat* did not catch a fish. *Boat* is the object of the preposition *in.*)

To find the verb of a sentence, look for a word that shows action. If you do not find an action word, look for a word from the lists below. The following words are usually verbs or a part of a verb phrase. Memorize these!

Linking or Helping		Action or Helping		Helping		Action or Linking		
am	were	have	do	shall	may	taste	look	grow
is	be	has	does	will	might	feel	appear	remain
are	being	had	did	should	must	smell	become	stay
was	been			would	can	sound	seem	
					could			

Exercise A **(1) Draw a vertical line between the complete subject and the complete predicate. (2) Draw one line under the simple subject and two lines under the simple predicate.**

Example: Many cattlemen | prefer Angus for good quality beef.

1. The saltwater crocodile | is one of the world's most dangerous crocodiles.
2. North American caribou | are much different from European reindeer.
3. Each autumn, the ruby-throated hummingbird | flies nonstop across the Gulf of Mexico to South America.

(continued)

Exercise A, cont.

4. The curiosity of the bat-eared fox often brings it near human activities.
5. Black bears may beg food from tourists in national parks.
6. Beaver dams are good examples of engineering skill.
7. The elephant is the largest of all existing land animals.
8. The tallest animal in the world is the giraffe.
9. The powerful golden eagle has been called the "king of birds."
10. The shy pygmy hippopotamus is very hard to find.

Exercise B

(1) Draw two lines under the simple predicate (verb). Be sure to include helping verbs. (2) Draw one line under the simple subject. Use the procedure that is given on page 37 for finding subjects and verbs.

1. The first settlers in America faced the probability of an early death.
2. Until the mid 1800s, many children died in early childhood.
3. During a smallpox epidemic in Boston in 1721, American medicine made its first significant advance.
4. Dr. Zabdiel Boylston successfully inoculated 235 people against smallpox.
5. During the mid 1800s, many doctors believed in bloodletting as a cure for ailments.
6. For years, doctors did not follow sanitary procedures during patient examinations and during surgery.
7. As a result, approximately half of all surgery patients died from infection.
8. In 1865, Dr. Joseph Lister introduced antiseptic procedures during surgery.
9. In 1842, Dr. Crawford Long performed a painless operation on a patient under ether gas.
10. The cause of yellow fever was discovered in 1900 by Dr. Walter Reed.
11. Pellagra, once a dreaded disease, has now been practically eliminated.
12. For years, Johns Hopkins Medical School was the only acceptable medical institution in America.
13. Wilhelm Roentgen's discovery of X-rays greatly aided doctors in their diagnoses.
14. The discovery of radium by Pierre and Marie Curie has saved the lives of many cancer victims.
15. Today, American medicine is recognized as the finest in the world.

Note: In all of the following lessons in this book, the word *subject* will mean simple subject, and the word *verb* will mean simple predicate.

Grammar G: Overcoming Problems in Locating Subjects & Verbs

UNIT 3

1 **The subject of a sentence normally comes *before* the predicate. When the predicate or any part of the predicate comes before the subject, the sentence is in *inverted order.* Inverted order usually occurs in *interrogative sentences* and in sentences that begin with *there* or *here.* The words *there* and *here* are rarely used as subjects.**

Are you trusting in the Lord? (interrogative sentence)

There is no escape from judgment. (The word *there* is not the subject.)

In interrogative sentences, the subject is usually between the parts of the verb phrase. It is easier to find the subject if you change the question into a declarative sentence:

You are trusting in the Lord.

2 **The *subject* of an *imperative sentence* is the word *you,* understood but not written.**

Be not greedy of popular applause.

(You) Be not greedy of popular applause.

Develop patience, courage, and perseverance.

(You) Develop patience, courage, and perseverance.

3 **Sometimes the *verb phrase* is *interrupted* by other words. Be careful to find all the words that make up the verb phrase. Include only the words that show action and words that are in the verb lists you have memorized (p. 37).**

An easy path will never build strong character. (The word *never* does not show action, neither is it in the verb lists.)

Inattention does not encourage learning. (*Not* and *n't* are never verbs.)

Exercise

(1) Draw two lines under each verb. Be sure to underline all the verbs in a verb phrase. (2) Draw one line under each subject. If the subject is *you,* understood, write *(you)* at the beginning of the sentence.

1. Didn't many wealthy Americans once go on the grand tour of Europe?
2. After graduation from college, students would often visit the famous places in Europe.
3. There are magnificent, quiet moorlands in England.
4. *(you)* Travel the fiords of Norway for breathtaking scenery.
5. Do the ruins of ancient Greece still exist?
6. Yes, in Athens a visitor can readily visit the old temples and amphitheaters.
7. Visitors to the Louvre in Paris will always have an enjoyable time.
8. Have you ever seen the tulip fields of Holland in the spring?
9. There are quaint, old canals in the beautiful city of Venice.
10. *(you)* Do not overlook the catacombs of Rome, those secret meeting places of early Christians.

Grammar

Diagraming Subjects & Verbs

Drawing a diagram reveals how well you can analyze the parts of a sentence. If you cannot place a part correctly, you do not fully understand something. Diagraming quickly shows you what you know and what you do not know, thus allowing you to give your full attention to your individual difficulties.

Follow these steps in diagraming subjects and verbs, and you will have few problems.

1. **Draw a horizontal line divided by a short vertical line.**
2. **Find the verb first and write it to the right of the vertical line.**
3. **Find the subject and write it to the left of the vertical line.**
4. **Read the subject and verb together to see if you have chosen sensible answers.**
5. **Retain all capitalization, but omit punctuation marks.**

God is good to me. (declarative sentence)

God | is

With the righteous dwells peace. (inverted sentence)

peace | dwells

Why do you complain? (interrogative sentence)

you | do complain

There are no disappointments in Christ. (The word *there* is not the subject.)

disappointments | are

Decide at once upon a noble purpose. (imperative sentence)

x | Decide

Note: The *x* in the diagram above and the *x*'s in other diagrams throughout this book indicate an ellipsis (the omission of a word or words necessary for complete grammatical analysis, but understood in the context). The understood subject *you* has been omitted.

Exercise A

(1) Diagram the subjects and verbs in each of the following sentences. Remember to find the verb first, then the subject. (2) After you have finished, read each diagram to see if you have chosen sensible answers.

1. Everyone must have proper food for good health. — Everyone | must have
2. Oxygen is obtained from fresh air. — Oxygen | is obtained
3. The body is kept in condition through exercise. — body | is kept
4. Cleanliness is a protection from illness. — Cleanliness | is
5. Good posture is an aid to good health. — posture | is
6. Adequate sleep restores expended energy. — sleep | restores

Exercise B Write sentences illustrating the following: (1) a declarative sentence having an interrupted verb phrase, (2) an inverted sentence, (3) an imperative sentence, (4) an interrogative sentence, (5) a sentence beginning with *there,* (6) an exclamatory sentence.

1. Answers will vary.
2.
3.
4.
5.
6.

Exercise C Diagram the subjects and verbs from the sentences you wrote for Exercise B.

1. Answers will vary.
2.
3.
4.
5.
6.

Exercise D For additional practice, diagram the subjects and verbs from the exercise on page 39.

1. Americans | Did go
2. students | would visit
3. moorlands | are
4. x | Travel
5. ruins | Do exist
6. visitor | can visit
7. Visitors | will have
8. you | Have seen
9. canals | are
10. x | Do overlook

Grammar

Recognizing Compound Subjects & Verbs

1 **A *compound subject* consists of two or more subjects connected by *and, or,* or *nor.* These subjects are used with the same verb.**

Hugs and kisses are important to grandparents. (The two parts of the subject are used with the same verb, *are.*)

2 **A *compound verb* consists of two or more verbs connected by *and, or, nor,* or *but.* These verbs are used with the same subject.**

The heart of the wise teacheth his mouth and addeth learning to his lips. (The two parts of the verb are used with the same subject, *heart.*)

Note: A sentence may contain both a compound subject and a compound verb.

Envy and strife are unneccessary and bring discontent.

Exercise A

Draw one line under each *compound subject* and two lines under each verb. Be sure to underline all the verbs in a verb phrase.

1. Ancient paintings and writings reveal much about early civilizations.
2. India and Pakistan formed their civilizations from the Indus Valley civilization.
3. Both Sargon and Hammurabi expanded the civilization at Sumer.
4. The idea of democracy and the study of philosophy were developed by the Greeks.
5. Greek armies and merchants formed many colonies along the Mediterranean Sea.
6. Roads, bridges, and aqueducts were built by the Romans.
7. Hinduism and Buddhism developed in India during the Mauryan period.
8. Over 1,700 years ago, Chinese philosophers and scholars composed a usable dictionary.
9. During the Middle Ages, the thoughts and devices of many civilized peoples were consolidated.
10. Commerce and travel abroad were encouraged by the famous ruler Kublai Khan.
11. The Americans and the British fought the Revolutionary War.
12. During the early 1800s, North America and South America freed themselves from European dominion.
13. The opera and the symphony were developed during the Age of Reason.
14. Faith and freedom provided inspiration for the colonists in America.
15. During the Industrial Revolution, many railroads and waterways were built.
16. Airplanes, radios, and refrigerators did not even exist in 1900.
17. World War I and World War II demonstrated the results of greed.
18. Canada and the United States maintain a peaceful border between them.
19. Hunger and illiteracy are still prevalent in certain countries.
20. Man's problems and heartaches can only be solved by applying the principles of God's Word.

Exercise B

(1) Draw two lines under each *compound verb*. Be sure to underline all the verbs in a verb phrase. (2) Draw one line under each subject.

1. In the past, men have lived in log houses and traveled in hollow-log canoes.
2. In some countries, elephants haul logs from the forest and stack them.
3. A forester organizes and supervises the management of a forest.
4. A lumberjack fells trees and transports the logs to a sawmill.
5. A sawmill in a new area could attract railroads and start new towns.
6. Early settlers cleared large areas in the forest and used these areas for farms.
7. Every year in the United States, fires mar and destroy over three million acres of forest land.
8. Men in helicopters can fly over a forest fire and determine its seriousness.
9. Animals often eat or trample young tree plants.
10. We have sufficient wood at the present time and are learning about conservation for the future.

Exercise C

Draw two lines under each verb and one line under each subject. Watch carefully for compound parts and verb phrases.

1. The visiting orphans ate and drank heartily.
2. James and John were called the Sons of Thunder.
3. Tennis and golf are popular sports and can be played by young or old.
4. Apples and oranges are picked by hand and put into a pail or bag.
5. Flying squirrels and flying lemurs stretch their webbed legs and glide from tree to tree.
6. Spain and France are separated by the Pyrenees Mountains.
7. Many Canadians and New Englanders hunt and fish for a living.
8. The father forgave the Prodigal Son and prepared a feast.
9. Heatstroke and heat exhaustion can overcome a person and cause real suffering.
10. During World War II, Anne Frank and her family were betrayed and taken to concentration camps.

Diagraming Compound Subjects & Verbs

COMPOUND SUBJECT

Justice and *judgment* are the habitation of Thy throne.

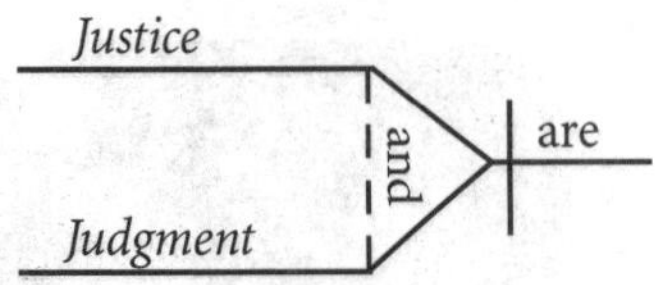

Days, months, and *years* soon expire.

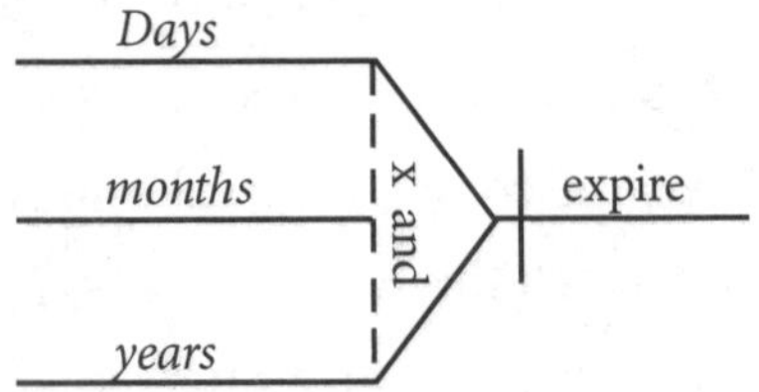

COMPOUND VERB

King Asa *destroyed* the idol and *burnt* it by the brook.

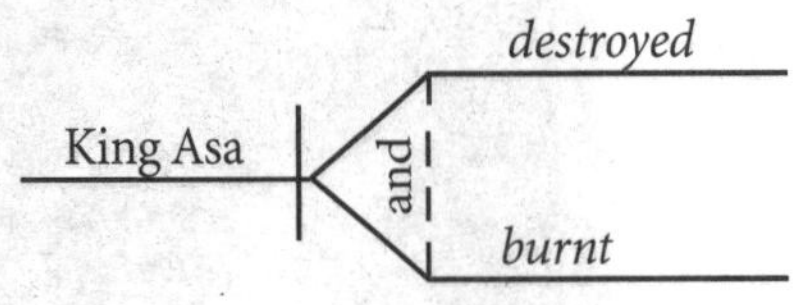

The Jews *had ignored* God's commands, *made* molten images, *worshiped* the stars, and *served* Baal.

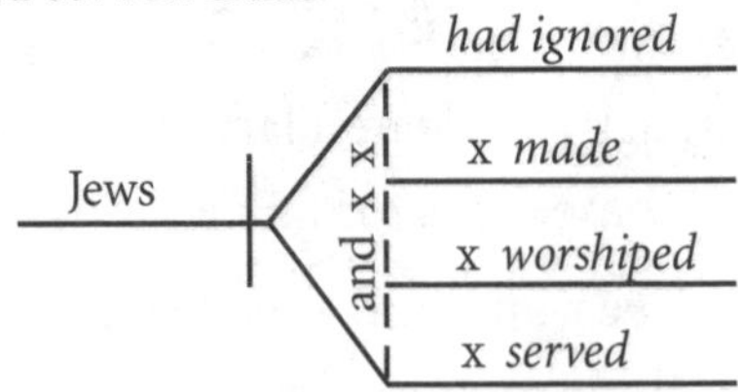

COMPOUND SUBJECT AND COMPOUND VERB

Jonathan and *David were* friends and *remained* unquestionably loyal.

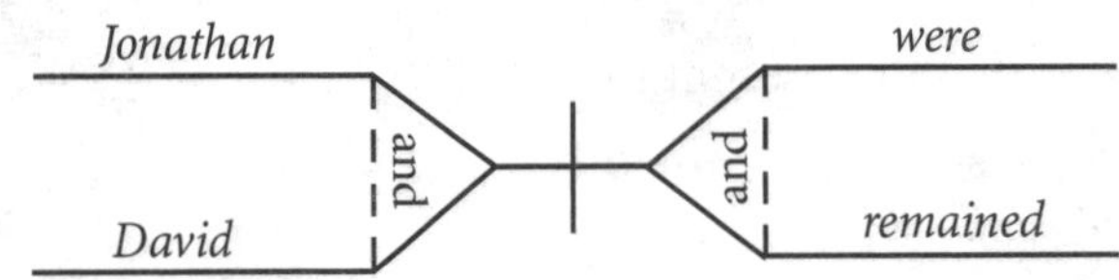

Note: The *x*'s in these diagrams are used to indicate an ellipsis (see p. 40).

Exercise A **On a separate sheet of paper, diagram the subjects and verbs from Exercise C, page 43.** (See *Supplement at back of this Teacher Key.*)

Exercise B **(1) Draw two lines under each verb and one line under each *compound subject.* (2) On a separate sheet of paper, diagram the subjects and verbs from these sentences.**

(See *Supplement.*)

1. In ancient times, Celts and other peoples lived in France.
2. Acetone and charcoal are two products of the forest.
3. California and Florida have large citrus industries.
4. John Smith and William Bradford wrote descriptions of colonial life.
5. Apples and pears can be severely damaged by the caterpillars of the codling moth.
6. Grant and Lee rank among the finest soldiers in U.S. history.

Diagraming Compound Subjects & Verbs

Exercise C **(1) Draw two lines under each *compound verb* and one line under each subject. (2) On a separate sheet of paper, diagram the subjects and verbs from these sentences.** (See *Supplement.*)

1. Spare moments of time may be discovered and used effectively.
2. One doctor translated a Latin work and rode his rounds at the same time.
3. Melanchthon, the reformer, noted every idle minute and redeemed it in good labor.
4. Sir Walter Scott was injured and confined to his bed.
5. He used his time and began his great poem "The Lay of the Last Minstrel."
6. The mayfly lives as an adult only a few hours but accomplishes its purpose in life in those moments.

Exercise D **(1) Draw two lines under each *verb* and one line under each *subject.* Watch closely for compound parts and verb phrases. (2) On a separate sheet of paper, diagram the subjects and verbs from these sentences.** (See *Supplement.*)

1. Cottonseed and soybeans are used as protein supplements for cattle.
2. Diesel engines burn cheap fuel and can perform heavy-duty work.
3. Electronic equipment and aircraft parts are manufactured in Dallas, Texas, a major center for such production.
4. Reservoirs and lakes often provide recreational areas for boating and swimming.
5. Operating from underwater laboratories, divers can live and work for weeks without surfacing.
6. Cranes and derricks lift and move heavy loads.
7. Most viruses can be seen only by means of a powerful electron microscope.
8. Computers on a space shuttle control the launch process and navigate the shuttle.
9. Both clams and oysters are classified as mollusks.
10. Iron reacts with oxygen in the air and forms rust.
11. Mercury becomes a liquid at room temperature and flows easily and rapidly.
12. Our kidneys filter approximately forty-five gallons of blood daily.
13. Scientists have named and described approximately 22,000 species of fish.
14. Miners may use several different methods in the extraction of salt.
15. Farmers feed salt to livestock and use it as a preservative for hay in storage.

Grammar

Locating Complements

Many times a subject and a verb are sufficient to express a complete thought.

The sun has risen.
The donkey balked.

But sometimes a third part, called a *complement,* is needed to complete the thought. This third part is called a complement because it completes the meaning begun by the subject and verb.

John is . . .
William broke . . .
Janice often rides . . .

In later lessons you will learn to *identify* the various kinds of complements. In this lesson you simply need to learn the procedure for *locating* complements. In general, you may locate a complement by asking the questions *who, whom,* or *what* after the verb.

Mr. Smith is our favorite teacher. (Mr. Smith is *what?* Mr. Smith is *teacher. Teacher* is the complement.)

Our team won the championship game. (Team won *what?* Team won *game. Game* is the complement.)

Sarah took Bethany to the store with her. (Sarah took *whom?* Sarah took *Bethany. Bethany* is the complement.)

Note: Complements cannot be within prepositional phrases.

Exercise

(1) Underline each subject once and each verb twice. (2) Draw a circle around each complement.

1. In 1783, a person used a parachute for the first time.
2. These early parachutes were large, rib-supported canvas umbrellas.
3. Exhibition jumpers first used parachutes with rip-cords in 1908.
4. The Wright brothers flew the first airplane in 1903.
5. John Alcock flew a plane from Newfoundland to Ireland sixteen years later.
6. Alcock and his navigator were the first men to fly nonstop across the Atlantic Ocean.
7. Charles Lindbergh crossed the Atlantic alone in 1927.
8. He was his own navigator on his flight.
9. That was the first solo, nonstop flight across the Atlantic Ocean.
10. The long flight was dangerous and lonely.
11. Lindbergh received a hero's welcome in Paris.
12. He won a large sum of money for his accomplishment.
13. Upon his return, Americans welcomed Lindbergh with a ticker-tape parade.

Recognizing Sentences & Fragments

1 **A *sentence* is a group of words that expresses a complete thought. It always has a subject and a predicate.**

A hopeful spirit will discern the silver lining of the darkest cloud.

2 **A *fragment* is a separated sentence part that does *not* express a complete thought.**

When all other things fail us. (fragment)
When all other things fail us, hope stands by us to the last. (sentence)
Running away from difficulties. (fragment)
Running away from difficulties, the man came to poverty. (sentence)
An island off the coast of Turkey. (fragment)
We visited Rhodes, *an island off the coast of Turkey.* (sentence)

UNIT 3

Exercise

In the blank before each number, write *s.* if the group of words is a sentence; write *frag.* if it is a fragment.

frag. 1. If the best man's faults were written on his forehead.
s. 2. Pride must have a fall.
frag. 3. While it aims at honor and reputation.
frag. 4. Trying to be somebody.
s. 5. Pride hardens the heart.
s. 6. Pride is founded on a high opinion of ourselves.
frag. 7. He that is proud.
s. 8. Pride is generally the effect of ignorance.
s. 9. All other virtues are choked by pride.
frag. 10. Rejecting the counsels of reason.
s. 11. Proud persons generally think of nothing but themselves.
frag. 12. Supposing that others think only of them.
frag. 13. When flowers are full of heaven-sent dew.
s. 14. They always hang their heads.
frag. 15. Taking absolutely no notice of him at any time.
frag. 16. As the sun appears largest when about to set.
s. 17. The fear of the Lord is the beginning of wisdom.
s. 18. We must all go from here.
s. 19. Humility softens the temper and the disposition.
frag. 20. When we realize that our life is but a moment compared to eternity.

Grammar

Correcting Fragments

The easiest way to correct a fragment is to rejoin it to the sentence from which it has been separated.

Wherever character is made a secondary object. Sensualism and crime prevail. (fragment)
Wherever character is made a secondary object, sensualism and crime prevail. (corrected)
The missionary took flying lessons. *To be able to fly into remote villages.* (fragment)
The missionary took flying lessons *to be able to fly into remote villages.* (corrected)

Exercise A

Each of the items below consists of two groups of words. If both are sentences, write *s.* in the blank. If one is a fragment, write *frag.* and correct the error.

Examples: s. 1. Be courteous. Good manners insure success.
frag. 2. Courage is fear/ ~~T~~t hat has said its prayers.

frag. 1. The enormous jewfish is a slow-swimming fish/ ~~T~~t hat stays close to the bottom of coastal waters.
s. 2. Some fish are very flat. Others can assume the shape of a balloon.
frag. 3. An archerfish spits drops of water at insects/ ~~R~~r esting above the surface of the water.
frag. 4. During its lifetime, ~~A~~a fish may increase several thousand times in size.
s. 5. A school of tuna may consist of fewer than twenty-five individuals. Schools of herring may number in the hundreds of millions.
s. 6. Some fish sleep on the bottom. Some sleep in midwater.
frag. 7. Occasionally, water temperatures drop suddenly, ~~K~~k illing many fish.

Exercise B

Make complete sentences of the fragments in the exercise on page 47. Before or after each fragment, add enough words to make a complete thought.

Answers will vary.

Correcting Run-on Sentences

A *run-on sentence* is two or more sentences written incorrectly as one sentence. (Sentences cannot be correctly written with *only* a comma between the sentences or with *no punctuation* between.) Notice how the run-on sentences below have been corrected.

Run-on	Every human being is a center of influence for good or evil no man can live unto himself. (no punctuation between the sentences)
Corrected	Every human being is a center of influence for good or evil. No man can live unto himself.
Run-on	Each young person should begin well, then the habit of doing well will become as easy as the habit of doing badly. (only a comma between the sentences)
Corrected	Each young person should begin well. Then the habit of doing well will become as easy as the habit of doing badly.
	Note: The word *then* is not a conjunction and cannot be used to join independent clauses.
Run-on	Every day is a little life our whole life is but a day repeated.
Corrected	Every day is a little life, and our whole life is but a day repeated.

Exercise A

Correct each of the following run-on sentences by supplying periods and capital letters.

Example: Do not give up. Keep on trying.

1. Birds with protective coloration are hidden from their enemies. They blend into their surroundings.
2. The hummingbird beats its wings sixty times a second. As a result, it can hover in the air like a helicopter.
3. Bird sanctuaries have been set up in many areas. These places of refuge protect the birds from their many enemies.
4. There were once millions of passenger pigeons. Now these wonderful creatures are extinct.
5. The wood duck builds its nest in a hollow tree. Often this nest is up to a mile from water.
6. The mother calls for each duckling to climb out of the nest. They are to jump to the ground.
7. Those ducklings that do not obey their mother's voice are left in the nest. There they will face possible death.
8. It takes courage to obey difficult instructions. The wise man will obey for his own good.
9. An eagle will fly with its young on its back. Then it will suddenly dive and leave the eaglets in midair.
10. The young eagles immediately begin to flutter their wings. It is in this manner that they learn to fly.

Exercise B

Some of the following groups of words are sentences. Others are run-ons. (1) Put *s.* before the number of a correctly written sentence and put *r.o.* before the number of a run-on sentence. (2) Correct the run-on sentences by supplying a period and a capital letter.

s. 1. An invention differs from a discovery, but they are closely related.

s. 2. An invention is the creation of something that never existed before.

r.o. 3. Most inventions have benefited mankind, [. S] some inventions, however, have caused harm.

r.o. 4. Eli Whitney invented the cotton gin [. T] this machine could remove cotton seeds fifty times as fast as men working by hand.

s. 5. Samuel Morse developed the dot-dash code, which made the telegraph commercially successful.

r.o. 6. Thomas Edison was perhaps the greatest inventor in history, [. H] his first invention was a vote recorder.

r.o. 7. Ottmar Mergenthaler patented the Linotype machine, [. H] his invention eliminated the need to set type by hand.

r.o. 8. The electric starter was invented by Charles F. Kettering, [. B] before this invention, automobile engines had to be cranked by hand.

r.o. 9. George Eastman's inventions made picture taking a family affair, [. T] then later Edwin Land developed a camera that would produce a finished print in one minute.

s. 10. Today, many pocket calculators can do the same job as the first electronic computer, which filled a large room.

Exercise C

Correct each of the following run-on sentences by supplying *a period and a capital letter* or by supplying *a comma and coordinating conjunction (and, but, or)*. You decide which is the better way to correct the sentences.

1. A penny is a very small amount, [but] the comfort of many families depends upon the proper saving and spending of pennies.
2. Economy is not merely saving [. I] it is foresight and arrangement.
3. It is every man's duty to live within his means [. T] this practice is the very essence of honesty.
4. Men are not ruined by what they want [. T] they are ruined by what they think they want.
5. Do not buy what you do not want, [or] you will soon want what you cannot buy.
6. Wealth does not make the man [. W] wealth should not be taken into account in our judgment of men.
7. Give your tithe to the Lord first [. T] then put some money into savings regularly.

8. Have high ambitions and richness of spirit. [T]this kind of wealth is far beyond all worldly possessions.

9. Economy is management of little things. [S]some men live better on twenty thousand dollars than others do on fifty thousand.

10. There is no virtue so unappreciated as economy, [and] a neglect of economy leads to poverty and sometimes to crime.

UNIT 3

Exercise D

Correct the run-on sentences in the following paragraphs by supplying *periods and capital letters* or by supplying *commas and coordinating conjunctions (and, but, or).*

The Lord told Jeremiah to go to the family of the Rechabites and to bring them into the temple in Jerusalem. Jeremiah did as God commanded him. [W]when he had brought them into a chamber, he set before them several jugs of wine. The prophet then invited this family to drink. [W]with one accord the Rechabites refused. They informed Jeremiah that their ancestor had commanded them not to drink wine, [and] they would obey his word. From this bold answer, the Lord showed his prophet a message for the people of Judah.

Almost two centuries before this, the Rechabite ancestor Jonadab, a relative of Moses' father-in-law, had given instructions to his family. [H]he had told them never to drink wine, nor live in houses, nor farm the land. [H]he wanted them to remain a simple people. Also, Jonadab knew that if they became involved in these things, they might turn to the worship of Baal. [T]this is what he most wanted to avoid. Since that time, the Rechabites had obeyed their forefather. [T]they lived in tents in the desert and herded sheep. [T]they also drank no wine at all.

Oh, that Judah had obeyed the Lord as faithfully as this family obeyed its ancestor! The Rechabites had been told only once, [but] they obeyed implicitly. Judah had been given God's commandments many times, [and] there had been many prophets who stood and proclaimed the Word of the Lord to backslidden Judah, [but] they refused to obey God. For this reason, Judah was conquered by heathen Babylon, [and] many of their people were taken as slaves. The Rechabites obeyed their father Jonadab, [and] God blessed them for it. Judah disobeyed God and was punished.

Exercise A

(1) Draw a vertical line between the complete subject and the complete predicate. (2) Draw two lines under each simple predicate (verb) and one line under each simple subject. Watch for compound parts and verb phrases.

1. The modern game of baseball | originated from the old English sport of rounders.
2. Alexander J. Cartwright | in 1845 compiled a set of rules and regulations for baseball.
3. The Boston Red Sox and the Pittsburgh Pirates | played in the first World Series in the fall of 1903.
4. The origin of the game of football | can be traced to the English game of rugby.
5. Walter C. Camp, a Yale undergraduate, | made many innovations and changes in the rules of football.
6. Football | is televised more than any other sport in the United States.
7. The game of basketball | originated in the United States in 1891.
8. Dr. James Naismith, the inventor of basketball, | tacked up two peach baskets and used a soccer ball for the first game.

Exercise B

(1) Underline each subject once and each verb twice. (2) Draw a circle around each complement. Remember that a complement cannot be in a prepositional phrase. One sentence does not have a complement.

1. Africa is the second largest (continent).
2. Trade between African coastal cities and Europe began in ancient times.
3. Before the nineteenth century, people knew very (little) about Africa's interior.
4. Europeans became (interested) in Africa's gold, diamonds, and ivory.
5. By 1914, many European nations had established (colonies) in Africa.

Exercise C

Write examples of each of the following kinds of sentences: (1) declarative, (2) exclamatory, (3) interrogative, (4) imperative, (5) simple sentence with compound subject, (6) simple sentence with compound verb, (7) simple sentence with compound subject and verb.

1. Answers will vary. __________
2. __________
3. __________
4. __________
5. __________
6. __________
7. __________

Exercise D

Some of the following items contain correctly written sentences. Others contain a sentence fragment. Others contain a run-on sentence. (1) Put *s.* before an item that contains correctly written sentences. Put *frag.* before an item that contains a fragment. Put *r.o.* before an item that contains a run-on sentence. (2) Correct each fragment and each run-on sentence.

frag. 1. Some unusual plants are carnivorous, which means "meat-eating."

frag. 2. They need insects to supply certain nutrients because they cannot get these nutrients from the soil.

s. 3. These plants also produce food for themselves through photosynthesis. This is in addition to that nourishment which they obtain from the trapped insects.

r.o. 4. Pitcher plants have leaves which form a bowl. The bowl collects water when it rains.

frag. 5. Being attracted by sweet substances on the leaves, bees often fall into the water.

r.o. 6. The insects drown in the water. Then the plant digests them with certain secreted fluids.

frag. 7. Juices on the hairs of the sundew plant trap insects, which are later suffocated by more liquid.

frag. 8. The Venus' flytrap has hinged leaves with sharp bristles along the edges.

r.o. 9. Many of these unique plants grow wild along the coasts of North and South Carolina, and they are often grown in greenhouses as curiosities.

s. 10. The Venus' flytrap often grows to a height of one foot.

Exercise E

Correct the fragments and run-ons in the following paragraph.

Russia is a land of unusual contrasts. The old and the new, the cultured and the rustic, the fertile and the arid all co-exist here. Nowhere is this contrast more evident than in its geography. Well watered by many rivers, eastern Russia is a broad, fertile land. Its once-grassy plains have been laid to the plow and now produce great quantities of grain. How different these gently rolling hills are from the vast, sandy deserts that extend along the southern tip of this vast nation! Northern and southern Russia also differ greatly. Far in the northern regions along the Arctic Ocean, such ports as Archangel and Murmansk are ice bound much of the year. On the southern border in the Crimean area, the climate is very temperate. This area greatly resembles southern California and, like California, abounds with citrus groves. Russia is well-nigh a world in itself, having almost every type of geography within its borders.

Exercise A Capitalization. Circle each letter that should be capitalized.

1. in 1770, captain james cook claimed possession of australia for britain.
2. on january 26, 1788, a group of english prisoners settled in sydney.
3. one of the prisoners, marcus clarke, wrote a novel about his experiences called *for the term of his natural life.*
4. robert ohara and william wills first crossed the continent from melbourne to the gulf of carpentaria.
5. many of the aborigines, the original inhabitants of Australia, have not yet been reached with the message of the lord jesus christ.
6. after world war II, many persons migrated to australia from austria, germany, great britain, greece, hungary, italy, holland, poland, and yugoslavia.

Exercise B Punctuation. Add all necessary punctuation to the following sentences.

1. Yes, Molly, you may reach her by writing to Route 3, Box 41, Pocahontas, Arkansas.
2. The huge cassowary bird of New Guinea and Australia, as a matter of fact, is the most dangerous of birds. it can cripple or kill a man with its sharp claws.
3. I recently read an article in the Atlantic Monthly, a fine magazine. it was entitled "Our Debt to the Past."
4. Mrs. Bass's son, a student at Pensacola Christian College, graduated on May 13, 1998.
5. In Psalm 93: 2, we read, "Thy throne is established of old. Thou art from everlasting."
6. We should be like David, the Psalmist of Israel, who said, "How sweet are Thy words unto my taste."
7. Ralph, in your essay I found thirty-three *and*'s and twelve *very*'s.
8. In 1 Kings 10: 22, we find that Solomon's treasures included the following: gold, silver, ivory, apes, and peacocks.

Exercise C Capitalization and Punctuation. (1) Draw a line through each incorrect small letter. Write a capital above it. (2) Add punctuation marks where needed.

1. In st. martinville, louisiana, you may see the evangeline oak, which was made famous by henry wadsworth longfellow.
2. On june 28, 1838, Queen Victoria began her long reign which lasted until january 22, 1901.
3. Oxford university, established in england in the 1100s, is one of the european universities that date from the middle ages.
4. In 1954, the nautilus, the world's first nuclear-powered submarine, was launched at groton, connecticut.

Exercise D Subject and Verbs. Draw two lines under each verb and one line under each subject. Watch carefully for compound parts and verb phrases.

1. Owls and cowbirds will often steal nests from other birds.
2. Flamingos scrape mud together and build a conelike nest.
3. The hummingbird's nest is the size of a golf ball.
4. It is made of plant down and spider webs and holds the tiny, pea-sized eggs.
5. The eagle's cliff-top nest is frequently mentioned in tales and stories.
6. Grasses and plant fibers compose the oriole's saclike nest.
7. The robin often returns to the same spot each year and builds its nest.
8. Wrens will nest in such unusual places as an old hat or a mailbox.
9. Martins send out scouts for good houses.
10. Upon arrival, the females can immediately settle into their new homes.

UNIT 3

Exercise E Diagraming. On a separate sheet of paper, diagram the subjects and verbs from the sentences in Exercise D. (See *Supplement.*)

Exercise F Complements. Underline the subject once and the verb twice. Circle any complements. Not all sentences contain complements.

1. The Bay of Bengal and the Arabian Sea form India's eastern and western borders.
2. The Himalaya Mountains separate India from the rest of Asia.
3. Because of this separation, India is called a subcontinent.
4. For centuries, India was isolated from the rest of the world.
5. As a result, Indians developed a unique culture.
6. The Ancient Indian civilization was a very advanced civilization.
7. Ancient Indians had well-planned cities, indoor plumbing, and extensive drainage systems.
8. India's most famous building is the beautiful Taj Mahal.

Exercise G The Sentence. In the blank before the number, write *s.* for sentences, *frag.* for fragments, or *r.o.* for run-ons.

r.o. 1. Herman Melville wrote several stories about the sea *Billy Budd* is one of the best.
frag. 2. Although I also like his book *Moby Dick.*
s. 3. Moby Dick was a gigantic white whale.
r.o. 4. Captain Ahab wanted to kill Moby Dick, it had crippled him.
r.o. 5. I enjoy Robert Louis Stevenson's books they are full of action and interesting to read.
s. 6. His book *The Black Arrow* is a fascinating story about the War of the Roses.
frag. 7. Because it has a good ending.

Unit 4 *Verbs & Their Uses*

Grammar

Recognizing Parts of Speech

In our language, there are eight kinds of words called **parts of speech: verbs, nouns, pronouns, adjectives, adverbs, prepositions, conjunctions,** and **interjections.** We will study these one at a time in separate units. In order to do well in English, you must know the eight parts of speech. Determine now to master these basic tools of your language.

The first step in mastering the parts of speech is to memorize their definitions. The definitions are listed below. Memorize these now and review them often throughout the year.

Definitions of the Eight Parts of Speech

1. A **verb** is a word that ***shows action, links*** a word to the subject, ***helps*** another verb, or merely ***indicates existence.***
2. A **noun** is a word that ***names*** a person, place, thing, or idea.
3. A **pronoun** is a word that ***takes the place of a noun.***
4. An **adjective** is a word that ***modifies a noun or a pronoun.*** It answers the questions ***what kind, which one, how many, how much*** or ***whose.***
5. An **adverb** is a word that ***modifies a verb,*** an ***adjective,*** or another ***adverb.*** It answers the questions ***where, when, how, how often, to what extent.***
6. A **preposition** is a word that shows how a noun or a pronoun ***is related*** to some other word in the sentence.
7. A **conjunction** is a word that ***joins*** words or groups of words.
8. An **interjection** is an ***exclamatory word*** that is not related to the other words in a sentence.

Before you begin to study the various parts of speech, take the following diagnostic test to help you determine how much you already know.

Exercise **Identify the parts of speech of the italicized words. Write *v.* for verb, *n.* for noun, *pro.* for pronoun, *adj.* for adjective, *adv.* for adverb, *prep.* for preposition, *conj.* for conjunction, *interj.* for interjection.**

"Yea, *joyfully*[1] shall *I*[2] *go*,"[3] *were*[4] the *words*[5] spoken *by*[6] a *courageous*[7] *Quaker*[8] *woman*[9] after a *Boston*[10] magistrate *condemned*[11] *her*[12] as a *heretic*[13] and *sentenced*[14] her to die. *She*[15] had *narrowly*[16] *escaped*[17] the *gallows*[18] once before, *but*[19] *this*[20] time the governor *would*[21] *not*[22] grant a reprieve. The *next*[23] day, *Mary Dyer*[24] was hanged because she would not compromise her *conscience*.[25]

1. adv.	6. prep.	11. v.	16. adv.	21. v.
2. pro.	7. adj.	12. pro.	17. v.	22. adv.
3. v.	8. adj.	13. n.	18. n.	23. adj.
4. v.	9. n.	14. v.	19. conj.	24. n.
5. n.	10. adj.	15. pro.	20. adj.	25. n.

Grammar

UNIT 4

Recognizing Action Verbs

Of all the parts of speech, the verb is the most important. It is the part around which all other elements are built. It is essential that you be able to identify verbs and use them correctly.

1 **A *verb* is a word that *shows action, links* another word to the subject, *helps* another verb, or merely *indicates existence.***

Joan *prepared* dinner. (action verb—shows what the subject is doing)
The stew *smells* delicious. (linking verb—links *delicious* to the subject *stew*)
We ***will*** *enjoy* the meal. (helping verb—***will*** helps the verb *enjoy* to show action)
Our new neighbors *are* here. (merely indicates the existence of neighbors)

2 **An *action verb* expresses *physical* or *mental action.***

walk, sit, laugh, swim, eat, jog (physical action verbs)
consider, trust, dream, realize, appreciate (mental action verbs)

Exercise A

Draw a circle around each action verb. Note: It is acceptable for students not to circle helping verbs.

1. Behold, I (stand) at the door and (knock). If any man (hear) My voice and (open) the door, I (will come) in to him and (will sup) with him, and he with Me.
2. If ye (shall ask) any thing in My name, I (will do) it.
3. If ye (love) Me, (keep) My commandments.

Exercise B

Fill in each blank with an appropriate action verb. Answers may vary.

1. Noah studied diligently for his math test.
2. Our basketball team won the game for the district championship.
3. We play chess when it rains.
4. The little boy dreamed about the day he would become a fireman.
5. The custodian swept the hall floor.
6. Most bears hibernate during the cold winter months.
7. Mr. Dunn assigned three exercises for homework.
8. Pollen causes people with hay fever to sneeze.
9. John opened the garage door for his father.
10. The homesick girl ran to meet her parents.

Grammar

Recognizing Linking Verbs

1 **A *linking verb* does not express action. It *links* a word in the predicate to the subject.**

The pizza *smells* delicious. (The verb *smells* links *delicious* to the subject *pizza.*)

Frank *is* a good student. (The verb *is* links *student* to the subject *Frank.*)

Linking Verbs				
am	were	taste	look	grow
is	be	feel	appear	remain
are	being	smell	become	stay
was	been	sound	seem	

2 **The verbs *am, is , are, was, were, be, being, been* are forms of the verb "be." These "be" verbs may be used as helping verbs as well as linking verbs.**

We *are* a happy family. (The verb *are* links *family* to the subject *we.*)

We ***are*** *serving* the Lord. (The verb ***are*** helps the verb *serving* to show action.)

3 **The verbs *taste, feel, smell, sound, look, appear, become, seem, grow, remain, stay* may be used as action verbs as well as linking verbs, depending on the sense of the sentence.**

Mary *looks* pretty in that dress. (*Looks* is a linking verb that links *pretty* to the subject *Mary.*)

Mary *looks* for attractive but modest clothing. (*Looks* is an action verb. The subject is performing the action of looking.)

Exercise A

(1) Insert a linking verb in each blank. Use a different verb each time. (2) Draw an arrow to indicate the word in the predicate that is linked to the subject.

Verbs may vary.

Example: I hope our country remains strong.

1. I am the true vine, and My Father is the husbandman.
2. My brother will become a missionary after he finishes college.
3. To those ignorant of the Scriptures, the future seems uncertain.
4. The chocolate cake tasted delicious to the three hungry boys.
5. Can you remain calm throughout difficult circumstances?
6. Christians are members of God's family.
7. Maria was very confident about the outcome of the essay contest.
8. Honesty is always the best policy.
9. Daniel stayed true to his principles.
10. After eight hours of sleep, you should look refreshed.

Recognizing Linking Verbs

Exercise B **(1) At the end of each sentence, write *action* if the italicized verb shows action; write *linking* if the verb links. (2) For the linking verbs, draw an arrow to indicate the word that is linked to the subject.**

Example: The animal *appears* tame. linking

1. Gideon *sounded* the charge to attack the Midianites. action
2. In 1820, Maine *became* the twenty-third state in the Union. linking
3. Adam *looked* distressed as he saw the work piled high before him. linking
4. Frank *looked* in the Bible for words of comfort. action
5. They *grew* excited at the prospects of visiting their state capital. linking
6. He *tasted* defeat as his ski caught the flag in the slalom race. action
7. Jennifer *appeared* confident backstage before the performance. linking
8. This *has been* a wonderful year of new experiences. linking
9. My little sister Gretchen *is growing* like a weed. action
10. The Israelites *tasted* the bitter waters of Marah. action
11. Julie always *feels* a surge of patriotism as the flag passes by. action
12. The purple lilacs *are* fragrant and beautiful. linking
13. Terry *seemed* greatly concerned about his friend Jeff. linking
14. Ruth *remained* faithful to her mother-in-law Naomi. linking
15. Catherine *looked* daily to the Lord for wisdom and guidance. action

Exercise C **For each of the following verbs, write two sentences. Use the verbs as action verbs in the first sentence and as linking verbs in the second. (1) taste, (2) feel, (3) smell, (4) look.**

1. (action) Answers will vary.
   (linking) ______
2. (action) ______
   (linking) ______
3. (action) ______
   (linking) ______
4. (action) ______
   (linking) ______

UNIT 4

Recognizing Helping Verbs

1 A *helping verb helps* the main verb to make a statement.

Christians ***must obey*** God's Word. (The verb ***must*** helps the main verb *obey* to show action.)

Christians ***must be*** obedient to God's Word. (The verb ***must*** helps the main verb *be* to link *obedient* to the subject *Christians.*)

We ***will be*** there today. (The verb ***will*** helps the main verb *be* indicate existence.)

Helping Verbs					
am	were	have	do	shall	may
is	be	has	does	will	might
are	being	had	did	should	must
was	been			would	can
					could

Note: The forms of "be" may be linking as well as helping verbs. The forms of "have" and "do" may also be action verbs.

2 A *verb phrase* is a main verb and its helping verbs.

3 A *verb phrase* is sometimes *interrupted* by adverbs. The adverb *not* is a common interrupter.

He *will* **readily** *agree* to the plan.

Discouragement *does* **not** *come* from God.

4 The *subject* of an interrogative sentence usually interrupts the verb phrase.

Where *does* **discouragement** *come* from?

Exercise A

Underline the verb phrases in the following sentences. Do not underline a word unless it shows action or unless it is one of the words in the verb lists that you have memorized.

1. The cowboy could easily be one of the most misrepresented figures in history.
2. Although a figure of many romantic legends, the cowboy did face many dangers.
3. Stampedes, which were often caused by thunderstorms, were greatly feared by the cowboy.
4. The cowboy has been almost completely replaced by the prairie farmer.
5. The cotton gin was invented by Eli Whitney.
6. The horse-drawn reaper was invented by Cyrus McCormick.
7. Tractors had almost replaced draft animals by 1930.
8. The following innovations were used by the prairie farmer: barbed wire, the steel-tipped plow, and the windmill.
9. Could the Dust Bowl have been avoided if farmers had exercised soil conservation techniques?
10. Today, farming has developed into a highly scientific procedure.

Exercise B

Underline the verb phrases in the following paragraph. Do not underline a word unless it shows action or unless it is one of the words in the verb lists that you have memorized.

We should always be cheerful. The times may be difficult, but a sad and gloomy countenance will not make them easier. The flower is made by the sunshine; it is not made by the clouds. Our hearts can be filled with warmth from the good things around us. We may have troubles, but we should not allow discouragement. No one can be completely free from problems; we should extract courage and fortitude from them. We should look on the bright side of everything, and then we can receive the maximum happiness from each day.

Exercise C

(1) Underline the verb phrases in the following sentences. (2) At the end of each sentence, write *linking* if the phrase is a linking verb phrase; write *action* if the phrase is an action verb phrase. The last word in the phrase determines the kind of phrase. If the last word is an action verb, the phrase is an action verb phrase; if the last word is a linking verb, the phrase is a linking verb phrase.

1. I will guide thee with mine eye. action
2. Ye shall be hated of all men for My name's sake. action
3. Thy statutes have been my songs. linking
4. Ye have set at nought all my counsel. action
5. They may be a witness unto Me. linking
6. I will be their God. linking
7. He is risen from the dead. action
8. How is Babylon become a desolation among the nations! linking
9. A wise man will increase learning. action
10. They were armed with bows. action

Distinguishing Verbs from Verbals

Sometimes verb *forms* are not used as verbs but *as verbals.* A *verbal* is a verb *form* used as a noun, adjective, or adverb. Later you will learn some details about verbals, but here you simply need to learn to *distinguish verbs from verbals.*

1 **To distinguish verbs from verbals, remember two things: (1) a *verb* has a subject; a verbal generally does not, (2) a *verbal* functions as a noun, adjective, or adverb.**

In the following paragraph, the subjects have been underlined once and the verbs have been underlined twice. The verbals have been circled. Carefully study each verbal, noticing its function in the sentence.

Thomas Alva Edison (s.) made (v.) significant contributions to modern life with his inventions. Edison (s.) never claimed (v.) (to be) (n.) a great scientist, but he was a technological genius. (Using) (adj.) scientific principles in a practical way, he (s.) invented (v.) many things and patented 1,093 of those inventions. Edison is best remembered for (inventing) (n.) the incandescent electric light bulb. Other popular inventions were the (talking) (adj.) phonograph and the motion picture machine.

Exercise A

In each sentence, a verb and a verbal are italicized. Decide which italicized word is a verb and write it in the blank.

woke 1. The *chirping* birds *woke* me early this morning.

requires 2. *Playing* the piano skillfully *requires* great diligence.

are praying 3. We *are praying* that your *broken* leg will heal quickly.

reached 4. *Praying* earnestly, the Taylors *reached* a decision.

wanted 5. John *wanted* to *sweep* the porch.

enjoy 6. Many Alaskans *enjoy fishing* for salmon.

showed 7. The architect *showed* us the *revised* plans.

has been mailed 8. The package *containing* my latest manuscript *has been mailed* to the publisher.

plans 9. The mayor *plans* to *attend* the dedication.

received 10. For *winning* the event, the boys each *received* a trophy.

Distinguishing Verbs from Verbals (cont.)

A *participle* is one kind of verbal. It functions as an adjective. Participles will be studied in detail later in this book. At this point, you simply need to learn to recognize participles and be able to tell them from verbs.

2 **A *participle* is a verbal used as an *adjective* to modify a *noun* or a *pronoun.* A participle has an ending similar to a verb *(-ing, -d, -ed, -t,* or *-en),* but functions as an adjective in the sentence.**

Nicholas is *studying* in the library. (*Is studying* is the verb in this sentence.)

Studying in the library, Nicholas lost track of time. (*Lost* is the verb because the sentence is about the action of *losing.* The verb form *studying* is an adjective describing the noun *Nicholas. Studying* is a *participle.)*

The pirates *buried* the treasure. (*Buried* is a verb.)

We found the *buried* treasure. (*Found* is the verb because the sentence is about the action of *finding.* The verb form *buried* is an adjective describing the noun *treasure. Buried* is a *participle.)*

The toast, *burnt* to a crisp, was not edible. (*Was* is the verb. The verb form *burnt* is an adjective describing the noun *toast. Burnt* is a *participle.)*

Hidden away in the attic, my skis became moldy. (*Became* is the verb. The verb form *hidden* is an adjective describing the noun *skis. Hidden* is a *participle.)*

Exercise B

(1) Draw two lines under each verb or verb phrase. (2) Draw a circle around each participle. (3) Draw an arrow from each participle to the noun or pronoun that it modifies.

1. Bitten by a rabid dog, Joseph Meister was exposed to the rabies virus.
2. Learning of Joseph's injuries, his parents became very distraught.
3. The French scientist Louis Pasteur, working diligently in his laboratory, had developed a possible vaccine for rabies.
4. The mother brought her injured son to Pasteur's laboratory in Paris.
5. Yielding to the mother's pleas, Pasteur finally consented to treat the child.
6. Feeling somewhat reluctant, Pasteur vaccinated the boy with the new serum.
7. Watching every symptom of the child, Pasteur continued the treatment for several weeks.
8. The lad, undergoing this treatment, never developed rabies.
9. Dr. Pasteur's vaccine almost eliminated a disease feared all over the world.
10. Many great discoveries have been made through methods involving trial-and-error procedures.

Grammar

Using Principal Parts I

Verbs have four *principal parts:* the *present,* the *present participle,* the *past,* and the *past participle.*

1 **All verbs may be classified as *regular* or *irregular* verbs, depending on the way that the past and past participle are formed.**

2 ***Regular verbs* form the past and past participle by adding *-ed, -d,* or *-t* to the present.**

use, use***d***, (have) use***d*** start, start***ed***, (have) start***ed*** mean, mean***t***, (have) mean***t***

3 ***Irregular verbs* form the past and past participle in irregular ways other than by adding *-ed, -d,* or *-t* to the present.** (Memorize the forms of the irregular verbs on page 65.)

go, went, (have) gone ride, rode, (have) ridden burst, burst, (have) burst

4 **Both regular and irregular verbs form the *present participle* by adding *-ing* to the *present.***

talk, talk***ing*** burn, burn***ing*** carry, carry***ing***

5 **Sometimes *spelling changes* must be made before adding *-ing* or *-ed* to verbs.**

a. For verbs ending in silent *e,* drop the *e* before adding *-ing.*

save, sav***ing*** hope, hop***ing*** **Exceptions:** canoeing, hoeing

b. For verbs ending in *y* preceded by a consonant, change the *y* to *i* before adding *-ed.*

sp***y***, sp***i***ed, sp***i***ed hurr***y***, hurr***i***ed, hurr***i***ed

c. For verbs ending in a single consonant preceded by a single vowel, usually double the final consonant before adding *-ed* or *-ing.*

flip, flip***p***ing, flip***p***ed, flip***p***ed plan, plan***n***ing, plan***n***ed, plan***n***ed

Exercise A

Write the principal parts of the following verbs. Use the helping verb *am* with the present participle and the helping verb *have* with the past participle to remind you that these two principal parts are always used with helping verbs.

Present	Present Participle	Past	Past Participle
1. try	(am) trying	tried	(have) tried
2. support	(am) supporting	supported	(have) supported
3. ask	(am) asking	asked	(have) asked
4. permit	(am) permitting	permitted	(have) permitted
5. shield	(am) shielding	shielded	(have) shielded
6. fill	(am) filling	filled	(have) filled
7. nourish	(am) nourishing	nourished	(have) nourished

Exercise B

Write sentences illustrating the following: (1) the present participle of *drop,* (2) the past of *risk,* (3) the past participle of *work.*

1. Answers will vary. ____________________

2. ____________________

3. ____________________

Using Principal Parts I

Learn the principal parts of these irregular verbs. The present participle has been omitted because it presents no problem. It always ends in *-ing*. When learning the forms, it is helpful to include a helping verb with the past participle.

Irregular Verbs

Present	Past	Past Participle	Present	Past	Past Participle
beat	beat	(have) beaten	pay	paid	(have) paid
begin	began	(have) begun	ride	rode	(have) ridden
bite	bit	(have) bitten	ring	rang	(have) rung
blow	blew	(have) blown	rise	rose	(have) risen
break	broke	(have) broken	run	ran	(have) run
bring	brought	(have) brought	say	said	(have) said
build	built	(have) built	see	saw	(have) seen
burst	burst	(have) burst	set	set	(have) set
buy	bought	(have) bought	shake	shook	(have) shaken
choose	chose	(have) chosen	shine	shone, shined[2]	(have) shone, shined[2]
come	came	(have) come	show	showed	(have) shown
do	did	(have) done	shrink	shrank	(have) shrunk
draw	drew	(have) drawn	sing	sang	(have) sung
drink	drank	(have) drunk	sink	sank	(have) sunk
drive	drove	(have) driven	sit	sat	(have) sat
eat	ate	(have) eaten	speak	spoke	(have) spoken
fall	fell	(have) fallen	spring	sprang	(have) sprung
fly	flew	(have) flown	steal	stole	(have) stolen
freeze	froze	(have) frozen	swear	swore	(have) sworn
get	got	(have) got, gotten[1]	swim	swam	(have) swum
give	gave	(have) given	swing	swung	(have) swung
go	went	(have) gone	take	took	(have) taken
grow	grew	(have) grown	tear	tore	(have) torn
hold	held	(have) held	think	thought	(have) thought
know	knew	(have) known	throw	threw	(have) thrown
lay	laid	(have) laid	wear	wore	(have) worn
lead	led	(have) led	weep	wept	(have) wept
leave	left	(have) left	win	won	(have) won
lie	lay	(have) lain	wring	wrung	(have) wrung
lose	lost	(have) lost	write	wrote	(have) written

[1]The first form is the form used in British English; both forms are used in America.

[2]*Shine, shined, shined* are the principal parts when *shine* means "to polish."

Grammar

Using Principal Parts II

6 **Do not confuse the *past* with the *past participle.* Never use helping verbs with the past. Always use helping verbs with the past participle.**

Gerald *taken* algebra last year. (incorrect)
Gerald *took* algebra last year. (correct)
Gerald *has took* algebra before. (incorrect)
Gerald *has taken* algebra before. (correct)

7 **Do not use such incorrect forms as the following: *attackted, brung, busted, clumb, drownded, drug,* (for *dragged*), *et, aten, growed, snuck, stoled, throwed, thunk.***

Tim brought (not *brung*) his lunch to school today.
Wesley broke (not *busted*) his leg when he fell from the tree.
The fishermen dragged (not *drug*) in their nets.
We sneaked (not *snuck*) in and sat down on the back row.
Billy thought (not *thunk*) carefully before he answered.

8 **Refer often to page 65 to make sure that you are using the correct forms for irregular verbs.**

Exercise A **Cross out each incorrect verb form in parentheses.**

1. Daniel (ran, ~~run~~) twelve laps during P.E. today.
2. The Philistines (~~attackted~~, attacked) the Israelites in the valley of Elah.
3. While riding in the woods, Brad (came, ~~come~~) upon several deer.
4. Father's wheat crop (~~growed~~, grew) well, but that late rain (brought, ~~brung~~) disaster.
5. When the ball (rang, ~~rung~~), I was still not in class.
6. Don's charcoal drawing (did, ~~done~~) very well in the art contest.
7. Papa, what would happen if that opossum (~~come~~, came) down out of that tree?
8. I (~~thunk~~, thought) a lot about heaven that day I almost (~~drownded~~, drowned).
9. Jordan (did, ~~done~~) his job before he (ate, ~~et~~) breakfast.
10. My books (fell, ~~fallen~~) out of my locker and (broke, ~~busted~~) my history project.
11. I (~~seen~~, saw) the Carlsbad Caverns last year on a trip out West.
12. You have (~~did~~, done) much better this semester, Joseph; you (~~brung~~, brought) up your grade from a *C-* to a *B+*.
13. It (began, ~~begun~~) to snow, so we (~~driven~~, drove) home immediately.
14. Andrew (came, ~~come~~) up to the snake from the front, while Paul (~~snuck~~, sneaked) up from the rear.
15. The water in the pipes has (~~frozed~~, frozen), and the pipes have (~~busted~~, burst).

Exercise B **Cross out each incorrect verb form and write the correct form above it.**

1. I ~~done~~ have done my homework and I have also ~~wrote~~ written a letter to Grandpa.
2. Ben Franklin and several mischievous friends had ~~drug~~ dragged some building stones to the bay and had ~~began~~ begun a small wharf.
3. We ~~seen~~ saw the groundhog come up out of his burrow.
4. A bandit has ~~snuck~~ sneaked into the house and has ~~stoled~~ stolen several valuables.

5. Several bears ~~come~~ came up to the tent and ~~et~~ ate some food from our provisions.
6. Each woman that ~~come~~ came to the church social ~~brung~~ brought a covered dish.
7. I don't ~~got~~ have any pets except one old turtle.
8. Daniel Boone was ~~attackted~~ attacked several times by creatures of the forest.
9. Have you ever ~~aten~~ eaten roast turkey with oyster dressing?
10. God ~~forgiven~~ forgave David his sin because he confessed it.
11. The fireman ~~clumb~~ climbed to the fourth floor and rescued an elderly gentleman.
12. Every summer, several people are ~~drownded~~ drowned simply because they do not observe safety rules.
13. Miss Baker has ~~showed~~ shown us the photographs of her journey to Burma.
14. We ~~et~~ ate a fine lunch of hamburgers, french fries, and apple pie.
15. Noah ~~builded~~ built the ark because of his faith in God.

Exercise C

Fill in the blanks with the correct form of the verbs in parentheses.

1. Dad bought me a Scofield Bible for Christmas. *(buy)*
2. Robert Moffat brought the good news of the Gospel to Africa. *(bring)*
3. Mr. Judson has drawn a unique picture with chalk. *(draw)*
4. Charles Lindbergh flew non-stop from New York to Paris in 1927. *(fly)*
5. You have held up your end of the bargain very bravely. *(hold)*
6. Einstein led the way into the modern nuclear age. *(lead)*
7. Ben has lost his science paper somewhere. *(lose)*
8. I shined Father's shoes so that he would look good during his business trip. *(shine)*
9. The cougar sprang at the frightened antelope. *(spring)*
10. Our President has thought through this important question deliberately. *(think)*

Exercise D

Write sentences using the form of the verbs indicated in parentheses.

1. (past tense of *attack*) Answers will vary.
2. (past tense of *eat*) ____________
3. (past tense of *drown*) ____________
4. (past tense of *throw*) ____________
5. (past tense of *burst*) ____________
6. (past participle of *ring*) ____________
7. (past participle of *sneak*) ____________
8. (past participle of *run*) ____________
9. (past participle of *do*) ____________
10. (past participle of *bring*) ____________

Grammar

Using Verb Tenses

The *tense* of a verb *indicates* the *time* expressed by the verb. (*Tense* means *time.*) A verb tells when things happen: past, present, or future. The verb changes form to express six different tenses.

Present tense: I *see.* (He *sees.*)
Past tense: I *saw.*
Future tense: I *shall* (or *will*) *see.*

Present perfect tense: I *have seen.* (He *has seen.*)
Past perfect tense: I *had seen.*
Future perfect tense: I *shall* (or *will*) *have seen.*

Exercise A **In the blank, write the form of the verb indicated in parentheses.**

Example: Joseph __remained__ faithful to his master. (past of *remain*)

1. Behold, I __stand__ at the door and knock. (present of *stand*)
2. He gave them their request; but __sent__ leanness into their soul. (past of *send*)
3. I __will bless__ the Lord at all times. (future of *bless*)
4. We have committed iniquity; we __have done__ wickedly. (present perfect of *do*)
5. The waters had overwhelmed us; the stream __had gone__ over our soul. (past perfect of *go*)
6. When this corruptible __shall have put__ on incorruption . . . then shall be brought to pass the saying that is written, "Death is swallowed up in victory." (future perfect of *put*)
7. The Lord Himself __shall descend__ from heaven with a shout. (future of *descend*)
8. He __came__ unto His own, and His own received Him not. (past of *come*)
9. When they __had crucified__ Him, they parted His garments. (past perfect of *crucify*)
10. I __have refrained__ my feet from every evil way that I might keep Thy Word. (present perfect of *refrain*)

Exercise B **Write sentences illustrating the following: (1) the present tense of *sing,* (2) the past tense of *work,* (3) the future tense of *write,* (4) the present perfect of *fall,* (5) the past perfect of *wash,* and (6) the future perfect of *break.***

1. Answers will vary.
2. __________
3. __________
4. __________
5. __________
6. __________

Observing Verb Tense Consistency

When you are writing, select one tense and *do not change to a different tense* without good reason. If you begin writing in the past tense, do not switch to the present. If you begin with the present, do not switch to the past.

Not consistent	Chuck *caught* the ball and *throws* it over the first baseman's head. (*Caught* is past tense; *throws* is present tense.)
Consistent	Chuck *caught* the ball and *threw* it over the first baseman's head. (Both verbs are in the past tense.)
Not consistent	When he *spoke,* he *wins* the approval of the audience. (*Spoke* is past tense; *wins* is present tense.)
Consistent	When he *spoke,* he *won* the approval of the audience. (Both verbs are in the past tense.)
Consistent	When he *speaks,* he *wins* the approval of the audience. (Both verbs are in the present tense.)

Exercise A **The following paragraph should be written in past tense. Cross out and correct any verbs that are not in the past tense.**

George Müller, the famous founder of the Bristol Orphans' Home, always trusted God without question. He ~~tells~~ told only God what he ~~needs~~ needed, and his heavenly Father always ~~supplies~~ supplied. This life of faith often led him into some strange experiences. One morning, Mr. Müller was confronted by the cook who ~~tells~~ told him that there was nothing left for breakfast. The faithful leader beckoned the children to breakfast as usual. They ~~bow~~ bowed their heads and ~~thank~~ thanked God for the morning meal. During the prayer, the doorbell rang. When the cook ~~answers~~ answered it, she found a milkman standing there. He said, "My wagon broke down, and I wondered if you folks wanted the extra milk." The milk ~~is~~ was gratefully received, and the children ~~are~~ were fed. This was one of many miracles God performed in answer to George Müller's prayers.

Exercise B **On a separate sheet of paper, write an account of something that has actually happened to you. The following are so me suggestions that may remind you of an interesting experience: (1) The Day I Broke the Window, (2) An Unforgettable Vacation, (3) My First Serious Injury, (4) My First Attempt to Ride a Horse. Be sure to maintain verb tense consistency throughout your paragraph.**

Grammar

Using Sit & Set Correctly

Three pairs of verbs cause more trouble than any others: *sit* and *set, rise* and *raise, lie* and *lay.* In order to use these verbs correctly, you must learn the ***principal parts*** and the ***definitions*** of these words.

1 **The verb *sit* means "to be seated." Its principal parts are *sit, sitting, sat, (have) sat.*** (The verb *sit* rarely requires an object.)

Let's *sit* near the front.
The campers *are sitting* in the shade.
The monkey *sat* on the limb.
We *have sat* here long enough.

2 **The verb *set* means "to put or place something." Its principal parts are *set, setting, set, (have) set.*** (The verb *set* usually requires an object.)

Set the **bowl** on the table. (*Bowl* is the object.)
They *are setting* the ***props*** in place. (*Props* is the object.)
Joe carefully *set* his ***project*** on the floor. (*Project* is the object.)
They *have set* the ***date*** for the performance. (*Date* is the object.)

Exercise A Cross out each incorrect verb form in parentheses.

1. (~~Sit~~, Set) the vase in the center of the table.
2. They are (sitting, ~~setting~~) close to the front of the auditorium.
3. The man (set, ~~sat~~) the books on the librarian's desk.
4. The stage crew has (set, ~~sat~~) the chairs on the platform.
5. Let's (sit, ~~set~~) down on the park bench and watch the squirrels.
6. Were the books (sitting, ~~setting~~) on the shelf yesterday?
7. Timothy (~~set~~, sat) patiently through the long performance.
8. We have (set, ~~sat~~) the date for our class outing.

Exercise B Fill in the blanks with the correct form of *sit* or *set.*

1. Please ___set___ the salad on the buffet table.
2. Are the craft displays ___sitting___ too close to the wall?
3. Taylor ___sat___ down beside his broken-down car.
4. The teacher has ___set___ the deadline for our projects.
5. The man was ___sitting___ on the bench in the bus station.
6. Do you know if anyone will be ___sitting___ in this seat?

Exercise C Write sentences using the verb forms in parentheses.

1. *(have sat)* Answers will vary.
2. *(sat)* ______________________
3. *(are setting)* ______________________
4. *(set)* ______________________

Grammar

G. Using Rise & Raise Correctly

3 **The verb *rise* means "to go up" or "to get up." Its principal parts are *rise, rising, rose, (have) risen.*** (The verb *rise* never requires an object.)

> The dead in Christ *shall rise* first.
> All Christians *will be rising* to meet the Lord in the air.
> Christ died and *rose* again.
> He *has risen* as He said.

4 **The verb *raise* means "to lift something" or "to push up something." Its principal parts are *raise, raising, raised, (have) raised.*** (The verb *raise* usually requires an object.)

> Each morning we *raise* the ***windows.*** (*Windows* is the object.)
> Our neighbors *are raising* ***vegetables.*** (*Vegetables* is the object.)
> Confederate forces *raised* the sunken ***Merrimac.*** (*Merrimac* is the object.)
> My friend *has raised* an ant ***colony.*** (*Colony* is the object.)

UNIT 4

Exercise A **Cross out each incorrect verb form in parentheses.**

1. Christ (raised, ~~rose~~) Jairus' daughter to life again.
2. The Navy has recently (~~risen~~, raised) a sunken ship in the Pacific.
3. A kind man was (raising, ~~rising~~) the small child in his arms so that the child could see the parade.
4. Smoke from a thousand campfires (~~raised~~, rose) into the clear African sky.
5. Dr. Livingstone often (raised, ~~rose~~) his eyes toward heaven and prayed for the lost heathen tribes.
6. The morning fog has (~~raised~~, risen), and the day is now bright.
7. Ralph is (raising, ~~rising~~) tomatoes to sell in the community market.
8. Jesus has (~~raised~~, risen) from the grave and now sits at the Father's right hand.

Exercise B **Fill in the blanks with the correct form of *rise* or *raise*.**

1. The boys ____raise____ the flag to the top of the flagpole.
2. Submarines ____rise____ to the surface by emptying water from their ballast tanks.
3. The oil from a spill always ____rises____ to the top of the water.
4. Danielle ____raised____ her hand to ask a question in class today.
5. Everyone, please ____rise____ and pray with me the Lord's Prayer.
6. Mother ____raised____ the window shades in my bedroom this morning.
7. Your balloon is ____rising____ over that tree, Benjamin.

Exercise C **Write sentences using the verb forms in parentheses.**

1. *(has raised)* Answers will vary.
2. *(rose)* ________________
3. *(has risen)* ________________
4. *(raised)* ________________

Using Lie & Lay Correctly

The verbs *lie* and *lay* are probably the most misused of all verbs. You can master them by learning their principal parts and their definitions.

5 The verb *lie* means "to recline." Its principal parts are *lie, lying, lay, (have) lain.* (The verb *lie* never requires an object.)

Do not *lie* down on the job.
The lion *is lying* in wait.
The turtle *lay* asleep under the bush.
He *had lain* motionless for hours.

6 The verb *lay* means "to put or place something." Its principal parts are *lay, laying, laid, (have) laid.* (The verb *lay* usually requires an object.)

Lay your ***briefcase*** on the table. (*Briefcase* is the object.)
We are laying new ***carpet*** in the den. (*Carpet* is the object.)
He *laid* his ***notes*** aside. (*Notes* is the object.)
The girl *has laid* her ***apron*** back into the drawer. (*Apron* is the object.)

Exercise A **Cross out each incorrect verb form in parentheses.**

1. Elijah was tired, so he (lay, ~~laid~~) down under a juniper tree.
2. Francis (laid, ~~lay~~) aside his life of warfare and became a servant of the Lord.
3. Peter was (lying, ~~laying~~) on the housetop when God showed him a special dream.
4. Has Sarah (laid, ~~lain~~) her paper on your desk yet?
5. (~~Lay~~, Lie) down for a while, and perhaps you will feel better.
6. You have (lain, ~~laid~~) in bed long enough, young man.
7. The Princess (~~laid~~, lay) on a mattress of goose down in a bed of ivory.
8. The Mississippi Valley (lies, ~~lays~~) between the Appalachian Mountains and the Rocky Mountains.

Exercise B **Fill in the blanks with the correct form of *lie* or *lay*.**

1. Naboth's vineyard ___lay___ next to the king's palace.
2. Coveting the vineyard, Ahab was ___lying___ on his bed.
3. The fisherman, John, ___laid___ his nets down and followed Jesus.
4. Abraham had ___laid___ Isaac on the altar of rough stones.
5. Our Lord ___laid___ down His life for our redemption.
6. Steven has ___lain___ in that hammock all afternoon.
7. Susanna is ___laying___ the quilts on the porch to air.

Exercise C **Write sentences using the verb forms in parentheses.**

1. *(are laying)* Answers will vary.
2. *(laid)* ______
3. *(is lying)* ______
4. *(has lain)* ______

Grammar

Using Other Troublesome Verbs Correctly

1 ***Bring* or *take*? *Bring* indicates movement toward you. *Take* indicates movement away from you.**

Bring the newspaper inside. *Take* the hamburgers out to the patio.

2 ***Can* or *may*? *Can* refers to ability. *May* refers to permission.**

Can you play tennis very well? *May* I play awhile before dinner?

3 ***Learn* or *teach*? *Learn* means "to obtain knowledge." *Teach* means "to give instruction."**

Learn as much as you can. You are being *taught* well.

4 ***Let* or *leave*? *Let* means "to allow." *Leave* means "to go away from" or "to cause to remain."**

Let me help you. *Leave* the car in the garage.

UNIT 4

Exercise A

Cross out each incorrect verb form in parentheses.

1. (~~Can~~, May) I (teach, ~~learn~~) you how to remember those definitions?
2. (~~Bring~~, Take) Mrs. Hudson this letter and (let, ~~leave~~) me know her feelings about it.
3. Parents must (teach, ~~learn~~) their children to obey God's Word.
4. (Can, ~~May~~) you (~~bring~~, take) this vase to the closet without dropping it, Stan?
5. My grandfather (~~learned~~, taught) me that I (can, ~~may~~) do all things through Christ.
6. (Let, ~~Leave~~) me (~~bring~~, take) these flowers to Linda in the hospital.
7. You should (~~teach~~, learn) how to (~~let~~, leave) your room neat and orderly.
8. (Let, ~~Leave~~) me finish my mopping, and I will then be happy to (~~bring~~, take) you to the grocery store.
9. Greg, you (can, ~~may~~) draw better than anyone I have ever (taught, ~~learned~~) before.
10. A good ambassador of Christ (can, ~~may~~) (~~bring~~, take) the Gospel to those around him.
11. My mother (~~learned~~, taught) me this verse, "(Let, ~~Leave~~) the wicked forsake his way, and the unrighteous his thoughts."
12. If you will (bring, ~~take~~) me your paper, I (~~may~~, can) show you your grammar mistakes.

Exercise B

Write sentences using the verbs *take, may, teach,* and *let.*

1. Answers will vary. __________
2. __________
3. __________
4. __________

Grammar

Avoiding Common Errors in Verb Usage

1 **Do not use *ain't* and *aren't I.***

He *ain't* here. (incorrect) I am here, *aren't I?* (incorrect)
He *isn't* here. (correct) I am here, *am I not?* (correct)

2 **Do not use *better* for *had better.***

We *better* leave now. (incorrect)
We *had better* leave now. (correct)

3 **Do not use *didn't go to* for *didn't mean to* or *didn't intend to.***

Billy *didn't go to* break Mom's vase. (incorrect)
Billy *didn't mean to* break Mom's vase. (correct)

4 **Do not use *took sick* for *became ill.***

Debbie *took sick* and went to the clinic. (incorrect)
Debbie *became ill* and went to the clinic. (correct)

5 **Do not use *used to could* for *used to be able to.***

He *used to could* memorize easily. (incorrect)
He *used to be able to* memorize easily. (correct)

6 **Do not use *want in, want out, want on, want off,* or *want through.***

Jack wants *in* the club. (incorrect) Stop. I want *off.* (incorrect)
Jack wants *to join* the club. (correct) Stop. I want *to get off.* (correct)

Exercise

Cross out and correct all errors in verb usage.

1. You ^had better get a doctor because Pierce ~~took sick~~ became ill a few moments ago.
2. Sammy ~~ain't~~ isn't here yet; we ^had better wait for him.
3. I am the only painter here, ~~aren't I?~~ am I not?
4. Clear this road; the king wants ~~through~~ to go through.
5. We ^had better try to display a Christlike attitude.
6. Trent used to ~~could~~ be able to sing well.
7. President William Harrison ~~took sick~~ became ill on his inauguration day and died one month later.
8. Elizabeth wants ~~off~~ to get off the seesaw. Since she ~~took sick~~ became ill, she has been unable to play as much as she used to ~~could~~ be able to.
9. That ~~ain't~~ isn't the correct answer to that problem.
10. Spot didn't ~~go to~~ mean to damage Mama's rose bushes.
11. I am the student you wanted to see, ~~aren't I?~~ am I not?
12. You ^had better stop the bus; several people want ~~off~~ to get off.
13. Grandmother used to ~~could~~ be able to work in the garden, but since she ~~took sick~~ became ill she has been in bed.
14. I didn't ~~go to~~ mean to start an argument; I was only giving my opinion.

Using Exact & Vivid Verbs

The surest way to attract and hold a reader's interest is to use exact and vivid words. Choose verbs with action and color to create mental pictures in the reader's mind. Notice the following sentence: "He *went* down the road." The verb *went* is a general word that does not show any specific action. Observe how the mental pictures change when *exact verbs* are substituted for the word *went*.

He *strutted* down the road.
He *plodded* down the road.
He *staggered* down the road.
He *stumbled* down the road.
He *sprinted* down the road.
He *rambled* down the road.

UNIT 4

Exercise A

In the space after each sentence, write three verbs that could replace the italicized verb to make the action more colorful and special. How does each new verb change the meaning of the sentence? Answers will vary.

1. The truck *came* to a stop. screeched, jolted, roared
2. The feeble old man *walked* out of the room. stumbled, meandered, sneaked
3. She *looked* at her rival across the room. stared, peeked, glared
4. May I *cook* the hamburgers? fry, broil, grill
5. Billy always *eats* his food. gobbles, devours, munches

Exercise B

Write a short paragraph describing a visit to the dentist. Use exact and colorful verbs to suggest the sounds made by the dentist's equipment and to indicate your feelings and reactions.

Answers will vary.

Reviewing Verbs & Their Uses

Exercise A

Underline the verbs in the following paragraphs. Watch for compound parts and verbs phrases.

Then Nebuchadnezzar spake and said, "Blessed be the God of Shadrach, Meshach, and Abednego who hath sent His angel and delivered His servants that trusted in Him and have changed the king's word and yielded their bodies that they might not serve nor worship any god except their own God. Therefore I make a decree that every people, nation, and language which speak anything amiss against the God of Shadrach, Meshach, and Abednego shall be cut in pieces and their houses shall be made a dunghill because there is no other God that can deliver after this sort."

Then the king promoted Shadrach, Meshach, and Abednego in the province of Babylon.

Exercise B

(1) At the end of each sentence, write *action* if the italicized verb shows action; write *linking* if the verb links. (2) For the linking verbs, draw an arrow to indicate the word that is linked to the subject.

Example: The student *grew* tired. linking

1. Don *tasted* the lemon pie before the party. action
2. The earth *looks* small compared to some other planets. linking
3. A black bear *was running* after Uncle Ed. action
4. The sequoia *is* a giant evergreen tree. linking
5. The Brunswick stew *tasted* delicious. linking
6. The little boy *had become* weary after a day at Grandma's house. linking
7. The giraffe *looked* around for some food. action
8. We *smelled* the aroma of steak cooking. action
9. Raphael *was* an Italian painter and architect. linking
10. Jennie *appeared* radiant after winning the swim meet. linking

Exercise C

(1) Draw a circle around each participle. (2) Draw an arrow from each participle to the word it modifies.

1. Walking down the hall, John tripped on his shoelace.
2. Luis saw a snake, slithering across the lawn.
3. Breaking from its mooring, the ship slowly drifted away from the dock.
4. Carrying their friend on a stretcher, the men arrived at the medic's tent.
5. Bursting into song, the little bird celebrated the arrival of spring.
6. The batter, trying for a home run, struck out.
7. The house, battered by the storm, could not be repaired.
8. Grinning joyfully, Laura accepted her award.
9. The float, bobbing crazily, signaled a catch.
10. Leaving her old life behind, Christine determined to serve the Lord.

Exercise D Cross out the incorrect verb form in parentheses.

1. Several sharks (~~raised~~, rose) from the ocean bottom and (attacked, ~~attackted~~) the bait that had been (~~throwed~~, thrown) overboard.
2. While Eduardo (climbed, ~~clumb~~) the tree, James (sat, ~~set~~) down and (ate, ~~et~~) a candy bar.
3. State troopers (dragged, ~~drug~~) the branch away which had (lain, ~~laid~~) in the road since the storm.
4. An usher (brought, ~~brung~~) the visitor into church and (showed, ~~shown~~) him where to (~~set~~, sit).
5. The boy that (~~stoled~~, stole) my bicycle has (~~gave~~, given) it back at the request of the police department.
6. Tina has (set, ~~sat~~) on the cabinet a bouquet of flowers which she (~~growed~~, grew) herself.
7. Aunt Alice's crystal bowl has (~~fell~~, fallen) from the shelf and has (broken, ~~busted~~).
8. An area of ground in our town has (~~sank~~, sunk), and groundwater has (~~rose~~, risen) to fill the cavity.
9. Our dog, which usually (~~lays~~, lies) on the front steps, (sneaked, ~~snuck~~) into the house during the storm.
10. A reckless driver (ran, ~~run~~) his auto off the pier and (~~drownded~~, drowned).
11. Since the sun has (~~rose~~, risen), the temperature has (~~began~~, begun) to (rise, ~~raise~~).
12. Before Robert Scott had (~~froze~~, frozen) to death, he had (~~wrote~~, written) in his diary why he (~~thunk~~, thought) the expedition had failed.
13. Mrs. Snell (~~lay~~, laid) a tub of ice cream on the table, and before long we had (~~aten~~, eaten) it all.
14. The traveler had been (beaten, ~~beat~~) and was (~~laying~~, lying) beside the Jericho road.
15. Although Tom has (swum, ~~swam~~) often, he is still cautious, to avoid being (drowned, ~~drownded~~).
16. An ancient Jew would have (~~teared~~, torn) his garment and (wept, ~~weeped~~) bitterly in time of grief.

Exercise E Cross out each incorrect verb and write the correct form above it.

1. Since Albert ~~took sick~~ [became ill], he has just ~~left~~ [let] his work ~~lay~~ [lie] there.
2. He ^[had] better quit ~~lying~~ [laying] his cleats on the coffee table.
3. I didn't ~~go to set~~ [mean to sit] on your hat, Mr. Bere.
4. Mrs. Maxwell used to ~~could~~ [be able to] play the piano well, but she ~~ain't~~ [isn't] able to now because of arthritis in her fingers.
5. Before Tom ~~took sick~~ [became ill], he ~~used to could~~ [use to be able to] work a ten-hour day at the lumber mill.
6. I am the one who will be ~~learning~~ [teaching] you to paint, ~~aren't I?~~ [am I not?]
7. ~~Can~~ [May] I ~~bring~~ [take] you to the shopping center, Aunt Betsy?
8. You ^[had] better ~~learn~~ [teach] Wally to sing, or he ~~ain't~~ [isn't] going to be in the choir.
9. "Pilot, please ~~sit~~ [set] this plane down; I want ~~off~~ [to get off]," the frightened passenger pleaded.
10. Sean ~~learned~~ [taught] his dog to ~~lay~~ [lie] down and roll over.

UNIT 4

Exercise A

Capitalization and Punctuation. (1) Draw a line through each incorrect small letter. Write a capital above it. (2) Add punctuation marks where needed.

M U J M F L E W M
1. Yes, michael, my uncle jesse left miami, florida, for london, england, on wednesday, may 18, at 4:30 p.m.

F G S G A P
2. The following courses will be offered this summer: french, german, spanish, greek, algebra II, and philosophy 402.

D A S G V
3. dear aunt susie,   gentlemen: very truly yours,

D G
4. "doth god exact day labor, light denied?"

I B
i fondly ask. but Patience, to prevent

T G
that murmur, soon replies, "god doth not need

E
either man's work, or His own gift; who best

B
bear His mild yoke, they serve Him best." —*John Milton*

J P J B R B S S N S
5. john paul jones's flagship bonhomme richard fought a bloody battle with the british ship serapis on september 23, 1779, in the north sea.

Exercise B

The Sentence. In the blank before the number, write *s.* for sentences, *frag.* for fragments, or *r.o.* for run-ons.

frag. 1. Whatever advice you give to those waiting to hear from you.

s. 2. I am Alpha and Omega, the beginning and the end, the first and the last.

r.o. 3. Never buy what you do not need, wastefulness is as great a sin as covetousness.

frag. 4. Sailing across the North Atlantic on her maiden voyage.

r.o. 5. The guns and cannon roared, the men could not see the other lines because of the smoke.

Exercise C

The Sentence. Underline each subject once and each verb twice. Circle the complement.

1. Rikki-Tikki-Tavi was a mongoose.
2. A small boy found Rikki-Tikki-Tavi and brought him into the bungalow.
3. Rikki-Tikki-Tavi protected the boy's family from dangerous snakes.
4. In spite of his small size, Rikki-Tikki-Tavi was very brave.

5. He killed two cobras and destroyed their eggs.
6. After that, no cobras entered the bungalow's garden.

Exercise D

Using Verbs. In the following sentences, (1) underline all action verbs. (2) Circle all linking verbs. (3) Draw a box around all participles.

UNIT 4

1. Pulling into the station, the train gave a loud blast from its whistle.
2. My brother is the boy closing the curtain.
3. In the countries bordering on the North Sea, fishermen are quite numerous.
4. The dog given to me by my father ran away.
5. Forests, destroyed by our carelessness, are not easily replaced.

Exercise E

Using Verbs. Cross out each incorrect verb form in parentheses.

1. Howard (~~drug~~, dragged) the (~~busted~~, broken) cart back up the hill.
2. He (lay, ~~laid~~) down on the sofa and (~~thunk~~, thought) about what he had heard.
3. Our den master (~~learned~~, taught) us boys how to (~~rise~~, raise) and lower the flag correctly.
4. Matt (~~took sick~~, became ill) and (~~wanted off~~, wanted to get off) the roller coaster.
5. I (~~better~~, had better) finish my homework.
6. (~~Can~~, May) we take this stray dog home or should we (~~let~~, leave) him here?
7. Several vandals (sneaked, ~~snuck~~) in and (~~stoled~~, stole) the famous painting.
8. Mrs. Bowman (~~took~~, brought) a rattan chair from the Philippines.
9. Brittany, (sit, ~~set~~) here and (~~leave~~, let) me make us a pot of tea.
10. A girl in the second row (raised, ~~rose~~) her hand and asked Mr. Turkington a question.

Unit 5 Nouns & Their Uses

Grammar

Recognizing Nouns

1 **A *noun* is a word that names a person, place, thing, or idea.**

persons — *sister, pilot, Don, missionary*
places — *Georgia, meadow, country, state*
things — *river, sand, air, bush*
ideas — *friendliness, honor, hope, gratitude*

2 **A *compound noun* is two or more words used as a single noun.** Some are written as separate words; some are hyphenated; some are solid. (Consult your dictionary for the correct spelling.)

Ben Jones *Pilgrim's Progress* horseshoe self-will Ivan the Terrible

3 **A *collective noun* names a group and is singular in form.**

audience class family flock herd team

Exercise A **Circle the nouns in the following paragraph. Words such as *he, we, they, them* are not nouns.**

Catherine the Great was born in Prussia. Her royal family ruled a tiny area of that German state. When she was a teenager, Catherine married Peter, successor to the Russian throne. He was a weakling, both mentally and physically. Through various plots, Peter was overthrown, and Catherine was made ruler of the empire. She ruled during the Age of Reason. She built hospitals and schools, encouraged education for women, and urged her people to be inoculated against smallpox. However, Catherine did nothing to alleviate the misery of the serfs. The physical and economic burdens placed on them became even greater. Catherine favored the rich aristocracy, while she ignored the masses.

Exercise B **(1) Circle the compound nouns. (2) Draw a box around the collective nouns. (3) Underline the remaining nouns.**

Charles John Huffam Dickens was born in Portsmouth, England, in 1812. When he was an infant, he moved with his family to London where he spent most of his life. He attended school off and on until the age of fourteen, and then he started to work. One of his first jobs was as a newsman. He wrote articles and reported on debates in Parliament. During his reporting days, Dickens sharpened his ability to write natural conversation and make accurate characterizations. His first literary success was *The Pickwick Papers*, a humorous book. Other well-known books by Dickens include the following: *A Christmas Carol, Great Expectations, David Copperfield,* and *A Tale of Two Cities*. His greatest literary work is *Bleak House*. Dickens was able to electrify an audience with a reading of his own works.

Grammar

UNIT 5

Recognizing Common & Proper Nouns

1 A *common noun* names a person, place, thing, or idea, but does not say which particular one.

man state ship hog horse truth

2 A *proper noun* names a *particular* person, place, or thing and always begins with a capital letter.

Robert Borden Arkansas *Titanic* Yorkshire Morgan

Exercise A

For each of the common nouns listed below, write a proper noun naming a person, place, or thing that you know well.

Examples: city Portland

lake Big Stone Lake

1. state Answers will vary.
2. country
3. desert
4. ocean
5. boy
6. holiday
7. street
8. magazine
9. mountain
10. store

Exercise B

In the following paragraph, underline all the common nouns and draw a circle around the proper nouns.

Let us take an imaginary journey down the Kanawha River. We will begin our trip near Charleston and head toward Point Pleasant and the mighty Ohio. As we start our journey, we notice the capitol building. It is beautiful. Especially note its gold dome. After passing the capitol, we see the buildings of the capital city. We also observe the workmen building the new interstate bridges. The chemical plants of South Charleston are now coming into view. This city ranks as one of the largest chemical centers in the South. Our journey down the river will lead us past many towns, communities, and rural farm areas. The majestic, scenic hills serve as a backdrop for each scene we pass. Our journey is almost over. We pass Huntington and its glass factories, and travel to the point where the Kanawha meets the Ohio.

Making Verbs Agree with Noun Subjects I

The verb of a sentence must *agree* with the subject in **number.** Learn the following rules so that you will know when to use a singular verb and when to use a plural verb.

1 ***Singular subjects* take *singular verbs; plural subjects* take *plural verbs. Nouns* ending in *s* are usually *plural; verbs* ending in *s* are usually *singular.***

The frog croaks loudly. (singular) The frogs croak loudly. (plural)

2 **The number of a subject is not usually affected by phrases between the subject and the verb.** (For exceptions, see p. 84, rule 7.)

The cookies (in the jar) tempt me. (The plural subject *cookies* takes the plural verb *tempt.* The singular object of the preposition *jar* does not affect the number of the subject.)

The caramel (in the cookies) gives them flavor. (The singular subject *caramel* takes the singular verb *gives.* The plural object of the preposition *cookies* does not affect the number of the subject.)

Exercise **Cross out the incorrect form in parentheses.**

1. The boys in the room down the hall (~~helps~~, help) Mr. Stephens every day.
2. The bush (blooms, ~~bloom~~) beautifully every year.
3. The books inside locker fifty-seven (~~belongs~~, belong) to Benjamin.
4. Several bags of groceries (~~needs~~, need) to be brought inside.
5. The silverware (is, ~~are~~) inside the left drawer.
6. The artist (draws, ~~draw~~) several pictures a month.
7. Dad, with the help of my two brothers, (mows, ~~mow~~) the lawn.
8. Our seats for the opera (~~was~~, were) in the balcony.
9. The teachers of our school (~~teaches~~, teach) more than just academic subjects.
10. The school's principal (takes, ~~take~~) the seniors to Washington, D.C.
11. The animals of the forest (~~was~~, were) running from the ravages of the forest fire.
12. Faith (is, ~~are~~) the substance of things hoped for, the evidence of things not seen.
13. An obstinate man (does, ~~do~~) not hold opinions; the opinions (~~holds~~, hold) him.
14. Trying times (~~is~~, are) times for trying.
15. Charlemagne, one of the Carolingian kings, (was, ~~were~~) crowned emperor by Pope Leo III.
16. The birds in that large tree (~~sings~~, sing) sweetly.
17. The students in Chemistry 101 (~~brings~~, bring) the equipment for their lab period.
18. The women of the church (~~prays~~, pray) regularly for the church missionaries.
19. My eight cousins (~~lives~~, live) in Pasadena.
20. Famous people (~~lectures~~, lecture) on college campuses every day.

Making Verbs Agree with Noun Subjects II

3 ***Compound subjects* joined by *and* take a plural verb.**

Michelle *and* Barb are good friends. (compound subject joined by *and*)

Note: Sometimes subjects joined by *and* refer to only one person or are considered as one thing. Use a singular verb in this situation.

The captain and center on our team is Bart Richards. (Bart is both the captain and the center.)

Spaghetti and meatballs is a favorite of many people. (Spaghetti and meatballs is only one dish.)

4 **When a *compound subject* is joined by *or* or *nor*, the verb agrees with the nearer subject.**

Either the boys or Mr. White is ready to help. (The subject closer to the verb is singular; therefore the verb is singular.)

Either Mr. White or the boys are ready to help. (The subject closer to the verb is plural; therefore the verb is plural.)

Exercise

Cross out the incorrect form in parentheses.

1. Bacon and eggs (is, ~~are~~) my favorite breakfast.
2. Neither the lion nor the bears (~~comes~~, come) out of their cages.
3. Joseph and Erin (~~does~~, do) errands for Mr. Sutton, a shut-in.
4. Abraham Lincoln and Lyndon B. Johnson (~~was~~, were) the tallest U.S. Presidents.
5. Either Michelle or the boys (have, ~~has~~) the key to the house.
6. Archery and swimming (~~is~~, are) two favorite camp activities.
7. The director and producer of the play (is, ~~are~~) Mr. Pattison.
8. Neither the scouts nor their leader (has, ~~have~~) seen the exhibition.
9. Mom and Dad (~~takes~~, take) us to church every Wednesday and Sunday.
10. Both a train and an airplane (~~travels~~, travel) faster than a car does.
11. Either Kelsey or Kayla (has, ~~have~~) to clean this room.
12. Science and history (~~was~~, were) assigned for homework.
13. Neither those stories nor that author (is, ~~are~~) found in this book.
14. The pianist and soloist (is, ~~are~~) her sister Sue.
15. William Bradford and Anne Bradstreet (~~was~~, were) early contributors of American literature.

Grammar

Making Verbs Agree with Noun Subjects III

5 ***Collective nouns* may be either singular or plural.** A collective noun names a group and is *singular in form.* (For example: *jury, team, class, family.*) When the collective noun acts as a *unit,* it is *singular;* but when the members of the group act *individually,* the collective noun is *plural.*

The herd is in the south pasture. (The herd is thought of as a unit; therefore the noun is singular.)

The herd run in different directions when they hear thunder. (Each animal is acting individually; therefore the noun is plural.)

6 **The words *there* and *here* are rarely used as subjects.** When a sentence begins with *there* or *here,* you must look carefully to find the subject.

There are many devices in a man's heart. (*Devices* is the subject; *are* is the verb.)

Here is the map you lent me. (*Map* is the subject; *is* is the verb.)

7 **Expressions stating *amounts* (fractions, measurements, money, time) *may be singular* or *plural.***

Five dollars was the amount we settled for.

Eight hours is enough time for sleep.

Three fourths of the cake is gone.

Three fourths of the boys are going.

8 ***Titles* of literary works, works of art, organizations, and countries are usually singular even if they are plural in form.**

Nighthawks is a painting by Edward Hopper.

The Girl Scouts was established in 1928.

The Philippines is an island country in the Pacific Ocean.

9 ***Doesn't, isn't,* and *wasn't* are singular and must be used with singular subjects. *Don't, aren't,* and *weren't* are plural and must be used with plural subjects.**

Frank doesn't like shrimp. They don't digest easily for him.

10 **A few words, although plural in form, take singular verbs. *Mathematics, civics, rickets, measles, mumps,* and *news* are examples of such words.**

Civics is an interesting course. Measles is extremely contagious.

Remember: *Verbs* ending in *s* are usually *singular.*

Exercise A **Cross out the incorrect form in parentheses.** (Rules 5, 6, 7)

1. Here (is, are) the plants you wanted for the garden.
2. The jury (has, have) handed down its decision.
3. Fifty dollars (is, are) not too much to pay for a good pair of shoes.
4. The team (plays, play) its best on the home court.
5. There (comes, come) to our lives many opportunities for witnessing about Christ.
6. Thirty-three years (was, were) all that Jesus lived on this earth.
7. Do you think there really (is, are) a "Big Foot"?
8. Two minutes (is, are) the longest that I can hold my breath.
9. The homeroom class (elects, elect) its representatives next week.
10. Here (is, are) some reasons why you may not go on the trip.

Exercise B Cross out the incorrect form in parentheses. (Rules 8, 9, 10)

1. Hot Springs, a city in Arkansas, (is, ~~are~~) a noted health resort.
2. The newspaper *London Times* (was, ~~were~~) founded in 1785.
3. *Great Expectations* (is, ~~are~~) a lengthy novel by Charles Dickens.
4. The evening news (airs, ~~air~~) at 6 o'clock in Pensacola.
5. (~~Wasn't~~, Weren't) the team members ready to play?
6. Mathematics (is, ~~are~~) a difficult subject for many students.
7. The Netherlands (is, ~~are~~) another name for Holland.
8. Rickets (~~cause~~, causes) bones to bend into unnatural shapes.
9. *The Canterbury Tales* (portrays, ~~portray~~) early English characters.
10. (Doesn't, ~~Don't~~) our town have a beautiful park?

Exercise C Cross out the incorrect form in parentheses. (Rules 1–10.)

1. Line *A* and line *B* (~~is~~, are) parallel in problem thirty-two.
2. (~~Doesn't~~, Don't) the period and the comma always go inside the quotation marks?
3. My shoes (~~is~~, are) untied and I can't bend down to tie them.
4. The founder and director of the organization (is, ~~are~~) Mrs. J. W. Wells.
5. Neither the kitten nor the dogs (~~remains~~, remain) inside the house.
6. Five gallons of ice cream (was, ~~were~~) not enough to feed such a large crowd.
7. Civics (explains, ~~explain~~) the obligations of a citizen to his town and country.
8. Ham and cheese (is, ~~are~~) Dad's favorite sandwich.
9. The church (has, ~~have~~) decided to build a new building on Ninth Street.
10. There (~~isn't~~, aren't) too many more days remaining in this month.
11. The pictures in this new magazine (~~shows~~, show) the rugged beauty of the West.
12. The Organization of American States (has, ~~have~~) its headquarters in Washington, D.C.
13. The lug nuts on the front wheel (~~wasn't~~, weren't) properly tightened.
14. Either the choir or Mrs. Johnson (sings, ~~sing~~) the special music on Sunday nights.
15. The Mississippi River and the Ohio River (~~forms~~, form) important river systems.
16. (~~Doesn't~~, Don't) the students need to be in their seats by eight o'clock?
17. Our family (choose, ~~chooses~~) different parts of the paper to read.
18. Measles (is, ~~are~~) caused by a virus.
19. *The Prince and the Pauper* (was, ~~were~~) written by Mark Twain.
20. The windows in the living room (~~was~~, were) shattered by the storm.
21. There (~~is~~, are) thirty-one days in most of the months of the year.
22. Neither the man nor the little girls (~~was~~, were) injured in the accident.
23. My hair (doesn't, ~~don't~~) need to be cut in back, but my bangs are too long.
24. Fifty-five cents (isn't, ~~aren't~~) a large enough tip for our waitress.
25. The Great Plains (is, ~~are~~) a region of the United States.

Grammar

Using Nouns as Predicate Nominatives

1 **A *predicate nominative* is a noun (or a pronoun) that follows a *linking verb* and *renames* or *explains* the subject.** This noun (or pronoun) means the same thing or person as the subject.

Rebecca was the *leader.* *(Leader* is a noun that means the same person as the subject *Rebecca.)*

2 **In a sentence containing a predicate nominative, you can always replace the verb with the word *equals.***

Alaska *is* the largest state in the United States. *(Alaska equals state.)*
Robert E. Lee *was* a great general. *(Robert E. Lee equals general.)*

3 **Predicate nominatives can *never* be *in prepositional phrases.***

Alaska is the largest *state* (P.N.) ***in the United States*** (Prep. Phrase). *(State* is the predicate nominative, not *United States.)*

4 **Predicate nominatives *may be compound.***

The members of the debate team are *Charles, Matthew,* and *Shane.*

5 **Predicate nominatives are sometimes called *subject complements.* Subject complements always follow linking verbs.** Have you memorized the following list of linking verbs? If not, you need to memorize them now.

Linking Verbs

am	were	taste	look	grow
is	be	feel	appear	remain
are	being	smell	become	stay
was	been	sound	seem	
(May also be used as helping verbs.)		(May also be used as action verbs.)		

Note: Some of the verbs in the last three columns above are not used with predicate nominatives, but with predicate adjectives, which you will study later.

Exercise A

(1) Underline the linking verbs. (2) Draw a circle around the predicate nominatives. To find a predicate nominative, first find the verb. Then ask *who* or *what* after the verb.

Example: Angie is our secretary. (Angie is *who* or *what?* Angie is *secretary. Secretary* is the predicate nominative.)

1. Edison was the inventor of the phonograph.
2. One of the smallest countries is San Marino.
3. Peter became a great preacher after Pentecost.
4. The Amalekites were Israel's enemies.
5. Charles Dickens remains a well-known novelist.
6. Walter Mondale was our Vice-President.
7. Jesus is the resurrection and the life.
8. I am the way, the truth, and the life.
9. The Lord is my light and my salvation.
10. Ye are My witnesses.

Using Nouns as Predicate Nominatives

Exercise B **(1) Underline the linking verbs. (2) Draw a circle around the predicate nominatives. Four of the sentences do not contain predicate nominatives. Do not do anything with these sentences.**

1. Dwight L. Moody was a great American evangelist.
2. Presbyterian missionaries were the first white settlers in Hawaii.
3. Jeremiah was the weeping prophet of Israel.
4. The men's choir did an excellent job this morning.
5. The Copperheads were Northerners opposed to President Lincoln's policies.
6. France is a country with many tourist attractions.
7. Elisha was given a double portion of the spirit of Elijah.
8. David was a man after God's own heart.
9. The Lord Jesus is the Shepherd and Bishop of our souls.
10. Michael is an archangel of the Lord.
11. Adoniram and Ann Judson became pioneer missionaries to Burma.
12. William Carey is credited with beginning modern missions work.
13. You are known by the company you keep.
14. Wasn't Clara Barton the founder of the American Red Cross?
15. Methodist circuit riders became carriers of the Gospel to frontier communities.

UNIT 5

Exercise C **Write sentences containing predicate nominatives. Then check your sentences by applying Rule 2.**

Example: He is a friend of the family. (He equals friend.)

1. Answers will vary.

2.

3.

4.

5.

6.

Diagraming Predicate Nominatives

Study the following examples carefully.

PREDICATE NOMINATIVE

Jim was the *winner.*

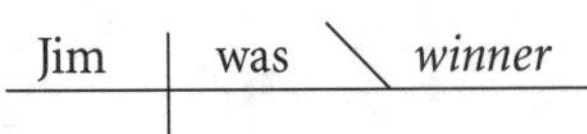

COMPOUND PREDICATE NOMINATIVE

The losers were *Chad* and *Nate.*

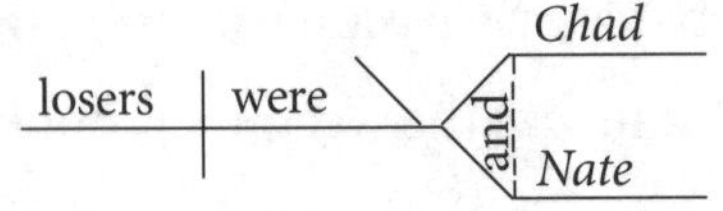

Notice the slanted line between the verb and the predicate nominative. This slanted line points toward the subject indicating that the predicate nominative refers to the subject.

Exercise A **Diagram the subjects, verbs, and predicate nominatives in the following sentences.**

1. The kings of France were absolute rulers of their realms.
2. Moses was the meekest man on earth.
3. Australia is the home of many rare species of birds and animals.
4. Johann Bach was a devoted father and a great composer.
5. He was also a very devout Christian man.
6. The gorilla is the largest member of the ape family.
7. Noah Webster was the compiler of the original *Webster's Dictionary.*
8. Spain and Portugal became the first nations to have colonies in America.
9. Gandhi was the leader of the Indian independence movement.
10. Greenland is the largest island in the world.

1. kings | were \ rulers
2. Moses | was \ man
3. Australia | is \ home
4. Johann Bach | was \ father and composer
5. He | was \ man
6. gorilla | is \ member
7. Noah Webster | was \ compiler
8. Spain and Portugal | became \ nations
9. Gandhi | was \ leader
10. Greenland | is \ island

Exercise B **For additional practice, diagram the subjects, verbs, and predicate nominatives from exercises A and B on pages 86–87.** (See *Supplement.*)

Grammar

Using Nouns as Direct Objects

There are two kinds of complements that follow *action* verbs: direct objects and indirect objects.

1 **A *direct object* is a noun (or a pronoun) that follows an action verb and receives the action from that verb. It answers the questions *whom* or *what* after the verb.**

Cleopatra lost her kingdom. (*Lost* is an action verb, so there may be a direct object. Cleopatra lost *what?* The answer is *kingdom,* so *kingdom* is the direct object.)

2 **If no word answers the questions *whom* or *what* after the action verb, the sentence does not have a direct object.**

Columbus could swim well. (Did Columbus swim anything? No; *well* is an adverb telling how he swam.)

3 **Direct objects can *never* be in prepositional phrases.**

Beavers build their *lodge* (**D.O.**) ***by some stream.*** (**Prep. Phrase**) (Beavers build *what?* Beavers build *lodge. Lodge* is the direct object. Beavers did not build the stream. *Stream* is the object of the preposition *by.*)

4 **Direct objects *may be compound.***

We nominated Ted and Donna. (We nominated *whom? Ted* and *Donna. Ted* and *Donna* is the compound direct object.)

UNIT 5

Exercise A

Draw a circle around the direct objects in the following sentences. Find the action verb and ask *whom* or *what* after the verb. Remember that a direct object cannot be in a prepositional phrase. Watch for compound direct objects.

1. Alone, Captain Joshua Slocum sailed his sloop around the world.
2. Nathaniel Bowditch published a famous book on the subject of navigation.
3. Captain Robert Gray inaugurated the Northwest coast-Hawaii-China trade.
4. Captain Gray named the Columbia River after his ship, the *Columbia.*
5. American shipwrights and fishermen perfected the schooner.
6. Frederic Tudor, a Boston merchant, sold ice, tea, and spices.
7. Whaling brought large profits during the 1700s and 1800s.
8. The head of a sperm whale provided pure oil and spermaceti.
9. Until the introduction of kerosene in 1860, whale oil lamps gave the best light.
10. David Bushnell built the first American underwater craft.
11. Jacques Piccard designed the *Trieste* for underwater research.
12. At 35,820 feet, the *Trieste* touched the bottom of the ocean.
13. The submarine U.S.S. *Tennessee* can launch missiles without surfacing.
14. The Navy did not use airplanes and aircraft carriers extensively until World War II.

Exercise B

Draw a circle around the direct objects in the following sentences. There may be more than one direct object in each sentence.

1. Frogmen can destroy underwater mines and beach obstacles.
2. Planes from aircraft carriers can destroy enemy shipping and disrupt communications.

(continued)

Exercise B, cont.

3. Paratroopers drop behind enemy lines and demolish bridges and cut supply lines.
4. Armored vests protect combat flyers and soldiers during wartime.
5. Logistic units provide cold-weather clothing, boots for arctic wear, and uniforms for use in temperate climates.
6. Infantrymen must throw grenades and fire various weapons.
7. The artillery protects the troops and neutralizes the enemy's fire.
8. Rockets also provide support for troops in the field.
9. The U.S. Army Infantry Center at Fort Benning, Georgia, conducts airborne and ranger training courses.
10. Army aircraft can spot enemy targets for the artillery and can provide rapid transportation to and from the front line.
11. The U.S. Army Airborne Center at Fort Rucker, Alabama, trains pilots and maintenance men for various aircraft.
12. Soldiers use gas masks and airtight clothing as protection from chemical warfare.
13. The men in the Special Forces infiltrate enemy positions and train local people in guerrilla warfare.
14. Engineers repair roads, build bridges, and construct landing strips.

Exercise C

Circle the direct objects in the following paragraphs. Not all sentences contain a direct object.

The first Monday in September is Labor Day. On this day, we give thought to those who work with their hands. Think what workers have done for our country. They felled the trees. They plowed the fields. They dug the mines and made the steel rails and laid the railroads and built the ships. There are two sides to every undertaking. The bird must have the air; the ship must have the sea; the seed must have the soil; and the mill must have its grain. One without the other is useless and dead.

The statesman may plan vast cities where today there is none; the captain of industry may desire the trade of the world; the farmer may plot his vast acres as he sits by the winter's fire; the poet may write, and the dreamer may dream. Of what avail is all this if workers do not fulfill the dreams?

Exercise D

(1) Write sentences illustrating Rules 3 and 4. (2) Underline the action verbs and circle the direct objects.

1. (Rule 3) Answers will vary. __________
2. (Rule 3) __________
3. (Rule 4) __________
4. (Rule 4) __________

Diagraming Direct Objects

Study the following examples carefully.

DIRECT OBJECT

The Chinese invented wood-block *printing*.

Chinese | invented | *printing*

COMPOUND DIRECT OBJECT

Antony defeated *Brutus* and *Cassius* at Philippi.

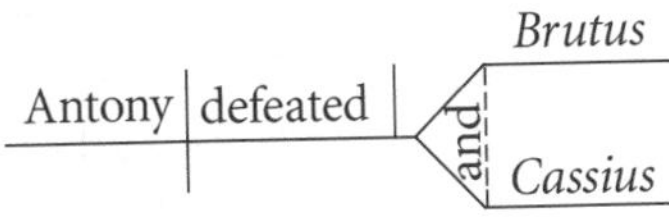

Notice the vertical line between the action verb and the direct object.

Exercise A Diagram the subjects, verbs, and direct objects in the following sentences.

1. Shakespeare wrote plays based on historical legends.
2. Mount Etna in Sicily erupted recently and spewed ash over the nearby villages.
3. Michelangelo painted the ceiling of the Sistine Chapel.
4. The Pennsylvania Dutch still maintain many traditional customs.
5. Robin Hood and his merry men robbed the rich and helped the poor.
6. The President hired Lewis and Clark as explorers of the Western frontier.
7. By 1871, Garibaldi had united the country of Italy.
8. Shah Jahan built the Taj Mahal as a memorial to his favorite wife.
9. Rome ruled the world until A.D. 476.
10. Blind Milton wrote sonnets and epics.

1. 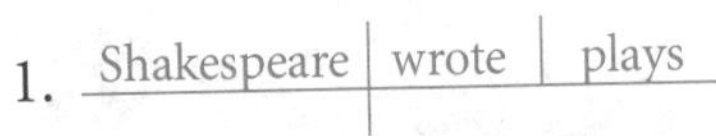

2. 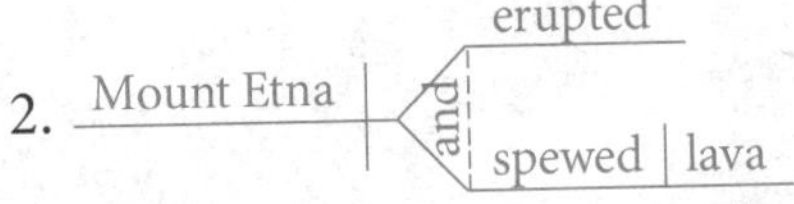

3. Michelangelo | painted | ceiling

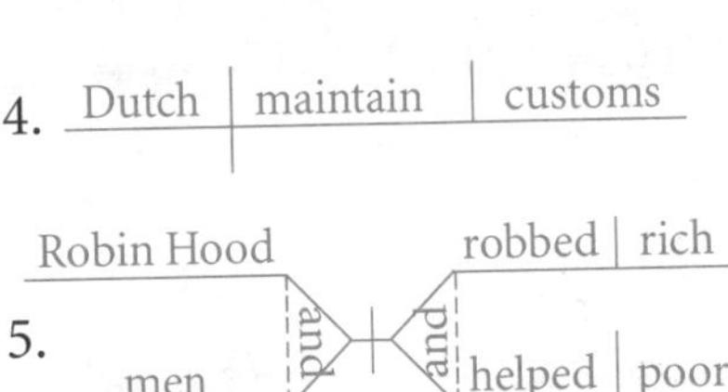

6. President | hired | Lewis and Clark

7. Garibaldi | had united | country

8. Shah Jahan | built | Taj Mahal

9. Rome | ruled | world

10. Milton | wrote | sonnets and epics

Exercise B For additional practice, diagram the subjects, verbs, and direct objects from Exercises A and B on pages 89–90. (See *Supplement*.)

Grammar

Using Nouns as Indirect Objects

1 **An *indirect object* is a noun or a pronoun (not in the possessive case) that precedes the direct object and tells *to whom* or *for whom,* or *to what* or *for what* the action of the verb is done.**

Dad bought our car a new battery. (Dad bought *what?* Dad bought *battery. Battery* is the direct object. Dad bought *for what* the battery? Dad bought for the *car* a battery. *Car* is the indirect object.)

Dad removed our car's dead battery. (Dad removed *what?* Dad removed *battery. Battery* is the direct object. Dad removed *for what* the battery? There is no answer to that question. *Car's* is not an indirect object. Possessive case nouns can never be used as indirect objects or as direct objects.)

2 **Indirect objects can *never* be in *prepositional phrases.***

Andy gave Mom (**I.O.**) a new toaster (**D. O.**). (*Mom* is an indirect object telling to whom Andy gave the toaster. Notice that the indirect object always comes between the action verb and the direct object.)

Andy gave a new toaster (**D.O.**) *to Mom* (**Prep. Phrase**). (*Mom* is not an indirect object in this sentence. *Mom* is in a prepositional phrase and is the object of the preposition *to.*)

3 **Indirect objects *may be compound.***

The teacher gave *Jed* and *Ted* much encouragement.

4 **Always look for the direct object first, and then find the indirect object. If there is no direct object, there can be no indirect object.**

Exercise A

In the sentence below draw a circle around each noun used as a direct object and underline each noun used as an indirect object. Not all of the sentences have indirect objects.

1. I gave Dad a watch for Father's Day.
2. Miss Wilson's class took a history test last Friday.
3. Eric sent his family a post card from Arizona.
4. Paul wrote the Corinthian church two letters.
5. King Darius cast Daniel into the lions' den.
6. God sent the Israelites manna every morning.
7. Samuel anointed David for the throne of Israel.
8. Arabia sells America many gallons of oil each day.
9. Peter preached a powerful sermon on the day of Pentecost.
10. Mother read the children several bedtime stories.

Exercise B

Write three sentences containing nouns used as indirect objects. Remember that your sentence must also contain a direct object.

1. Answers will vary. ______________________________
2. ______________________________
3. ______________________________

Diagraming Indirect Objects

Study the following examples carefully.

INDIRECT OBJECT

The store offered *Gretchen* a summer job.

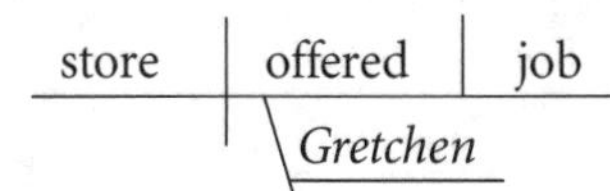

COMPOUND INDIRECT OBJECT

The company awarded *Jake* and *Diana* the scholarships.

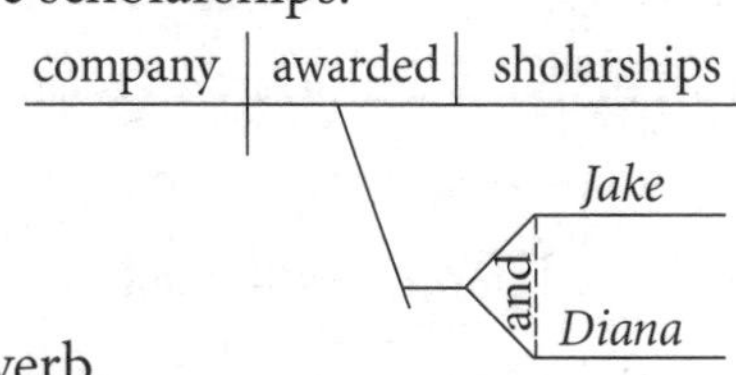

Notice that the indirect object goes underneath the action verb.

Exercise A

Diagram the subjects, verbs, direct objects and indirect objects in the following sentences.

1. Mrs. Davis mailed Alan a gift for graduation.
2. A faithful Christian will give the Lord a tithe of his income.
3. The postman delivered our family a package today.
4. A distant cousin bequeathed Paul some property in Germany.
5. The government often grants farmers the grazing rights to government property.
6. Have you yielded Christ your life?
7. Mr. Deese assigned our class a unique geography project.
8. Father handed Jenny a note for the teacher.
9. The first runner handed Don the baton.
10. Our society presented Charity Hospital a check for a thousand dollars.

1. Mrs. Davis | mailed | gift — Alan
2. Christian | will give | tithe — Lord
3. postman | delivered | package — family
4. cousin | bequeathed | property — Paul
5. government | grants | rights — farmers
6. you | Have yielded | life — Christ
7. Mr. Deese | assigned | project — class
8. Father | handed | note — Jenny
9. runner | handed | baton — Don
10. society | presented | check — Charity Hospital

Exercise B

For additional practice, diagram the subjects, verbs, direct objects, and indirect objects from Exercise A on page 92. (See *Supplement*.)

Reviewing Direct & Indirect Objects

Exercise A

(1) Circle the direct objects in the following sentences. (2) Underline the indirect objects.

1. Miss Peterson offered Kate some cookies and milk.
2. Grace handed Ethan his math book.
3. The Lord sent John a vision of the end of the world.
4. An officer showed the tourists the way to the courthouse.
5. Good parents will teach their children the value of obedience.
6. Solomon built the Lord a magnificent temple in Jerusalem.
7. We lent our neighbors our aluminum ladder.
8. Grandma made Dawn a new skirt of blue cotton.

Exercise B

(1) Circle the direct objects in the following paragraphs. (2) Underline the indirect objects. Not every sentence contains objects.

After David had committed sin with Bathsheba, God sent the king a message. Nathan, the prophet, approached David and told the following story. "There were two men in the same city, one rich and one poor. The rich man had many flocks of sheep, but the poor man had only one small lamb. One day a traveler visited the rich man. The rich man prepared his visitor a feast, but instead of using one of his own sheep, he killed the poor man's lamb and prepared the meal."

When David heard this story, he became very angry. He recommended the death sentence for such a man. Then Nathan said to King David, "Thou art the man."

King David had every possession he needed, yet he had taken another man's wife. God sent David many troubles and heartaches because of his sin. Not even a king can sin and get away with it.

Exercise C

Write four sentences containing direct objects and indirect objects.

1. Answers will vary. ______________________________

____

2. ______________________________

____

3. ______________________________

____

4. ______________________________

____

Grammar G

Distinguishing Indirect Objects from Objects of Prepositions

1 A *phrase* is a group of related words that *does not contain a subject and a verb.*

2 A *prepositional phrase* consists of a preposition, its noun (or pronoun) object, and any modifiers of the object. (See Unit 9 for a list of commonly used prepositions.)

Prep. N. Obj.
The horses stood quietly **inside** *the huge* **corral.**

3 A prepositional phrase *may have a compound object.*

Prep. Obj. Obj.
We talked *about the* **Grecians** *and the* **Romans.**

4 You can tell the difference between an indirect object and an object of a preposition by noting the location of the noun to be identified. An indirect object is always *between* the verb and the direct object; an object of a preposition comes *after* a preposition.

UNIT 5

Exercise A

If the italicized word is an indirect object, write *i.o.* above the word; if it is the object of a preposition, write *o.p.* above the word.

1. We sang a hymn of the early *Church.* (o.p.)
2. Mr. Newman wired his *daughter* enough money for her ticket. (i.o.)
3. We sent our offerings to the African *missionaries.* (o.p.)
4. The Israelite women sang praises to *God* by the Red Sea. (o.p.)
5. God gave *Hezekiah* an extra fifteen years of life. (i.o.)
6. The lad brought *Andrew* the lunch of loaves and fishes. (i.o.)
7. A package arrived for *Sarah* yesterday. (o.p.)
8. God delivered the Ten Commandments to *Moses.* (o.p.)
9. Moses took the *children* of Israel these new commandments for living. (i.o.)
10. President Ford placed a wreath at the *Lincoln Memorial.* (o.p.)

Exercise B

Write (1) one sentence using *Justin* as an indirect object; (2) one sentence using *Justin* as the object of a preposition; (3) one sentence using *frog* as an indirect object; (4) one sentence using *frog* as the object of a preposition.

1. Answers will vary. ______________________
2. ______________________
3. ______________________
4. ______________________

Grammar G

Using Nouns as Appositives & as Nouns of Direct Address

1 **An *appositive* is a word that follows a noun and explains or identifies that noun.**

Berlin, Germany's largest *city,* was once divided by a wall. (*City* is an appositive that identifies the noun *Berlin.*)

William *the Conqueror* won the Battle of Hastings in 1066. (The compound noun *William the Conqueror* consists of the noun William with the appositive *the Conqueror.*)

2 **An appositive *may be compound.***

The Twin Cities, *Minneapolis* and *St. Paul,* are the two largest cities in Minnesota.

3 **An *appositive phrase* is an appositive with all its modifiers.**

Helsinki, *the* ***capital*** *of Finland,* is dark most of the time during the winter.

4 **A *nonessential appositive phrase* is *set off by commas* because it is not closely related to the word it follows. An appositive which is closely related to the word it follows is *essential* and should not be set off by commas.**

Betty, *my* ***cousin*** *from Columbus,* got married last night. (*My cousin from Columbus* is a nonessential appositive phrase.)

The poem "A Forest Hymn" was written by William Cullen Bryant. (*"A Forest Hymn"* is an essential appositive.)

Note: Appositives that follow proper nouns are usually nonessential.

5 **A *noun of direct address* is the name of the person to whom a sentence is directed. It is set off by commas.**

Did they tell you, Bert, when the plane will arrive? (The sentence is directed to *Bert. Bert* is the noun of direct address.)

6 **Nouns of direct address *may be compound.***

Don't sit down, *Jack* and *Joe,* until the ladies are seated.

Exercise A

(1) Write *d.a.* above each noun of direct address. (2) Write *ap.* above each appositive. (3) Put parentheses around the word that the appositive identifies. (4) Insert commas where necessary.

1. (John) the [ap.] Baptist baptized Jesus in the Jordan River.
2. (Mary), the [ap.] mother of Jesus, watched Him die on the cross.
3. Jesus said unto Mary, "[d.a.] Woman, behold thy Son!"
4. Learn your verses today, [d.a.] James; do not wait any longer.
5. Molly gave the flowers to (Mrs. Smathers), our Sunday school [ap.] teacher.
6. [d.a.] Mom, may we invite (Lindsey), our new [ap.] neighbor, to the youth meeting?
7. Did you know, [d.a.] Heather, that (West Virginia), the "[ap.] Mountain State," was the thirty-fifth state to join the Union?
8. (World War I), "the [ap.] war to end all wars," did not and could not eliminate the threat of war.

Exercise B

Write two sentences, one with *Steve* as an appositive and one with *Steve* as a noun of direct address.

1. Answers will vary. __________
2. __________

Diagraming Appositives

Study the following examples carefully.

APPOSITIVE

Milton, the great *poet*, became blind.

Milton (*poet*) | became \ blind

COMPOUND APPOSITIVE

Two girls, *Terri* and *Jess*, planned the party.

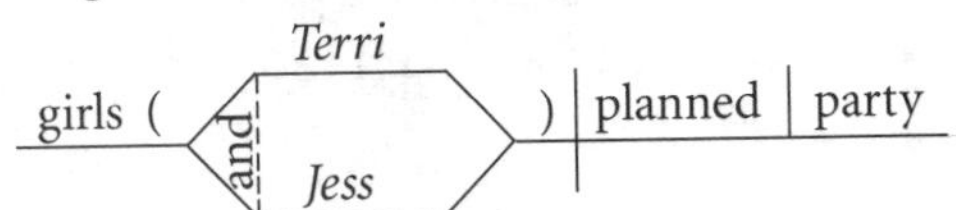

Notice that the appositive is enclosed within parentheses.

UNIT 5

Exercise **Diagram all the sentence parts that you have studied thus far this year.**

1. Shakespeare, the greatest playwright, wrote many sonnets.
2. We took Aunt Meg, Mother's sister, a chocolate cake.
3. My two brothers, Dave and Greg, hit home runs in yesterday's game.
4. Ladybugs, the farmer's friends, destroy many insect pests.
5. Olympia, the capital of Washington, was first settled in 1840.
6. Luke, the beloved physician, was also a writer.
7. My sister Melissa is a caretaker at the San Diego Zoo.
8. Two water fowls, the duck and the swan, are graceful swimmers.
9. The teacher of the year is Mr. Steele, the biology teacher.
10. Sewing, Sharon's hobby, is a useful skill.

1. Shakespeare (playwright) | wrote | sonnets

2. We | took | cake
   \ Aunt Meg (sister)

3. brothers (Dave and Greg) | hit | home runs

4. Ladybugs (friends) | destroy | pests

5. Olympia (capital) | was settled

6. Luke (physician) | was \ writer

7. sister (Melissa) | is \ caretaker

8. fowls (duck and swan) | are \ swimmers

9. teacher | is \ Mr. Steele (teacher)

10. Sewing (hobby) | is \ skill

Grammar

Using Exact & Vivid Nouns

The wise choice of nouns helps attract and hold your reader's interest. Choose nouns that name persons, places, and things *exactly.* Do not use general terms such as *workman* or *a man who works on pipes* when you mean *plumber.* Notice some exact nouns for the word *group: army, galaxy, flock, herd, brood, covey.* Some of these words may be made even more exact. For example, a more exact word for *galaxy* would be the *Milky Way.*

Exercise A

For each general noun below, list three exact nouns.

1. flower Answers will vary. ________ ________
2. animal ________ ________ ________
3. cloth ________ ________ ________
4. vegetable ________ ________ ________
5. building ________ ________ ________

Exercise B

Write a paragraph describing a house, a building, or a room with which you are familiar. It might be your dad's workshop, your doctor's office, your barn, or your family room. Name specific persons and things in the room or building that will present to your reader a clear and interesting picture.

Answers will vary.

Reviewing Nouns & Their Uses

Exercise A **(1) Underline the subject in each sentence. (2) Put parentheses around all proper nouns.**

1. The (Lord) sent (Jonah) to the city of (Nineveh).
2. The boys sang in the (Cherub Choir).
3. (John the Beloved) was exiled on the lonely (Isle of Patmos).
4. The story of (Deborah) and (Barak) is found in the book of (Judges).
5. (Henry) and (Russell) work for my father in his shop.
6. (King Edward) and (Prince Charles) battled each other for several years.
7. The (*Titanic*) sank on its maiden voyage.

Exercise B **Cross out the incorrect verb form in parentheses.**

1. The congregation of that church (~~are~~, is) very friendly.
2. "Soldiers of Christ, Arise" (is, ~~are~~) a beautiful hymn by Charles Wesley.
3. Fifty dollars (~~seem~~, seems) like a large price for so small an item.
4. Civics (is, ~~are~~) the study of our government and its operation.
5. *Little Women* (was, ~~were~~) first published in 1868.
6. Our class (was, ~~were~~) discussing the merits of capitalism.
7. Here (~~is~~, are) the books I've been looking for.

Exercise C **(1) Write *p.n.* above each predicate nominative. (2) Write *d.o.* above each direct object. (3) Write *i.o.* above each indirect object.**

1. Mr. Steinbach is our school's new principal [p.n.].
2. David told God [i.o.] his troubles [d.o.] as he fled from King Saul.
3. Daniel became the highest Persian ruler [p.n.] under the emperor.
4. Nathan Hale would not divulge any secrets [d.o.] to the British.
5. I am the Good Shepherd [p.n.]. The Good Shepherd giveth His life [d.o.] for His sheep.
6. Joseph of Arimathaea gave Jesus [i.o.] his tomb [d.o.].
7. Our Lord chose the unlearned Peter [d.o.] and the well-educated Paul [d.o.]; He can use any clean vessel [d.o.].

Exercise D **For the italicized nouns in the following sentences, write *p.n.* for predicate nominative, *d.o.* for direct object, *i.o.* for indirect object, *o.p.* for object of a preposition, *ap.* for appositive, and *d.a.* for noun of direct address.**

1. In the *autumn* [o.p.], New England becomes a glorious *wonderland* [p.n.] of color.
2. John Quincy Adams, *son* [ap.] of President John Adams, also became *President* [p.n.].
3. *Max* [d.a.], wasn't Albert Einstein, the famous *scientist* [ap.], a German Jew?
4. Yes, but he lived in the *United States* [o.p.] after 1933; he became a United States *citizen* [p.n.] in 1940.
5. Israeli leaders offered *Einstein* [i.o.] the *presidency* [d.o.] in 1952.
6. Edward the Confessor, the last *descendant* [ap.] of Alfred the Great, promised *Duke William* [i.o.] the *throne* [d.o.] of England.
7. At the Battle of Hastings, William defeated *Harold* [d.o.], who also wanted the *throne* [d.o.].

UNIT 5

Exercise A Capitalization and Punctuation. (1) Draw a line through each incorrect small letter. Write a capital above it. (2) Add punctuation where needed.

1. nathaniel hawthorne wrote the novel the scarlet letter.
2. the first american prisoner taken in the korean war was col. jack moore.
3. in the civil war, the following states were among those who left the union: south carolina, georgia, alabama, mississippi, and virginia.
4. each morning, the bell rings at 10:05 A.M. for chapel.
5. I have final exams on the following days: monday, tuesday, and wednesday.
6. my sister enjoys reading the poetry of edgar allan poe; however, i like percy bysshe shelley.
7. 1 john 5:3 reads, "for this is the love of god, that we keep his commandments."
8. Dear Aunt Kay, Dear sir: Sincerely yours,
9. there were twenty-nine contestants in the recent american legion speech contest.
10. no, you may not leave english class early to go to the baseball game.

Exercise B Subjects, Verbs, and Participles. (1) Draw two lines under each verb. (2) Draw one line under each subject. (3) Circle each participle.

1. Christianity was officially recognized by the Roman emperor Constantine in A.D. 313.
2. Leading the Scots against the English, Robert Bruce defeated Edward II's forces and won the Battle of Bannockburn.
3. During the Second Punic War, Hannibal of Carthage crossed the Alps and invaded Italy.
4. Special rafts built by Hannibal and his forces carried their elephants across the Rhone River.

Exercise C The Sentence. In the blank before the number, write *s.* for sentence, *frag.* for fragment, or *r.o.* for run-on.

frag. 1. Ichabod Crane pursued by the relentless Headless Horseman.

r.o. 2. America stands for work, the early settlers found a wilderness and had to work to make something from it.

s. 3. The history of America is a story of work and workers.

frag. 4. Many times when Daniel Boone was out exploring in the forests of Kentucky.

s. 5. Standing firmly upon the statements of Scripture was Martin Luther.

Exercise D Principal Parts. Write the principal parts of the following verbs. Use helping verbs with the present participle and the past participle.

Present	Present Participle	Past	Past Participle
1. talk	(am) talking	talked	(have) talked
2. run	(am) running	ran	(have) run
3. try	(am) trying	tried	(have) tried
4. set	(am) setting	set	(have) set
5. risk	(am) risking	risked	(have) risked

UNIT 5

Exercise E Using Verbs. Cross out each incorrect verb form in parentheses.

1. King Saul (lay, ~~laid~~) down in the mouth of a cave.
2. The sharks (~~attackted~~, attacked) the fish that were (~~throwed~~, thrown) into their tank.
3. Abraham (taught, ~~learned~~) his son Isaac to trust God.
4. We (climbed, ~~clumb~~) to the top of the ridge and (sat, ~~set~~) down to rest.
5. A lifeguard (swam, ~~swum~~) to the child and rescued her before she (drowned, ~~drownded~~).
6. I have (~~sat~~, set) my affection to the house of my God.
7. Mark (~~brung~~, brought) his coat and (laid, ~~lay~~) it on the sofa.
8. (May, ~~Can~~) I (~~bring~~, take) this book back to the library?
9. A thief (~~snuck~~, sneaked) up to the house and (raised, ~~rose~~) a window.
10. The students (~~raised~~, rose) from their seats and said the Pledge of Allegiance.

Exercise F Using Verbs. Cross out each incorrect verb form and write the correct verb form above it. (Some verbs may be corrected in more than one way.)

1. You ~~better~~ [had better] go inside before you ~~take sick~~ [become ill].
2. My brother used to ~~could~~ [be able to] lift heavier weights than he can now.
3. ~~Ain't~~ [Aren't] you the person who wanted ~~on~~ [to get on/to board] the bus this morning?
4. I am the shortest student in the class, ~~aren't I~~ [am I not]?
5. Annie didn't ~~go to~~ [mean to] break that cup, so you ~~better~~ [had better] apologize for getting upset.
6. Since Father ~~took sick~~ [became ill], he can't work like he used to ~~could~~ [be able to].
7. Several drivers want ~~through~~ [to get through] this intersection, but they ~~ain't~~ [aren't] going to make it.
8. Some vandals ~~busted~~ [broke] into the house and ~~et~~ [ate] our food.

Exercise G Subject and Verb Agreement. Cross out the incorrect verb form.

1. "Night Clouds" (is, ~~are~~) the name of a poem written by Amy Lowell.
2. Mathematics (was, ~~were~~) one of my favorite courses in high school.
3. The last group (is, ~~are~~) leaving tomorrow at noon.
4. Several houses on Ninth Street (~~was~~, were) destroyed by fire.
5. The granite blocks in the monument (~~is~~, are) beginning to separate.
6. Tammy (doesn't, ~~don't~~) like watermelon, but I do.
7. Trouble and anguish (~~has~~, have) taken hold on the wayward boy.
8. Either Jack or his brothers (~~is~~, are) going to rake the yard.

Exercise H Identifying Complements. For each italicized noun, write *d.o.* for direct object, *i.o.* for indirect object, and *p.n.* for predicate nominative.

p.n. 1. Lady Jane Grey was the *cousin* of Edward VI, Henry the VIII's successor.

i.o. 2. On his deathbed, Edward VI gave *Jane* the crown of England.

d.o. 3. This action angered *Mary Tudor,* Edward's sister.

p.n. 4. Jane Grey became *queen,* but the people did not accept her.

d.o. 5. Mary raised an *army* and sent Jane a demand for surrender.

i.o. 6. After only nine days as queen, Jane yielded *Mary* the throne.

Exercise I Using Nouns. Above each italicized noun, write *p.n.* for predicate nominative, *d.o.* for direct object, *i.o.* for indirect object, *o.p.* for object of a preposition, *ap.* for appositive, and *d.a.* for noun of direct address.

1. Johannes Kepler, a German *astronomer* [ap.] and *mathematician,* [ap.] discovered three *laws* [d.o.] of planetary *motion.* [o.p.]
2. I will sing a new *song* [d.o.] unto *Thee,* [o.p.] O *God.* [d.a.]
3. Dad and Mom gave my *sister* [i.o.] a beautiful *sweater* [d.o.] for her birthday.
4. The Lord is my *strength* [p.n.] and my *shield.* [p.n.]
5. An Australian nurse, *Elizabeth Kenny,* [ap.] developed a new *method* [d.o.] of treating polio.
6. The ancient Greeks were great *poets,* [p.n.] *politicians,* [p.n.] and *philosophers.* [p.n.]
7. Make no *friendship* [d.o.] with an angry *man.* [o.p.]
8. I sent my *cousin* [i.o.] in Chicago some *photographs* [d.o.] of our *family.* [o.p.]

Exercise J Diagraming. Diagram the subjects, verbs, appositives, and complements of ex. I, numbers 1–4. (See *Supplement.*)

UNIT 5

Exercise A

Capitalization and Punctuation. (1) Draw a line through each incorrect small letter. Write a capital above it. (2) Add punctuation where needed.

1. J C B H C
julius caesar led an invasion of britain. he described his victories in his book commentaries
G W
on the gallic war.
2. W
wasn't it he who said,"I came, I saw, I conquered"?
3. B C R
because of his military successes, caesar was made dictator of rome.
4. A R O L
after his death, the following three men became leaders of rome: octavian, lepidus, and
M A
mark antony.
5. T
the three men briefly shared power; however, it was not long before they were fighting each other.
6. O
octavian, who won the power struggle, was a strong, effective ruler during his forty-four years as emperor.
7. P R G S
Octavian's reign began the pax romana, a time of peace during which god's son came to earth.

Exercise B

Subjects, Verbs, and Participles. (1) Draw two lines under each verb. (2) Draw one line under each subject. (3) Circle each participle.

1. The Greek navy was victorious at the Battle of Salamis, destroying the Persian fleet completely.
2. Hittite and Egyptian armies fought a great battle at Kadesh about 1285 B.C.
3. The Civil War in America was a tragic conflict between the North and the South.
4. Flourishing less than ten years after its completion, the Erie Canal proved a great success.
5. Remembered by many for his novel *A Christmas Carol,* Charles Dickens also wrote several other famous works.

Exercise C

The Sentence. In the blank before the number, write *s.* for sentence, *frag.* for fragment, or *r.o.* for run-on.

frag. 1. The very first man to sail completely around the world alone.

frag. 2. Patented by John Deere in 1837.

s. 3. Although the *Titanic* was supposed to be unsinkable, she sank less than three hours after striking an iceberg.

r.o. 4. Mark Twain is a well-known author he wrote about life along the Mississippi.

s. 5. Hitler's plan to invade Britain was called Operation Sea-Lion.

Exercise D

Action and Linking Verbs. (1) Write *action* if the italicized verb shows action; write *linking* if the verb links. (2) For the linking verbs, draw an arrow to indicate the word that is linked to the subject.

action 1. The energy in foods *is measured* in Calories.

action 2. Some foods *contain* more energy, and thus more Calories, than other foods.

linking 3. Fats and oils *are* high-Calorie foods.

action 4. For this reason, we *must* carefully *monitor* our fat intake.

linking 5. Excess Calories in our diet *become* excess fat.

action 6. We *use* Calories all day long.

action 7. We even *burn* approximately 60 Calories during each hour of sleep.

linking 8. A low-Calorie diet and exercise *are* an important part of a healthy lifestyle.

Exercise E

Principal Parts. In the blank, write the correct principal part of the verb indicated in parentheses.

1. Jamie swims each day at this time. (present of *swim*)
2. Gary called three times before he got an answer. (past of *call*)
3. Larry has answered all of my questions. (past participle of *answer*)
4. I am running in the next race. (present participle of *run*)

Exercise F

Using Verbs. Cross out each incorrect verb form and write the correct verb form above it. (Some verbs may be corrected in more than one way.)

1. Those vines have ~~growed~~ grown over the doorway, but I have ~~brung~~ brought a machete to cut them.
2. I am the only one who ~~thunk~~ thought of the answer, ~~aren't I~~ am I not?
3. Moses ~~rose~~ raised his rod toward heaven, and the battle was won.
4. My brother ~~better~~ had better stop eating so much, or he will have ~~aten us~~ eaten us out of house and home.
5. I ~~seen~~ saw Gene laying those bricks for the patio.
6. The captives wanted ~~out~~ to get out/to escape so badly that they ~~drug~~ dragged a log to the gate and ~~busted~~ broke it down.
7. Sammy didn't ~~go~~ mean to tear up the garden, Papa; he ~~ain't~~ isn't a bad dog.
8. The monkey ~~clumb~~ climbed to the top of the tree, ~~set~~ sat down, and ~~et~~ ate his banana.
9. We had thought of several ways to ~~rise~~ raise the sunken vessel.
10. The President ~~throwed~~ threw out the first ball, and the baseball season ~~begun~~ began.
11. We had better tell the bus driver that we want ~~off~~ to get off at the next stop.
12. I used to ~~could~~ be able to play the *Moonlight Sonata* from memory.

Exercise G Subject and Verb Agreement. Cross out each incorrect verb form in parentheses.

1. Footprints in the sands of time (~~was~~, were) not made by people sitting down.
2. Either the librarian or her assistants (~~is~~, are) always on duty.
3. Goodness or evil (is, ~~are~~) the inheritance of the home.
4. Neither the students nor the teacher (was, ~~were~~) aware that a bird had flown into the room.
5. The class (~~has~~, have) finished their science projects.
6. Fred (doesn't, ~~don't~~) like corn bread and turnip greens.
7. There (~~is~~, are) my suitcases by the ticket counter.
8. Four hours (was, ~~were~~) sufficient time to fly to Houston.

UNIT 5

Exercise H Uses in the Sentence. (1) Underline each subject once and each verb twice. (2) Above each italicized noun in the following sentences, write *p.n.* for predicate nominative, *d.o.* for direct object, *i.o.* for indirect object, *o.p.* for object of a preposition, *ap.* for appositive, and *d.a.* for noun of direct address.

1. Ben Jonson, an English *playwright* [ap.] and *poet,* [ap.] was a *friend* [p.n.] of William Shakespeare.
2. Mrs. Wilson made chocolate chip *cookies* [d.o.] and purchased *soft drinks* [d.o.] for our class party.
3. Deanna gave her *brother* [i.o.] a striped *tie* [d.o.] on his birthday.
4. Before the *end* [o.p.] of *class,* [o.p.] William gave the *teacher* [i.o.] his test *paper.* [d.o.]
5. Reason and judgment are the *qualities* [p.n.] of a leader.
6. My English teacher, *Mr. Lowery,* [ap.] used an overhead *projector.* [d.o.]
7. Kristen and Sarah were class *officers* [p.n.] this fall.
8. Mike, our starting *center,* [ap.] has sprained his *ankle.* [d.o.]
9. NaCl is the chemical *formula* [p.n.] for table *salt.* [o.p.]
10. The book is an edited edition of the original book *The Spirit of America.* [ap.]
11. The documentary featured a story [d.o.] of a great white shark. [o.p.]
12. These sharks constantly replace old, worn *teeth* [d.o.] with sharp, new ones.

Exercise I Diagraming. Diagram the subjects, verbs, appositives, and complements of ex. H, numbers 1–8. (See *Supplement.*)

Grammar

Recognizing Pronouns

1 **A *pronoun* is a word that takes the place of a noun.**

Jesus Christ is God. *He* died to atone for our sins. (The pronoun *He* takes the place of the noun *Jesus Christ.*)

2 **An *antecedent* is the word for which a pronoun stands.**

Jesus Christ is God. He died to atone for our sins. (*Jesus Christ* is the antecedent of the pronoun *He.*)

Note: The antecedent is not always stated.

Did *you* enjoy your trip? (The antecedent of *you* is not stated.)

3 **There are various kinds of pronouns.**

a. **Personal pronouns** refer *to the speaker (I, me, we, us, my, mine, our, ours); the person spoken to (you, your, yours);* and *the person spoken about (he, she, it, they, him, her, them, his, hers, its, their, theirs).*

b. **Interrogative pronouns** are used to ask a question *(who, whom, whose, which, what).*

c. **Demonstrative pronouns** point out the person or thing referred to *(this, that, these, those).*

d. **Indefinite pronouns** point out indefinite persons or things and do not usually have antecedents *(each, either, one, anybody, some, more, all, etc.).*

e. **Compound pronouns** are pronouns combined with *self* or *selves (myself, ourselves, yourself, yourselves, himself, herself, itself, oneself, themselves).*

f. **Relative pronouns** are used to introduce dependent clauses *(who, whom, whose, which, that).*

Note: Many of the words called pronouns on this page may also function as adjectives (see pages 113 and 122).

Exercise

(1) Circle each pronoun in the following sentences. (2) Draw a box around the antecedent of each pronoun. Some antecedents may have more than one pronoun referring to them. Some pronouns may not have an antecedent in the sentence.

1. Dad said he would not let Mary cross the street by herself.
2. "Marie, will you be able to help me on Saturday?" asked Elise.
3. Which of the disciples did Andrew himself bring to Christ?
4. The girls prepared themselves a complete meal during home economics class.
5. After looking through all of the stores, Katie finally found herself a new dress and bought it.
6. After Saul disobeyed God's Word, he tried to excuse himself by saying he had spared the sheep in order to sacrifice them to the Lord.
7. The Bible tells us to rest in the Lord, and wait patiently for Him.
8. What must one do to be born again?
9. A man is a sluggard if he asks for what he himself can find.
10. And the angel said unto them, "Fear not: for, behold, I bring you good tidings of great joy."

Grammar

Making Verbs Agree with Pronoun Subjects I

Memorize the following lists of pronouns.

1 **These *indefinite pronouns* are *singular* and take a singular verb: *each, either, neither, one, everyone, everybody, no one, nobody, anyone, anybody, someone, somebody.***

Each of the birds *has* an identifying tag.
Either of the ties *is* suitable.
Everyone in the group *was* fully *prepared.*

2 **These *indefinite pronouns* are *plural* and take a plural verb: *both, few, several, many.***

Both of the chairs *were* antiques.
Several of the visitors *have* chauffeur-driven cars.

3 **These *indefinite pronouns* may be either *singular* or *plural: some, any, none, all, most.* To determine the number of these words, look at the context of the sentence.**

None of the corn *has been harvested.* (singular)
None of the cows *have been milked.* (plural)
Most of the game *is* usually exciting. (singular)
Most of the spectators *have arrived.* (plural)

Note: Verbs ending in *s* are usually singular.

UNIT 6

Exercise A **Cross out the incorrect form in parentheses.**

1. One of the windows on the car (is, ~~are~~) broken.
2. Few of the sale items (~~was~~, were) really bargains.
3. Most of the big game animals (~~is~~, are) found south of the river.
4. No one in the room (was, ~~were~~) aware of the storm raging outside.
5. (~~Is~~, Are) any of the coins dated 1808?
6. Neither of the books (is, ~~are~~) suitable for a book report.
7. Many of the letters (~~was~~, were) destroyed in the fire.
8. Most of the tourists (~~is~~, are) leaving by chartered bus.
9. Someone in the office (has, ~~have~~) a brown sedan.
10. Few of the students (~~has~~, have) learning difficulties.
11. None of the term papers (~~is~~, are) ready for grading.
12. Most of the paint (has, ~~have~~) flaked off the old car.
13. Several of the students (~~has~~, have) completed the correspondence course.
14. Everyone in the United States (has, ~~have~~) opportunity to succeed.
15. All of the potato fields (~~is~~, are) ready to be harvested.
16. Some of the lakes (freeze, ~~freezes~~) in the winter.
17. Both of the paintings (look, ~~looks~~) professional.
18. (Does, ~~Do~~) either of the welders know how to weld stainless steel?

Exercise B **Write one sentence to illustrate each of the rules above.**

1. Answers will vary. ______________________
2. ______________________
3. ______________________

Grammar

Making Verbs Agree with Pronoun Subjects II

4 ***Doesn't, isn't,* and *wasn't* are *singular* and must be used with singular subjects. *Don't, aren't,* and *weren't* are *plural* and must be used with plural subjects.** (Exception: Use *don't* with the pronouns *I* and *you.*)

Incorrect: He *don't* want any spinach.
Correct: He *doesn't* want any spinach.
Correct: They *don't* want any spinach.

Note: Most errors occur when *don't* is used incorrectly with *he, she,* or *it.*

5 **The verb agrees with the subject, not the predicate nominative.** Do not be confused by a predicate nominative that differs in number from the subject.

One of my real difficulties *is* cumulative exams. (The predicate nominative *exams* is plural, but that has no effect on the subject-verb agreement.)

Exercise A Cross out the incorrect form in parentheses.

1. Many still (~~doesn't~~, don't) have peace.
2. (Doesn't, ~~Don't~~) he know how to drive yet?
3. She (doesn't, ~~don't~~) take care of children under the age of two.
4. It (doesn't, ~~don't~~) have to be ready until Thursday.
5. She (wasn't, ~~weren't~~) expecting the sharp curve in the road.
6. It (isn't, ~~aren't~~) proper to interrupt when others are speaking.
7. I am not driving my car home for the Christmas holidays since it (doesn't, ~~don't~~) run well in the winter.
8. (~~Aren't~~, Isn't) anyone going to help that man unload his furniture?
9. You (don't, ~~doesn't~~) really need all the things you have on that list.
10. They (~~wasn't~~, weren't) able to finish eating the ice cream before it melted.
11. He (~~don't~~, doesn't) think he can finish raking before lunch.
12. Many of the guppies (~~was~~, were) bait for larger fish.
13. They (don't ~~doesn't~~) want to go to the concert with us.
14. (~~Wasn't~~, Weren't) they the explorers who brought President Jefferson two grizzly bear cubs?
15. It (~~don't~~, doesn't) matter which way you insert it.
16. (~~Don't~~, Doesn't) everyone know what to do?
17. Many of his coughing seizures (~~is~~, are) a result of poor health habits.
18. She (~~don't~~, doesn't) know how to keep house.
19. (~~Don't~~, Doesn't) he like lemon meringue pie?
20. They (~~wasn't~~, weren't) expecting him to arrive so soon.

Exercise B (1) Use *doesn't* in two sentences with pronoun subjects and *don't* in two sentences with pronoun subjects. (2) Write a sentence illustrating Rule 5.

1. Answers will vary.
2. ______
3. ______
4. ______
5. ______

Using Nominative Case Pronouns I

1 **Pronouns may be used as *subjects.***

She and *I* have begun nurses' training.

2 **Pronouns used as subjects must be nominative case pronouns. Memorize the list below.**

NOMINATIVE CASE PRONOUNS	
Singular	**Plural**
I	we
(you)	(you)
he, she, (it)	they

Note: The pronouns in parentheses are also objective case pronouns (see pp. 111–112).

3 **Most problems occur when the subject is *compound.* It is helpful to try the pronoun alone in the sentence.**

Jake and (he, him) played on the varsity.
Him played on the varsity. (incorrect)
He played on the varsity. (correct)
Jake and *he* played on the varsity.

4 **Sometimes the subject is *followed by an appositive.* It is helpful to try the pronoun apart from the appositive.**

(We, Us) boys have done our share.
Us have done our share. (incorrect)
We have done our share. (correct)
We boys have done our share.

UNIT 6

Exercise A **Cross out each incorrect pronoun in parentheses.**

1. John and (he, ~~him~~) are going to the state track meet next week.
2. Susie and (she, ~~her~~) are baking cakes for the bake sale.
3. (We, ~~Us~~) girls will help with the spring cleaning.
4. (She, ~~Her~~) and (he, ~~him~~) are planning a surprise party for their parents' anniversary.
5. (We, ~~Us~~) girls must learn a variety of household skills.
6. Mr. Jones and (I, ~~me~~) found a new method of caring for lawns.
7. Gary and (he, ~~him~~) are the tallest members of our family.
8. (We, ~~Us~~) boys must learn the fine art of being gentlemen.
9. Both (they, ~~them~~) and (we, ~~us~~) were participants in the relay race.
10. Yesterday, Grace and (they, ~~them~~) returned from a three-week vacation.
11. (We, ~~Us~~) boys mowed and raked Mrs. Anderson's yard for her.
12. My dad and (I, ~~me~~) are going deep-sea fishing.

Exercise B **Write sentences using pronouns as indicated in parentheses.**

1. (compound subject) Answers will vary. ______________________________

____

2. (subject followed by appositive) ______________________________

____

Using Nominative Case Pronouns II

5 **Pronouns may be used as *predicate nominatives.*** (Predicate nominatives follow linking verbs and rename the subject.)

The next group will be *they.*

6 **Pronouns used as predicate nominatives must be nominative case pronouns.**

NOMINATIVE CASE PRONOUNS	
Singular	**Plural**
I	we
(you)	(you)
he, she, (it)	they

Note: The pronouns in parentheses are also objective case pronouns (see pp. 111–112).

7 **Predicate nominatives *may be compound.***

The finalists are *he* and *she.*

8 **The expression *It is me* or *It's me* is now commonly used in everyday conversation. However, in formal writing follow the rule and write *It is I.***

Exercise A

Cross out each incorrect pronoun in parentheses.

1. The new doctors in town are Dr. Rabold and (he, ~~him~~).
2. Raymond answered, "It is (they, ~~them~~)."
3. No one knew that it was (we, ~~us~~) girls.
4. The shepherds in the play were (he, ~~him~~) and some of his friends.
5. The members of the play cast are Meg, James, Sheila, and (I, ~~me~~).
6. Go and see if it is (he, ~~him~~).
7. Carrie insisted that the thief was (he, ~~him~~).
8. Mr. Green was sure that it was (she, ~~her~~) who had taken the call.
9. The new club officers were Karen, Jeff, and (she, ~~her~~).
10. The foreign correspondent knew it was (she, ~~her~~) that had sold top military secrets.
11. The new youth leaders are Andy and (he, ~~him~~).
12. The Good Shepherd is (He, ~~Him~~) that gives His life for His sheep.
13. If that had been (they, ~~them~~), I would have recognized their car.
14. Was it Rodney or (he, ~~him~~) who did the best work?
15. The student with the best science project was (he, ~~him~~).
16. Is it (she, ~~her~~) who teaches eighth grade history?
17. The only passengers on the small chartered plane were (he, ~~him~~) and (she, ~~her~~).
18. The people invited to the reception are you and (they, ~~them~~).
19. No one ever knew that it was (we, ~~us~~) boys who did most of the work.
20. That might have been (they, ~~them~~) whom we just met.

Exercise B

Write three sentences using pronouns as predicate nominatives. One of the sentences should contain a compound predicate nominative.

1. Answers will vary. ____________________
2. ____________________
3. ____________________

Grammar

G: Using Objective Case Pronouns I

1 Pronouns may be used as *direct objects* and as *indirect objects.*

The Lord delivered *them.* (*Them* is a direct object following the action verb *delivered.*)

The Lord gave *them* deliverance. (*Them* is an indirect object between the action verb *gave* and the direct object *deliverance.*)

2 Pronouns used as objects must be objective case pronouns. Memorize this list.

OBJECTIVE CASE PRONOUNS	
Singular	**Plural**
me	us
(you)	(you)
him, her, (it)	them

Note: The pronouns in parentheses are also nominative case pronouns (see pp. 109–110).

UNIT 6

3 Most problems occur when the objects are *compound.* It is helpful to try each pronoun alone in the sentence.

The Lord comforts you and (I, me).
The Lord comforts *I.* (incorrect)
The Lord comforts *me.* (correct)
The Lord comforts you and *me.*

4 Sometimes the object is *followed by an appositive.* It is helpful to try the pronoun apart from the appositive.

Mom took (we, us) girls to the sewing class. (Omit the appositive *girls* and the sentence reads thus: Mom took *us* to the sewing class.)

Exercise A **Cross out each incorrect pronoun in parentheses.**

1. Matthew will bring you and (~~she~~, her) the message.
2. The Bible tells (~~we~~, us) people the right methods for living.
3. Moses commanded (~~he~~, him) and his nation to set the people free.
4. Miss Atkins told (~~we~~, us) students about the special assignment.
5. Show my family and (~~I~~, me) Thy truth, O Lord.
6. Misty mailed Jenny and (~~I~~, me) a letter from London.
7. Forgive (~~we~~, us) mortals our debts as we forgive our debtors.
8. Headmaster Thompson taught (~~we~~, us) boys to be gentlemen.
9. The old man watched Ted and (~~he~~, him) playing in the snow.
10. Nebuchadnezzar placed Shadrach and (~~they~~, them) in the fiery furnace.
11. The curator of the museum lectured (~~we~~, us) visitors about ancient Egypt.
12. Sam showed (~~she~~, her) and Kristy his coin collection.

Exercise B **Write sentences using pronouns as indicated in parentheses.**

1. (compound direct object) Answers will vary. ____________________

2. (compound indirect object) ____________________

3. (direct object followed by an appositive) ____________________

Using Objective Case Pronouns II

5 Pronouns may be used as *objects of prepositions.* (See the lists of prepositions in Unit 9.)

Mildred went over and sat *beside **her.***

6 Pronouns used as objects must be objective case pronouns.

OBJECTIVE CASE PRONOUNS	
Singular	**Plural**
me	us
(you)	(you)
him, her, (it)	them

Note: The pronouns in parentheses are also nominative case pronouns (see pp. 109–110).

7 Most problems occur when the object is *compound.* It is helpful to try each pronoun alone in the sentence.

We enjoy being with Tom and (they, them).
We enjoy being with *they.* (incorrect)
We enjoy being with *them.* (correct)
We enjoy being with Tom and *them.*

8 Sometimes the object is *followed by an appositive.* It is helpful to try the pronoun apart from the appositive.

The positions were made available to (we, us) girls.
The positions were made available to *we.* (incorrect)
The positions were made available to *us.* (correct)
The positions were made available to *us* girls.

Exercise A **Cross out each incorrect pronoun in parentheses.**

1. The game continued without Grant and (~~he~~, him).
2. Mom gave the presents to (~~we~~, us) girls.
3. Everyone was there except Joy and (~~she~~, her).
4. The award will be presented to (~~they~~, them) or (~~we~~, us).
5. Do you have any projects for Jan and (~~I~~, me)?
6. A spirited debate developed between (~~we~~, us) and (~~they~~, them).
7. He sold the tomatoes to (~~he~~, him) and his friend.
8. He let everyone leave except (~~we~~, us) boys.
9. Alan went hunting with Uncle Nathan and (~~they~~, them).
10. Everything worked out great for (~~they~~, them) and (~~we~~, us).
11. We saw the bear heading straight toward (~~we~~, us) campers and the ranger.
12. The branch was just a bit too high for (~~we~~, us) berry pickers to reach.
13. Only one minute problem stands between (~~we~~, us) and the board of directors.

Exercise B **Write sentences using pronouns as indicated in parentheses.**

1. (compound object) Answers will vary.
2. (object followed by appositive)

Grammar

Using Possessive Case Pronouns

***Possessive case pronouns* show ownership or relationship.** The underlined pronouns in the list below are used as adjectives. Some authorities refer to them as possessive adjectives. *His* and *its* may be used as pronouns or as adjectives.

POSSESSIVE CASE PRONOUNS	
Singular	**Plural**
my, mine	our, ours
your, yours	your, yours
his, her, hers, its	their, theirs

Note: Possessive case pronouns do not use apostrophes to show possession. The possessive form of the pronoun *it* is written ***its.*** The contraction of the words *it is* is written ***it's.***

Mr. Johnson gave his boys some tools. (adj.)
Was that project yours, Carolyn? (pro.)

UNIT 6

Exercise **(1) Circle the possessive pronouns that are used as pronouns. (2) Underline the possessive pronouns that are used as adjectives.**

1. The winner from their class beat our champion in the spelling bee.
2. I am sure that my answer is correct, but is hers?
3. President Carter sent his wife to represent him at the dedication.
4. We raised our voices and called to anyone who might hear our cry.
5. Children, obey your parents in all things, for this is well pleasing unto the Lord.
6. Andrew Carnegie gave much of his fortune to build libraries in our country.
7. I have been young and now am old, yet have I not seen the righteous forsaken nor his seed begging bread.
8. Is this book mine, or is it yours, Alex?
9. I say unto you, "Love your enemies; bless them that curse you."
10. Everyone agreed that Allison knew her speech very well.
11. The male sea horse carries its offspring in a small pouch, much like a kangaroo carries hers.
12. His mercy is on them that fear Him from generation to generation.
13. It is better to be elevated by your humbleness, than to be lowered by your pride.
14. Her brother brought two pink roses he had grown in his experimental garden.
15. Marie, are these shells yours, or did you borrow them from your brother?
16. Several squirrels had built their nests in our large oak tree.
17. Dorcas used her needlework to provide for many of her friends.
18. Let your light so shine before men that they may see your good works.
19. The mouse had built her nest in my father's hard hat.
20. The aging gardener spent most of his time taking care of our lawn for us.

Grammar

Diagraming Pronouns

Study the following examples carefully.

PRONOUN USED AS SUBJECT

She is a homemaker.

She | is \ homemaker

PRONOUN USED AS PREDICATE NOMINATIVE

The homemaker is *she*.

homemaker | is \ she

PRONOUN USED AS DIRECT OBJECT

The people elected *him*.

people | elected | him

PRONOUN USED AS INDIRECT OBJECT

The people gave *him* enthusiastic applause.

people | gave | applause
him

Notice that pronouns are diagramed as nouns are.

Exercise

Diagram the subjects, verbs, predicate nominatives, direct objects, and indirect objects in the following sentences.

1. Dave gave him a watch for Christmas.
2. They are taking a trip to Texas.
3. The deacon presented it to the visitor.
4. This old stamp is one of a kind.
5. We gave them a ride to the airport.
6. Who were the Cambridge Poets?
7. Don gave her a lovely necklace for Mother's Day.
8. Sue and I invited her to the revival.
9. The Lord showered us with blessings.
10. I must tell you about my problem.

1. Dave | gave | watch
him

2. They | are taking | trip

3. deacon | presented | it

4. stamp | is \ one

5. We | gave | ride
them

6. Cambridge Poets | were \ Who

7. Don | gave | necklace
her

8. Sue
and
I | invited | her

9. Lord | showered | us

10. I | must tell | you

Grammar

UNIT 6

1 **Pronouns used as *subjects* or *predicate nominatives* must be in the *nominative* case. Remember that a subject or a predicate nominative can never be in a prepositional phrase.**

NOMINATIVE CASE PRONOUNS: *I, he, she, we, they.* (*You* and *it* are in the nominative case and in the objective case.)

2 **Remember that *predicate nominatives* come only after *linking verbs.***

LINKING VERBS

am	were	taste	look	grow
is	be	feel	appear	remain
are	being	smell	become	stay
was	been	sound	seem	

3 **Pronouns used as *direct objects, indirect objects,* or *objects of prepositions* must be in the *objective case.***

OBJECTIVE CASE PRONOUNS: *me, him, her, us, them.* (*You* and *it* are in the objective case and in the nominative case.)

4 **Remember that *direct objects* and *indirect objects* come only after *action verbs* and can never be in prepositional phrases.**

5 **In order to know which pronoun to select, you must first determine how the pronoun is used in the sentence. Then you select the pronoun from the correct case.**

The leaders in the parade will be Kim and (she, her). [*Kim and (she, her)* is used as a compound predicate nominative. Therefore, you must select the nominative case pronoun *she.* The leaders in the parade will be Kim and *she.*]

Note: See complete procedure for analyzing a sentence on page 143.

Exercise A **(1) In the blank before each sentence, write the use of the pronoun. Write *s.* for subject, *p.n.* for predicate nominative, *d.o.* for direct object, *i.o.* for indirect object, and *o.p.* for object of preposition. (2) Cross out the incorrect pronoun in parentheses.**

__o.p.__ 1. The doctor prescribed some medicine for (~~she~~, her) and the others.
__s.__ 2. Dad and (I, ~~me~~) went on a camping trip in the Colorado Valley.
__i.o.__ 3. Mrs. Johnson sent Oscar and (~~they~~, them) a package of homemade cookies.
__o.p.__ 4. Mr. Nickson gave tennis lessons to Claire and (~~she~~, her).
__p.n.__ 5. The top two finishers are Jack and (he, ~~him~~).
__i.o.__ 6. Mr. Hawkins asked Karl and (~~he~~, him) a different question.
__i.o.__ 7. Uncle James sent his niece and (~~they~~, them) a letter from England.
__s.__ 8. (She, ~~Her~~) and Julie are going shopping tonight after supper.
__d.o.__ 9. Mrs. Williams instructed (~~we~~, us) girls in the fine arts.
__i.o.__ 10. Mr. Macon told Edwin and (~~he~~, him) a funny joke.
__d.o.__ 11. Did Mr. Jones defeat Dr. Roberts and (~~they~~, them) in the county elections?
__d.o.__ 12. Mr. Lakin took (~~we~~, us) students on a nature hike.
__s.__ 13. Bryn and (I, ~~me~~) did some sewing this weekend.

(continued)

Exercise A, cont.

d.o. 14. The mayor presented Mrs. Abbot and (~~she~~, her) with the key to the city.

s. 15. Mom and (they, ~~them~~) gave Dad a fishing rod for Father's Day.

o.p. 16. The mural on the wall was done by Wes and (~~he~~, him).

p.n. 17. The winner of the contest is (she, ~~her~~).

s. 18. Are (they, ~~them~~) the ones who will take us to the concert?

o.p. 19. Isn't the Lord wonderful to (~~we~~, us) Christians?

p.n. 20. It will be (he, ~~him~~) who will receive recognition.

i.o. 21. Grandma sent (~~she~~, her) and Lisa dolls for Christmas.

d.o. 22. The band director asked (~~we~~, us) band members about our future plans.

s. 23. Laurie and (she, ~~her~~) made a huge bowl of potato salad for the picnic.

s. 24. From the inner courts of the castle came (she, ~~her~~) and the king.

i.o. 25. Would you present (~~she~~, her) and the scout troop the award?

o.p. 26. The boxes in the attic belong to Jim and (~~they~~, them).

d.o. 27. The president advised (~~we~~, us) students concerning successful living.

p.n. 28. They knew it was (he, ~~him~~) who had given the anonymous gift.

s. 29. (We, ~~Us~~) children found the lost puppy in the woods.

s. 30. (He, ~~Him~~) is a champion defense lawyer.

Exercise B

Cross out each incorrect pronoun in the following twenty-five sentences and write the correct pronoun form above it. Seven of the sentences are correct; write *C* in front of them.

1. Dan sent Paul and ~~he~~ him a package from Colorado.
2. Didn't Dad and ~~them~~ they give that planter to Mom for Mother's Day?
3. C We seventh graders must have the poem "If" memorized by Monday.
4. The teacher gave the jobs to ~~she~~ her and Jamie.
5. It is ~~him~~ he and ~~me~~ I who have to do the grocery shopping.
6. Weren't Howard and ~~her~~ she elected to the student council from our class?
7. Mrs. Adams gave ~~we~~ us boys some gingerbread to eat.
8. C A worried Mr. Cary sent Philip to look for Spot and us.
9. Was it you or ~~them~~ they?
10. Lynn and ~~me~~ I spent our vacation with missionaries in the Dominican Republic.
11. Our parents are helping my sister and ~~I~~ me through college.
12. C The babysitter put Tony and him into highchairs in order to feed them.
13. ~~Us~~ We girls are a part of the scout troop that earned a citation.
14. C He and Stonewall Jackson gave their lives for the cause they believed in.
15. General Stuart sent ~~they~~ them and the scouts around the enemy lines.

C 16. We seniors had a great time on the senior trip.

17. He asked Gretchen and ~~she~~ her about their summer jobs.

18. The play *Our Town* was produced by ~~we~~ us drama team members.

19. Sharon and ~~him~~ he are attending the honor club meeting.

20. No, it was not ~~him~~ he that you saw.

C 21. Achievement tests will be given to us students tomorrow.

22. Her mom made the costumes for Ellen and ~~I~~ me.

23. The Statue of Liberty was a gift to ~~we~~ us Americans from France.

24. Peter and ~~him~~ he were two of the greatest czars in Russia.

C 25. It was for Greg and me that she made the chocolate pie.

UNIT 6

Exercise C Cross out each incorrect pronoun in the following sentences.

1. He (doesn't, ~~don't~~) want to go fishing until the weather is warmer.
2. Each of us (is, ~~are~~) planning to bring something for the fundraising bake sale on Tuesday.
3. Both of the entries (~~was~~, were) excellent, but Tracy's won first place.
4. One of Paul's piano pieces (is, ~~are~~) extremely difficult.
5. It (doesn't, ~~don't~~) make any difference which bus you ride on.
6. They (~~wasn't~~, weren't) able to finish the project on time.
7. Many of my classmates (~~was~~, were) planning to attend the ball game.
8. All of the schools in our area (~~was~~, were) closed because of bad weather.
9. None of this food (is, ~~are~~) going to be wasted because all of us (~~is~~, are) hungry.
10. Everyone in our church (enjoys, ~~enjoy~~) our Independence Day picnic.
11. I hope that most of the citizens (~~is~~, are) planning to vote in the election.
12. (~~Does~~, Do) either of you know where I can find my economics book?
13. In spite of the rain, she (doesn't, ~~don't~~) want to cancel the picnic because there is a large pavilion in the park.
14. I know that all of us (~~wants~~, want) the best solution to the problem.
15. Many of the museum's paintings (~~was~~, were) a gift from the governor.
16. Hers (was, ~~were~~) the best set of photographs in the contest.
17. I believe that no one in the class (is, ~~are~~) going to miss this question.
18. Neither of the decisions (was, ~~were~~) made hastily.
19. (Is, ~~Are~~) any of that cheesecake left?
20. This baseball season he (doesn't, ~~don't~~) want to miss a single practice.

Exercise A

Capitalization and Punctuation. (1) Draw a line through each incorrect small letter. Write a capital above it. (2) Add punctuation where needed.

1. joseph ward, a congregational minister, led the drive for south dakota's statehood.
2. didn't izaak walton, an english puritan, write the compleat angler, a book on fishing?
3. i'm sure you've read life on the mississippi by mark twain.
4. in judges 12:5–6, we find that the gileadites forced the ephraimites to say the word *shibboleth* as a test.
5. yes, noah webster's dictionary helped standardize american spelling.
6. on october 30, 1967, a tornado struck our town; however, no one was hurt.
7. "the novel the yearling was written by marjorie kinnan rawlings, a florida author," answered kurt.
8. in the novel little women, we read about the following characters: jo, meg, beth, and amy.
9. noah, job, and daniel are recorded in ezekiel 14:14 as being righteous men.
10. alexander the great conquered most of the civilized world, yet he died in babylon at the age of thirty-three.

Exercise B

Subjects and Verbs. (1) Draw two lines under each verb. (2) Draw one line under each subject.

1. The songs of Stephen Foster are perhaps the best known in America.
2. The "Star Spangled Banner" was composed during the War of 1812.
3. Early Appalachian mountain folk borrowed much of their music from their English forebears.
4. The temple choirs of Israel sang psalms as praises to God.
5. Palace musicians of ancient China used such instruments as the lute, flute, and xylophone.
6. Anabaptist singers and Moravian musicians produced many hymns in the early seventeenth century.
7. We do not know the composer of "Greensleeves," a lovely English folk song.
8. In Europe during the Middle Ages, the practice of part-singing was developed.

Exercise C

The Sentence. In the blank before the number, write *s.* for sentences, *frag.* for fragments, or *r.o.* for run-ons.

s. 1. Antarctic explorers treated the penguins as pets.

frag. 2. Building a vivarium, a large glass container to keep snakes and other reptiles in.

r.o. 3. Caracalla, a Roman emperor, kept a pet lion, his name was Scimitar.

frag. 4. Which trained falcons to bring down game birds in flight.

r.o. 5. Small pets can be properly taken care of indoors, an aquarium is a good choice for apartment dwellers.

s. 6. Cleanliness is a vital part of caring for any pet.

frag. 7. President Roosevelt's Scottish terrier Fala, running around the White House.

Exercise D **Using Verbs. Cross out each incorrect verb form in parentheses.**

1. Molly (sneaked, ~~snuck~~) out of the house and (~~laid~~, lay) down in the meadow and looked up at the stars overhead.
2. Ben and Lydia (chose, ~~chosed~~) to (~~lie~~, lay) that green carpet in the master bedroom.
3. (Let, ~~Leave~~) me (lay, ~~lie~~) out my clothes now, so that we (can, ~~may~~) leave before the sun (~~raises~~, rises).
4. That fort (~~may~~, can) not be (attacked, ~~attackted~~) except through the marshes.
5. Aunt Nancy has (~~took sick~~, become ill) and now cannot even (sit, ~~set~~) up in bed.
6. Carl Zelter (taught, ~~learned~~) Mendelssohn to play the piano.
7. Because I have (~~did~~, done) this job before, I can (~~learn~~, teach) you how to do it.
8. We (~~better~~, had better) make camp now; we have (~~clumb~~, climbed) enough for one day.
9. He (~~lay~~, laid) his nets on the right side of the ship and (brought, ~~brung~~) the catch to land.
10. Evidently, Mr. Vinelli (ate, ~~et~~) something that was spoiled, for he (~~took sick~~, became ill) and went home.
11. Justin (~~ain't~~, isn't) the one who (raises, ~~rises~~) the curtain in the auditorium.
12. The hunter, who was nearly (~~froze~~, frozen), was (dragged, ~~drug~~) into the sleigh by the rescuers.
13. Neil (shined, ~~shone~~) his shoes, so he could (~~bring~~, take) them on his trip to Lansing.
14. Kate caught the ball, (~~brought~~, took) it quickly to second base, and (~~throwed~~, threw) it to third for a triple play.
15. The balloon (rose, ~~raised~~) into the air, but, snagging on a tree limb, it (~~busted~~, burst).

Exercise E **Subject and Verb Agreement. Cross out each incorrect verb form in parentheses.**

1. "The Pit and the Pendulum" (is, ~~are~~) a classic short story by Edgar Allan Poe.
2. The teacher, not the students, (gives, ~~give~~) out the test papers.
3. Her illness (makes, ~~make~~) caring for her children very difficult.
4. Neither the boys nor Dad (seems, ~~seem~~) to know we are here.

(continued)

UNIT 6

Exercise E, cont.

5. Civics and mathematics (~~is~~, are) her favorite subjects at the academy.
6. The students sitting in the last row (~~is~~, are) not able to see the chalkboard clearly.
7. The news from the battlefields (was, ~~were~~) encouraging.
8. (~~Doesn't~~, Don't) they understand the principles of democracy yet?
9. Many flocks of birds (~~flies~~, fly) south for the winter.
10. (Is, ~~Are~~) *Pride and Prejudice* written by Jane Austen or Emily Brontë?
11. The prices on the stock market (~~rises~~, rise) and (fall, ~~falls~~) every minute.
12. Christians (need, ~~needs~~) to take God at His Word and trust Him.
13. Stephanie (writes, ~~write~~) her grandmother a long letter each week.
14. David and Jonathan (~~is~~, are) examples of true friends.
15. No harm can come to us unless our heavenly Father (wills, ~~will~~) it so.

Exercise F

Using Nouns. For the italicized nouns in the following sentences, write *s.* above each subject, *p.n.* above each predicate nominative, *d.o.* above each direct object, *i.o.* above each indirect object, *o.p.* above each object of a preposition, *ap.* above each appositive, and *d.a.* above each noun of direct address.

1. Miss White sent the *students* [d.o.] to the *library* [o.p.].
2. Mark, her little *brother* [ap.], fell out of a *tree* [o.p.] and broke his *leg* [d.o.].
3. John Huss was an early Bohemian *martyr* [p.n.] for the *faith* [o.p.].
4. Do you know, *David* [d.a.], the *way* [d.o.] to the auditorium?
5. The woman wished to touch the hem of Jesus' *garment* [o.p.].
6. Father attended *college* [d.o.] at a small Midwestern *school* [o.p.].
7. The nurse gave the *child* [i.o.] *penicillin* [d.o.] to fight the infectious germs.
8. Of course, *Austin* [d.a.], you will be required to finish this assignment.
9. Grandfather sent the model *airplanes* [d.o.] to us *boys* [ap.].
10. The Return of the Native is a *novel* [p.n.] set in the English *moorlands* [o.p.].
11. Da Vinci and Michelangelo were famous *artists* [p.n.] during the Italian *Renaissance* [o.p.].
12. The *ladies* [s.] in our Women's Missionary Society are truly *servants* [p.n.] to the *missionaries* [o.p.] our church supports.
13. Mr. Chou wired his *daughter* [i.o.] the necessary *funds* [d.o.] to purchase the rare vase.
14. We visited *Williamsburg* [d.o.], the restored colonial *town* [ap.], during our *trip* [o.p.] to the East Coast.
15. *Alyssa* [d.a.], you should rewrite these *exercises* [d.o.] neatly.

Exercise G Using Pronouns. (1) In the blank before each sentence, write the use of the pronoun. Write *s.* for subject, *p.n.* for predicate nominative, *d.o.* for direct object, *i.o.* for indirect object, and *o.p.* for object of preposition. (2) Cross out the incorrect pronoun in

s. 1. (She, ~~Her~~) and the other girls prepared a special dinner for their mother.

d.o. 2. Why didn't you tell Jan and (~~I~~, me) about this before?

i.o. 3. Mrs. MacIntosh told (us, ~~we~~) students a story of her childhood.

p.n. 4. The best fishermen in this family are (he, ~~him~~) and dad.

o.p. 5. Nurse Wilkins gave directions to Peter and (~~they~~, them).

s. 6. Jeff and (I, ~~me~~) are working on a special project for Spanish class.

d.o. 7. Father took (us, ~~we~~) children to the museum.

o.p. 8. We sent a gift to Allan and (~~she~~, her) on their anniversary.

i.o. 9. Mr. Schwartzkoff sent Brooke and (~~he~~, him) some photographs taken on his Hawaiian tour.

p.n. 10. It was (we, ~~us~~) boys who mowed the church yard, Pastor.

UNIT 6

Unit 7 Adjectives & Their Uses

Grammar

Recognizing Adjectives

1 **An *adjective* is a word that modifies a noun or a pronoun. It answers the questions *what kind, which one, how many, how much,* or *whose.*** (A modifier makes the meaning of another word more specific by describing or limiting that word.)

joyful people (what kind) *that* apple (which one) *my* shoes (whose)

three exams (how many) *sufficient* rest (how much)

2 **Most adjectives come before the words they modify as in the examples above. In some sentences adjectives come after the words they modify.**

Mark's hair is *curly.* (predicate adjective)

Alex, *strong* and *muscular,* hits many home runs. (appositive adjectives)

3 **Several adjectives may modify the same word.**

The *long, hot* summer can become *tiresome.*

4 **The words *a, an,* and *the* are always adjectives. They are called *articles.*** (Do not confuse *an* with *and. And* is a conjunction; *an* is an adjective.)

5 **Possessive nouns and certain possessive pronouns** (page 106) **are usually called adjectives.**

Emily's bug collection is complete, but *her* brother has not even started *his* collection.

6 **A *participle* is a verb form used as an adjective.** (See page 63.) **Participles have endings similar to a verb *(-ing, -d, -ed, -t,* or *-en),* but they function as an adjective to modify a noun or pronoun.**

The *burning* barn lighted up the night sky.

The English book *found* on the bus was returned to its owner.

Exercise A

(1) Underline all the adjectives in the following sentences (except the articles *a, an,* and *the*). (2) Draw arrows to the nouns or pronouns that the adjectives modify.

1. The people prayed a joyful prayer of thanksgiving when they learned of the war's end.
2. Their small pond, filled with blue and green fish, is near the rose garden.
3. The three desperate men faded into the dim shadows of the forest.
4. A cold, icy wind tore savagely at the woman's scarf.
5. The house, warm and cozy, sheltered the shivering children from the wind's frigid breath.
6. The cool leafy shade of the oak tree provided a refreshing relief from the unrelenting rays of the summer sun.
7. A small, white country church stood on the grassy slope of the narrow dirt road.
8. Karen's idea to make red cushions was readily accepted by the ladies' sewing circle.

9. His long vacations provided sufficient time for him to find a profitable summer job.
10. The little, white kitten mewed dejectedly through the metal bars of its cage.
11. Dana's unique doll collection intrigues her younger cousins when they visit.
12. The old, godly prophet rebuked the wicked, grasping king.
13. Young Rehoboam was foolish; he would not obey the wise counsel of Solomon's advisers.
14. Pagan, barbarous tribesmen overran the Roman Empire in A.D. 476.
15. The mighty empire became a mere name in world history.

Exercise B

In the story below fill each blank with an appropriate adjective. Answers will vary.

Today, our Thanksgiving celebrations usually consist of a ________ meal made up of a ________, ________ turkey, ________ dressing, ________ pies, and many other ________ foods. But the first Thanksgiving was different. The ________ Pilgrims that came to the ________ wilderness of America had gone through their first ________ winter in the new land. By working the ________ soil and planting crops with the aid of ________ Indians, the Pilgrims brought forth their first ________ harvest. The Pilgrims had a feast to lift ________ hearts in praise to God. The ________ meal of the first Thanksgiving is commemorated in the ________ feasts of today, but the purpose of Thanksgiving remains the same.

Exercise C

(1) Write a brief paragraph describing a ballpoint pen. Assume that you are writing to someone who has never seen such a thing. (2) Underline all the adjectives in your paragraph (except articles).

Answers will vary.

UNIT 7

Grammar

Recognizing Proper Adjectives

A *proper adjective* is a word formed from a proper noun and, like a proper noun, begins with a capital letter.

Proper nouns	Proper adjectives
Japan	*Japanese* food
Elizabeth	*Elizabethan* customs
Ephesus	*Ephesian* church

Exercise A

In the following sentences, underline all the proper nouns and draw a circle around the proper adjectives.

1. The members of the band from Highlands, North Carolina, were dressed in Scottish kilts.
2. During the Victorian period of English literature, such writers as Dickens, Thackeray, and Tennyson were very prolific.
3. Messianic promises are found throughout the Old Testament, especially in the Psalms.
4. Near Bethlehem on the Judean hillside, the angel announced the birth of Christ to some shepherds.
5. Roman government, Greek culture, and Jewish religion all combined to crucify Jesus Christ.
6. The Russian author, Alexander Solzhenitsyn, was exiled from his homeland because he wrote against the Siberian concentration camps.
7. Failure of the potato crops in 1845–46 caused thousands of Irish immigrants to come to America.
8. The Spenserian sonnet was developed by Edmund Spenser, an English poet.
9. Henry VII, the first Tudor king, brought peace to Britain after the Wars of the Roses.
10. Miguel de Cervantes authored perhaps the greatest Spanish novel, *Don Quixote.*

Exercise B

(1) Write five sentences containing proper adjectives. (2) Circle each proper adjective in your sentences.

1. Answers will vary.
2. __________
3. __________
4. __________
5. __________

Grammar G

Distinguishing Adjectives from Nouns & Pronouns

Many times the same word can be used as different parts of speech. You cannot tell what part of speech a word is until you determine its *use in a sentence.*

Pro. *Each* of the players did well.	**Adj.** *Each* player performed well.
N. This *tire* is a radial tire.	**Adj.** The *tire* marks were examined.
Pro. I exchanged my book for *his.*	**Adj.** That is *his* book.
N. *Mary* is my best friend.	**Adj.** *Mary's* hair always looks attractive.

Exercise A

In the blank before each number, identify the part of speech of the italicized word. Write *n.* for noun, *pro.* for pronoun, and *adj.* for adjective.

UNIT 7

pro. 1. *Several* of the graduates gave their testimonies.

adj. 2. We traveled to *several* states during our vacation.

adj. 3. *Train* tracks run along our back campus.

n. 4. I will need to leave at 4:20 P.M. to catch my *train.*

n. 5. From the *fence,* we could see acres of pastures.

adj. 6. A white squirrel was sitting on one of the *fence* posts.

pro. 7. *This* is the day which the Lord hath made.

adj. 8. *This* day is thy soul required of thee.

n. 9. For a newly arrived immigrant, Mr. Dien can speak *English* remarkably well.

adj. 10. Every educated person should be able to use the *English* language effectively.

adj. 11. Many perfumes are produced from *flower* petals.

n. 12. *Flower* in the crannied wall, I pluck you out of the crannies. —*Tennyson*

pro. 13. The Father calls *some* of His children to lay down their lives for Him.

adj. 14. Despite the many witnesses, *some* people refuse to accept Jesus as Savior.

adj. 15. The *mountain* settlers were rugged individualists.

n. 16. Moses was called to the *mountain* to receive the tables of the Law.

adj. 17. I do not really like *either* color.

pro. 18. *Either* of these books would be suitable for your report, Don.

adj. 19. A *Christian* scholar will do all his schoolwork to the glory of God.

n. 20. God calls every *Christian* to be separated from this sinful world.

Distinguishing Adjectives from Nouns & Pronouns

Exercise B **In the blanks, write the part of speech of the italicized words. Write *n.* for noun, *pro.* for pronoun, and *adj.* for adjective.**

Americans[1] have, since the *early*[2] days of the *nation*[3], been involved in the *missionary*[4] movement. As early as 1745, *David Brainerd*[5] had begun to work with the Indians of the Northeast. *He*[6] was just one of our many home missionaries. Later, such workers as Jason Lee and Marcus and Narcissa Whitman pushed to the *Pacific*[7] Northwest. In fact, they were the first white *settlers*[8] to cross the Rocky Mountains. In 1812, five *young*[9] men dedicated themselves to spreading the Gospel to *heathen*[10] lands beyond our own shores. *One*[11] of *these*[12] young men, Adoniram Judson, and his wife Ann went to *Burma*[13]. There *they*[14] labored for *many*[15] years. After a *long*[16], hard struggle, they were given fruit for *their*[17] labor. While these faithful *servants*[18] were busy in *other*[19] nations, God raised up men in the United States to preach *His*[20] word. These "circuit riders" went even to the remotest frontier *village*[21] with the *Word*[22] of God. Only in heaven will *we*[23] be fully able to realize the *great*[24] value of these *labors*[25].

1. n.	6. pro.	11. pro.	16. adj.	21. n.
2. adj.	7. adj.	12. adj.	17. adj.	22. n.
3. n.	8. n.	13. n.	18. n.	23. pro.
4. adj.	9. adj.	14. pro.	19. adj.	24. adj.
5. n.	10. adj.	15. adj.	20. adj.	25. n.

Exercise C **Write ten sentences, using the following words as instructed. Underline the given word in each sentence.**

1. (*tree* as a noun) Answers will vary.
2. (*tree* as an adjective) ______
3. (*one* as a pronoun) ______
4. (*one* as an adjective) ______
5. (*light* as a noun) ______
6. (*light* as an adjective) ______
7. (*some* as a pronoun) ______
8. (*some* as an adjective) ______
9. (*iron* as a noun) ______
10. (*iron* as an adjective) ______

Grammar

Recognizing Predicate Adjectives I

1 A ***predicate adjective*** **is an adjective that follows a** ***linking verb*** **and** ***modifies*** **the subject.**

The sky is *blue.* *(Blue is a predicate adjective modifying the subject sky.)*

2 **Predicate adjectives** ***may be compound.***

The Word of God is *quick* and *powerful.*

3 **Predicate adjectives are sometimes called** ***subject complements.*** Subject complements always follow linking verbs. Have you memorized the following list?

Linking Verbs

am	were	taste	look	grow
is	be	feel	appear	remain
are	being	smell	become	stay
was	been	sound	seem	
(May also be used as helping verbs)		(May also be used as action verbs)		

4 **To find a predicate adjective, first locate the verb. Then ask the questions** ***what*** **or** ***how*** **after the verb.** (See page 143 for a complete procedure for locating complements.)

UNIT 7

Exercise

(1) Underline the linking verbs. (2) Draw a circle around the predicate adjectives.

1. A child of the Savior should be friendly and helpful to everyone he meets.
2. Saul was tall and handsome, yet he was not obedient.
3. Miss Adams is certainly knowledgeable on this subject.
4. Wash me, and I shall be whiter than snow.
5. The law of the Lord is perfect.
6. The prayers of the saints are sweet to our Savior.
7. His description of a sailing vessel was both accurate and clear.
8. A clipper ship was slender and swift.
9. The Lord is not slack concerning His promises.
10. The Church of Ephesus was patient and diligent.
11. Absalom was rebellious; his rebellion led to an untimely death.
12. Wasn't today simply lovely, Rhonda?
13. The old man was tall, thin, and somewhat bald.
14. I am terribly sorry to hear of your illness, May.
15. This winter's storms were greater in number and more severe than those of past winters.

Grammar G

Recognizing Predicate Adjectives II

The verbs *taste, feel, smell, sound, look, appear, become, seem, grow, remain, stay* may be used either as linking verbs or as action verbs. You may easily determine whether these words are action or linking by asking yourself the following question: "Is the subject in this sentence performing any action?"

A.V. **D.O.**
We *smelled* the *steak* cooking. (Is the subject *we* performing the action of smelling something? Yes. *We* is performing the action of smelling the steak. *Smelled* is an action verb and *steak* is the direct object.)

L.V. **P.A.**
The steak *smelled delectable.* (Is the subject *steak* performing the action of smelling something? No. *Smelled* is a linking verb, linking the predicate adjective *delectable* to the subject *steak.*)

Exercise A

(1) Identify the verbs in the following sentences by writing *a.v.* above action verbs and *l.v.* above linking verbs. (2) In those sentences that contain linking verbs, draw a circle around the predicate adjectives.

1. Miriam tasted (a.v.) the strawberry preserves.
2. That freshly baked bread smells (l.v.) (delicious)!
3. Banquo's ghost appeared (a.v.) to Macbeth at the banquet.
4. It seems (l.v.) (warmer) today than yesterday.
5. Aunt Molly grows (a.v.) zinnias, asters, and nasturtiums in her front yard.
6. The *1812 Overture* sounds (l.v.) very (bold) and (warlike).
7. The blind girl put (a.v.) out her hand and felt (a.v.) the lamb's wool.
8. I have felt (l.v.) somewhat (ill) since lunch.
9. Two-year-old children become (l.v.) (restless) easily.
10. You should remain (l.v.) (helpful), no matter what your position in life.

Exercise B

Write four sentences, using the following words as instructed.

1. (*taste* as an action verb) Answers will vary.
2. (*taste* as a linking verb) ______
3. (*sound* as an action verb) ______
4. (*sound* as a linking verb) ______
5. (*look* as an action verb) ______
6. (*look* as a linking verb) ______
7. (*grow* as an action verb) ______
8. (*grow* as a linking verb) ______

Grammar

Diagraming Adjectives

Study the following examples carefully.

Her lovely black and *red* dress was *expensive.*

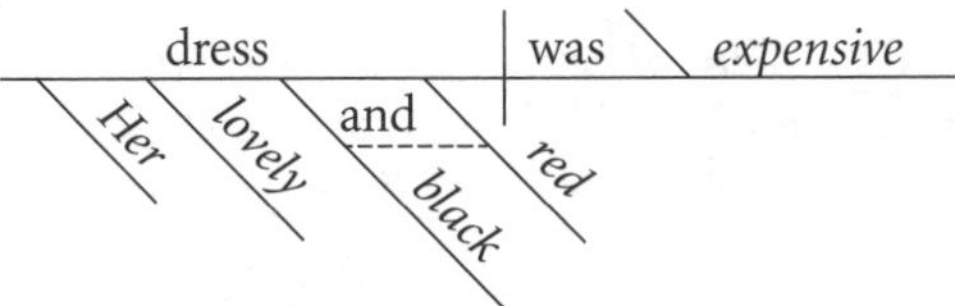

Good Christians are *kind* and *cheerful.*

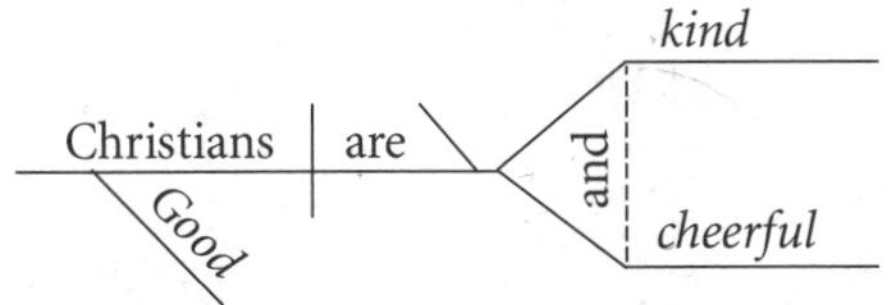

Notice in the diagrams above that the predicate adjectives *expensive, kind,* and *cheerful* are diagramed exactly as a predicate nominative is diagramed, with the line slanting toward the subject. Also notice in the first example how the compound adjective *black* and *red* is diagramed.

The galloping horse had *a beautiful brown* and *white* coat.

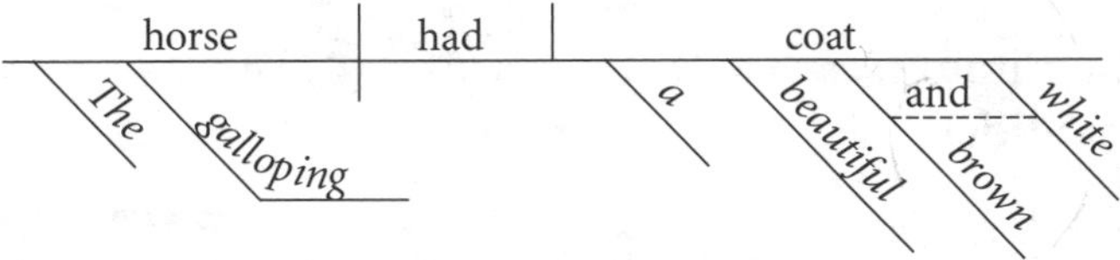

Notice how the participle *galloping* is diagramed.

Exercise

Diagram the following sentences on a separate sheet of paper. (See *Supplement.*)

1. That ancient Ming porcelain had a slight crack.
2. The mad rushing waters overflowed the pioneer's tiny boat.
3. The persecuted Christians were joyful and courageous.
4. Cowardly Shimei hurled several awful curses.
5. One great storm destroyed the invincible Armada.
6. New England maple trees produce magnificent orange and red leaves.
7. The Jewish Holy Place contained a tall golden candlestick.
8. The guilty sinners were miserable.
9. A noble Hebrew woman saved her entire race.
10. The wandering tribes were victorious.

UNIT 7

Grammar

Using Prepositional Phrases as Adjectives

1 **A *phrase* is a group of words that is used as one part of speech. A phrase does not contain a subject and verb.**

Adjective
Prep. Adj. N.
Cary is the boy with red hair. (*With red hair* is the phrase. *With* is a preposition. *Red* is an adjective. *Hair* is a noun. The three words in the phrase are used together to modify the noun *boy;* therefore, the group of words is *used* as *one* part of speech—an adjective.)

2 **A *prepositional phrase* consists of a preposition, its noun or pronoun object, and any modifiers of the object.** (Memorize the list of commonly used prepositions in unit 9.)

He spilled the can *of paint.*

The boy *with the ready smile* is well liked.

3 **The object of a preposition *may be compound.***

The salad *of lettuce and tomatoes* was delicious.

4 **A prepositional phrase that modifies a noun or a pronoun is called an *adjective phrase.* An adjective phrase answers the questions *what kind, which one, how many, how much,* or *whose.***

The house *with the green shutters* is ours.

Exercise A

(1) Draw a box around each adjective phrase. (2) Draw an arrow to the noun or pronoun that the phrase modifies.

1. David was a descendant of the noble Ruth.
2. The seminar in Richmond was profitable.
3. My horse is the chestnut mare with the white star on its forehead.
4. Hymns are Scriptural songs of praise.
5. Our ride in the mountains gave me great pleasure.
6. The road through the village was rutted and overgrown.
7. A speaker from Washington addressed our local farm board.
8. Our new neighbor is that fellow in the green jacket.
9. Acreage around the lake is marshy and uninhabitable.
10. Only one of the healed lepers was thankful.

Exercise B

(1) Write four sentences, each containing an adjective phrase. Use the prepositions given below. (2) Circle the phrases and draw arrows to the words modified.

1. *(on)* Answers will vary.
2. *(across)* ______
3. *(with)* ______
4. *(by)* ______

Grammar

Using Participial Phrases

1 A *participle* is a verb form used as an *adjective* to modify a *noun* or a *pronoun.* Participles end in *-ing, -d, -ed, -t,* or *-en.* (See p. 63 to review verbals.)

In her haste, Sarah broke the vase. (*Broke* is the verb.)

The *broken* vase lay at Sarah's feet. (*Broken* is a participle because it is used as an adjective: it modifies the noun *vase.*)

Balking at the sight of the angel's sword, the donkey saved Balaam's life. (*Balking* is a participle because it is a verb form used as an adjective: it modifies the noun *donkey.*)

2 A *participial phrase* consists of the participle together with its modifiers or complements. The modifiers may be single adverbs or prepositional phrases.

Part. I.O. D.O.
Handing Bill the present, Mom smiled broadly. (*Handing* is the participle. *Bill* is the indirect object and *present* is the direct object of *handing.*)

Part. Adv.
Smiling broadly, Mom handed Bill the present. (*Smiling* is the participle. *Broadly* is a single adverb that modifies *smiling.*)

Part. Prep. Phrase
Smiling at Bill, Mom gave him the present. (*Smiling* is the participle. *At Bill* is the prepositional phrase that modifies *smiling.*)

3 Notice in all the examples above that the entire participial phrase acts as an adjective to modify a noun or a pronoun.

UNIT 7

Exercise A

(1) Draw a box around each participial phrase. (2) Draw an arrow to the noun or pronoun that it modifies.

1. The lad holding the horse's reins was small.
2. Cowering to a maid, Peter denied his Lord.
3. Workers skilled in metallurgy were imported from Tyre.
4. Pleased with the news, the old gentleman smiled.
5. The saints tread upon a road paved with pure gold.
6. Daniel, thrown into the lion's den, still trusted God.
7. Blown over during the storm, the ancient oak destroyed a small home.
8. Waving at the ship, the children stood at the dock.
9. Trained in obedience, Samuel could be trusted.
10. Crying quietly, the little girl sat on the street curb.

Exercise B

(1) Write two sentences containing participial phrases. (2) Circle the phrases and draw an arrow to the noun or pronoun that each modifies.

1. Answers will vary.
2. ______

Diagraming Adjective Phrases

ADJECTIVE PHRASE

The boy *with red hair* grinned.

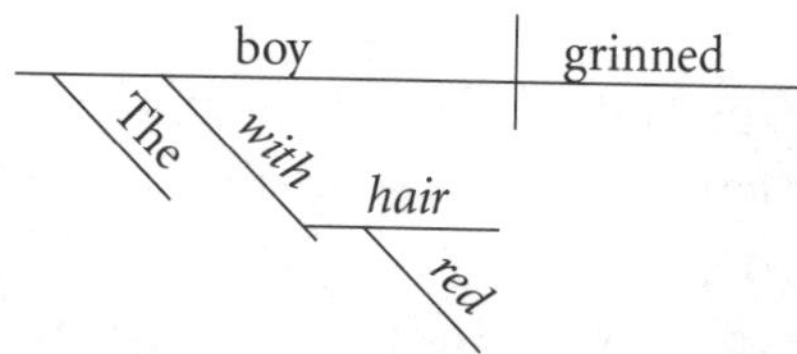

ADJECTIVE PHRASE WITH COMPOUND OBJECT

The boy *with red hair and blue eyes* grinned.

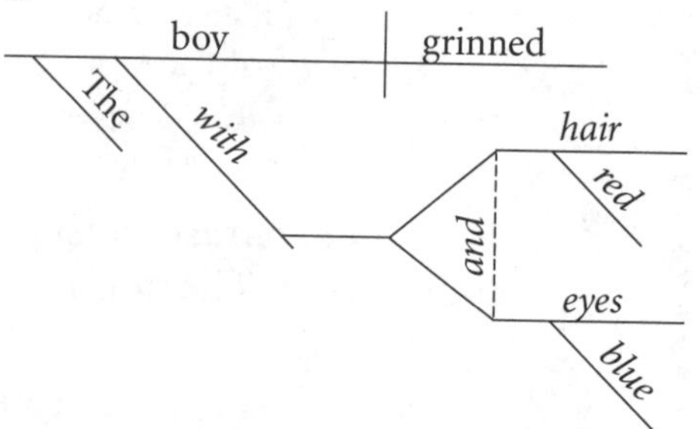

PARTICIPIAL PHRASE WITH ADVERB AND PREPOSITIONAL PHRASE MODIFIERS

Smiling broadly at Bill, Mom gave him the present.

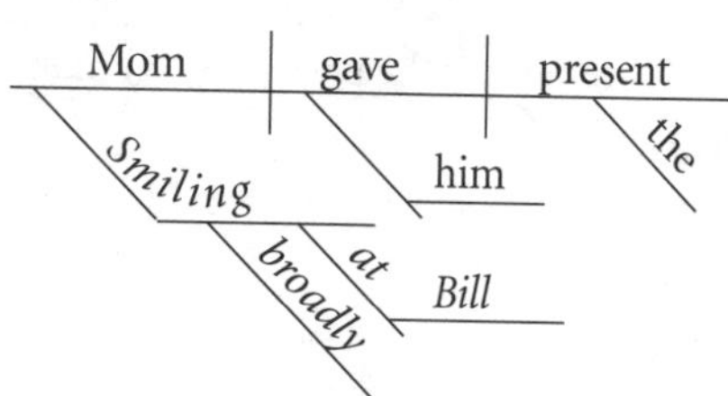

PARTICIPIAL PHRASE WITH INDIRECT AND DIRECT OBJECT

Handing Bill the present, Mom smiled.

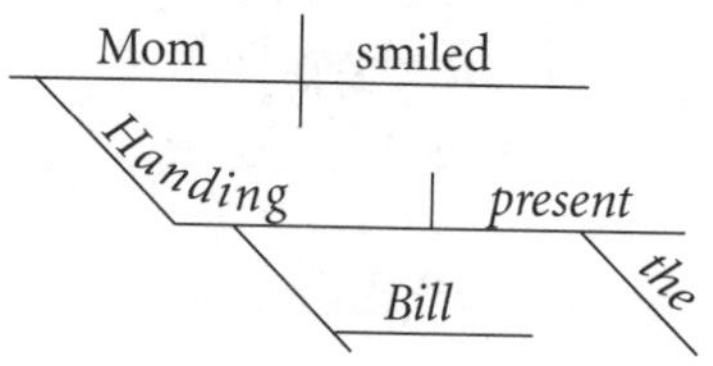

Note: In the diagram of a *prepositional* phrase, the slanted line extends past the horizontal line; but in a *participial* phrase, the slanted line meets the horizontal line.

Exercise A **On a separate sheet of paper, diagram the following sentences.** (See *Supplement.*)

1. The mirror in the golden frame sparkled.
2. John Alden married the Pilgrim girl with golden hair and blue eyes.
3. Sneezing loudly during the service, Ralph disturbed the entire congregation.
4. Sweeping the kitchen floor, Mom whistled a tune.
5. Our God is Ruler of heaven and earth.
6. Mr. Gower was the editor of the local newspaper.
7. Giving his clerk little pay, Scrooge expected long hours of work.
8. Visited by three ghosts, Ebenezer changed his ways.
9. A woman with a large hat asked me a question.
10. Walking slowly up the street, Kyle examined each shop window.

Exercise B **If additional practice is needed, you may diagram the sentences on pages 130 and 131.** (See *Supplement.*)

Grammar

Using Adjective Clauses

1 A *clause* is a group of words that contains both a subject and a verb. It is used as a part of a sentence.

2 An *independent clause* expresses a complete thought and can stand alone as a sentence.

Greg is the last contestant who will give a speech.

3 A *dependent* (subordinate) *clause* does not express a complete thought and cannot stand alone as a sentence.

These are the definitions *that we should learn.*

4 A dependent clause that modifies a noun or a pronoun is called an *adjective clause.*

Here is the book *that I bought for you.*

5 Adjective clauses are introduced by words called *relatives. Who, whom, which,* and *that* are relative pronouns. *Whose* is a relative adjective.

6 A relative serves two purposes: (1) It introduces the clause. (2) It serves a grammatical function within the clause.

She is the one ***who*** *will help us.* (*Who* is the subject of *will help.*)

He is the boy *to* ***whom*** *the scholarship was granted.* (*Whom is the object of the preposition to.*)

A Christian is a person ***whose*** *conduct should be above reproach.* (*Whose modifies the noun conduct.*)

There is the painting ***that*** *I really want.* (*That is the direct object of want.*)

UNIT 7

Exercise A

(1) Underline each subject one time and each verb two times. (2) Circle each relative. (3) Put parentheses around each adjective clause. (4) Draw an arrow to the noun or pronoun that the clause modifies.

1. Arthur was the only one (that could pull the sword from the stone.)
2. The person (who is elected to this office) will represent our class at the council meeting.
3. Andrew Jackson is the President (whom we studied today.)
4. The incandescent light bulb is an invention (that revolutionized our nation.)
5. South Carolina was the first state (which seceded from the Union.)
6. Mr. Foxhall is the gentleman (with whom we made the agreement.)
7. There went with Saul men (whose hearts God had touched.)
8. Our dog, (which escaped last month,) returned home last night.
9. Space remains as a frontier (that we can explore.)
10. Vikings were the first settlers of that land (which is now known as Iceland.)
11. The land (to which we journey) is a place of rest for God's children.
12. William Shakespeare, (who wrote 37 plays and over 150 sonnets,) is the most famous of all English writers.

(continued)

Exercise A, cont.

13. Our best friends are they (who tell us of our faults.)
14. A mummy (which was recently discovered) is on display in the museum.
15. The Bible, (which was written by forty authors,) is, of course, the Word of God.
16. The Bretons, (whose ancestors were Celts,) speak a language somewhat like Gaelic.
17. Students (who won scholarships) will have their photograph taken this afternoon.
18. The pilgrims (with whom Chaucer traveled) were a diverse group.

Exercise B

The following paragraphs contain 10 adjective clauses. (1) Put parentheses around each adjective clause. (2) Draw an arrow from each relative to the word that the adjective clause modifies.

The islands (which compose the country of Japan) have a unique climate unlike the Asian mainland and the other Pacific islands. Japan's temperate weather can be compared to that of the United States. The residents of Kyushu and Shikoku, (whose island homes lie in the southern tip of the nation,) can enjoy the same type weather as those (who live in Florida.) They have cool winters and extremely warm summers.

The largest island, Honshu, (on which Tokyo is situated,) is much like the states (that form our eastern seaboard.) The summers there are warm; but the winters in northern Honshu bring much snow, (which makes the area a haven for skiers.) The southern area of Honshu has winters (which are much more mild.)

The northernmost island, Hokkaido, (which has frigid winters and cool summers), can be compared with New England. These harsh temperatures combine with the poor soil, (which is mainly sands and volcanic ash,) to produce an uninhabitable area. Only five percent of all people (that live in Japan) make Hokkaido their home.

Exercise C

Combine each pair of sentences into one sentence by using an adjective clause.

Answers may vary.

1. Matt was on the varsity baseball team. He often hit home runs. Matt, who often hit home runs, was on the varsity baseball team.
2. That building is being torn down. It has been condemned. That building, which has been condemned, is being torn down.
3. He is my friend. I would do anything for him. He is my friend for whom I would do anything.

Diagraming Adjective Clauses

Grammar

Diagram the independent clause first. Then diagram the adjective clause below the independent clause. Draw a dotted line from the relative pronoun or relative adjective to the noun or pronoun that the clause modifies.

Jason's sister, who won the contest, had an excellent project.

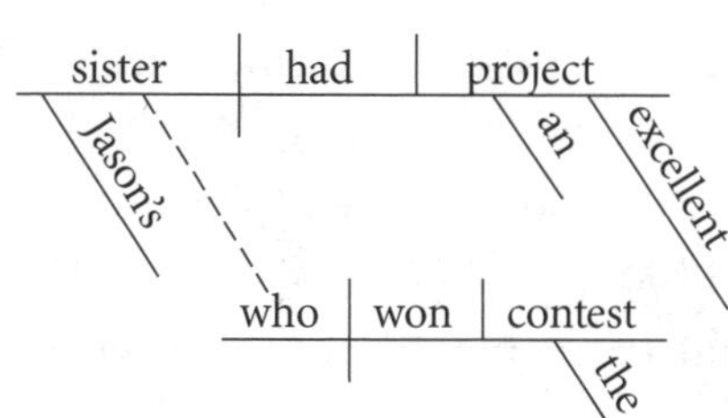

Jessica is the one whose place I took.

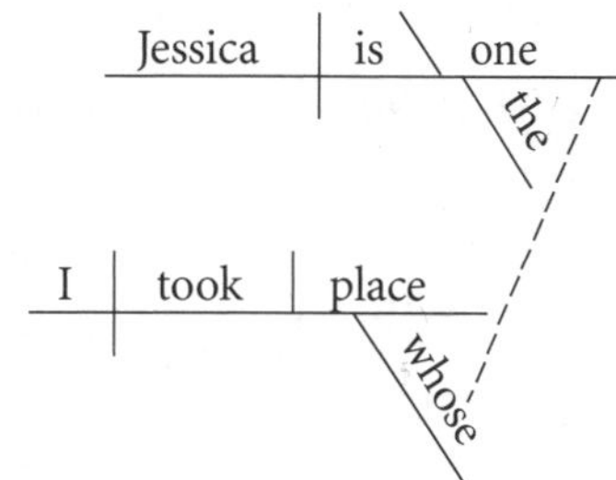

We played a game that I really enjoyed.

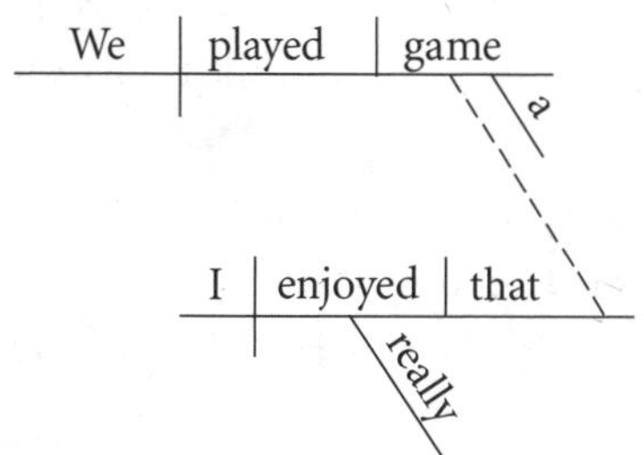

Teresa is the girl to whom the seat was assigned.

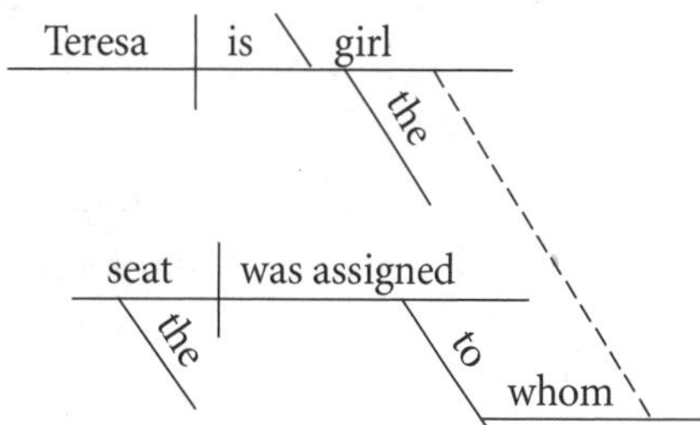

UNIT 7

Exercise A **Diagram the following sentences.** (See *Supplement*.)

1. The world contains many countries that are extremely small.
2. Monaco is a small country whose ruler is a prince.
3. Monte Carlo, which is the capital of Monaco, is a famous tourist resort.
4. Two tiny countries in Italy that maintain their own distinctiveness are Vatican City and San Marino.
5. Vatican City, in which few people live, is the world's smallest independent state.
6. San Marino, which occupies a mountain in central Italy, is the world's oldest republic.
7. El Salvador is the Western Hemisphere's smallest country that is not an island.
8. The Bahamas, whose economy depends largely on tourism, comprises a chain of small islands near Cuba.

Exercise B **For additional practice, diagram numbers 1–6 in Exercise A on p. 133.** *Supplement.*)

Grammar G:

Placing & Punctuating Adjective Modifiers

1 **Make sure to *place adjective modifiers* so that they sensibly modify the noun or pronoun that you intend.** Notice how the meaning of the following sentence changes as the adjective phrase *from Australia* is placed after different nouns.

The representative *from Australia* showed a film about kangaroos.

The representative showed a film *from Australia* about kangaroos.

The representative showed a film about kangaroos *from Australia.*

2 **Adjective phrases and adjective clauses should come immediately after the words they modify.**

The hunter shot the deer *with the red hat.* (misplaced phrase)

The hunter *with the red hat* shot the deer. (corrected)

The postman delivered a package to my neighbor *that weighed only twelve ounces.* (misplaced clause)

The postman delivered a package *that weighed only twelve ounces* to my neighbor. (corrected)

3 **Participial phrases may come immediately after the words they modify or they may be at the beginning of the sentence.** If a participial phrase comes at the beginning of a sentence, it must modify the subject of the sentence that follows it. Otherwise the sentence will have a dangling participle.

I can see the neighbor's travel trailer *looking through my window.* (misplaced)

Looking through my window, I can see the neighbor's travel trailer. (corrected)

Spinning out on the last turn, the race was lost by the favored driver. (dangling)

Spinning out on the last turn, the favored driver lost the race. (corrected)

4 **Nonessential adjective clauses and nonessential participial phrases should be set off by commas.** The adjective clause or participial phrase is nonessential if it can be removed from the sentence without changing the meaning of the independent clause.

Sam Brown, *who is now a graduate student,* enjoys doing research. (nonessential clause)

No one *who rejects Christ* will go to heaven. (essential clause)

Treasure Island, *written by Robert Louis Stevenson,* is a very popular book. (nonessential phrase)

The book *written by Robert Louis Stevenson* is a very popular book. (essential phrase)

Note: Participial phrases at the beginning of a sentence are always set off by commas.

Exercise A

The following sentences contain misplaced adjective phrases or adjective clauses. Circle each misplaced modifier and draw an arrow to the place where it should be.

1. The moon can be fully seen on a clear night, which reflects the light of the sun.
2. The small girl went to see the doctor with the broken arm.
3. Mrs. Gleason made cookies for the children with chocolate chips in them.
4. These roads were built by the Romans which are paved with cobblestones.
5. Emily bought a bushel of peaches at the wayside market which cost $5.00.
6. My brother's car was given him by our father which is a small sport model.

Placing & Punctuating Adjective Modifiers

Exercise B **In the blank write *E* if the adjective clause or participial phrase is essential. Write *N* if the modifier is nonessential. Set off the nonessential phrases and clauses by commas.**

N 1. James Schneider,who was my father's accountant,moved to Atlanta, Georgia.

N 2. The snow, glistening in the morning sun,is beautiful.

E 3. All men working at the Circle Ranch will be under the supervision of Roy Garret.

N 4. Theodore Roosevelt,who was the leader of the Rough Riders,became President of the United States.

E 5. The book for which you are looking is on the counter.

Exercise C **The following sentences contain dangling participles. Rewrite them correctly. Remember that participial phrases at the beginning of sentences are set off by commas.**

UNIT 7

1. Peering into the telescope, a pirate ship was seen at a distance.
   Peering into the telescope, he could see a pirate ship at a distance.
2. Standing on his tiptoes, the queen's coach could barely be seen.
   Standing on his tiptoes, he could barely see the queen's coach.
3. Hitting the ball as far as he could, the point was scored and the game was won.
   Hitting the ball as far as he could, Bill scored a point and won the game.
4. Trusting God implicitly, Goliath was killed by young David.
   Trusting God implicitly, young David killed Goliath.
5. Traveling down river, a waterfall stopped us.
   Traveling downriver, we were stopped by a waterfall.

Exercise D **Combine each pair of sentences into one sentence by using an adjective clause or a participial phrase. Use commas to set off the nonessential phrases or clauses.**

Answers may vary.

1. Pearl S. Buck won the Pulitzer Prize. She wrote *The Good Earth*.
   Pearl S. Buck, who wrote *The Good Earth,* won the Pulitzer Prize.
2. Smitty was grinning wickedly. He was eyeing the sizzling steaks.
   Smitty, eyeing the sizzling steaks, was grinning wickedly.
3. The girl is a member of prayer band. She sits behind me in math class.
   The girl who sits behind me in math class is a member of prayer band.

Exercise E **On a separate sheet of paper, write five sentences that contain *misplaced* modifiers like the sentences in Exercise A, page 136. Exchange papers with someone sitting close to you. Rewrite each other's sentences correctly.**

Grammar: Using Adjectives Correctly I

1 **There are three degrees of comparison: *positive, comparative,* and *superlative.***

2 **The *positive* degree is used when no comparison is expressed.**

> This room is *cold.*
> She is very *pleasant.*
> Gilbert is *diligent.*

3 **The *comparative* degree is used when *two people or things* are being compared.** Most *one-syllable* and some *two-syllable* adjectives form the comparative degree by adding *-er* to the positive. Most *two-syllable* adjectives form the comparative degree by using the word *more.* All adjectives of *three or more syllables* form the comparative degree by using the word *more.*

> This room is *colder* than the one next door.
> She is *more pleasant* than her sister.
> Gilbert is *more diligent* than his friend.

4 **The *superlative* degree is used when *three or more people or things* are being compared.** Most *one-syllable* and some *two-syllable* adjectives form the superlative degree by adding *-est* to the positive. Most *two-syllable* adjectives form the superlative degree by using the word *most.* All adjectives of *three or more syllables* form the superlative degree by using the word *most.*

> This is the *coldest* room in the building.
> She is the ***most** pleasant* person I have met.
> Gilbert is the ***most** diligent* of all the students.

Note: If in doubt about using the *-er, -est* endings on 2-syllable words, check your dictionary. It gives the *-er, -est* endings when they can be used.

5 **The comparative and superlative degrees of a few adjectives are formed *irregularly.*** Learn this list of *irregular modifiers.*

POSITIVE	COMPARATIVE	SUPERLATIVE
good	better	best
well	better	best
bad	worse	worst
ill	worse	worst
many	more	most
much	more	most

Exercise A

In the blank write *p.* if the adjective is in the positive degree, *c.* if the adjective is in the comparative degree, and *s.* if the adjective is in the superlative degree.

c. 1. more distant	p. 4. late	s. 7. most absorbent
s. 2. driest	s. 5. toughest	p. 8. little
c. 3. worse	c. 6. better	c. 9. higher

Exercise B

Cross out the incorrect adjective in parentheses.

1. Dover is the (~~faster~~, fastest) horse in our stables.
2. David was (~~more short~~, shorter) than the giant of Gath.
3. Of the two cities, Tulsa and Galveston, Galveston is certainly (more humid, ~~most humid~~).

4. David was a (friendlier, ~~more friendly~~) person than Nabal.
5. Mr. Douglas arrived (later, ~~more late~~) than I.
6. This is the (~~dirtier~~, dirtiest) room I have ever seen!
7. Death Valley is the (~~lower~~, lowest) spot in the United States.
8. Nero was perhaps the (~~more wicked~~, most wicked) Roman ruler.
9. The love of God is (greater, ~~more great~~) than mortal mind can comprehend.
10. Isn't Mont Blanc the (highest, ~~most high~~) mountain in Europe?
11. It is (better, ~~best~~) to be a doorkeeper in the house of the Lord than to dwell in the tents of the wicked.
12. Why is this novel (more expensive, ~~expensiver~~) than that one, Haley?
13. Today is supposed to be the (hottest, ~~most hot~~) day of the year.

Exercise C **Cross out the incorrect form of the irregular adjectives in the sentences below.**

1. Do you feel (~~gooder~~, better) today, Blake?
2. These are the (~~more~~, most) visitors we have had in several months.
3. Of the ten girls, Becky is the (best, ~~better~~) seamstress.
4. The weather is (~~badder~~, worse) today than yesterday.
5. She is the (worst, ~~baddest~~) tennis player I have ever seen.

Exercise D **In the blank write the correct form of the adjective in parentheses.**

1. Tim is the ___best___ pianist in our class. *(good)*
2. Always be ___more courageous___ than cowardly Barak was. *(courageous)*
3. I believe this is the ___heaviest___ trunk here, Joe. *(heavy)*
4. Didn't Paul say that the Bereans were ___more noble or "nobler"___ than the Thessalonians because they searched the Scriptures? *(noble)*
5. The ruby is ___more brilliant___ than the onyx. *(brilliant)*
6. Wasn't he one of the ___wisest___ men of his time? *(wise)*
7. Hercules was the ___strongest___ of the heroes of Greek legend. *(strong)*
8. Of all those tools, the jigsaw will be ___most useful___ to you. *(useful)*
9. The chimpanzee is one of the ___funniest___ of all creatures. *(funny)*
10. Job was the ___most righteous___ man of his day. *(righteous)*

Exercise E **Write four sentences using the adjectives as indicated below.**

1. (comparative of *ill*) Answers will vary.
2. (superlative of *good*) ______
3. (superlative of *practical*) ______
4. (comparative of *mountainous*) ______

Using Adjectives Correctly II

6 **Avoid the *double comparison.* Never use *-er* and *more* together or *-est* and *most* together. Only one form is needed.**

My dog is *more bigger* than yours. (incorrect)

My dog is *bigger* than yours. (correct)

That is the *most beautifulest* sunset I have ever seen. (incorrect)

That is the *most beautiful* sunset I have ever seen. (correct)

7 **When comparing a person with a group of which that person is a member, use *other* or *else* with the comparative.**

Jack is smarter than any student in the class. (incorrect—Jack is a member of the class. He cannot be smarter than himself.)

Jack is smarter than any *other* student in the class. (correct)

Jane is more reliable than anyone in her family. (incorrect—Jane is a member of her family. She cannot be more reliable than herself.)

Jane is more reliable than anyone *else* in her family. (correct)

8 **Use *fewer* with items that can be counted; use *less* with a quantity of a substance.**

There are *fewer* players on that team. That team needs *less* help.

9 ***Them* is never used as an adjective; use *those* instead.**

Them planes are too noisy. (incorrect)

Those planes are too noisy. (correct)

Exercise A Cross out the incorrect adjective in parentheses.

1. Use (~~fewer~~, less) flour in this recipe, Tammy.
2. Elise is the (~~most wittiest~~, wittiest) person I know.
3. Peter was more headstrong than (~~any~~, any other) of our Lord's apostles.
4. Have you finished grading (~~them~~, those) papers, class?
5. Gettysburg was the (bloodiest, ~~most bloodiest~~) battle of the Civil War.
6. Justin can bat better than (~~anyone~~, anyone else) on his team.
7. The snail is the (slowest, ~~most slowest~~) land creature.
8. This problem is (~~more difficulter~~, more difficult) than I had imagined.
9. It takes (~~fewer~~, less) effort to do something right the first time, than to do it over.
10. (Those, ~~Them~~) ruins once composed Caesar's lavish palaces.
11. This room is (~~more tidier~~, tidier) than (~~any~~, any other) room in the house.
12. Father is taller than (~~any~~, any other) member of our family.
13. (Fewer, ~~Less~~) bricks will be needed than you suppose.
14. My mother taught me (~~them~~, those) songs.
15. Solomon had greater riches than (~~anyone~~, anyone else) in history.

Using Adjectives Correctly II

Exercise B

The following sentences contain errors in the use of adjectives. Cross out any incorrect words and make corrections where necessary.

1. New York is the ~~most~~ largest city in the United States.
2. I borrowed all ~~them~~ those books from the public library.
3. The Pharisees, more than anyone else in Israel, should have welcomed the Messiah.
4. There are ~~less~~ fewer Moslems than Hindus in India.
5. Many synthetic fibers are ~~more~~ stronger than our natural materials.
6. Listening to others is one of the ~~most~~ finest arts.
7. By Tuesday, we should have learned all three of ~~them~~ those verses.
8. The mayor told ~~them~~ those rioters to disperse quietly.
9. Since the price of beef has risen, our family has eaten ~~less~~ fewer steaks.
10. Extending some 2,300 miles, the Volga is the ~~most long~~ longest river in Europe.
11. Hawaii raises more pineapples than any other region in the world.
12. Franklin D. Roosevelt served the ~~longer~~ longest term of any American President.
13. Father, Jeff, and I are going to rake ~~them~~ those leaves in the front yard.
14. There are ~~less~~ fewer boys than girls in my study hall.
15. Your report was the ~~bestest~~ best one in the class, Cyrus.
16. ~~Less~~ Fewer nails may be used in ~~them~~ those planks, Ken.
17. Detroit produces more automobiles than any other city in the United States.
18. Kay can spell better than any other student in her school.
19. A Christian should be ~~more happy~~ happier than a worldling.
20. Abraham Lincoln, at 6'4" was our ~~most~~ tallest President.
21. The Day of Atonement was the ~~most~~ holiest day of the Hebrew year.
22. ~~Them~~ Those bales of cotton were shipped here from India.
23. Wasn't Alexander the Great the ~~most young~~ youngest world conqueror?
24. There are ~~less~~ fewer sails on a sloop than on a schooner.

Exercise C

Write sentences illustrating Rules 7, 8, and 9 from page 140.

1. (Rule 7) Answers will vary. __________
2. (Rule 7) __________
3. (Rule 8) __________
4. (Rule 8) __________
5. (Rule 9) __________

UNIT 7

Grammar

Using Exact & Vivid Adjectives

In Units Four and Five, we learned that using exact verbs and nouns is the careful writer's first consideration. Nevertheless, many times adjectives are also necessary to help nouns present a clear mental picture of a person, place, or thing. Adjectives cannot make up for poorly selected nouns, but they are often necessary to give preciseness in description.

1 **Carefully select the exact adjective needed to express your idea.** Notice the differences in meaning of the following synonyms.

earthly—of the earth as contrasted with *heavenly*

worldly—of material concerns as contrasted with *spiritual*

mundane—the commonplace aspects of life on earth

2 **Be sparing in the use of adjectives.**

In spite of his success, the senator is still a *friendly, cheerful, neighborly country* boy at heart. (poor)

In spite of his success, the senator is still a *jovial country* boy at heart.

Exercise A

Fill in the blanks in the following sentences with exact and vivid adjectives.

Answers will vary.

1. The ________________ preacher was a very ________________ speaker.
2. The ________________ lawyer presented a ________________ case.
3. It is ________________ to make ________________ decisions.

Exercise B

(1) Write a brief paragraph describing the cheering section at a basketball game. Choose adjectives carefully, and do not include any that are unnecessary. (2) Underline the adjectives in your paragraph.

Answers will vary.

Grammar

Reviewing Complements

Learn this procedure for finding and identifying complements.

1 *Find the verb* in the sentence.

2 Ask *who* or *what* before the verb to *find the subject.*

3 Ask yourself if the verb is an *action verb* or if it is a *linking verb.*

4 If the verb is an *action verb,* look for a noun or a pronoun that answers *whom* or *what* after the verb. (Say the verb. Say *whom* or *what.*) If there is a word that answers one of those questions, it is the *direct object.*

5 Say the *subject, verb,* and *direct object* together to see if you have chosen sensible answers.

6 If the sentence does have a direct object, look for a noun or a pronoun between the action verb and the direct object that answers *to whom* or *for whom,* or *to what* or *for what* after the verb. If there is a word that answers one of those questions, it is the *indirect object.* (If a sentence does not have a direct object, it cannot have an indirect object.)

7 Say the *subject, verb, indirect object,* and *direct object* together to see if you have chosen sensible answers.

8 If the verb is a *linking verb* (see page 58), look for a noun or a pronoun that follows the verb and renames the subject. If there is one, it is the *predicate nominative.*

9 If there is no predicate nominative, look for an adjective that follows the *linking verb* and describes the subject. If there is one, it is the *predicate adjective.*

10 Not all verbs need a complement, but look for one just in case.

UNIT 7

Exercise A

Use the procedure above to find and identify the complements in the following sentences. (1) Underline each complement. (2) Identify the complements by writing *d.o., i.o., p.n.,* or *p.a.* above them.

1. The author of Aesop's Fables was a Greek slave. (p.n.: slave)
2. Aristotle taught Alexander much of Greek knowledge. (i.o.: Alexander; d.o.: much)
3. Steinway pianos are well known throughout the world. (p.a.: known)
4. The king of Siam offered President Lincoln two elephants. (i.o.: President Lincoln; d.o.: elephants)
5. An ostrich has only two toes on each foot. (d.o.: toes)
6. That cloud over there looks unusual. (p.a.: unusual)
7. We mailed Aunt Agatha a shawl for her birthday. (i.o.: Aunt Agatha; d.o.: shawl)
8. The widow of Nain was sorrowful over the loss of her son. (p.a.: sorrowful)
9. John Chrysostom was an early Christian leader. (p.n.: leader)
10. The sweet singer of Israel gave God praise for all His benefits. (i.o.: God; d.o.: praise)

Exercise B

(1) Draw one line under each linking verb. (2) Draw a circle around each predicate nominative and draw a wavy line under each predicate adjective.

Examples: Gail is a girl. Gail is good. **Remember that predicate nominatives *equal* the subject, but predicate adjectives *describe* the subject.**

1. Nova Scotia or "New Scotland" is one of the most picturesque areas of Canada.
2. Jeremy has been late for school every day this week.
3. The Macedonians became the first European Christians.
4. Nicholas II was the last czar of imperial Russia.
5. The judgments of the Lord are true and righteous altogether.

Exercise C

(1) Draw one line under each linking verb and draw a circle around the predicate nominative. (2) Draw two lines under each action verb and draw a box around the direct object.

Examples: Chester is a senior this year. Chester will attend a Christian college.

1. We are playing Beethoven's Fifth Symphony in the city-wide youth orchestra.
2. The narcissus is a delicate, white flower.
3. Mrs. Mackay painted her bureau a brilliant shade of blue.
4. The editors were writing feature stories for the school newspaper.
5. Celtic tribes were some of the earliest inhabitants of Britain.
6. Standing on the Acropolis, Paul preached the Word of God.
7. Returning to his riches, the rich young man forsook Christ.
8. Dwight D. Eisenhower was the thirty-fourth President of the United States.
9. Cyrus Vance was once secretary of state.
10. Mike Lyons will be playing his accordian at the young people's service at church.

Exercise D

Draw one line under all linking verbs. Above each predicate nominative write *p.n.* and above each predicate adjective write *p.a.* (2) Draw two lines under all action verbs. Above each direct object write *d.o.* and above each indirect object write *i.o.*

David Livingstone was perhaps the most famous missionary (p.n.) of the nineteenth century. Born into a poor family, Livingstone began work (d.o.) in a cotton mill when he was very young (p.a.). He greatly desired an education (d.o.), and with his first wages he purchased a Latin grammar (d.o.) and studied it (d.o.) on his own. He eventually went to college and studied medicine (d.o.) and theology (d.o.). In 1840, he became a missionary (p.n.) to Africa, where he gave the people (i.o.) the message (d.o.) of salvation. Livingstone's extensive exploration of the interior of Africa paved the way (d.o.) for other missionaries. When Livingstone died, Africans buried his heart (d.o.) in a jungle clearing and carried his body (d.o.) back to the coast. Because Livingstone gave Africa (i.o.) his life (d.o.), many Africans received Christ (d.o.) as Savior.

Exercise

Diagram the subjects, verbs, and complements in the following sentences.

1. Dr. Franklin became postmaster general in 1775.
2. Any of Picasso's paintings are costly.
3. Mrs. Nobles deeded the church a parcel of land.
4. I grew weary of her excuses.
5. Many of the committee members were late.
6. President Nixon sent Henry Kissinger to Moscow.
7. The largest states in the U.S. are Alaska and Texas.
8. Robert Walpole was the first English prime minister.
9. Isaiah gave Hezekiah God's message.
10. Pastor Blaurock is the minister of our church.
11. Do any task with all your might.
12. These watermelons are not ripe.
13. Aquila and Priscilla left Rome and fled to Corinth.
14. The Mayo brothers were the founders of the famous Mayo Clinic.

1. Dr. Franklin | became \ postmaster general

2. Any | are \ costly

3. Mrs. Nobles | deeded | parcel
church

4. I | grew \ weary

5. Many | were \ late

6. President Nixon | sent | Henry Kissinger

7.

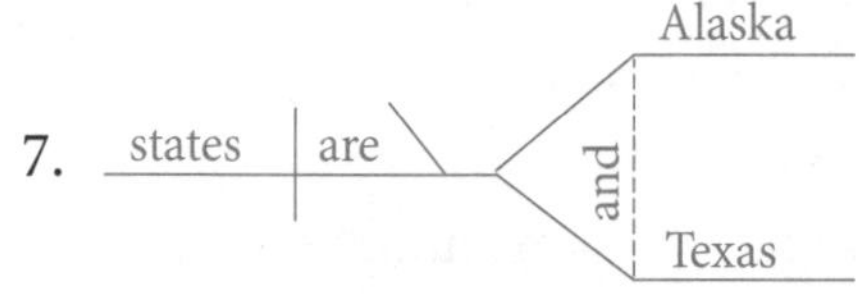

8. Robert Walpole | was \ prime minister

9.

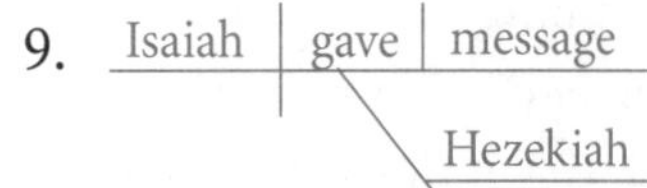

10. Pastor Blaurock | is \ minister

11. x | Do | task

12. watermelons | are \ ripe

13.

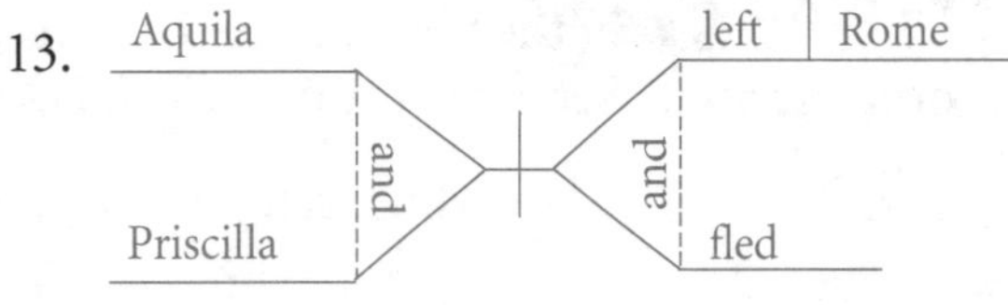

14. brothers | were \ founders

UNIT 7

Exercise A

(1) Circle all one-word adjectives (except articles). This includes predicate adjectives. (2) Draw arrows to the words modified.

1. The early Italian settlers were known as the Etruscans.
2. Etruscan farm villages dotted the Apennine hillsides.
3. One small village became great by conquering others.
4. Roman warriors soon conquered the other native peoples.
5. Many Etruscan clay sculptures have been located and are now world famous.

Exercise B

For the following groups of words, put *p.* if the entire group of words is a *phrase;* put *c.* if the group of words is a *clause;* and put *s.* if the group of words could be punctuated as a complete *sentence.*

p. 1. From the banks of the mighty "Father of Waters," the Mississippi River.
c. 2. Which is made of slippery, silken glass.
s. 3. The flowers which bloom in early spring seem to announce nature's return to the throne.
p. 4. With a white shirt and black trousers.
p. 5. Practicing his speech for tomorrow's contest.
s. 6. Spectacular ruins of the ancient cities of Athens and Rome can still be seen.
c. 7. That dwell in trees and eat fruits and nuts.
s. 8. Of all the units of society, the family is the most important.
s. 9. Hoping to remove his own guilt, the thief accused someone else.
c. 10. Which we have seen with our eyes.
s. 11. In the month of October, a baby was born into the Rutledge home.
p. 12. Bitten by Jon's golden Labrador retriever.
s. 13. That man who dressed so plainly is Pastor Holmstead.
c. 14. Whose lives were given to the service of Christ.
s. 15. The lad with quiet manners was finally recognized as a true scholar.
c. 16. Who loves his God, his family, and the souls of men.
s. 17. Karen was the one who received the award for service to our school.
p. 18. Praising the Lord for his deliverance.

Exercise C

In the blank write *E* if the adjective clause is essential; write *N* if the clause is nonessential. Set off the nonessential clauses with commas.

E 1. The boy whose father is crippled works on Uncle Nathan's farm.
N 2. Cassie Wharton, who is my cousin, will be visiting us next week.
E 3. He that trusts in the Lord Jesus Christ will not be condemned.
N 4. The giraffe, which is the tallest living land creature, has the same number of neck bones as the field mouse.
N 5. Alexander Fleming, who discovered penicillin in 1929, received the Nobel prize for his work in medicine.

Exercise D (1) Circle all adjective phrases. (2) Put parentheses around all adjective clauses. (3) Draw a box around all participial phrases. (4) Draw arrows to the words modified.

1. A person with a contrite heart is the only one (whom God will forgive.)
2. Wanting a glimpse of the President, spectators surrounded the building (in which he was staying.)
3. The American Preservation Society is the owner of this home, (which once belonged to Daniel Boone.)
4. Smitten with leprosy, Miriam, (who had rebelled against her brother,) left the camp of Israel.
5. He (that would wear the crown) must first bear the cross.
6. The people of France are descendants of the ancient Gauls (with whom Caesar fought.)
7. The house destroyed in yesterday's fire was the home of one of our church elders.
8. Matthew, (whose book bears his name,) had once been a collector of Roman taxes.
9. The peace (that God gives) passes all the understanding of man.
10. The sons of Abraham produced the peoples of Israel and Arabia.
11. Holding back the rain, God punished Ahab, the wicked king of Israel.
12. Noah Webster, a teacher in New England, wrote the first dictionary for Americans.

Exercise E (1) Cross out each incorrect or misplaced modifier. (2) Make all necessary corrections.

1. ~~Them~~ Those buildings are the ~~most~~ biggest ones I have ever seen.
2. Berlin is ~~more~~ larger than any other city in Germany.
3. I will hang that picture of horses in the middle of the living room wall ~~of horses.~~
4. There are ~~less~~ fewer potatoes in my sack than there are in yours.
5. The professor required four reports on the Himalayan Mountains from an encyclopedia ~~on the Himalayan Mountains.~~
6. Zachary is ~~more~~ taller than anyone else on the basketball team.
7. ~~Lying on the dresser,~~ I found my gloves lying on the dresser.
8. The aircraft carrier USS *Theodore Roosevelt* is ~~more~~ longer than three football fields.
9. Women today spend ~~fewer~~ less time in the kitchen than women thirty years ago did.
10. *Ben-Hur: A Tale of the Christ* is the ~~most~~ greatest novel that I have ever read.
11. I bought a purse which cost only twelve pesos in Mexico at an open market ~~which cost only twelve pesos.~~
12. My friend who lives in Alaska sent me some moccasins of reindeer skin ~~who lives in Alaska.~~

UNIT 7

Exercise A

Capitalization and Punctuation. (1) Draw a line through each incorrect small letter. Write a capital above it. (2) Add punctuation where needed.

1. tricia, kelly, and sarah all read the book alice in wonderland for their book reports.
2. joshua asked, "do you know what happened at kitty hawk, north carolina, in 1903?"
3. kevin's father sent him to the store for the following items: milk, heinz catsup, and oscar mayer hot dogs.
4. hudson taylor is known for his work with the chinese people; moreover, he is remembered for founding the china inland mission.
5. ninety-four more signatures are needed before we can present this bill to the oklahoma senate.
6. angie's parents are scheduled to arrive on a delta airline jet at 9:45 P.M.
7. the american writer ralph waldo emerson once stated, "there is always a best way of doing everything."
8. margaret, doesn't dr. o. h. willowby, the professor from south africa, teach zoology 403 at donaldsville community college?

Exercise B

Subjects and Verbs. (1) Draw two lines under each verb. (2) Draw one line under each subject.

1. The Pygmy tribe is unlike other native African tribes.
2. Bombers in World War II destroyed many ancient gothic cathedrals.
3. Didn't Philip baptize the Ethiopian eunuch?
4. Rich and poor alike must come as paupers to the coffers of Christ.
5. Christ knelt and washed His disciples' feet.

Exercise C

The Sentence. In the blank before the number, write *s.* for sentences, *frag.* for fragments, or *r.o.* for run-ons.

frag. 1. A rich man clothed in purple and fine linen.

s. 2. Poor Lazarus lay at the rich man's gate and begged.

s. 3. Lazarus died and went to paradise, but the wealthy man lifted up his eyes in hell.

frag. 4. Could receive no respite from the awful tortures of that place.

r.o. 5. Every man receives his own reward we certainly do reap what we sow.

Exercise D **Using Verbs. Cross out each incorrect verb form in parentheses.**

1. (~~Can~~, May) I (~~leave~~, let) Rachel finish my chores for me, Papa?
2. Pat (~~didn't go to~~, didn't mean to) break the window, but he (~~better~~, had better) learn to be more careful.
3. (~~Bring~~, Take) this letter to Mr. Collins, Hudson, and (~~take~~, bring) me back his reply.
4. Cynthia (~~rose~~, raised) the window and straightened her closet, but she (~~leaved~~, left) her clothes (~~laying~~, lying) on the bed.
5. Star, our horse, (~~used to could~~, used to be able to) run an excellent race, but since she (~~took sick~~, became ill) I have (~~left~~, let) her stay in the pasture.
6. (~~Lying~~, Laying) his head on the hard stone, Jacob fell asleep.
7. Young Arthur (~~growed~~, grew) into a fine king and (~~brung~~, brought) peace to his realm.
8. I (thought, ~~thunk~~) that this willow tree would have (~~growed~~, grown) somewhat by now.

UNIT 7

Exercise E **Using Verbs. Cross out each incorrect verb form and write the correct verb form above it.**

1. We [had] better stop the ferris wheel, folks; that little girl wants [to get off] ~~off~~.
2. I am the one who [brought] ~~brung~~ in this story, [am I not?] ~~aren't I?~~
3. Jesus [sat] ~~set~~ down on the side of the well and [began] ~~begun~~ to talk with the woman.
4. Later, she [left] ~~leaved~~ her waterpot and [went] ~~gone~~ away, having received living water.
5. The Indians [taught] ~~learned~~ the Pilgrims how to plant corn.
6. The disciples were [taught] ~~learned~~ to rely solely upon God and not man.
7. Aaron [jumped] ~~jumps~~ into the lake and saved the woman that had almost [drowned] ~~drownded~~.
8. Katherine [brought] ~~brung~~ in some flowers and [set] ~~sit~~ them on the table.
9. The congregation [sang] ~~sung~~ a hymn, and then the pastor [began] ~~begun~~ his sermon.
10. I [am not] ~~ain't~~ the one who [threw] ~~throwed~~ that stone, Mrs. Handford.

Exercise F **Subject and Verb Agreement. Cross out each incorrect verb form in parentheses.**

1. Neither silver nor gold (~~have~~, has) obtained our redemption.
2. *Little Women* (is, ~~are~~) excellent reading material, especially for young ladies.
3. Here (are, ~~is~~) those shoes which you wanted, Tina.
4. Either Erica or the boys (~~has~~, have) arrived at the correct answer.
5. Fifty thousand pounds (~~are~~, is) the maximum load for this truck.
6. Today's news (~~seem~~, seems) worse than usual.

(continued)

Exercise F, cont.

7. Fifty-five dollars (is, ~~are~~) a lot to spend for one shirt.
8. A wild horse from the high plateaus (was, ~~were~~) sighted today by a small boy.
9. There (~~is~~, are) many who go down the broad, easy way.
10. The Master's Men (~~are~~, is) our church layman's organization.
11. That bowl filled with nuts (~~were~~, was) a gift from Dean's mother.
12. *Pilgrims Going to Church* (~~show~~, shows) a scene from American colonial history.
13. Rickets (is, ~~are~~) a disease of the skeletal system.
14. A ship containing 115 crates of tea (~~have~~, has) docked at Boston Harbor.
15. There (are, ~~is~~) few men who could have served in Moses' place.

Exercise G

Using Nouns. Above each italicized word write its use. Abbreviate as follows: *s.* (subject), *p.n.* (predicate nominative), *d.o.* (direct object), *i.o.* (indirect object), *o.p.* (object of preposition), *ap.* (appositive), and *d.a.* (direct address).

s. ap. p.n. o.p.
1. *Frank*, my *brother-in-law*, is a *teacher* at a mission school in *Arizona*.

d.o. d.a.
2. Didn't Edward VIII abdicate the English *throne* in 1936, *Joel?*

s. o.p.
3. *President Ford* served as President without being elected to that *office*.

ap. d.o.
4. Paul, the great *missionary*, preached *Christ* crucified.

i.o. d.o.
5. Dr. Petri read the *congregation* the *parable* of the Good Samaritan.

d.a. d.o. o.p.
6. *Elaine*, please give me the *answer* to this *question*.

Exercise H

Using Pronouns. Cross out the incorrect pronoun in parentheses.

1. Rodney and (I, ~~me~~) will help you move the sofa, Tanya.
2. Blessed is (he, ~~him~~) whose transgression is forgiven.
3. (We, ~~Us~~) members of the church are praying for you, Mrs. Jackson.
4. We sent (~~she~~, her) and her family a basket of fruit from Florida.
5. Mr. O'Leary asked for (~~they~~, them) and (~~we~~, us) to come to the office immediately.
6. For (~~we~~, us) Christians, life is based on eternal values.
7. Mother told Andrew and (~~I~~, me) the meaning of that Latin phrase.
8. (He, ~~Him~~) and Silas visited Philippi on their missionary journey.
9. Father and (she, ~~her~~) have gone to the mountains for a short rest.
10. I received a letter from Leah and (~~he~~, him) this morning.
11. Mr. Lawson did not give (~~we~~, us) students an assignment over the holidays.
12. (They, ~~Them~~) who work hard succeed.

13. With Doug and (~~I~~, me) beside him, Brad asked Jesus to come into his heart.
14. We picked these flowers especially for (~~she~~, her) and Anna.
15. The Lord went up the mountainside with Andrew, John, and (~~he~~, him).

Exercise **Using Adjectives. (1) Cross out each incorrect or misplaced modifier. (2) Make all necessary corrections.**

1. You should use ~~less~~ fewer bricks if you want to save more money.
2. ~~Them~~ Those bees can inflict quite painful wounds.
3. The farmer with the red cap won the turkey shoot ~~with the red cap~~.
4. Keith presented his speech better than any other speaker in his age bracket.
5. Brian Myrowitz, whose father is mayor, sits behind me in math class. ~~whose father is mayor.~~
6. ~~Written in hieroglyphics,~~ Professor Judson discovered an ancient tablet, written in hieroglyphics.
7. Jonathan was ~~more~~ friendlier to David than David was to him.
8. ~~Them~~ Those clouds look ~~worst~~ worse than they did one hour ago.
9. A large audience in the stands was watching the porpoise ~~in the stands~~.
10. The Challenger Deep is the ~~most~~ deepest spot in all the oceans.
11. A bear with several cubs must provide a ready supply of food ~~with several cubs~~.
12. I carried the dog with a broken leg to the veterinarian's office ~~with a broken leg~~.
13. Hurry, Charlie; we have ~~less~~ fewer minutes now in which to finish.
14. The apostle John was perhaps the ~~most~~ closest earthly friend of Jesus.
15. ~~Inside the cage~~ We watched the boa constrictor inside the cage.

Q18

Grammar

Recognizing Adverbs

1 **An *adverb* is a word that modifies a verb, an adjective, or another adverb. It answers the questions *where, when, how, how often, to what extent.*** (A modifier makes the meaning of another word more specific.)

hid *there* (where) left *later* (when) walked *softly* (how)

usually wins (how often) *fully* understood (to what extent)

2 **The word *not* or its contraction *n't* is a frequently used adverb.**

did *not* stay wasn*'t* asked

3 **Adverbs modify *verbs* most of the time. An adverb that modifies a verb may be *before or after* the verb it modifies; it may be *in the middle of a verb phrase* that it modifies; or it may be *at the beginning of the sentence,* nowhere near the verb it modifies.**

Jerry *often* reads biographies about great Christians.

Ann realized *later* that she had mailed the wrong package.

Communists can *not* be trusted to keep their word.

Yesterday, after the assembly, we moved the risers from the stage.

To locate adverbs, first find the verb. Then ask the questions which adverbs answer.

Yesterday, after the assembly, we moved the risers from the stage. (*Moved* is the verb. Moved *when? Yesterday. Yesterday* is the adverb that answers the question *when.* We moved *yesterday.*)

Many adverbs are formed by adding *-ly* to adjectives: quick***ly,*** quiet***ly,*** careful***ly,*** silent***ly***. However, not all words that end in *-ly* are adverbs. Some are adjectives *(friendly, lovely),* and some can be either adverbs or adjectives *(early, daily).* Some frequently used adverbs do not end in *-ly;* therefore, when identifying adverbs, do not depend on the *-ly* ending. Use the procedure mentioned above to locate adverbs.

4 **Adverbs also modify *adjectives.* When adverbs modify adjectives, they are located *immediately* before those adjectives and usually tell *how* or *to what extent.***

To find adverbs that modify adjectives, first find the adjective. Then ask the questions *how* or *to what extent.*

During a snowstorm, drivers should expect *extremely* slippery roads. (*Slippery* is an adjective because it modifies the noun *roads. Extremely* is an adverb because it modifies the adjective *slippery,* telling *to what extent* the roads are slippery.)

5 **Adverbs occasionally modify *other adverbs.* When adverbs modify other adverbs, they are located *immediately before* those adverbs and usually tell *how.***

The pianist played *unusually* well. (*Well* is an adverb because it modifies the verb *played. Unusually* is an adverb because it modifies the adverb *well,* telling *how* well the pianist played.)

Exercise A

(1) In the first blank, write the adverb. (2) In the second blank, write the verb or verb phrase that the adverb modifies. (3) Read the adverb and the verb that is modified to see if they make sense together.

Adverb	Verb Modified	
majestically	sang	1. The heralding angels sang majestically.
calmly	stood	2. Jesus stood calmly before His accusers in Pilate's hall.
quickly	shaped	3. The potter quickly shaped a water jar from clay.
immediately	erupted	4. Immediately there erupted a flood of lava.
blindly	go	5. The lost go blindly down the road of destruction.
tomorrow	will arrive	6. Our cousins will arrive in Waukegan tomorrow.
cheerfully	gave	7. The widow gave her two mites cheerfully.
deeply	was concerned	8. James Chalmers was deeply concerned for the lost men of New Guinea.
gradually	slopes	9. The mountain slopes gradually to the plain below.
early	rose	10. Abraham rose early and took Isaac to Mount Moriah.
simply	live	11. Refrain from putting on airs; live simply.
daily	memorizes	12. My sister Carolyn memorizes Scripture daily.

UNIT 8

Exercise B

(1) Underline the adverbs that modify adjectives. (2) Draw an arrow to the adjective that is modified.

1. The extremely fragile jade bowl was enclosed in a glass case.
2. Hitler committed especially heartless crimes against the Jews.
3. An unusually heavy snow was forecast on the evening news.
4. The tiny violet is delicately beautiful.
5. Dolly Madison was a tremendously popular First Lady.
6. Mr. Henrikson's peaches are slightly green.
7. After the ordeal, he looked remarkably well.
8. This quilt is too lovely to be put away; let's use it as a wall hanging.
9. Chancellor Bismarck was known as an imperiously proud man.
10. Science during the Middle Ages was relatively nonexistent in Europe.

Exercise C

(1) Underline the adverbs that modify other adverbs. (2) Draw an arrow to the adverb that is modified.

1. Cornelius Vanderbilt's home, The Breakers, was a very extravagantly decorated mansion.
2. Jenny Lind sang more beautifully than anyone I had ever heard.
3. John loves this game because he very rarely loses.
4. Quakers were persecuted most shamefully by the Puritans.
5. Phil's four-year-old brother can read amazingly well.
6. David confessed his sin most contritely after Nathan's speech to him.
7. His convictions were implanted unusually deep in his heart.
8. He that tarries too long at his work cannot expect to receive his reward with the others.
9. Tim's church is much farther away from my house than Mike's church is.
10. Sullivan made that remark perfectly innocently.

Exercise D

(1) Draw one line under the adverbs that modify verbs. (2) Draw a circle around the adverbs that modify adjectives. (3) Draw a box around the adverbs that modify adverbs.

1. Hudson Taylor could rarely visit his family in England.
2. The baby walked toward his father most timidly.
3. Jesus rather frequently used parables to illustrate a point.
4. The builders of the Tabernacle meticulously followed the Lord's instructions.
5. God sees our problems much differently from the way we see them.
6. A very shoddy product is an extremely difficult item to sell.
7. The woman who anointed Jesus' feet loved Him greatly, for she had been completely forgiven of her sins.
8. The person most completely responsible for rebuilding the wall was probably Nehemiah.
9. The grebe always dives deeply into the water when attacked by other animals.
10. Job walked perfectly in the eyes of the Lord.
11. That was an unusually heavy rain this afternoon.
12. I will praise Thee, for I am fearfully and wonderfully made.
13. God deals severely with those who stubbornly disobey His commands.
14. Had David acted too hastily he would most assuredly have been captured by the Philistines.

Exercise E

(1) Write six sentences using the following adverbs as directed. (2) Draw an arrow from each adverb to the word it modifies.

1. (*never* modifying a verb) Answers will vary.
2. (*incredibly* modifying an adjective) __________
3. (*very* modifying an adverb) __________
4. (*persistently* modifying a verb) __________
5. (*unusually* modifying an adjective) __________
6. (*much* modifying an adverb) __________

Grammar

Diagraming Adverbs

Adverbs are diagramed on a line below the verb, adjective, or adverb that they modify.

MODIFIES VERB

Jake yelled *excitedly.*

Jake | yelled
excitedly

MODIFIES ADJECTIVE

Joan is an *unusually* talented speller.

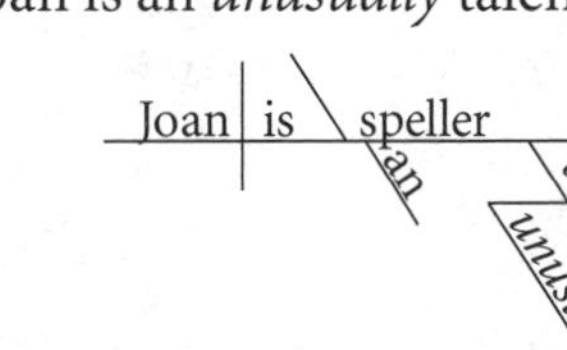

MODIFIES ADVERB

They stopped *too* soon.

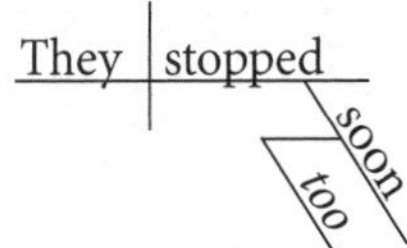

Exercise

Diagram the following sentences.

1. You should never speak too hastily.
2. Our visitors will soon be here.
3. The painfully slow process finally ended.
4. An unusually large amount of rain has fallen today.
5. Always do your work neatly.
6. A very tiny girl has been waiting quite patiently.
7. Their very bountiful crop has already been gathered.
8. Job was very sorely tempted.

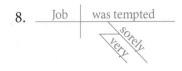

1.

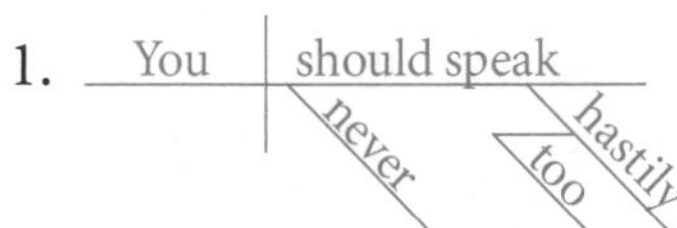

2.

visitors | will be
Our
soon
here

3.

process | ended
The
slow
painfully
finally

4.

amount | has fallen
An
large
unusually
of
rain
today

5.

6.

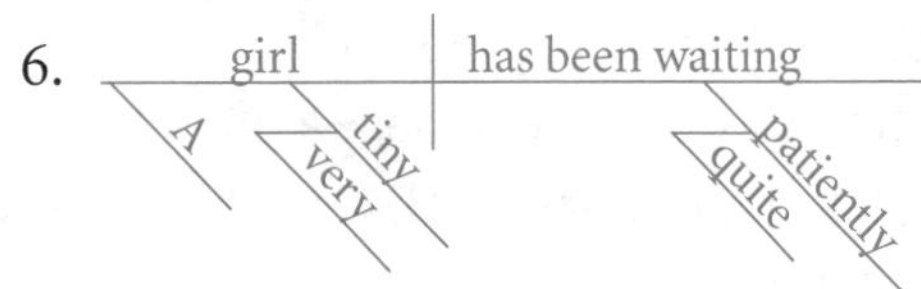

7.

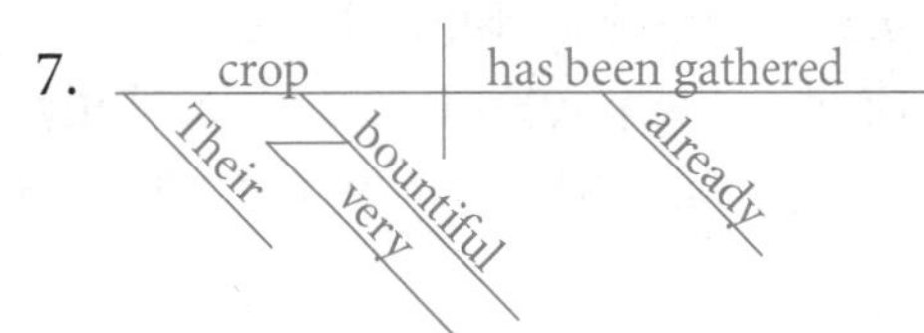

8.

Job | was tempted
sorely
very

UNIT 8

Grammar

Distinguishing Adverbs from Adjectives

1 **Use *adjectives* to modify *nouns or pronouns.* Use *adverbs* to modify *verbs, adjectives,* or *adverbs.***

He is a *logical* thinker. (adjective) He thinks *logically.* (adverb)

2 **Use a predicate adjective after linking verbs.**

The purple flower smells *fragrant.* (not *fragrantly*)
The grits and eggs tasted *delicious.* (not *deliciously*)

3 **Distinguish between *good* and *well.* Always use the word *good* as an adjective. *Well* is an *adverb* when it modifies a verb; *well* is an *adjective* when it refers to a person's health.**

The little baby is being especially *good.* (adjective)
On a hot day, water tastes *good.* (adjective)
The helpful boy finished the job *well.* (adverb modifying the verb)
I think Granddad is completely *well.* (adjective referring to the person's health)

4 ***Sure, real,* and *bad* are not usually used as adverbs.**

I am *surely* glad to see you. (not *sure*)
Jasper is *really* fast in a Sword drill. (not *real*)
Eric plays his trumpet *badly.* (not *bad*)

Exercise A **Cross out each incorrect form in parentheses.**

1. My cousin had the flu last week, and he still doesn't seem (well, ~~good~~).
2. The baby lay in the carriage very (~~contented~~, contentedly).
3. On this test, it is important that you follow the directions very (~~careful~~, carefully).
4. The odor of burning sulfur smells (~~real~~, really) (bad, ~~badly~~).
5. Mark, you (~~sure~~, surely) wouldn't hit your little sister, would you?
6. I need a new coat very (~~bad~~, badly).
7. The music box played Brahms's *Lullaby* very (~~soft~~, softly).
8. Our pastor's delivery is (good, ~~well~~).
9. I (~~sure~~, surely) would like to have a giant banana split.
10. "Patrick, that book looks (~~real~~, really) interesting," said Mrs. Strychalski.
11. The leper could not reenter the camp until he was (~~good~~, well).
12. The soprano really sang quite (~~bad~~, badly).
13. This lemonade tastes too (bitter, ~~bitterly~~).
14. You look (happy, ~~happily~~) this morning, Holly.
15. Jennifer did (~~good~~, well) on her piano solo.

Exercise B **Write sentences using the words in parentheses correctly.**

1. *(good)* Answers will vary.
2. *(well)* ______
3. *(surely)* ______
4. *(really)* ______

Grammar

Using Prepositional Phrases as Adverbs

1 A *prepositional phrase* consists of a preposition, its noun or pronoun object, and any modifiers of the object. See Unit 9 for a list of commonly used prepositions.

2 A prepositional phrase that modifies a verb, an adjective, or an adverb is called an *adverb phrase.* An adverb phrase usually answers the questions *where, when, how,* or *why.*

> *In A.D. 70,* the temple at Jerusalem was destroyed. (The adverb phrase modifies the verb *was destroyed,* telling *when.*)
>
> His hair is gray *around the temples.* (The adverb phrase modifies the adjective *gray,* telling *where.*)
>
> The fishermen rose early *in the morning.* (The adverb phrase modifies the adverb *early,* telling *when.*)

3 Adverb phrases modify verbs more often than they modify adjectives or adverbs.

UNIT 8

Exercise A

(1) Draw a circle around each adverb phrase. (2) Draw an arrow to the word that the phrase modifies. Do not circle adjective phrases.

1. This cheese is hard on the edges.
2. A diligent man will not sleep late in the mornings.
3. The skies are magnificent in the evenings.
4. Jesus calls us from the worship of the vain world's golden store.
5. Early in the morning my song shall rise to Thee.
6. Christ came from the splendor of heaven to a sinful earth.
7. Serve the Lord with fear and rejoice with trembling.
8. They that sow in tears shall reap in joy.
9. The Pharisees in Christ's day were clean on the outside but corrupt on the inside.
10. The mutineers set Captain Bligh adrift in the Pacific.
11. He sendeth springs into the valleys.
12. Peter climbed from the boat and walked on the water.
13. At the voice of Thy thunder, they hastened away.
14. David was happy in his soul when the ark was returned to Jerusalem.
15. I will sing of mercy and judgment; unto Thee, O Lord, will I sing.

Exercise B

(1) Write four sentences, each containing an adverb phrase. Use the prepositions given below. (2) Circle the phrases. Draw arrows to the words modified.

1. *(about)* Answers will vary. __________
2. *(against)* __________
3. *(beyond)* __________
4. *(near)* __________

Diagraming Adverb Phrases

MODIFIES ADJECTIVE
His hair is gray *around the temples.*

MODIFIES ADVERB
The fishermen rose early *in the morning.*

MODIFIES VERB
The raft floated *beyond Lamar and me.*

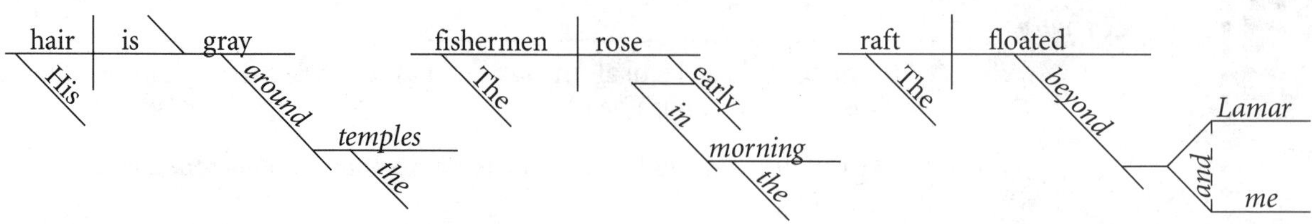

Exercise

Diagram the following sentences.

1. Peter, James, and John were fishing on the Sea of Galilee.
2. I received the assignment later in the afternoon.
3. Mrs. Parker played the piano with grace and ease.
4. In the attic, I found a biography about Adoniram Judson.
5. This book was published in 1956 by a Christian publisher.
6. Place the slide on the microscope.
7. Joseph was sold by his brothers into Egypt.
8. Jesus may come at any moment.

1. 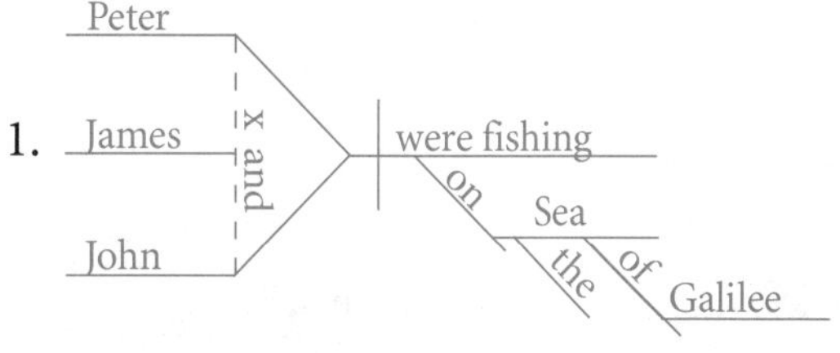

2. 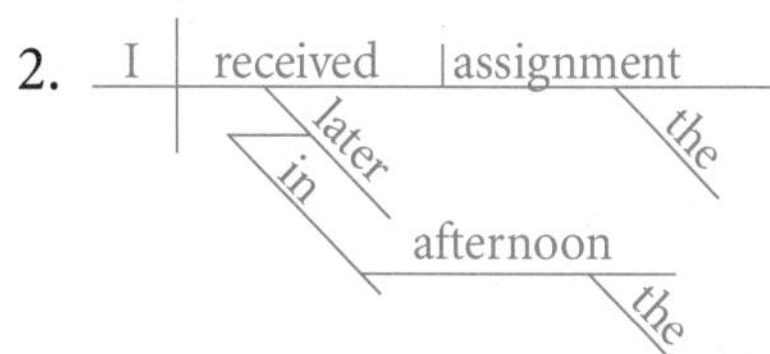

3. 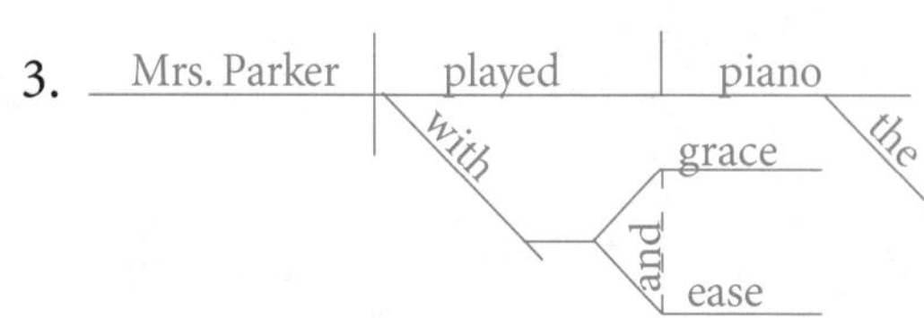

4. 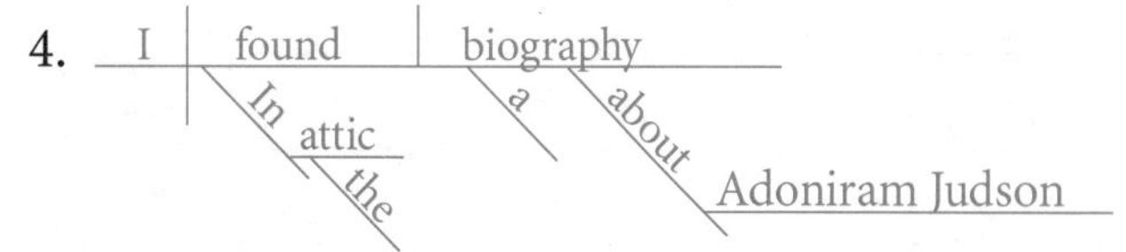

5. 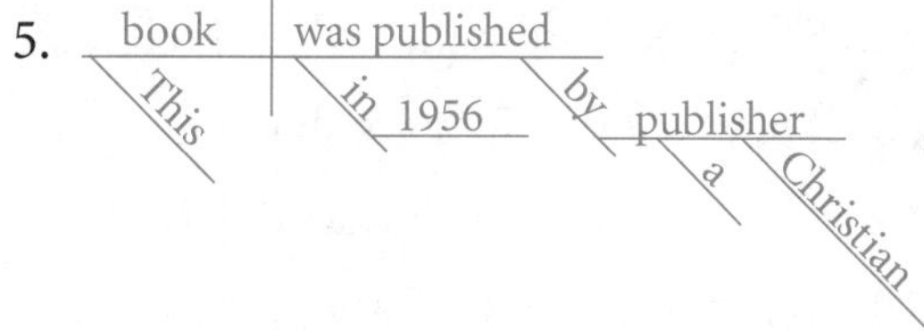

6. 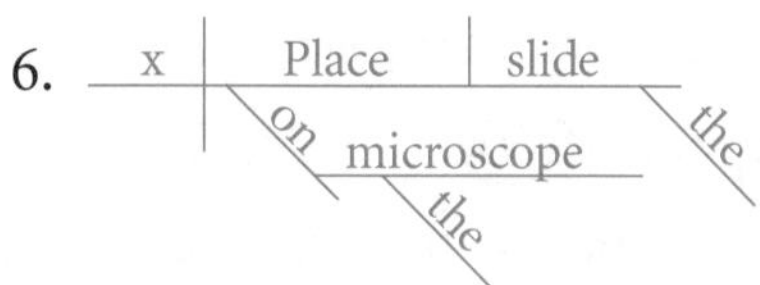

7. 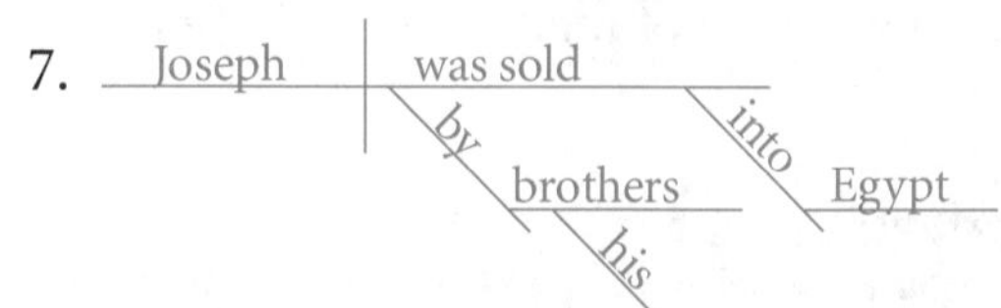

8. 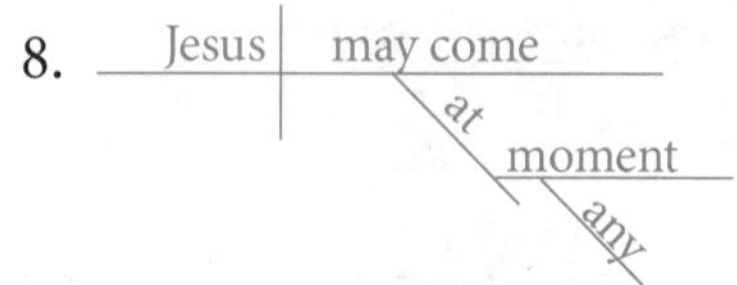

Distinguishing between Adverb & Adjective Phrases

Exercise A

(1) Circle each prepositional phrase. (2) Draw an arrow to the word modified. (3) On each line, write *adj.* if the phrase is an adjective, or write *adv.* if it is an adverb.

adj. 1. The young man in that novel symbolizes goodness.

adv. 2. General Braddock's men cut a pathway through the forest.

adj. 3. Pastures and fields beyond these mountains must be irrigated heavily.

adv. 4. The continental shelf extends several hundred miles underneath the ocean.

adj. 5. We finally finished painting the fence around the churchyard.

adv. 6. Christians should spread the gospel throughout the whole earth.

adv. 7. Charles Lindbergh crossed the Atlantic in his single-engine plane.

adv. 8. Through our troubles, we learn patience.

adv. 9. A beautiful rainbow appeared across the distant horizon.

adj. 10. The tares among the wheat were finally detected.

adv. 11. Beneath the calm surface, a nuclear submarine was lurking.

adj. 12. The man on the shore was waving frantically.

adv. 13. After the earthquake, the city was rebuilt.

adj. 14. The men of Jabesh-gilead recovered Saul's body.

Exercise B

(1) Circle all the prepositional phrases in the following sentences. (2) Write *adj.* above the adjective phrases and *adv.* above the adverb phrases.

adj. adv. adv.
1. Buffalo Bill, one of the most well-known frontiersmen, was born in Iowa in 1846.

adv.
2. During Bill's early years, his father died.

adj.
3. Bill later became a rider for the Pony Express.

adv. adj.
4. He obtained his name from his skill in buffalo hunting.

adv.
5. Buffalo Bill could bring down a buffalo with a single shot.

adv.
6. In 1883, Bill began his famous "Wild West" show.

adv.
7. His show, which included Indians and sharpshooters, traveled in the United States and even

adv.
to Europe.

adj. adj. adv.
8. This hunter of buffaloes from the American West became well known in many parts

adj.
of the world.

adv.
9. Buffalo Bill traveled with his show and managed it.

adv. adj. adj.
10. He finally retired to his ranch in the plains of Wyoming.

Distinguishing between Adverb & Adjective Phrases

Exercise C **There are two prepositional phrases in each sentence. (1) Draw a box around each phrase. (2) Mark each phrase *adj.* or *adv.* and draw an arrow to the word each phrase modifies.**

Example: The battle [of the giants] (adj.) was fought [in the valley.] (adv.)

1. The whales are the largest species [of creatures] (adj.) which exist [on earth.] (adv.)
2. Whaling developed [among the Basques] (adv.) [in the 1200s.] (adv.)
3. The colonists [of New Bedford, Massachusetts,] (adj.) started whaling [about 1760.] (adv.)
4. Soon this small village [in New England] (adj.) was the whaling capital [of the world.] (adj.)
5. [From the whale] (adv.) was also obtained an oil which was burned [in colonial lamps.] (adv.)
6. Whalebone, a strong, elastic substance, was a component [of hoopskirts,] (adj.) devices which extended the large skirts [of American women.] (adj.)
7. Soon the production [of petroleum] (adj.) increased, and it became more accessible [to American homes.] (adv.)
8. Very little whaling is now done [by Americans] (adv.) because the demand [for these products] (adj.) is very small.
9. Herman Melville, a literary genius [of the nineteenth century,] (adj.) glamorized whaling [in his novel *Moby Dick.*] (adv.)

Exercise D **(1) Write five sentences containing adjective phrases and five sentences containing adverb phrases. (2) Circle the phrases and draw arrows to the words modified.**

1. Answers will vary.
2. ______
3. ______
4. ______
5. ______
6. ______
7. ______
8. ______
9. ______
10. ______

Grammar G

Using Adverb Clauses

1 A *clause* is a group of words that contains both a subject and a verb. It is used as a part of a sentence.

2 An *independent clause* expresses a complete thought and can stand alone as a sentence.

3 A *dependent* (subordinate) *clause* does not express a complete thought and cannot stand alone as a sentence.

4 A dependent clause that modifies a verb, an adjective, or an adverb is called an *adverb clause.* Adverb clauses usually answer the questions *where, when, how, why, to what extent,* or *under what condition.*

She came *when I called.* (modifies the verb *came*)

David is as reliable *as his dad is.* (modifies the adjective *reliable*)

Chase worked faster *than Paul did.* (modifies the adverb *faster*)

5 Adverb clauses are introduced by *subordinating conjunctions: after, although, as, as if, as much as, as long as, as soon as, because, before, if, in order that, since, so that, than, though, unless, until, when, whenever, where, wherever, while.* (Some of these words may also be used as other parts of speech.)

6 Introductory adverb clauses are set off by commas. Adverb clauses at the end of a sentence do not usually require commas.

Because he was exhausted, he sat down to rest.
I will go with you *if the contest is held on Saturday.*

UNIT 8

Exercise A

(1) Underline each subject one time and each verb two times. (2) Circle each subordinating conjunction. (3) Put parentheses around each dependent clause.

1. (Although the other senses are important,) eyesight controls most of a person's activities.
2. (Whenever light rays hit the eye,) an image is sent to the visual centers of the brain.
3. The iris controls the light entering into the eye (so that exactly the right amount enters.)
4. The light rays, (when they have entered the eye,) travel to the retina.
5. (Whenever the light hits the retina,) light rays move through the nerve cells to reach the rods and cones.
6. The cones do the majority of one's seeing during the day (because they are sensitive to fairly bright light.)
7. (Although the dots of light blend together,) the rods and cones receive separate light rays from different parts of the object.
8. The light rays bend (so that the image comes in upside down.)
9. (When the light hits a rod or cone,) a signal is sent to the visual center of the brain.
10. The visual center, (after it has received the signal,) turns the image right-side-up.

Using Adverb Clauses

Exercise B **(1) Circle each subordinating conjunction. (2) Put parentheses around each adverb clause. (3) Draw an arrow to the word that the clause modifies.**

1. (Although everything seemed calm,) we were actually in the eye of a hurricane.
2. Moses could not enter the promised land (because he had disobeyed God.)
3. The teacher, (when he had received the homework,) resumed his lecture.
4. (Because it has no outlet,) the Dead Sea has a large concentration of salt.
5. The nation expressed deep sorrow (when President Lincoln died.)
6. Katherine was working (so that she could go to college.)
7. (Although Abraham loved Isaac,) he was willing to sacrifice his son.
8. (Wherever Hope went,) she kept a smile on her face.
9. (Whenever the cloud moved,) the Israelite nation moved.
10. (Because the people were against Christ,) they provoked Pilate to crucify Him.

Exercise C **In the following paragraph, identify the adverb clauses. (1) Circle each subordinating conjunction. (2) Draw a line under each adverb clause.**

Although he was only fifty-one years old, Captain Joshua Slocum found himself without a ship to command. Because he loved the sea so much, he could not bear the thought of being separated from it. In order that he might be near his beloved sea, Captain Slocum contrived the fanciful idea of sailing around the world—alone. He found an abandoned oyster boat, and with $600 worth of repairs he made her navigable. After he left the New England coast, he sailed across the Atlantic to Gibraltar, and then recrossed the ocean to South America. He made it through the Straits of Magellan although he had a stormy time. As soon as he was in the calmer Pacific, he made up for lost time. Before he arrived home again, he had visited Samoa, Australia, and South Africa. Captain Slocum finally arrived in Newport, Rhode Island, on June 27, 1898, after he had been at sea for three years and twenty-five days.

Exercise D **Combine each pair of sentences into one sentence by using an adverb clause. The first one is done for you.**

1. Frank had a headache. He kept on working. Although Frank had a headache, he kept on working.
2. The girls arrived in Rome. They rented a car. When the girls arrived in Rome, they rented a car.
3. We were late to the game. Our car ran out of gas. We were late to the game because our car ran out of gas.
4. The shirt is too small. We will want to return it. Because the shirt is too small, we will want to return it.

Grammar

Diagraming Adverb Clauses

Diagram the independent clause first. Then diagram the adverb clause below the independent clause. Draw a dotted line from the verb in the dependent clause to the word modified in the independent clause. Write the subordinating conjunction on the dotted line. Use an *x* to indicate the omission of any word from the sentence (for example, the word *you* in an imperative sentence).

Before they moved away, Sandra would often visit the Andersons.

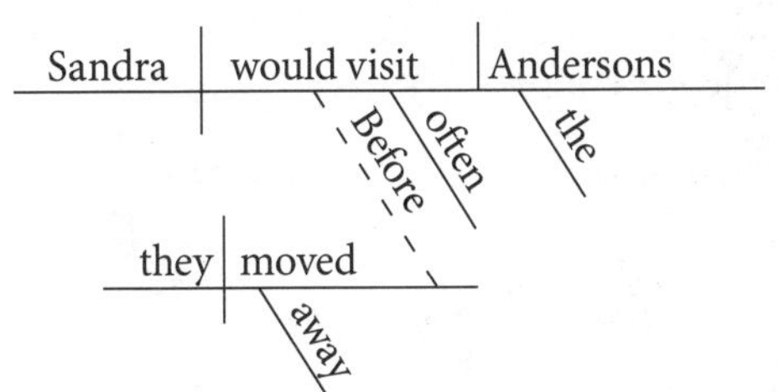

If ye love me, keep my commandments.

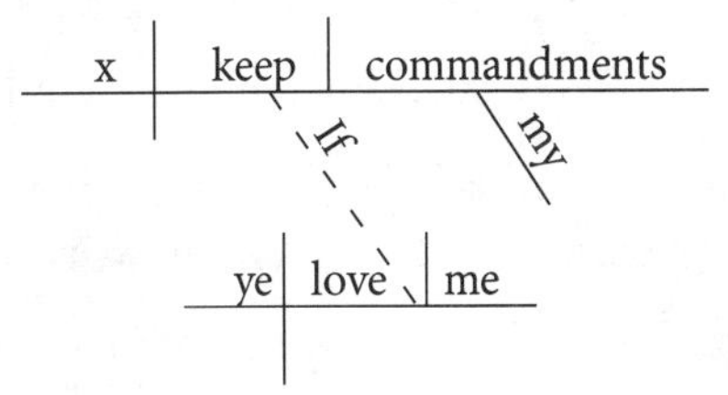

Mom gave me a snack *after I finished my homework.*

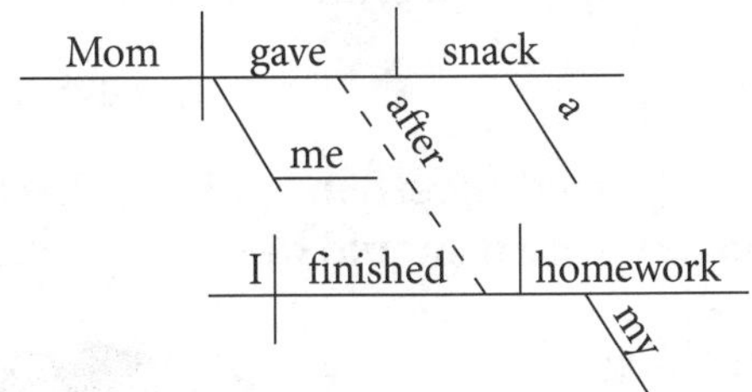

Thomas became a youth pastor *after he graduated from college.*

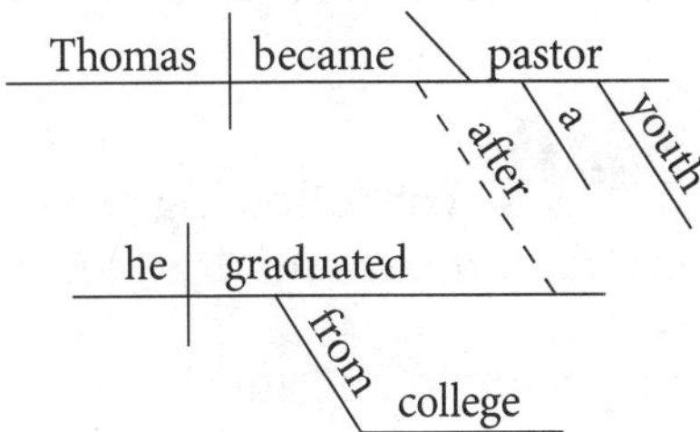

UNIT 8

Exercise A **Diagram the following sentences.** (See *Supplement.*)

1. When David Livingstone went to Africa in 1841, few Europeans had penetrated Africa's interior.
2. While many Europeans desired Africa's vast riches, Livingstone sought lost souls.
3. Livingstone thoroughly explored Africa's interior as he traveled between villages.
4. Many newspapers wrote stories about Livingstone's travels because Europeans were very much interested in his explorations.
5. Soon many Europeans went to Africa for wealth, although others became missionaries to the African people.
6. Because explorers discovered gold, diamonds, and ivory in Africa, many nations established colonies there.
7. After World War II ended, many of these colonies became independent nations.
8. Africa contained over sixty independent countries before the twentieth century closed.

Exercise B **For additional practice, diagram numbers 1–6 in Exercise B on p. 162.** (See *Supplement.*)

Grammar

Placing Adverb Modifiers

Place adverb modifiers so they clearly modify the word you intend.

1 **An adverb phrase or clause that *modifies a verb* may be placed *before or after* the verb it modifies, but *not between* two verbs that it might modify.**

When the rain stops, you may go outside. (modifier before the verb—correct)

You may go outside *when the rain stops.* (modifier after the verb—correct)

Dad said *on Wednesday* we would have a picnic. (modifier between two verbs that it might modify—incorrect)

On Wednesday, Dad said that we would have a picnic. (corrected)

Dad said that we would have a picnic *on Wednesday.* (corrected)

2 **An adverb phrase or clause that *modifies an adjective* or *an adverb* is usually placed immediately *after* the word it modifies.**

He was prosperous *beyond his wildest dreams.* (modifies adjective)

Speedy runs faster *than his brother does.* (modifies adverb)

3 **Place adverb modifiers as close as possible to the words they modify.**

I read that the FBI captured a criminal *in today's newspaper.* (misplaced)

In today's newspaper, I read that the FBI captured a criminal. (better)

Exercise A

The following sentences contain misplaced adverb modifiers. Circle each misplaced modifier and draw an arrow to the place where it should be.

1. Doug promised on Saturday he would take me fishing. or
2. Mr. Sturgis said on Monday he would help with the yard work. or
3. I heard that the police had arrested the thief on the radio.
4. Mom saw a lovely kitten on her way to the beauty parlor.
5. Marshall told me on his vacation where he would be staying.
6. I told Gary today I would teach him how to swim. or
7. They left town before the hurricane struck on the bus.
8. I enjoy listening to music while resting on the stereo.
9. The boys saw a painting done by Grandma Moses in the museum.
10. It was reported that a plane had been hijacked to Angola by the newscaster.

Exercise B

Write two sentences containing adverb phrases and two sentences containing adverb clauses. Make sure to place the modifiers correctly.

1. Answers will vary. __________
2. __________
3. __________
4. __________

Grammar G

Using Adverbs in Comparisons

1 ***Most adverbs*** **form the comparative and superlative degrees by using** ***more*** **and** ***most.***

POSITIVE	COMPARATIVE	SUPERLATIVE
frantically	*more* frantically	*most* frantically
beautifully	*more* beautifully	*most* beautifully

2 ***A few adverbs*** **form the comparative and superlative degrees by adding** ***-er*** **and** ***-est.***

POSITIVE	COMPARATIVE	SUPERLATIVE
late	lat***er***	lat***est***
low	low***er***	low***est***
close	clos***er***	clos***est***

3 **A few adverbs are** ***irregular*** **in form.**

POSITIVE	COMPARATIVE	SUPERLATIVE
well	better	best
much	more	most
badly	worse	worst
little	less	least
far	farther	farthest

4 **Remember to use the** ***comparative*** **degree when** ***only two*** **things are being compared.**

UNIT 8

Exercise A **In each blank, write the correct degree of the adverb in parentheses.**

1. Hebron lay closer to Shechem than Beer-sheba did. *(close)*
2. This plastering was done better than the other work you did for me. *(well)*
3. The snail travels more slowly than the energetic ant. *(slowly)*
4. Of all the men in Congress, he acted most courageously. *(courageously)*
5. This plane flew lower than the helicopter did. *(low)*
6. The baby began crying more loudly as he became more hungry. *(loudly)*
7. Polycarp died more nobly than his persecutors lived. *(nobly)*
8. Solomon ruled most wisely of all the kings of Israel. *(wisely)*
9. The Good Samaritan behaved more kindly than the other travelers did. *(kindly)*
10. We had to walk farther to get home than Joel did. *(far)*

Exercise B **Write sentences using adverbs as indicated in parentheses. Make sure they modify verbs, adjectives, or adverbs.**

1. (comparative of *far*) Answers will vary.
2. (comparative of *little*) ____
3. (superlative of *much*) ____
4. (superlative of *well*) ____

G: Using Adverbs Correctly

1 **Avoid the *double comparison.* Never use *-er* and *more* together or *-est* and *most* together. Only one form is needed.**

This plane flies *more faster* than that one. (incorrect)
This plane flies *faster* than that one. (correct)
He lives *most farthest* from school. (incorrect)
He lives *farthest* from school. (correct)

2 **Use the *comparative* degree when comparing *two* persons or things. Use the *superlative* when comparing *three or more* persons or things.**

Of the two girls, Marie types *faster.* (not *fastest*)

3 **Avoid the *double negative.* The following words are called negatives: *no, not* (or *n't*), *none, never, no one, nothing, hardly, scarcely.* Do not use two negative words in the same statement.**

They *don't* see *none* to fit them. (incorrect)
They *don't* see any to fit them. (correct)
or They see *none* to fit them. (correct)

We can*not scarcely* see through the fog. (incorrect)
We can *scarcely* see through the fog. (correct)

Exercise A **Cross out each incorrect form in parentheses.**

1. There aren't (no, any) figs on these trees at all.
2. Beth sings (most, more) beautifully than her sister does.
3. The pioneers pushed (more farther, farther) into the open plains.
4. Of the two horses, Star can run (faster, fastest).
5. I cannot find (no one, anyone) who knows where that street is.
6. A diamond sparkles (brilliantlier, more brilliantly) than a ruby.
7. Of the four cars, this one rode (more, most) quietly.
8. We (couldn't, could) hardly raise our tent because of the strong wind.
9. Charles can speak (more forcefully, more forcefullier) than anyone I know.
10. Samuel Adams spoke out (more bravely, most bravely) than any other Bostonian.
11. Several workers stayed (later, more later) than normal to finish the job.
12. I can't (never, ever) find (nothing, anything) in this store.
13. My cousins live (more nearer, nearer) to the coast than I do.
14. Many people give to others (more freelier, more freely) after they themselves have been helped.
15. Tad (hadn't, had) scarcely arrived when his father telephoned.
16. The Arctic tern flies (farther, farthest) of any bird.
17. Life will be over (sooner, more sooner) than you think.
18. The birds that fly the (most highest, highest) of all are geese.
19. Of the two teams, theirs played (more, most) fairly.
20. At first, Franklin didn't receive (no, any) help from the French government.
21. I arose (more earlier, earlier) than usual today.

Using Adverbs Correctly

Exercise B **The following sentences contain errors in the use of adverbs. Cross out any incorrect words and make corrections where necessary.**

1. Jesus did not want ~~no~~ any money changers in the temple.
2. The Conestoga wagon traveled ~~slowlier~~ more slowly than the steam engine.
3. David would ~~not~~ fear no one, because God was with him. or "would not fear anyone"
4. The geology class lasted ~~more~~ longer than the archaeology class.
5. Those scientists have pursued this question ~~more~~ further than anyone else in the field.
6. The doctor couldn't do ~~nothing~~ anything for the boy who was hit by the car. or "could do nothing"
7. Of the three swimmers, Leigh swam ~~more~~ most quickly.
8. Jesus, the Son of God, ~~never~~ did no wrong while He was here on earth. or "never did wrong"
9. Of all the patriarchs, Abraham is noted for serving God ~~more~~ most faithfully.
10. Peter replied that he had ~~never~~ eaten nothing unclean. or "never eaten anything"
11. Methuselah walked ~~more~~ longer on this earth than any other human being.
12. Karen sews ~~more~~ better than her sister Susan.
13. The barometric pressure goes ~~more~~ lower in the mountains than in the plains.
14. I can't think of ~~nothing~~ anything else to do, can you? or "can think of nothing"
15. The party of hunters had ~~not~~ hardly seen any game.
16. The Spanish settled in the Americas ~~more~~ earlier than any other group.
17. A lazy man won't ~~never~~ ever see God's blessing on his life. or "will never"
18. Abraham and Sarah had ~~not~~ had no children until Isaac was born. or "had not had any"
19. Of all the hosts, Mr. Smallay spoke the ~~most~~ friendliest.
20. Edison worked ~~more~~ harder at his inventions than we can imagine.
21. Arriving ~~more~~ sooner than the other hikers, Jordan sat down under a tree.
22. There was ~~not~~ no one absent in our Sunday school class this morning.
23. There were~~n't~~ scarcely any people around the house.
24. Of the twenty patients, Philip was hurt ~~more badly~~ worst.
25. I couldn't do ~~nothing~~ anything to help her out of the predicament. or "could do nothing"

Exercise C **Write sentences illustrating Rules 1, 2, and 3 from page 166.**

1. (Rule 1) Answers will vary. ________________
2. (Rule 2) ________________
3. (Rule 3) ________________

Grammar G

Using Exact & Vivid Adverbs

In previous units, we learned that using exact verbs and nouns is the first consideration of the careful writer. Nevertheless, many times *adverbs* are necessary to tell where, when, or how the action of a verb takes place. Adverbs can also give different shades of meaning to adjectives and other adverbs.

1 **Use the most *vivid* adverbs you can find. Adverbs that end in *-ly* are usually the most vivid.**

awkwardly, bullishly, clumsily, contentedly, dexterously, mysteriously

2 **Carefully select the *exact* adverb needed to express your idea.** For example, the word *easily* is a general word. Notice the following synonyms that will express the same idea more exactly: *effortlessly, gently, readily, smoothly.*

The sailboat glided *easily* across the water. (vague)

The sailboat glided *smoothly* across the water. (exact)

3 **The adverbs *very* and *really* are greatly overused.** As often as possible, substitute such synonyms as *decidedly, extremely, exceedingly, incomparably, indeed, intensely.*

He was *really* grateful for the gift. (trite)

He was *extremely* grateful for the gift. (better)

Exercise A

Supply a more vivid adverb for each italicized word below. Use your dictionary or a thesaurus. Answers will vary.

_______________ 1. The carpenters worked *hard.*

_______________ 2. He *easily* finished his homework.

_______________ 3. A little boy answered the question *nicely.*

_______________ 4. Brittany plays the organ *well.*

_______________ 5. Heather *surely* needs help with this project.

_______________ 6. The tugboat moved ahead *slowly.*

_______________ 7. Early Christians were *really* persecuted.

_______________ 8. The road was *very* rough.

_______________ 9. A cleaning woman moved *quietly* about the room.

_______________ 10. He spoke to her *badly.*

_______________ 11. The boys and girls sang *happily.*

_______________ 12. This *unusually* cold weather should end soon.

Exercise B

(1) Describe what it is like at your house during a severe storm. Describe the storm as well as your feelings and reactions. First select vivid verbs. Then use adverbs where necessary to add the right shade of meaning. (2) Circle each adverb.

Reviewing Adverbs

Exercise A

(1) Underline all one-word adverbs. (2) Circle all adverb phrases. (3) Put parentheses around each adverb clause.

1. Sorrowfully, Jeremiah lamented about the Israelite nation.
2. Stan ran swiftly to the church (because he did not want to be late.)
3. (Although the man once was blind,) with the touch of the Master he could now see.
4. The monkey stared at me curiously.
5. The leper shouted for joy (when he had been cleansed.)
6. Martha came into the room in which Mary was quietly listening to Jesus.
7. Peter went out and wept bitterly.
8. Matt, the boy in the blue shirt, trusted Christ today during Bible class.
9. The boys walked into the art gallery and looked about wonderingly.
10. Moses died in the land of Moab (because he did not obey God.)

Exercise B

Cross out each incorrect word in parentheses.

1. Justin ran (~~more farther~~, farther) than anyone else.
2. The veterinarian couldn't do (~~nothing~~, anything) to save the puppy.
3. There has never been (~~no~~, any) person who could get to heaven by good works.
4. Emma draws the (~~better~~, best) of any girl in our art class.
5. Of the three mansions in our town, the Colby House is the (~~more beautifully~~, most beautifully) decorated.
6. There is not (~~no one~~, anyone) living in that old house.
7. The Dog Star, Sirius, is seen the (~~more~~, most) clearly of any star.
8. The beggar's dime was (more, ~~most~~) freely given than the tycoon's hundred dollars.
9. It is reported that George Washington never told (~~no~~, a) lie.
10. I didn't find (~~none~~, any) of the tools where they should be.

Exercise C

The following sentences contain errors in the use of adverbs. Cross out any incorrect words and make corrections where necessary. If a modifier is misplaced, circle it and draw an arrow to where it should be.

1. Mrs. Patterson informed me on Monday that I was to come to work early. (or)
2. You ~~sure~~ surely write ~~good~~ well for an amateur, Hunter.
3. You ~~won't~~ will hardly find ~~nobody~~ anybody who can sketch ~~more~~ better than Meg.
4. The witness said that the defendant had ~~not~~ never been very honest. or "had not ever"
5. Professor Rushdoony ~~sure~~ surely spoke ~~intelligent~~ intelligently, didn't he?
6. Handle this china ~~careful~~ carefully because you can break it ~~easy~~ easily.
7. The camel can go ~~more~~ longer without water than a donkey can.
8. Miss Houseman saw that ancient Fort George is being renovated in a newspaper. (or)
9. These apples certainly taste ~~sourly~~ sour.
10. The latest submarine can dive ~~more~~ deeper in the ocean than the previous ones.

UNIT 8

Exercise A

Capitalization and Punctuation. (1) Draw a line through each incorrect small letter. Write a capital above it. (2) Add punctuation where needed.

1. last year, i read the book how we got our bible by w.h. griffith thomas.
2. my family lives in the small german town of frankenmuth, michigan, where my father works at transnational cracker corporation.
3. paul reinhart, the director of the choir, is dean at dickerson community college in dickerson, nebraska.
4. graham's electronics on goodell boulevard and the phonofixit shop at strickland mall are the two places you should go for new parts for your sony stereo.
5. "is it july 15 that we will be leaving for guatemala aboard the seafarer," asked dan, "or will we wait until august 10 and travel on the merchant ship dixie bell?"
6. on january 20, 1977, jimmy carter became president of the united states of america.

Exercise B

Subjects and Verbs. (1) Draw two lines under each verb. (2) Draw one line under each subject.

1. Paul went to Iconium, a city in Asia Minor, on one of his missionary journeys.
2. When Peter spoke on the day of Pentecost, many people were added to the Church.
3. The "Son of Thunder" was the title given to John the apostle.
4. John James Audubon and Grant Wood are two American painters whose paintings are well known.
5. One exquisite Chinese painting was done on a silk fan.
6. Thomas Hart Benton's murals cover huge walls.

Exercise C

The Sentence. In the blank before the number, write *s.* for sentences, *frag.* for fragments, or *r.o.* for run-ons.

__frag.__ 1. First at the church and later at the school.

__r.o.__ 2. The dik-dik is one of the smallest antelopes, it lives only in eastern Africa.

__r.o.__ 3. Marcus did not know the answer he asked the Lord to help him.

__s.__ 4. Jim drove to the bank to cash a check while Janelle walked to the grocery store.

__frag.__ 5. Although the ship had landed and had taken on fresh water and food.

Exercise D Using Verbs. Cross out each incorrect verb form in parentheses.

1. They (~~lay~~, laid) Jesus in Joseph's garden tomb.
2. Joy and Jon, we (had better, ~~better~~) leave now; we don't want to wear out our welcome.
3. Before we go, you (~~better~~, had better) (~~leave~~, let) Grandma pack your lunch.
4. Jesus (~~et~~, ate) with the disciples at the Last Supper.
5. When the teacher asked a question, all of her students (~~rose~~, raised) their hands.
6. On Sunday morning, my pastor spoke about the reality of Hell, and I (thought, ~~thunk~~) much about what he said.
7. When he (~~busted~~, broke) his arm, he had to be (taken, ~~took~~) to the hospital.
8. "No," said Tom, "I (~~ain't~~, am not) going to the art gallery today. I have a football game."
9. Several vandals (~~snuck~~, sneaked) into the house by (~~rising~~, raising) a window.
10. Since I (~~took sick~~, became ill), I can't get around so well; would you mind (~~bringing~~, taking) this package to the post office for me?

Exercise E Using Verbs. Cross out each incorrect verb form and write the correct form above it.

1. ~~Can~~ May I ~~sit~~ set these baskets in the garage, or should I ~~leave~~ let them ~~set~~ sit here?
2. David often had to protect his flock from animals which ~~attackted~~ attacked them.
3. Lisa ~~took sick~~ became ill while we were riding on the ferris wheel.
4. Do you know this subject well enough so that you ~~may learn~~ can teach other students?
5. A kind man ~~sat~~ set his own luggage aside and ~~drug~~ dragged an elderly lady's trunk up to the landing gate.

Exercise F Subject and Verb Agreement. Cross out each incorrect verb form in parentheses.

1. There (~~is~~, are) many characteristics which should identify a Christian.
2. Twenty dollars (is, ~~are~~) not enough to pay the bill.
3. "Songs in the Night" (is, ~~are~~) a favorite radio program of mine.
4. The congregation (~~is~~, are) discussing that proposal among themselves.
5. Neither faith nor good works (~~is~~, are) good by themselves.
6. The eyes of the Lord (~~is~~, are) over the righteous.
7. Mumps (is, ~~are~~) contagious to those exposed to it; so is a gripy attitude.
8. God (~~don't~~, doesn't) honor a selfish man's desires.
9. Here (are, ~~is~~) two of David's outstanding qualities: loyalty and faithfulness.
10. Our students (~~is~~, are) writing letters to Mr. Snyder, who is ill.

Exercise G

Using Nouns. Above each italicized word, write its use. Abbreviate as follows: *s.* (subject), *p.n.* (predicate nominative), *d.o.* (direct object), *i.o* (indirect object), *o.p.* (object of preposition), *ap.* (appositive), and *d.a.* (direct address).

d.a. o.p.
1. *John*, did you learn about photography in your journalism *class?*

ap. o.p. i.o. d.o.
2. Photography, the *art* of capturing images on *film*, can provide a *person* long *hours* of enjoyment.

s. ap. p.n.
3. *Composition*, the *arrangement* of the objects, is an important *part* of any photograph.

i.o. d.o.
4. The salesman showed *Doug* several new camera *models*.

p.n. s. o.p.
5. Julia Margaret Cameron was an early *photographer;* her *portraits* of famous *people* are known across the world.

Exercise H

Using Pronouns. Cross out the incorrect pronouns and write the correct pronouns above them. If a sentence is correct, write *C* beside the number of the sentence.

I
1. Every Friday night, Sharon and ~~me~~ give out tracts and witness to people in the shopping mall.

them
2. Translating the Bible from English to a native dialect was hard for Dr. Zimmer and ~~they~~.

C 3. The pastor thanked Carl and him for their hard work on the building project.

they
4. Jesus and ~~them~~ went to pray in the Garden of Gethsemane after nightfall.

We
5. ~~Us~~ Christians can go directly to the Lord Jesus Christ; we do not need a human intercessor.

he
6. The captain said that Ron and ~~him~~ are the best scuba divers on the entire crew.

C 7. For I know that my Redeemer liveth, and that He shall stand at the latter day upon the earth.

they
8. The Boswells and ~~them~~ went to the beach to see the glorious sunset.

he
9. Don and ~~him~~ were praying for me when I was so terribly ill last week.

us
10. Mrs. Howells and she taught ~~we~~ girls how to do embroidery.

Exercise I

Using Adjectives. The following sentences contain adjectives used incorrectly. Cross out any incorrect words and make corrections where necessary. If a modifier is misplaced, circle it and draw an arrow to where it should be.

1. The man will not find it difficult to obey God's commands (whose heart is right).

fewer
2. The use of ~~less~~ adjectives will improve your composition.

other
3. This dwelling is older than any ^ home in the area.

those
4. Show ~~them~~ boys the way to their room.

5. The lining was made of a purple velvet fabric (within the trunk).

better
6. It is ~~gooder~~ to die for something, than to live for nothing.

7. (Hanging on a hook in the closet), I could see my new tie.

8. Dad bought a small car from a salesman in the next town (that holds four people).

9. Arkansas produces more rice than any other state in the Republic.
10. Paul Bunyan was the ~~most~~ tallest man in American folklore.
11. That man in this picture with red hair is my uncle.
12. ~~Them~~ Those chickens are the ~~goodest~~ best ones we have ever raised on our farm.
13. A concerto has ~~less~~ fewer movements than a symphony.
14. Mr. Sedgewicke is ~~more~~ older than any other man in our neighborhood.
15. Anchorage, Alaska, is the ~~most cold~~ coldest city I have ever been in.
16. The boys jumped into the lake, laughing and hollering.
17. Tad had ~~less~~ fewer *A*'s on his report card than I did.

Exercise J

Using Adverbs. The following sentences contain errors in the use of adverbs. Cross out any incorrect words and make corrections where necessary. If a modifier is misplaced, circle it and draw an arrow to where it should be.

1. You can ~~sure~~ surely knit ~~good~~ well, Jan.
2. These persimmons taste ~~real~~ really bitter.
3. Buddy couldn't find ~~nothing~~ anything about the mongoose in this book. or "could find nothing"
4. Father told me on Wednesday afternoon we would plant the garden.
5. Of the three pieces, this composition sounds ~~more~~ most beautiful.
6. Elaine draws more ~~skillfullier~~ skillfully each day; one day she will paint ~~good~~ well, too.
7. That soloist sounded ~~real~~ really good, didn't he?
8. I read that Lebanon had declared war in the paper.
9. Jeremy did ~~real good~~ really well in math; in fact, he is the ~~goodest~~ best mathematician in our class.
10. The young preacher didn't seem to know where ~~none~~ any of his notes were.
11. Alexander sings really ~~good~~ well; in fact, of all the choir members he sings the ~~better~~ best.
12. Mr. Lowman said on Friday our papers would be due.
13. The tone of his language sounded ~~decided~~ decidedly harsh, but I am sure he didn't mean to speak ~~rough~~ roughly.
14. He writes ~~plain~~ plainly; you ~~sure~~ surely should be able to understand him.
15. Julius Caesar did not suspect ~~none~~ any of his friends of treachery.
16. I thought when the snow stopped that we could proceed on our journey.
17. Christ did not perform ~~no~~ any miracles in Nazareth because of the people's unbelief.
18. You should listen more ~~closelier~~ closely if you want to improve.
19. I ~~don't~~ want nothing to do with your childish pranks. or "do not want anything"
20. This stew tastes good; it must have been cooked ~~more~~ longer than the other.

Grammar

Recognizing Prepositions

1 **A *preposition* is a word that shows how a noun or a pronoun is related to some other word in the sentence.**

Mark sat *on* the barrel.
Mark stood *beside* the barrel.
Mark climbed *into* the barrel.
Mark crawled *through* the barrel.
Mark jumped *over* the barrel.

The prepositions *on, beside, into, through,* and *over* show how the word *Mark* is related to the noun *barrel.*

FREQUENTLY USED PREPOSITIONS

aboard	among	between	from	over	underneath
about	around	beyond	in	past	until
above	at	but	into	since	unto
across	before	by	like	through	up
after	behind	down	near	throughout	upon
against	below	during	of	to	with
along	beneath	except	off	toward	within
amid	beside	for	on	under	without

Some prepositions are *compound.* They consist of more than one word but should be considered as one word.

COMPOUND PREPOSITIONS

according to	by way of	in spite of	out of
as for	except for	instead of	regardless of
because of	in front of	on account of	with regard to

2 **A *prepositional phrase* consists of a preposition, its noun or pronoun object, and any modifiers of the object.**

The sun sparkled **on** (Prep.) the emerald *waters* (Obj.).

3 **The *object of a preposition* is the noun or pronoun that completes a prepositional phrase. A preposition must always have an object.**

The deer bolted **through** (Prep.) the *woods* (Obj.).

4 **A preposition may have a *compound object.***

We received a telegram **from** (Prep.) *Uncle Otis* (Obj.) and *Aunt Eunice* (Obj.).

Exercise A

Circle the prepositions. Count compound prepositions as one word. See if you can find all 24.

O come, let us sing (unto) the Lord; let us make a joyful noise (to) the rock (of) our salvation. Let us come (before) His presence (with) thanksgiving, and make a joyful noise (unto) Him (with) psalms.

The Lord is a great God, and a great King above all gods.

All the gods of the nations are idols, but the Lord made the heavens.

Sing unto the Lord a new song; sing unto the Lord, all the earth. Sing unto the Lord; bless His name; shew forth His salvation from day to day.

O Lord, our Lord, how excellent is Thy name in all the earth! Out of the mouth of babes and sucklings hast Thou ordained strength because of Thine enemies.

I will praise Thee, O Lord my God, with all my heart; for great is Thy mercy toward me, and Thou hast delivered my soul from the lowest hell.

Thy kingdom is an everlasting kingdom, and Thy dominion endureth throughout all generations.

Praise ye the Lord. Praise ye the Lord from the heavens; praise Him in the heights.

Exercise B **(1) Underline the prepositional phrases. (2) Circle the prepositions. (3) Draw a box around the objects of prepositions.**

UNIT 9

1. In the beginning God created the heaven and the earth.
2. Sing unto the Lord a new song, and His praise in the congregation of saints.
3. Prepare ye the way of the Lord; make straight in the desert a highway for our God.
4. The king's favour is toward a wise servant, but his wrath is against him that causeth shame.
5. He restoreth my soul; He leadeth me in the paths of righteousness for His name's sake.
6. I will put enmity between thee and the woman, and between thy seed and her seed.
7. He that dwelleth in the secret place of the most High shall abide under the shadow of the Almighty.
8. From the end of the earth will I cry unto Thee, when my heart is overwhelmed.
9. He escaped out of their hand and went away again beyond Jordan.
10. I will be exalted among the heathen; I will be exalted in the earth.

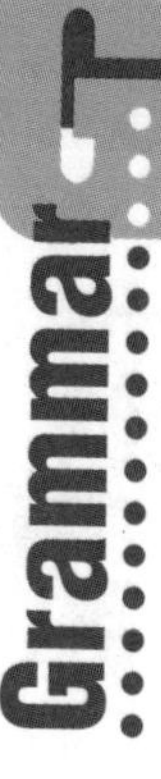

Recognizing Prepositions (cont.)

5 **Many of the words in the preposition list on page 174 can also be used as adverbs. It is easy to tell the difference. Prepositions always have objects. Adverbs never do.**

We jumped *off.* (adverb—no object)
We jumped *off* the diving board. (preposition—*board* is the object)

Exercise C **In the blank write *adv.* if the italicized word is an adverb. Write *prep.* if the word is a preposition.**

adv. 1. While visiting the island, the captain met the chief of the natives and brought him *aboard.*

prep. 2. A commander dressed in an elaborate uniform walked *aboard* the vessel.

prep. 3. When thou passest *through* the waters, I will be with thee.

adv. 4. The blockade runner finally succeeded in making it *through*.

prep. 5. The once-mighty ship sank *below* the crashing waves.

adv. 6. Has all the gear been stowed *below,* Captain Cook?

prep. 7. Millions of vehicles have passed *over* the Brooklyn Bridge.

adv. 8. Watch your balance; you don't want to fall *over*.

prep. 9. Centipedes can often be found *underneath* large, flat rocks.

adv. 10. The eternal God is thy refuge, and *underneath* are the everlasting arms.

Exercise D **(1) Write four sentences that contain prepositional phrases. Use at least one compound preposition. (2) Underline the phrases.**

1. Answers will vary.

2.

3.

4.

Using Prepositions Correctly I

Learn to distinguish carefully the prepositions in this lesson.

1 ***(beside, besides)*** ***Beside*** **means "by the side of";** ***besides*** **means "in addition to."**

Look at that boulder *beside* the road.

Are there other choices *besides* this one?

2 ***(between, among)*** **Use** ***between*** **in referring to two people or things; use** ***among*** **in referring to more than two.**

At the concert, I sat *between* my wife and my daughter.

I will praise Thee *among* much people.

3 ***(except, accept)*** ***Except*****, as a preposition, means "excluding."** ***Accept*** **is a verb and means "to receive" or "to agree to."**

All the cast was on stage *except* Dale.

Will you *accept* the goodness of God and not be thankful?

4 ***(in, into)*** **Use** ***in*** **for location within; use** ***into*** **for motion from outside to inside.**

I enjoy being *in* this class.

Did you lead the horse *into* the barn?

5 ***(of, have)*** ***Of*** **is a preposition and should not be used for the helping verb** ***have*****.**

We should *of* listened to Dad's instructions. (incorrect)

We should *have* listened to Dad's instructions. (correct)

6 ***(to, and)*** **Do not use the conjunction** ***and*** **after the words** ***try*** **and** ***sure*****. Use the word** ***to*** **instead.**

Try *and* be more patient. (incorrect)

Try *to* be more patient. (correct)

Be sure *and* arrive on time. (incorrect)

Be sure *to* arrive on time. (correct)

Exercise A **Cross out each incorrect form in parentheses.**

1. To (accept, ~~except~~) the gift of God is to live eternally.
2. Try (to, ~~and~~) be on time for the meeting, Geri.
3. Is there anything (~~among~~, between) you and the Savior?
4. The hot loaf of bread was divided evenly (~~between~~, among) the six hungry soldiers.
5. An enormous ocean liner sailed (into, ~~in~~) Charleston harbor.
6. All (except, ~~accept~~) Anthony are expected to attend.
7. (~~Among~~, Between) two friends there should be no misunderstandings.
8. I should (~~of~~, have) repented long before I did.
9. Who was translated to heaven (~~beside~~, besides) Enoch?
10. Be sure (to, ~~and~~) carry your luggage with you.
11. Father's train pulled (into, ~~in~~) the station.
12. If he had not been stricken on the Damascus Road, Saul might (~~of~~, have) never (accepted, ~~excepted~~) Jesus Christ.

(continued)

Exercise A, cont.

13. Esther stood (in, ~~into~~) the presence of King Ahasuerus.
14. You should (accept, ~~except~~) correction cheerfully.
15. You could (have, ~~of~~) stopped by the market on your way home.
16. Be sure (~~and~~, to) finish your essay for tomorrow's class.
17. Two wild geese were flying (~~besides~~, beside) each other in the autumn sky.
18. The Communists went (~~in~~, into) Poland and took away the people's freedom.

Exercise B

The following sentences contain errors in the use of prepositions. Cross out any incorrect words and make corrections where necessary.

1. Try ~~and~~ to answer each math problem correctly.
2. He leadeth me ~~besides~~ beside the still waters.
3. Let's not allow anything to come ~~among~~ between you and me, Sarah.
4. He might ~~of~~ have done great things for God, but he chose to be a quitter.
5. A spirit of jealousy arose ~~between~~ among the members of the baseball team.
6. Everyone ~~accept~~ except Harvey will be at the gathering.
7. Be sure ~~and~~ to bring your Bibles to church each Sunday.
8. We can now enter boldly ~~in~~ into the presence of God with our petitions.
9. One should ~~except~~ accept defeat with dignity and victory with humility.
10. A man nine feet tall stepped ~~in~~ into the arena of battle.
11. ~~Among~~ Between you and me, I think that you should not go there.
12. He could ~~of~~ have been a famous author, but he did not apply himself.
13. The graduates marched ~~in~~ into the auditorium solemnly.
14. Try ~~and~~ to read for pleasure besides doing your assigned homework.
15. A herd of gazelles were grazing ~~besides~~ beside a shallow water hole.
16. Demas could ~~of~~ have served God, but he turned back instead.

Exercise C

Write sentences illustrating the correct use of Rules 1–6, page 177.

1. Answers will vary. ______
2. ______
3. ______
4. ______
5. ______
6. ______

Grammar

Using Prepositions Correctly II

Avoid using unnecessary prepositions.

1 ***(amounts up to)*** **Omit the preposition *up*.**

Our grocery bill *amounted up to* $40.00. (incorrect)
Our grocery bill *amounted to* $40.00. (correct)

2 ***(at about)*** **Omit one of the prepositions.**

The game will begin *at about* three o'clock. (incorrect)
The game will begin *about* three o'clock. (correct)
The game will begin *at* three o'clock. (correct)

3 ***(had of)*** **Omit the preposition *of*.**

If you *had of* thought first, you would not have spoken. (incorrect)
If you *had* thought first, you would not have spoken. (correct)

4 ***(inside of*** **or** ***outside of)*** **Omit the preposition *of*.**

Spot was accidentally locked *inside of* his dog house. (incorrect)
Spot was accidentally locked *inside* his dog house. (correct)
Lepers had to be quarantined *outside of* the camp. (incorrect)
Lepers had to be quarantined *outside* the camp. (correct)

5 ***(Where . . . to)*** **Omit the preposition *to*.**

He did not realize *where* he was going *to.* (incorrect)
He did not realize *where* he was going. (correct)

6 ***(Where . . . at)*** **Omit the preposition *at*.**

Where did you say we should meet *at?* (incorrect)
Where did you say we should meet? (correct)

UNIT 9

Exercise A Cross out any unnecessary prepositions in the following sentences.

1. This confession amounts ~~up~~ to treason, Master Hale!
2. If you had ~~of~~ done your part, this job would now be finished, Son.
3. The horses inside ~~of~~ the corral were becoming frightened by the lightning.
4. Ponce de Leon met some Native Americans who supposedly knew where the Fountain of Youth was ~~at~~.
5. I arose ~~at~~ or ~~about~~ 3 o'clock this morning to go fishing.
6. The salmon didn't know where it was going ~~to~~; it merely followed its instincts.
7. Outside ~~of~~ the house, a violent tornado was destroying everything in its path.
8. If the authorities had ~~of~~ been aware of the weakness in the dam, the disaster might have been avoided.
9. Many Americans have no idea where they are going ~~to~~ when they die.
10. ~~At~~ or ~~about~~ the age of seventeen, my grandmother was already teaching school.
11. The Founding Fathers could not have realized where the paths of glory would take our nation ~~to~~.

(continued)

Exercise A, cont.

12. ~~At~~ or ~~about~~ noontime, the sky became dark as the Messiah took our punishment.
13. This bill amounts ~~up~~ to more than I can pay, sir.
14. The Pied Piper led the children outside ~~of~~ the town.
15. Can you tell me where the canned goods are at?
16. The price of the power mower and all its attachments amounts ~~up~~ to $600.
17. Several explorers wondered where the Seven Cities of Gold were ~~at~~.

Exercise B

Cross out any unnecessary prepositions in the following paragraphs.

At ~~about~~ suppertime one evening in 1735, the constable of New York and his men burst inside ~~of~~ the home of John Peter Zenger and arrested him. "Where are you taking him ~~to~~?" his wife pleaded.

"Where all who speak libelously about the king's governors go ~~to~~—to jail, ma'am."

For several months, Zenger, a printer, had been publishing the *Journal*, a local newspaper. In it, he had severely criticized the governor's haughty and dictatorial actions. If he had ~~of~~ retracted the statements, he would not have gone to jail. But as an honest man he could not recant. ~~At~~ about the age of 38, John Peter Zenger found himself inside ~~of~~ a dark prison cell.

At the trial nine months later, the prosecuting attorney read some of Zenger's writings. "This amounts ~~up~~ to libel, gentlemen. If these words had ~~of~~ been uttered on the street, they would ~~of~~ have been libelous. Hidden inside ~~of~~ the pages of a newspaper, they are also libelous."

When Zenger's lawyer, Andrew Hamilton, got up, he showed that the statements did not amount ~~up~~ to libel, but rather, the truth; and truth cannot be libel. The jury found Zenger innocent, and he was set free.

If a person were to visit New York City today, he could see where this battle for a free press occurred ~~at~~. It is a shrine of our liberty.

Exercise C

Write sentences illustrating the correct use of Rules 1–6, page 179.

1. Answers will vary.
2.
3.
4.
5.
6.

Grammar G

Recognizing Conjunctions

1 **A *conjunction* is a word that joins words or groups of words.**

2 **The following conjunctions are called *coordinating conjunctions: and, but, or, nor, for, yet.***

We like *bacon* **and** *tomato* sandwiches on toast. (conjunction joining words)

Should we put it *on the plate* **or** *in a separate bowl?* (conjunction joining phrases)

We went fishing, **but** *we caught no fish.* (conjunction joining two sentences)

3 **Some other coordinating conjunctions go in pairs: *either—or, neither—nor, both—and, not only—but also.* These conjunctions are called *correlative conjunctions.***

Both *Jack* **and** *Joe* bought bicycles with the money they earned. (correlative conjunction joining words)

4 ***Subordinating conjunctions* are used to introduce adverb clauses: *after, although as, as if, as much as, as long as, as soon as, because, before, if, in order that, since, so that, than, though, unless, until, when, whenever, where, wherever, while.***
(Some of these words may also be used as prepositions or as other parts of speech.)

Because *he had real determination,* he would not quit. (introduces adverb clause)

UNIT 9

Exercise A

(1) Underline the conjunctions, being sure to underline both parts of a correlative conjunction. (2) On the line before each sentence, write *W* if the conjunction joins *words;* write *P* if it joins *phrases;* write *S* if it joins *sentences;* write *D* if it introduces a *dependent clause.*

S 1. Cast thy burden upon the Lord, and He shall sustain thee.

S 2. Man proposes, but God disposes. *—Thomas à Kempis*

P 3. In quietness and in confidence shall be your strength.

D 4. Where liberty dwells, there is my country. *—Milton*

W 5. Good manners and soft words have brought many a difficult thing to pass. *—Aesop*

W 6. Principle is a passion for truth and right. *—Hazlitt*

W 7. Which hope we have as an anchor of the soul, both sure and steadfast.

S 8. Yea, they may forget, yet will I not forget thee.

D 9. If honor be your clothing, the suit will last a lifetime. *—Arnot*

P 10. Since infancy and until death, every man is altogether a sinner.

Exercise B

Write sentences using conjunctions as directed.

1. Use *and* to join the parts of a compound subject. Answers will vary.

2. Use *neither—nor* to join two nouns used as the subject.

3. Use *unless* to introduce an adverb clause.

Grammar G

Recognizing Interjections

1 **An *interjection* is an exclamatory word that is not related to the other words in a sentence.**

2 **An exclamation point is usually used after an interjection, but a comma may be used after a mild interjection.**

Hurrah! The war is over.

Boy, did he hit that ball!

Well! What do you know about that!

Note: If you punctuate an interjection with an exclamation point, capitalize the next word.

Exercise A

Write five sentences that contain interjections. Use the ones listed below.

1. *(Hey)* Answers will vary. ____________
2. *(Ouch)* ____________
3. *(Oh)* ____________
4. *(My)* ____________
5. *(Well)* ____________

Now that you've studied the eight parts of speech, check yourself. Do you fully understand them all? In order to do well in English, you must know the parts of speech and be able to identify them in sentences. The exercise below will help you check your knowledge of the parts of speech.

Review Exercise

Fill in the missing words in these definitions of the parts of speech.

1. An adverb is a word that modifies a verb, adjective, or another adverb.
2. A pronoun is a word that takes the place of a noun.
3. A preposition is a word that shows how a noun or a pronoun is related to some other word in the sentence.
4. An adjective is a word that modifies a noun or a pronoun.
5. A verb is a word that shows action, links another word to the subject, helps another verb, or merely indicates existence.
6. An interjection is an exclamatory word that is not related to any other word in the sentence.
7. A noun is a word that names a person, place, thing, or idea.
8. A conjunction is a word that joins words or groups of words.

Exercise A

Identify the italicized words in the following sentences by writing the part of speech above each word. Write *prep.* for prepositions, *conj.* for conjunctions, and *interj.* for interjections.

1. Hear my voice, *O* [interj.] God, in my prayer; preserve my life *from* [prep.] fear *of* [prep.] the enemy.
2. The thoughts *of* [prep.] the wicked are an abomination to the Lord, *but* [conj.] the words of the pure are pleasant words.
3. *Oh,* [interj.] a clear conscience *and* [conj.] a quiet spirit—these can be received only *at* [prep.] the storehouse of God.
4. Be not wise *in* [prep.] thine own eyes; fear the Lord, *and* [conj.] depart from evil.
5. *Both* [conj.] Demas *and* [conj.] John Mark turned back *to* [prep.] the "beggarly elements of the world," but fortunately Mark returned to the service of God.
6. *Behold,* [interj.] I stand *at* [prep.] the door *and* [conj.] knock; *if* [conj.] any man hear my voice *and* [conj.] open the door, I will come in *to* [prep.] him, *and* [conj.] will sup *with* [prep.] him, and he with me.
7. Many daughters have done virtuously, *but* [conj.] thou excellest them all.
8. *Oh,* [interj.] that the salvation *of* [prep.] Israel were come *out of* [prep.] Zion!
9. *Neither* [conj.] Thomas *nor* [conj.] the other disciples fully understood Jesus *when* [conj.] He said that He was going away.

Exercise B

Make whatever changes are necessary to correct the preposition usage in the following sentences.

1. Try ~~and~~ [to] be at the office ~~at about~~ [or] seven o'clock.
2. All the family ~~accept~~ [except] Mark was at a picnic ~~besides~~ [beside] the river.
3. I divided the apple ~~between~~ [among] my four younger brothers.
4. If you had ~~of~~ considered your financial situation, you would not have made purchases amounting ~~up~~ to so much money.
5. Outside ~~of~~ the door was the tool you could ~~of~~ [have] used.
6. A young man standing ~~besides~~ [beside] the counter wished to know where the next bus was going ~~to~~.
7. ~~At~~ [A] about halfway through the program, Joseph will ~~except~~ [accept] the award.
8. Be sure ~~and~~ [to] divide the reward evenly ~~among~~ [between] Ben and me.
9. ~~Beside~~ [Besides] our taxes, we also had to pay a bill which amounted ~~up~~ to $50.
10. You should ~~of~~ [have] taken your bicycle ~~in~~ [into] the garage before the storm, Eric.
11. The presidential nominee is scheduled to come ~~in~~ [into] the convention hall ~~at about~~ [or] eight o'clock on Friday night.
12. In 1899, the islands of Samoa were divided ~~among~~ [between] Germany and the United States.

UNIT 9

Remember, you cannot tell what part of speech a word is until you determine its *use in a sentence.*

We built a *tree* house in the back yard. (*Tree* is an adjective modifying the noun *house.*)

The men cut down the dead *tree.* (*Tree* is a noun because it names a thing.)

Exercise A

Identify the italicized words. Write *n.* for noun, *pro.* for pronoun, and *adj.* for adjective.

pro. 1. *Either* of these books will supply the information that you need.

adj. 2. *Either* blouse would look good with that skirt, Michelle.

n. 3. Her *dress* looks like what the pilgrims wore.

adj. 4. The *dress* rehearsal will be held Friday night after dinner.

adj. 5. I enjoy the *evening* services on Sunday best of all.

n. 6. In the Scottish moorlands, the fog rises in the *evening* and obscures all visibility.

adj. 7. Please hand a copy of this form to *each* student as he comes in.

pro. 8. *Each* of us made a comment on the poem we had just read.

pro. 9. *One* of the boys asked a question about the meaning of the title.

adj. 10. *One* bird in the hand is worth two in the bush.

Exercise B

Identify the italicized words. Write *adj.* for adjective and *adv.* for adverb.

adv. 1. *Yesterday,* we started reading The Oregon Trail by Francis Parkman.

adv. 2. The fields, woods, and mountains were *colorfully* decorated in the garb of spring.

adj. 3. An *early* frost hurt many of the area's crops.

adv. 4. The barge proceeded *slowly* down the river.

adj. 5. Thomas Edward Lawrence was an Englishman who lived with the *Bedouin* tribes of Arabia.

adj. 6. A *friendly* attitude is one mark of a Christian gentleman.

adj. 7. A *cowardly* Spartan soldier betrayed his comrades to the enemy.

adv. 8. This *unusually* morbid tale was written by Edgar Allan Poe.

adj. 9. Robert Herrick was a *courtly* gentleman who wrote poetry.

adv. 10. His actions were *much* more predictable than his wife's were.

Exercise C Identify the italicized words. Write *prep.* for preposition or *adv.* for adverb.

prep. 1. American settlers crossed *over* the Alleghenies prior to the Revolutionary War.

adv. 2. Dogs can be trained to roll *over* on command.

adv. 3. No one was home, but the water was running and the lights were turned *on.*

prep. 4. Thousands in Hannibal's armies perished *on* the slopes of the Alps.

adv. 5. Several skiers fell *down* and were thus disqualified from the contest.

prep. 6. The skier gracefully made her way *down* the hill.

prep. 7. A new heart also will I give you, and a new spirit will I put *within* you.

adv. 8. Only Christ can cleanse *within.*

prep. 9. When the drawbridge had been raised, the barge passed *through* the opening and into the harbor.

adv. 10. The bridge was lowered after the boat passed *through.*

prep. 11. He that dwelleth in the secret place of the most High shall abide *under* the shadow of the Almighty.

adv. 12. After leaving the harbor, the submarine went *under* and headed due north.

UNIT 9

Exercise D Identify all the words in the following sentences by writing the part of speech above each word. Write *n.* for noun, *pro.* for pronoun, *adj.* for adjective, *v.* for verb, *adv.* for adverb, *prep.* for preposition, *conj.* for conjunction, and *interj.* for interjection.

n. v. adj. adj. n. prep. n. prep. adj.
1. George Washington Carver made an amazing number of products from ordinary
n. prep. n. conj. adj. n.
substances like peanuts and sweet potatoes.

n. adv. v. prep. adj. n. conj. adj. n. v. v. adv.
2. Judson quickly moved out of the doorway so that the girls could go through.

adj. n. v. v. v. adv. prep. n.
3. Everyone's works shall be judged someday by Christ.

n. v. adj. n. adv. conj. pro. v. prep. adj. n.
4. Eric cleaned his room thoroughly before he went to the game.

pro. v. v. pro. conj. v. pro. conj. pro. v. v. prep. pro. prep. adj. adj. n.
5. Ye shall seek me and find me, when ye shall search for me with all your heart.

conj. n. conj. n. v. adv. v. prep. adj. adj. n. prep. adj. n.
6. Neither Michael nor Dan had ever fished from the long pier on the bay.

adj. adj. n. v. v. v. prep. adj. n. conj. n. pro. v. adj. adj. n.
7. "A daily award will be given to each boy or girl who memorizes the most Scripture,"
v. adj. adj. n.
said the camp director.

adj. n. prep. adj. n. prep. adj. n. v. prep. adj. adj. n.
8. The President of the United States, along with his bodyguards, went aboard the aircraft carrier.

conj. pro. v. v. n. adv. v. adj. n. prep. adj. n.
9. Until he was converted, Saul zealously persecuted the members of the Church.

interj. v. adv. pro. adj. adv. adj. n. pro. pro. v. adv. v. v. n.
10. "Oh, aren't these the most beautiful paintings that you have ever seen?" asked Allison,
conj. pro. v. prep. adj. adj. n.
as she walked through the art museum.

Exercise E

In the blanks below the following paragraphs, identify the parts of speech of the italicized words. Use the same abbreviations that you used for Exercise D. Be careful to determine the use of the word before you attempt to identify its part of speech.

Although[1] *it*[2] has *recently*[3] become *incredibly*[4] popular, the game of tennis *is*[5] over five hundred years old. The *French*[6] started playing tennis (then called jeu de paume) *in*[7] the 1200s by hitting a ball back *and*[8] forth *over*[9] a net *with*[10] the palms *of*[11] their *hands*[12]. Major Walter Clopton Wingfield, an *Englishman*[13], *brought*[14] tennis *to*[15] its *present*[16] form in the 1870s. People found it to be a sport that was both challenging *and*[17] *enjoyable*[18]. All over the country *British*[19] folk put down their *croquet*[20] mallets and took up tennis *racquets*[21]. In fact, tennis *has replaced*[22] *croquet*[23] *as*[24] England's most *popular*[25] sport.

One *sunny*[26] afternoon in 1874, *onlookers*[27] *at*[28] the Staten Island Cricket and Baseball Club in New York City *watched*[29] *curiously*[30] as Mary Ewing Outerbridge *used*[31] British-made tennis *equipment*[32] to set up the *first*[33] tennis court *in*[34] America. *Soon*[35] on *both*[36] sides of the *Atlantic*[37] amateur and *professional*[38] tennis *leagues*[39] were organized, *and*[40] *now*[41] more people *play*[42] tennis than ever before.

If[43] the French *dukes*[44] of the 1200s *could see*[45] the expensive clothing and *elaborate*[46] equipment used by millions of tennis players today, they would probably *gasp*[47] and say, "*My!*[48] Did *we*[49] start all *that?*[50]"

1. conj.	11. prep.	21. n.	31. v.	41. adv.
2. pro.	12. n.	22. v.	32. n.	42. v.
3. adv.	13. n.	23. n.	33. adj.	43. conj.
4. adv.	14. v.	24. prep.	34. prep.	44. n.
5. v.	15. prep.	25. adj.	35. adv.	45. v.
6. n.	16. adj.	26. adj.	36. adj.	46. adj.
7. prep.	17. conj.	27. n.	37. n.	47. v.
8. conj.	18. adj.	28. prep.	38. adj.	48. interj.
9. prep.	19. adj.	29. v.	39. n.	49. pro.
10. prep.	20. adj.	30. adv.	40. conj.	50. pro.

Exercise A **Capitalization and Punctuation. (1) Draw a line through each incorrect small letter. Write a capital above it. (2) Add all necessary punctuation.**

1. yes, the teacher of literature 404, dr. d. n. newman, attended oxford university.
2. mr. sanders, our latin teacher, received an illustrated copy of julius caesar's history of the gallic wars for his forty-second birthday.
3. julie, wasn't john f. kennedy, who was born may 29, 1917, the first president born in the twentieth century?
4. according to the u. s. department of agriculture, poultry amounts to one third of american meat consumption.
5. one painting which i especially like is a girl with a broom by rembrandt, a dutch artist.
6. the country of portugal, which shares its land mass with spain, produces one half of the world's supply of cork.

Exercise B **Subjects and Verbs. (1) Draw two lines under each verb. (2) Draw one line under each subject.**

1. In all labour there is profit, but the talk of the lips tendeth only to penury.
2. The stone which the builders refused has become the head of the corner.
3. The drunkard and the glutton shall come to poverty, and drowsiness shall clothe a man with rags.
4. I will sing of the mercies of the Lord for ever.

(You) 5. Cast out the scorner, and contention shall go out.

Exercise C **The Sentence. In the blank before the number, write *s.* for sentences, *frag.* for fragments, or *r.o.* for run-ons.**

frag. 1. Which only someone with a keen mind and trained eye could see.

s. 2. Our Creator would never have made such lovely days, and have given us the deep hearts to enjoy them, above and beyond all thought, unless we were meant to be immortal. —*Hawthorne*

s. 3. The ornament of a house is the friends that frequent it. —*Emerson*

frag. 4. In the North Sea off the coast of the Low Countries.

r.o. 5. There is no substitute for hard work genius is one percent inspiration and ninety-nine percent perspiration. —*Edison*

Exercise D **Using Verbs. Cross out all incorrect verb forms and make the necessary corrections.**

1. I (had) better bring (take) Kathy to her house; I fear that she has took sick (become ill) from whatever she et (ate).
2. Can (May) we learn (teach) you how to do this more easily?

(continued)

Exercise D, cont.

3. We [had] better ~~leave~~ [let] our plans wait until we find that child who has ~~snuck~~ [sneaked] off.
4. Eli did not ~~learn~~ [teach] his boys God's Word; somehow he ~~thunk~~ [thought] they would obey anyway.
5. Hank ~~lay~~ [laid] his hat on the table, ~~drug~~ [dragged] up a chair, and ~~set~~ [sat] down.
6. I'm the first one to arrive, ~~aren't I~~ [am I not]?

Exercise E

Subject and Verb Agreement. Cross out the incorrect verb forms in parentheses.

1. Prayer, thanksgiving, and praise (are, ~~is~~) ways in which we can worship God.
2. Each policy (~~carry~~, carries) a different number of benefits.
3. My closest friend and confidant (is, ~~are~~) leaving for Europe tonight.
4. There (~~is~~, are) many religious people who do not know the Lord.
5. The epistles of Peter (provide, ~~provides~~) the Church with a warning about false teachers.
6. *The Maids of Honor* (~~seem~~, seems) mysterious with its shadows and dark colors.

Exercise F

Using Nouns. Above each italicized word, write its use. Abbreviate as follows: *s.* (subject), *p.n.* (predicate nominative), *d.o.* (direct object), *i.o.* (indirect object), *o.p.* (object of preposition), *ap.* (appositive), and *d.a.* (direct address).

1. *Johann Bach,* [s.] a devout *Christian,* [ap.] was also a famous *composer.* [p.n.]
2. His *brother* [s.] gave *Bach* [i.o.] music *lessons* [d.o.] when *Bach* [s.] was only a young *boy.* [p.n.]
3. He was *organist* [p.n.] of New Church in *Arnstadt* [o.p.] from 1703 to 1707.
4. *Bach* [s.] often incorporated *hymns* [d.o.] into his compositions.
5. Yes, *Betty,* [d.a.] he gave the *world* [i.o.] over 300 choral *works,* [d.o.] or cantatas.
6. Johann Bach praised *God* [d.o.] through his *music.* [o.p.]

Exercise G

Using Pronouns. Cross out the incorrect pronouns in parentheses.

1. Gaius, Diotrephes, and (~~him~~, he) were the men mentioned in III John.
2. (We, ~~Us~~) girls made some clothes for the baby.
3. When Paul was in Jerusalem, he was tried by Felix and (~~he~~, him).
4. They asked Tom and (~~I~~, me) to come to lunch at their house.
5. Father told (~~we~~, us) boys about the new jobs for (~~they~~, them) and (~~we~~, us).

Exercise H

Adjectives and Adverbs. Cross out any incorrect words and make corrections where necessary.

1. Use ~~less~~ [fewer] pickles in your salad than ~~them~~ [those] other cooks did, Katherine.
2. David was ~~more~~ braver than any [other] Israelite in the camp.
3. I ~~sure~~ [surely] feel bad from my fall this morning.
4. The writing on the old letter could~~n't~~ hardly be read.

5. This pudding tastes ~~well,~~ good Mother; in fact, it is the ~~most~~ ~~bestest~~ best one you have ever made.
6. Hoping to please his teacher, the student worked ~~admirable~~ admirably hard.
7. This router is one of the most useful~~est~~ tools in my shop.

Exercise I

Identify the italicized words in the following sentences by writing the part of speech above each word. Write *prep.* for prepositions, *adv.* for adverbs, *conj.* for conjunctions, and *interj.* for interjections.

1. "*Oh,* (interj.) how nice!" exclaimed Mother when she saw what Jackie *and* (conj.) Carrie had made *for* (prep.) her.
2. Mary ran *quickly* (adv.) from the tomb *to* (prep.) the place where the disciples were.
3. Paige loved the people *across* (prep.) the street *although* (conj.) they were *sometimes* (adv.) disagreeable.
4. "Halt! Who goes *there?*" (adv.) the Roman sentry called.
5. *Not only* (conj.) carbohydrates *but also* (conj.) protein is needed *in order that* (conj.) your body may function well.
6. *Behold,* (interj.) I bring you good tidings of great joy which shall be *to* (prep.) all people.
7. *Neither* (conj.) Peter *nor* (conj.) the other disciples *fully* (adv.) comprehended Christ's prophecies of His death.

Exercise J

(1) Put parentheses ( ) around each prepositional phrase. (2) Put brackets [ ] around each adjective or adverb clause.

1. [Until William Harvey made his discovery,] few people [who lived (in Europe)] knew anything (about human blood.)
2. [When he was a small boy,] Moses was educated (in the courts) (of Pharaoh.)
3. Darius could not sleep [while Daniel was still (in the den) (of lions.)]
4. Bishop Latimer walked (to the stake) quietly [because his heart was right (with God.)]
5. Wait (on the Lord;) be (of good courage,) and He shall strengthen thine heart.

Exercise K

Make whatever changes are necessary to correct the preposition usage in the following sentences.

1. If you had ~~of~~ paid your bills on time, they would not amount ~~up~~ to so much now.
2. Jonathan realized that there was a problem ~~among~~ between his father and David.
3. Try ~~and~~ to be here ~~at about~~ or four o'clock, Angela.
4. Take these chairs ~~in~~ into the house, please.
5. Let's go inside ~~of~~ the office; it is there where we will find those papers ~~at.~~
6. The workers could ~~of~~ have come inside ~~of~~ the house for some cool water.
7. If Don had gone outside ~~of~~ the house, he would ~~of~~ have seen the fire engines.
8. Be sure ~~and~~ to ask where your hike will end ~~at~~ before you begin.

Grammar G

Recognizing Simple & Compound Sentences

1 A *clause* is a group of words that contains both a subject and a verb. It is used as a part of a sentence.

2 An *independent clause* expresses a complete thought and can stand alone as a sentence.

3 A *dependent (subordinate) clause* does not express a complete thought and cannot stand alone as a sentence.

4 A *simple sentence* contains one independent clause and no dependent (subordinate) clauses. Both subject and verb may be compound.

5 A *compound sentence* contains two or more independent clauses but no dependent (subordinate) clauses. Compound sentences may be joined by (1) a comma and coordinating conjunction or (2) a semicolon. (*And, but, or, nor,* and *for* are the most commonly used conjunctions; however, any of the coordinating conjunctions listed on page 181 may be used.)

Beauty may die, but it leaves traces behind it. (S V , but S V)

I recognize that car; I once owned it. (S V ; S V)

Why are the following sentences not compound sentences?

Time destroys cities and overthrows empires. (This is a simple sentence with a compound verb. S V and V)

Moses and Elijah appeared on the mount. (This is a simple sentence with a compound subject. S and S V)

Adam and Eve disobeyed God and forfeited paradise. (This is a simple sentence with a compound subject and a compound verb. S and S V and V)

Note: To spot a compound sentence, look for (1) a comma and coordinating conjunction or (2) a semicolon. If the sentence is compound, there will be a subject and a verb to the left of the comma and coordinating conjunction (or semicolon) and a subject and a verb to the right of the comma and coordinating conjunction (or semicolon).

S V , and SV   S V ; SV

Exercise A

(1) Draw one line under each subject and two lines under each verb. (2) Draw a box around the comma and conjunction (or semicolon) that joins the two parts of a compound sentence.

1. Mr. Adams left early, but his wife waited for us.
2. Holiness is not the way to Christ, but Christ is the way to holiness.
3. In the fear of the Lord is strong confidence, and His children shall have a place of refuge.
4. A winner never quits; a quitter never wins.
5. The eyes of the Lord are upon the righteous, and His ears are open unto their cry.

Exercise B

(1) Draw one line under each subject and two lines under each verb. (2) Draw a box around any commas and conjunctions (or semicolons) that join the two parts of compound sentences. (3) In the blank to the left of each sentence, write *S* if it is a simple sentence and *Cd* if it is a compound sentence.

S 1. In the center of the mall was a display of trading cards and other collectibles.

Cd 2. My brother was interested in the baseball cards, but I was attracted to the antique coins.

Cd 3. A soft answer turneth away wrath, but grievous words stir up anger.

S 4. Surely goodness and mercy shall follow me all the days of my life.

S 5. Charity suffereth long and is kind.

Cd 6. A man's heart deviseth his way, but the Lord directeth his steps.

S 7. Judas and Silas exhorted the brethren with many words and confirmed them.

Cd 8. Treasures of wickedness profit nothing, but righteousness delivereth from death.

Cd 9. Sleep is the best form of rest; a good night's sleep will refresh the body and the mind.

S 10. Most doctors recommend eight hours of sleep each night.

Exercise C

(1) Draw one line under each subject and two lines under each verb. (2) Draw a box around any commas and conjunctions (or semicolons) that join the two parts of compound sentences. (3) In the blank at the end of each sentence, write the formula that indicates the type of sentence. The first one has been done for you.

1. Lewis and Clark explored the western regions of our country between 1804 and 1806.
   S and S V = simple
2. He must increase, but I must decrease. SV , but SV = compound
3. Helen Keller overcame severe physical handicaps; she was an inspiration to thousands of handicapped people. SV ; SV = compound
4. The Lord is my strength and song, and He is become my salvation. SV, and SV = compound
5. Daniel Boone of Kentucky and Davy Crockett of Tennessee are two heroes from America's frontier days. S and S V = simple
6. The tongue of the wise useth knowledge aright, but the mouth of fools poureth out foolishness. SV, but SV = compound
7. Franklin D. Roosevelt ran against and defeated Wendell Willkie for the Presidency in 1940. SV and V = simple
8. I will praise Thee, O Lord, among the people; I will sing unto Thee among the nations.
   SV ; SV = compound
9. Emily Dickinson wrote many poems but did not become famous as a poet until after her death. SV but V = simple
10. Truly my soul waiteth upon God; from Him cometh my salvation. SV ; SV = compound

UNIT 10

Grammar

Diagraming Compound Sentences

A compound sentence is diagramed like two simple sentences, the first one placed above the second one. Study carefully the examples below.

Leisure is a beautiful garment, but it will not do for constant wear.

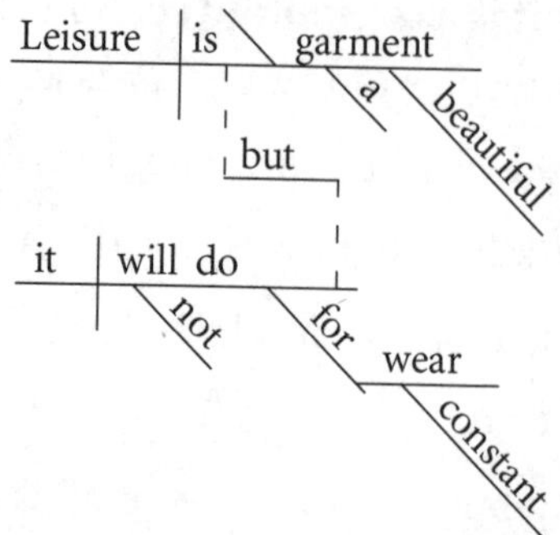

Friends greatly influence our thoughts and our actions; we should choose friends carefully.

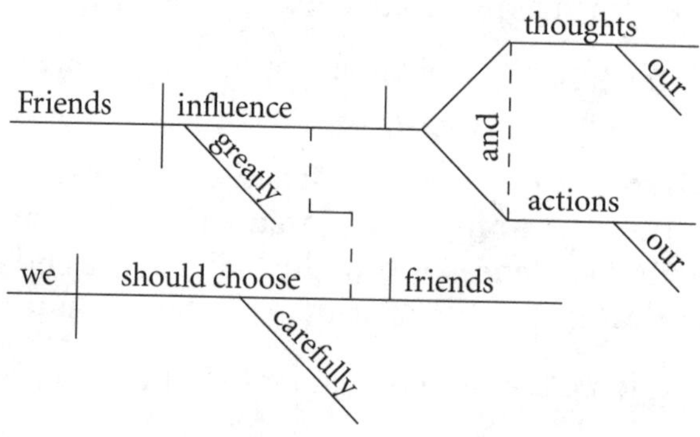

Note: If the sentences are joined by a semicolon, the lines are drawn the same way; but the semicolon is omitted.

Exercise

On a separate sheet of paper, diagram the following sentences. (See *Supplement*.)

1. Jules Verne wrote novels, but he did not write poetry.
2. Schubert was a German composer; Goethe was a German writer.
3. The eyes of the Lord preserve knowledge, and He overthroweth the words of the transgressor.
4. People ask you for criticism, but they only want praise. *—Maugham*
5. Idleness is death; activity is life.
6. Anger may rise momentarily in the heart of a wise man, but it remains in the heart of a fool.
7. Joy missed school yesterday, but she is here today.
8. I read *Little Women* for my last book report, and I may read *Little Men* for my next one.

Grammar

G Recognizing Complex Sentences

1 **A *complex sentence* contains one independent clause and one or more dependent (subordinate) clauses.**

2 **Dependent clauses always have introductory words (sometimes understood) that join them to an independent clause (*who, whom, which, that, whose, after, although, as, as if, because, since, when,* etc.).** (See pages 133 and 161.)

He [that spares the wicked] injures the good. (one independent clause and one dependent clause = complex sentence)

Independent clause = *He injures the good.*

Dependent clause = *that spares the wicked* (modifies *He*)

[When the Lord turned again the captivity of Zion,] we were like them [that dream.] (one independent clause and two dependent clauses = complex sentence)

Independent clause = *we were like them*

Dependent clauses = *When the Lord turned again the captivity of Zion* (modifies *were*) *that dream* (modifies *them*)

Exercise A

All the following sentences are complex sentences. (1) Underline all subjects once and all verbs twice. (2) Put brackets around each dependent clause.

1. The Congo River,[which is Africa's largest river in volume,]flows northward.
2. The Nile River,[which is Africa's longest river,]flows northward also.
3. [If I am faithful to the duties of the present,]God will provide for the future.
4. He[who is good at making excuses]is seldom good for anything else.
5. We would often be sorry[if our wishes were gratified.]
6. [When faithfulness is most difficult,]it is most necessary.
7. Nothing can be truly great[which is not right.]
8. Earth has no sorrow[that heaven cannot heal.]
9. He[that loveth pleasure]shall be a poor man.
10. [Since the wind is so strong,]all planes are grounded for now.

Exercise B

(1) Write one complex sentence containing an adjective clause, introduced by a relative. (2) Write a complex sentence that contains an adverb clause, introduced by a subordinating conjunction.

1. Answers will vary.

2.

UNIT 10

G Diagraming Complex Sentences

Study very carefully the examples given below.

Complex sentences are diagramed by placing the dependent clauses underneath the words that they modify. For adjective clauses, the dotted line goes upward from the relative pronoun or relative adjective to the word that is modified; nothing is written on the dotted line. For adverb clauses, the dotted line goes upward from the verb line of the dependent clause to the word that is modified, and the subordinating conjunction is written on the dotted line.

ADJECTIVE CLAUSE

He *who can suppress a moment's anger* may prevent a day of sorrow.

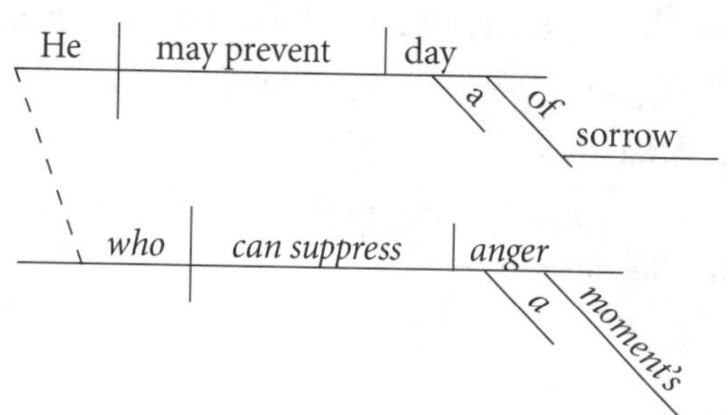

ADVERB CLAUSE

Anyone can hold the helm *when the sea is calm.*

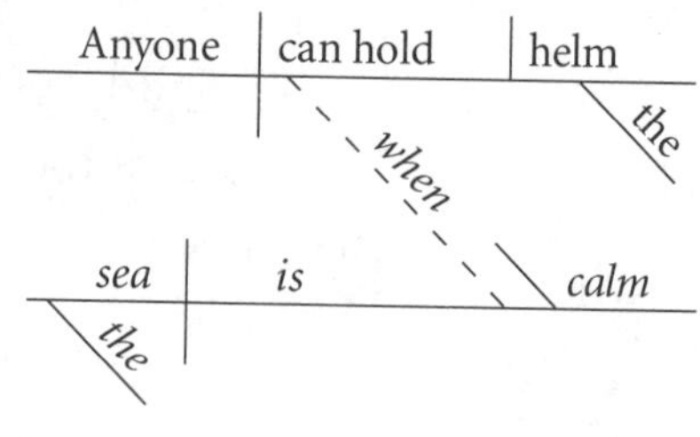

ADJECTIVE AND ADVERB CLAUSE

When we forget ourselves, we do things *that are remembered.*

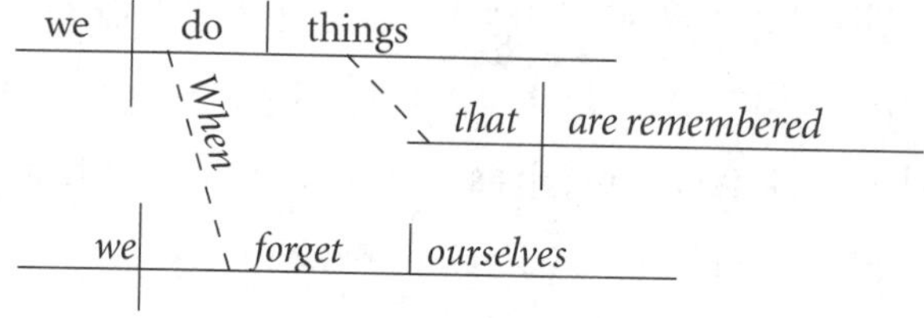

Exercise

On a separate sheet of paper, diagram the following sentences. (See *Supplement.*)

1. Never answer a letter while you are angry.
2. If I regard iniquity in my heart, the Lord will not hear me.
3. They always talk who never think.
4. He that trusteth in his riches shall fall.
5. If a man love Me, he will keep My words.
6. They that sow in tears shall reap in joy.
7. Happy is that people whose God is the Lord.
8. He who would be famous must be a hard worker while he is obscure.

Grammar

Recognizing Compound-Complex Sentences

1 A *compound-complex sentence* contains two or more independent clauses and one or more dependent (subordinate) clauses.

2 Dependent clauses are introduced by *relative pronouns* or by *subordinating conjunctions.*

3 Independent clauses are joined by a *comma and a coordinating conjunction* or by a *semicolon.*

[Before I was afflicted,] I went astray, but now have I kept Thy Word.
(two independent clauses and one dependent clause = compound-complex sentence)

He [that tilleth his land] shall have plenty of bread, but he [that followeth after vain persons] shall have poverty enough. (two independent clauses and two dependent clauses = compound-complex sentence)

Note: It is two or more *independent clauses* that make any sentence *compound.* It is one or more *dependent clauses* that make any sentence *complex.* When you have *both* of the above, you have a compound-complex sentence.

Exercise A

(1) Draw a box around each *comma and coordinating conjunction* (or *semicolon*) that joins independent clauses. (2) Underline every subject once and every verb twice. (3) Put brackets around each *dependent clause.* See the examples above.

1. Friends [that are true] listen with their heart; others listen only with their ears.
2. The wicked flee [when no man pursueth], but the righteous are bold as a lion.
3. The fruit of the righteous is a tree of life, and he [that winneth souls] is wise.
4. [As biologists search for answers,] they should examine a drop of blood, for within the blood lies the secret of life itself.
5. Righteous lips are the delight of kings, and they love him [that speaketh right.]
6. Faith is the root of all good works; a root [that produces nothing] is dead.
7. Sleep is important [because the brain requires sufficient rest]; the brain of a person [who is deprived of sleep] will not function properly.

Exercise B

(1) Write one compound-complex sentence c. (2) Mark your sentence according to the directions for Exercise A.

Answers will vary.

UNIT 10

Diagraming Compound-Complex Sentences

Compound-complex sentences are diagramed by putting the independent clauses underneath each other in the same order as they appear in the sentence. The dependent clauses are placed beneath the word they modify.

Lying lips are an abomination to the Lord, but they that deal truly are His delight.

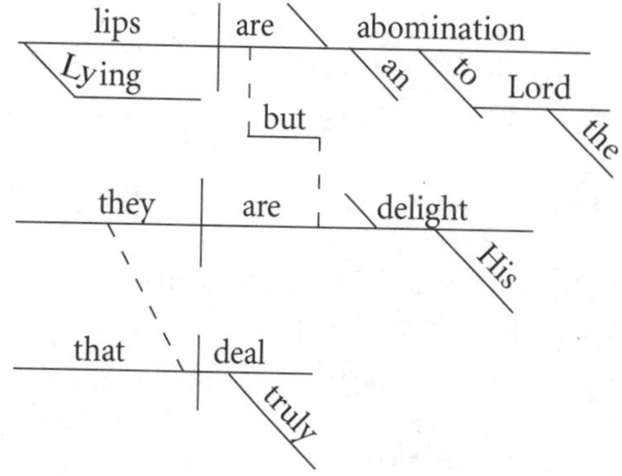

Aaron is younger than I am, but he is taller.

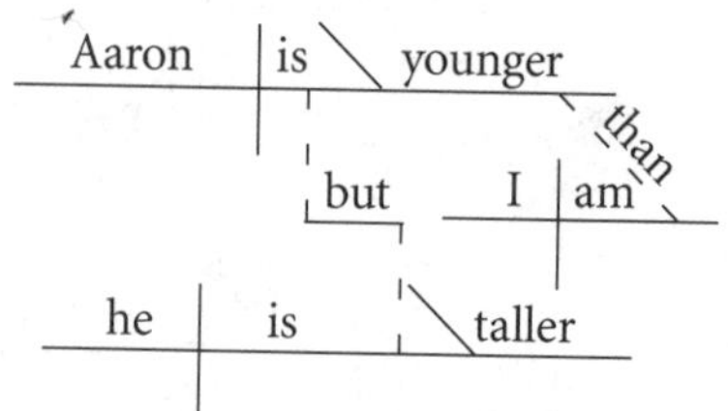

The book in which you can find the answers has been placed on reserve; you can use it when the library is open.

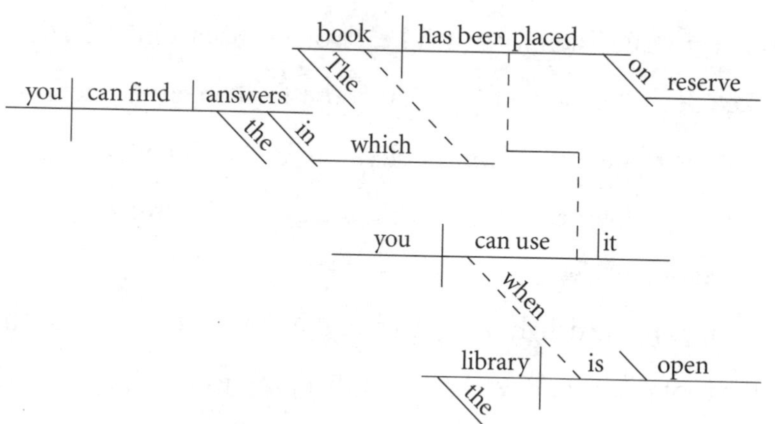

Exercise

Diagram the following sentences on a separate sheet of paper. (See *Supplement*.)

1. The auditorium was empty when the first guests arrived; after a few minutes, the auditorium became full.
2. Everyone that asketh receiveth, and he that seeketh findeth.
3. The crepe myrtles which bloom in Florida in June are lovely, but the spring azaleas are my favorite.
4. Our house was the right size for our family when my father built it, but now we must move to a larger home.

Reviewing Sentence Structure

Exercise A **(1) Draw a box around each *comma and coordinating conjunction* (or *semicolon*) that joins independent clauses. (2) Underline every subject once and every verb twice. (3) Put brackets around each *dependent clause.* (4) In the blank, write the pattern. Use the following abbreviations: *I* (independent), *D* (dependent), *S* (simple), *Cd* (compound), *Cx* (complex), *CdCx* (compound-complex). The first one has been done for you.**

D + I + D + I = CdCx 1. [When you set goals,] you should aim high; [if you do not give up,] you will stand a good chance of success.

I + I = Cd 2. I will bless the Lord at all times; His praise shall continually be in my mouth.

I = S 3. The devil knows his own and is a particularly bad paymaster.

I + D = Cx 4. One [who does not believe in God] does not believe at all.

I + I = Cd 5. (You) Keep thy heart with all diligence, for out of it are the issues of life.

I + D = Cx 6. Mercy and truth shall be to them [that devise good.]

I + I =Cd 7. Nobody ever outgrows Scripture; the book widens and deepens with our years.

I = S 8. Character building begins in our infancy and continues until death.

I + D = Cx 9. The land and climate of a region largely determine the kinds of plants and animals [that are found there.]

I = S 10. We should flee from the friendship of the wicked.

Exercise B **Identify the following sentences. Write *S* (simple), *Cd* (compound), *Cx* (complex), *CdCx* (compound-complex).**

S 1. Obedience is the mother of success and is wedded to safety.

Cx 2. When we lose a friend, we die a little.

Cx 3. He who runs from God in the morning will scarcely find Him the rest of the day.

S 4. In spite of its small size and famous neutrality, Switzerland has an impressive military organization.

CdCx 5. The spectacular Swiss Alps, which include the Matterhorn, cover the southern 50% of Switzerland; the Jura Mountains cover another 10% in the north.

Cd 6. You can hardly make a friend in a year, but you can easily lose one in an hour.

Cx 7. If once will not suffice, do it thrice!

Cx 8. Blessed is the man that walketh not in the counsel of the ungodly.

Cd 9. A faithful witness will not lie, but a false witness will utter lies.

S 10. Only the actions of the just smell sweet and blossom in the dust.

Exercise A Capitalization and Punctuation. (1) Draw a line through each incorrect small letter. Write a capital above it. (2) Add all necessary punctuation.

1. please write to me this summer at 5025 greenbriar road lansing michigan 48917.
2. dr jonas salk developed a vaccine for polio.
3. yes tom my mother did write an article for the readers digest i replied.
4. mr and mrs myron t hathaway rented a summer home near green cove last july.
5. maine pennsylvania and massachusetts are good states to visit during the summer florida, california and hawaii attract many visitors in the winter time.
6. william jenning bryan a statesman from nebraska served as secretary of state during the administration of president woodrow wilson.

Exercise B Subjects and Verbs. (1) Draw two lines under each verb. (2) Draw one line under each subject. (3) Circle any participles.

1. Death and life are in the power of the tongue.
2. Wealth gotten by vanity shall be diminished.
3. A wise man feareth and departeth from evil.
4. A flattering mouth worketh ruin.
5. The desire accomplished is sweet to the soul.

Exercise C The Sentence. In the blank before the number, write *s.* for sentences, *frag.* for fragments, or *r.o.* for run-ons.

frag. 1. The lesson about sentence fragments which creep into careless students' writing.

s. 2. The fashion of this world passeth away.

frag. 3. A star for every state and a state for every star.

r.o. 4. In Judah is God known, His name is great in Israel.

s. 5. The best way out of a difficulty is through it.

Exercise D Using Verbs. Cross out each incorrect verb form in parentheses.

1. (Bring, Take) this love offering to the missionary family so that they (can, may) return to the field.
2. (Leave, Let) me help you (bring, take) that firewood to Mr. Risch.
3. (Can, May) I (teach, learn) you how to embroider, Emily?
4. The boys (threw, throwed) horseshoes, (climbed, clumb) into trees, and (et, ate) watermelon.

5. Ben (isn't, ~~ain't~~) the one who (~~growed~~, grew) these potatoes.
6. We (~~better~~, had better) (~~sit~~, set) these ceramic pots down carefully.
7. We (can, ~~may~~) (~~rise~~, raise) this platform if it is not high enough.
8. The artist (~~drawed~~, drew) a picture of the deserted farmhouse.
9. I (gave, ~~give~~) him a call yesterday to see what he (~~thinked~~, thought).
10. The trapper (~~drug~~, dragged) his furs into the buying agent's office.

Exercise E Subject and Verb Agreement. Cross out each incorrect verb form in parentheses.

1. A hurricane with accompanying smaller storms (is, ~~are~~) sweeping across Florida.
2. Gilbert and Sullivan (~~was~~, were) writers of operettas in the nineteenth century.
3. All of the rugs and the furniture in the hallway (~~was~~, were) destroyed by fire.
4. There (~~goes~~, go) all my chances to be in the school play.
5. Mumps (~~cause~~, causes) swelling in the salivary glands.
6. Neither the orchestra members nor the conductor (has, ~~have~~) ever performed this symphony before.
7. Success in your classes (depends, ~~depend~~) upon your ability to finish the job.

UNIT 10

Exercise F Using Nouns. Above each italicized word write its use. Abbreviate as follows: *s.* (subject), *p.n.* (predicate nominative), *d.o.* (direct object), *i.o.* (indirect object), *o.p.* (object of preposition), *ap.* (appositive), and *d.a.* (direct address).

1. *Charles I* [s.] gave *Lord Baltimore* [i.o.] a *grant* [d.o.] of approximately ten million *acres* [o.p.] in *America* [o.p.].
2. *St. Augustine,* [s.] a Florida *city* [ap.] founded by the Spanish, is the oldest permanent *settlement* [p.n.] in America.
3. On a July *morning* [o.p.] in 1945, the explosion of the first atomic bomb shattered the *stillness* [d.o.] of a Nevada *desert* [o.p.].
4. *Neil Armstrong* [s.] was the first *man* [p.n.] to walk on the moon.
5. No, *Matt,* [d.a.] John Adams was the second *President;* [p.n.] it was not *Thomas Jefferson* [p.n.].
6. Aaron Copland, an American *composer* [ap.] who wrote many famous *pieces* [d.o.] about the West, was born in Brooklyn.
7. The *attack* [s.] on Fort Sumter by Southern *artillery* [o.p.] started the *Civil War* [d.o.].

Exercise G Using Pronouns. Cross out the incorrect pronouns in parentheses.

1. (We, ~~Us~~) boys have learned that practice makes permanent.
2. Several new agreements have been signed between (~~we~~, us) and (~~they~~, them).
3. The baby in this old family photograph is (he, ~~him~~).

(continued)

Exercise G, cont.

4. Melanie distributed the dress patterns to (~~we,~~ us) girls.
5. Between you and (~~I,~~ me), I think that in this election the best choice is (he, ~~him~~).
6. Sixteen of (~~we,~~ us) relatives welcomed (~~they,~~ them) at the airport.
7. If any of (~~them,~~ those) pictures are good, Peter, (we, ~~us~~) twins would like a copy.
8. Is it (they, ~~them~~) or Jared that you need for the photo?

Exercise H

Using Adjectives and Adverbs. Cross out the incorrect words in parentheses.

1. The food at the camp was (better, ~~more good~~) than ever.
2. We had an accident; but none of us were hurt very (~~bad,~~ badly).
3. The roast chicken tasted (good, ~~well~~).
4. Most of the class did (~~good,~~ well) on the last exam.
5. Out of the whole class, Anne did the (~~better,~~ best) job on the exam.
6. The (heavier, ~~heaviest~~) of the two boxes was filled with books.
7. I have not been to (any, ~~none~~) of the meetings.
8. My new record player sounds (~~real,~~ really) (good, ~~well~~).

Exercise I

Identify the italicized words in the following sentences by writing the part of speech above each word. Write *prep.* for prepositions, *adv.* for adverbs, *conj.* for conjunctions, and *interj.* for interjections.

1. She seeketh wool and flax *and* [conj.] worketh *willingly* [adv.] *with* [prep.] her hands.
2. *Both* [conj.] Joy *and* [conj.] Cindy made it *to* [prep.] the bottom safely, but unfortunately Hans fell *down* [adv.].
3. *"Oh,"* [interj.] said Elsa as she walked *into* [prep.] the store, "just look at these beautiful antiques."
4. The school year is *almost* [adv.] over; I cannot believe we are *near* [prep.] the end.
5. He shall cover thee *with* [prep.] His feathers, and *under* [prep.] His wings shalt thou trust: His truth shall be thy shield *and* [conj.] buckler.

Exercise J

Make whatever changes necessary to correct the preposition usage in the following sentences.

1. After Jesus gave thanks, He broke the bread and divided it ~~between~~ [among] the disciples.
2. All the employees of the firm were present at the meeting ~~accept~~ [except] for Hamilton Bernhoft.
3. The cost of the Bible and its case amounted ~~up~~ to $40.00.

4. At ~~about~~ seven o'clock, the race ~~among~~ between Trevor and Tracy will begin.
5. Jesus found money changers inside ~~of~~ the temple.
6. If Jonah had ~~of~~ obeyed God, he wouldn't have spent any time inside ~~of~~ the whale.
7. The meeting will begin at ~~about~~ seven o'clock this evening.
8. He was sitting ~~besides~~ beside me when it was time to get off ~~of~~ the bus.

Exercise K

Identify the following sentences. Write *S* (simple), *Cd* (compound), *Cx* (complex), *CdCx* (compound-complex).

__S__ 1. Great works are performed, not by strength, but by perseverance.

__CdCx__ 2. A man that hath friends must shew himself friendly, and there is a friend that sticketh closer than a brother.

__Cx__ 3. When the wise is instructed, he receiveth knowledge.

__Cd__ 4. Friends help; others pity.

__Cd__ 5. I have never gone to Africa, but I would like to.

__S__ 6. Individuality is the salt of common life.

__Cx__ 7. We would often see beauty if only we would look.

__Cd__ 8. Every wise woman buildeth her house, but the foolish plucketh it down with her hands.

__S__ 9. Honor the Lord with thy substance and with the firstfruits of all thine increase.

__Cx__ 10. If a man's eye is on the Eternal, his intellect will grow.

__Cx__ 11. When the bell rang, the halls became crowded with students who were changing classes.

__CdCx__ 12. A false witness shall not be unpunished, and he that speaketh lies shall perish.

__S__ 13. American cuisine may quite possibly be the most varied food in the world.

__Cd__ 14. Smoked salmon is a delicacy in the Pacific, and Boston clam chowder is a New England favorite.

__Cd__ 15. In Louisiana, they have jambalaya; in Texas they make the country's hottest chili; and Americans everywhere love Southern fried chicken.

UNIT 10

Part 2

Composition

Using Manuscript Form

Follow standard practice in writing or typing manuscripts (compositions).

1 Use appropriate materials.

a. *Paper.* Use white, wide-lined paper. If you type, use $8\frac{1}{2}$ by 11-inch typing paper.

b. *Ink.* Use blue, black, or blue-black ink.

2 Arrange your writing in orderly fashion on the page.

a. *Name, date, and subject.* Follow your school's policy for placing your name, the date, and the subject.

b. *Title.* If your paper has a title, center it on the line indicated by your instructor. Usually it will be placed on the first line. Do not underline the title or put quotation marks around it unless it is the title of a book or a quotation. Do not place a period after the title. Skip a line between the title and the first line of your composition.

c. *Margins.* Leave a margin of about one inch at the top, bottom, and sides of the paper. On the first page, leave two inches at the top.

d. *Indention.* Indent the first lines of paragraphs about an inch in longhand and five spaces in typewritten copy.

e. *Pagination.* Use Arabic numerals to number every page in the body of the paper. In longhand, center the number on the top line; in typewritten copy, center the number six lines from the top edge of the paper. Do not use a period or parentheses with the number.

> **Note:** On every page with a major heading (for example, the first page of the paper and the first page of the bibliography), place the number at the bottom of the page. In longhand, it will be on the bottom line; in typewritten copy, it will be six lines from the bottom edge.

f. *General appearance.* Write legibly. Form each letter distinctly so that it will not be confused with a similar letter. Be sure the capital letters stand out clearly from the lowercase letters. If you make an error, draw one or two neat lines through the entire word, and rewrite the word. If you have numerous corrections, you need to rewrite the entire page.

3 Observe these rules for using abbreviations.

a. Most words should be spelled out, but certain abbreviations are customary.

b. Use the following abbreviations before a name:

Mrs. Mr. Dr.

c. Use the abbreviation *Dr.* before a name, but spell it out when using it without a name.

I visited Dr. Johnson's office when I had the flu.

I visited the doctor's office when I had the flu.

d. Use abbreviations for scholastic degrees after a name. Notice that a comma precedes the abbreviation.

Joanna Vercelli, B.S. Charles Mayo, M.D. Pastor Robert, Ph.D.

e. Use the abbreviations *Jr., Sr., (Junior, Senior)* after a full name (first and last name). Notice that a comma precedes the abbreviation.

Donald Pendley, Jr. Mrs. Todd Jackson, Sr.

f. The titles *Reverend* and *Honorable* may be abbreviated if used with the full name.

Reverend Lewis (correct), but not Rev. Lewis

Rev. John Lewis (correct)

Honorable Davis (correct) but not Hon. Davis

Hon. Andrew N. Davis (correct)

Note: The titles *Reverend* and *Honorable* must be written out if preceded by *the.*

The Rev. John Lewis will be the speaker. (incorrect)

The Reverend John Lewis will be the speaker. (correct)

g. Use the abbreviations A.M. *(before noon),* P.M. *(after noon),* M. *(noon),* A.D. *(in the year of the Lord), and* B.C. *(before Christ)* for time and date designations. Do not use *o'clock* with A.M. or P.M. or with figures, and do not use *in the morning* with A.M. or *in the evening* with P.M. A.D. should precede the year number and B.C. should follow it.

We left Louisville at 9:00 A.M., ate lunch near Bowling Green at 12:00 M., stopped for dinner in Montgomery at 6:00 P.M., and finally arrived in New Orleans about 12:00 A.M. (Noon is written as 12:00 M. and midnight as 12:00 A.M.)

We left Louisville at nine o'clock in the morning.

The fall of Nineveh in 612 B.C. occurred about 1,100 years before the fall of Rome in A.D. 476.

h. Abbreviations for well-known organizations are acceptable.

PTM CIA YWCA FDA IRS

Note: It is now general practice to omit periods for abbreviations of organizations.

i. Do not use & or + for *and.*

4 Observe these rules for writing numbers.

a. In nonscientific writing, spell out all numbers of one or two words.

twenty thirty-seven three thousand fifty-six hundred

b. If you are writing several like numbers, some of them only two words and some more than two, use figures for all.

There were only 12 people in my tour group, but a total of 259 people visited the museum today.

We arrived at the museum at 2:00 P.M. and stayed for three hours.

c. Do not begin a sentence with figures.

2 of the college students lived over 5,500 miles away. (incorrect)

Two of the college students lived over 5,500 miles away. (correct)

d. Write out numbers like *first, sixth, forty-third,* and so on.

first (not 1st) sixth (not 6th) forty-third (not 43rd)

UNIT 11

Using Manuscript Form (cont.)

e. Names of numbered streets under one hundred are preferably written out.

Fourth Avenue   Twenty-sixth Street

Note: Year numbers and numbers referring to parts of a book are written as figures (except at the beginning of a sentence) and do not affect the writing of other numbers in the sentence.

4 B.C.   A.D. 120   page 41   chapter 7   unit 21

In the year 1976, our country celebrated two hundred years of independence.

5 **Divide words properly at the end of a line.** (See the dictionary for help when needed.)

a. Do not divide one-syllable words. *(walked,* not *walk-ed)*

b. Divide only between pronounceable syllables. *(prej-udice,* not *pre-judice)*

c. Do not divide after a single letter. *(against,* not *a-gainst)*

d. Do not carry over a two-letter syllable if it can be avoided. *(empty,* not *emp-ty)*

e. Divide words with prefixes after the prefix. *(post-graduate,* not *postgradu-ate)*

6 **Learn the following correction symbols.**

Symbol	Meaning	Symbol	Meaning
awk	awkward sentence	**ro**	run-on sentence
cap	use capital letter	**sp**	error in spelling
dict	see dictionary	**ss**	error in sentence structure
frag	sentence fragment	**t**	error in tense
gr	error in grammar	**ww**	wrong word
il	illegible writing	**x**	obvious fault
lc	use lower case, no capital	¶	begin new paragraph
ms	error in manuscript form	**No ¶**	run paragraphs together
nc	not clear	∧	something omitted
p	error in punctuation	⁀	join words
R	rewrite page or portion indicated	#	space between words

Exercise

Cross out any errors in manuscript form and make corrections where necessary.

1. The ~~Rev.~~ Reverend Paul Moore will preach in the church service tonight at 7:00 P.M. ~~in the evening.~~
2. ~~10~~ Ten of the Canadian provinces have more than one million people, ~~&~~ and Ontario has more than ten million.
3. Of the over 150 patients that Doctor Smith treated last week, only ~~three~~ 3 of them had the chickenpox.
4. There were ~~3~~ three sets of antique china at the store on the corner of Floyd Street and ~~2nd~~ Second Avenue.
5. By ~~100 A.D.~~ A.D. 100, all ~~66~~ sixty-six books of the Bible had been written.

Reviewing Manuscript Form

Exercise A **Cross out any errors in manuscript form in the following sentences and write the correction above it. Add periods or commas where needed. One sentence is correct.**

1. Before the ~~dr.~~ doctor began surgery, ~~Rev.~~ Reverend Montgomery prayed with the family members in the hospital waiting room.
2. Mr. Eric Anderson,B.A., will show slides to the ~~26~~ twenty-six students in Miss White's biology class.
3. C Did you know that a person who drinks 8 glasses of water each day will consume about 480 glasses of water over the course of two months?
4. The ~~Hon.~~ Honorable John R. Davis was reelected as the judge for our district.
5. For homework last night, Miss Mitchell assigned us to do ~~2~~ two exercises in unit 3.

Exercise B **Cross out the incorrect answer in the following sentences.**

1. (~~50~~, Fifty) miles from Alaska's west coast lies the country of Russia; Russia sold Alaska to the United States in (1867, ~~eighteen sixty-seven~~).
2. Chapter (6, ~~six~~) of our geography book says that the United States bought Alaska from Russia for approximately (~~2~~, two) cents an acre.
3. Alaska is the largest of the (~~50~~, fifty) states; Texas is the (~~2nd~~, second) largest.
4. Since the world was created about (~~B.C. 4,000~~, 4,000 B.C.), the earth is now about six thousand years old.
5. My little sister was born at (10:00 A.M., ~~10:00 A.M. in the morning~~), but we children were not allowed to see her until two hours later at (~~12:00 N.~~, 12:00 M.).

Exercise C **The following expressions are each given in two versions. Suppose that each expression appeared in a sentence. Choose the expression that correctly follows the rules of manuscript form, and write its letter (*A* or *B*) in the space at the left. If neither version is correct, write *N* (for neither) in the blank.**

		A	B
A	1.	my first choice	my 1st choice
B	2.	the Rev. James Cranston	the Reverend James Cranston
A	3.	130	one hundred thirty
N	4.	ten o'clock A.M.	10:00 A.M. in the morning
A	5.	the doctor's diagnosis	the dr.'s diagnosis
B	6.	Samuel Johnson Ph.D.	Samuel Johnson, Ph.D.
A	7.	unit 4	unit Four
B	8.	only twelve of the two hundred fifty five guests	only 12 of the 255 guests
B	9.	412 A.D.	A.D. 412
A	10.	the second one	the 2nd one

UNIT 11

Following the Writing Process

Is the ability to write well a mysterious gift granted by God to only a few, or can everyone learn how to write well? Even the most successful writers will tell you that good writing does not come easily for anyone. It is mainly the result of careful planning and hard work. No one naturally knows how to write well. You must learn how to do it.

Everyone can and should learn how to communicate his ideas clearly and effectively. You can do this by following the basic writing process as practiced by most experienced writers. In brief, the process consists of (1) focusing on a subject and planning what to say about it, (2) writing a first draft, (3) rewriting, and (4) editing.

1 The Writer Plans

The amateur writer often writes a first draft too soon. He gets a vague idea about a subject, gathers a small amount of information, and starts writing. The experienced writer spends a great amount of time ***focusing*** on a subject and ***planning*** what to say. He does not usually write a first draft until he has a good idea of what he wants to do and has an abundance of supporting information from which to choose.

2 The Writer Writes

When the focusing and planning seem complete, the writer writes the first draft. He writes the first draft as rapidly as possible, not allowing anything to interrupt. If he cannot think of the right word or is not sure of the spelling of a word, he does not stop to look it up. If he realizes that he has written a garbled sentence, he does not stop to straighten it out. If he recognizes that he does not have enough information, he does not stop to look for more; he just keeps writing. *In the first draft, the writer's goal is to get his ideas down onto paper*, no matter how clumsy and inadequate the wording may be. Later, he will go back and fill in the gaps in his thinking, straighten out twisted sentences, and find those words that will exactly express his meaning.

3 The Writer Rewrites

Often when the first draft has been completed the inexperienced writer thinks that he is finished, except for proofreading. The experienced writer knows that the writing has just begun. He knows that good writing results from rewriting again and again until the piece finally takes the desired shape. *Rewriting is an essential part of the writer's work.*

How then does a writer rewrite? First he looks at the work as a whole. He asks questions: Does the work have ***unity?*** (Do all the parts contribute to the single idea of the whole, or has some detail slipped in that is interesting but unrelated?) Does the work have ***coherence?*** (Are the ideas carefully distinguished from one another? Are the ideas in good order so that the thought flows smoothly from beginning to end? Are additional transitions needed?) Does the work have the proper ***emphasis?*** (Has each part been developed at a length in proportion to its importance in the composition?) In short, is the composition clear, complete, and effective?

The writer will indicate on the first draft what needs to be inserted, deleted, or rearranged. Sometimes he may have to make an outline of what he has written in order to straighten out the arrangement. The writer will then produce another full draft in order to see the effect of his revisions. He keeps rewriting until he knows that everything is there and in the right order. He then checks the transitions to make sure that all the major parts connect. When the rewriting of the whole is complete, the writer assumes the role of an editor.

4 The Writer Edits

Now the writer goes back and examines everything in the minutest detail. First he checks each ***paragraph*** for unity, coherence, and emphasis (unit 13). Next he checks each ***sentence*** for clarity, correctness, and effectiveness (units 3 and 20). At the same time, he checks the grammar and mechanics. Then he checks the ***phrases*** for accurate figures of speech and correct idioms. He eliminates jargon, triteness, and wordiness. Finally he checks the ***words.*** He checks to see that he has used vivid verbs and concrete nouns, and that his words are appropriate to his audience. He also checks for misspelled words. After all corrections have been made, the writer makes his final copy and proofreads it for mechanical accuracy.

Plan, write, rewrite, edit—these are the things that writers do.

Composition C

Introducing the Paragraph

Written compositions are made up of units of thought called paragraphs. A paragraph is a group of sentences developing one topic. The beginning of a new paragraph is signaled by an indention of the first line.

Some paragraphs are written as self-contained units; that is, they are like miniature essays. They have a beginning, a middle, and an end. The beginning consists of a topic sentence; the middle, a series of sentences developing the topic; and the end, a summarizing sentence.

Most paragraphs, though, are only parts of a larger composition. These paragraphs are essentially the same as the self-contained kind, except that the last sentence, instead of merely summarizing, links the present paragraph to the one that follows.

1 **Topic Sentence. A *topic sentence* is a sentence that states the topic (or main idea) of a paragraph.** Topic sentences are necessary to most kinds of writing and are usually placed at the very beginning of the paragraph. (Some kinds of writing deliberately omit topic sentences and allow the reader to infer the topic from the details in the paragraph.)

2 **Summarizing Sentence. A *summarizing* (or clincher) *sentence* may be used at the end of a paragraph if the paragraph is long or if the paragraph is written as a self-contained unit.** This sentence is essentially a restatement of the topic of the paragraph.

Exercise

(1) Underline the topic sentence in each of the following paragraphs. (2) Two of the paragraphs have a summarizing sentence. Put parentheses around this sentence.

1. The name of Crane was not inapplicable to his person. He was tall, but exceedingly lank, with narrow shoulders, long arms and legs, hands that dangled a mile out of his sleeves, feet that might have served for shovels, and his whole frame most loosely hung together. His head was small and flat at top, with huge ears, large green glassy eyes, and a long snipe nose, so that it looked like a weathercock perched upon his spindle neck to tell which way the wind blew. To see him striding along the profile of a hill on a windy day, with his clothes bagging and fluttering about him, one might have mistaken him for the spirit of famine descending upon the earth, or some scarecrow eloped from a cornfield.

—Washington Irving, *The Legend of Sleepy Hollow*

2. The hand is one of the most wonderful features of the human body. The hand is so unique and so wonderful in its construction and function that it alone marks man as apart and distinct from every other creature. No other creature in the world, not even the ape, is

equipped with an instrument comparable to the human hand. Normal human life without the hand would be inconceivable. . . . Without it our civilization would be impossible. (In everything that man has created, his hands in one way or another have been involved.)

—Alfred M. Rehwinkel, *The Wonders of Creation* (Minneapolis: Bethany House, 1976)

3. That word *imagination* brings me to the chief use of poetry, an even more important one than the re-creation of language. When we are very young, the world, nature, people are mysterious to us. Give a baby an orange. He stares at it, fingers it, dribbles on it, drops it, howls for you to pick it up again. To him, it is a beautiful, round coloured object, with a strange smell, which is heavy to hold and stays put on the floor when he drops it, instead of walking away like a cat. A baby uses all his senses to make such discoveries; he is like an explorer in a new world, full of wonder and surprise at the novelty of everything. In a way, a poet is a man who never grows out of that sense of wonder. (It keeps his imagination constantly on the stretch and quivering at the mysteriousness and beauty of the world; and thus his poetry helps *us* to understand the world by sharpening our own senses, by making us more sensitive to life.)

—C. Day Lewis, *Poetry for You* (New York: Oxford University Press, 1947)

Paragraph Development

3 *Development.* To develop a paragraph, write sentences with details that support the idea of the topic sentence. The following are three ways of developing paragraphs: giving *examples,* telling *incidents,* and giving *reasons.* (More than one of these methods may be used in a paragraph.)

Examples: **The following paragraphs are developed by *examples* that support the topic sentences. Look for the examples used.**

Paragraph • 1

Because Job refused to turn from God when everything seemed against him, God later blessed him abundantly. The Lord blessed Job with twice as much wealth as he had lost, giving him fourteen thousand sheep, six thousand camels, a thousand yoke of oxen, and a thousand donkeys. The Lord gave him seven sons and three daughters to replace those that had been killed. He also restored Job's health and allowed him to live a hundred and forty years in peace and prosperity.

Paragraph • 2

A number of desert creatures employ unusual means of fighting or evading their enemies. If molested, the chuckwalla, or puff-lizard, of Arizona will dart into a rock crevice and there inflate its lungs so that it cannot be pulled out—even if the chuckwalla's enemy pulls its tail off! Kangaroo rats have been observed to protect their burrows against invading rattlesnakes by kicking sand and gravel into the snakes' faces. The trap-door spider of Arizona and California desert areas fashions a kind of waferlike trapdoor over its burrow both for protection and camouflage. Made of layers of earth and spun silk, this trapdoor wedges as tightly as a cork into the spider's bottlenecked hole. It also aids the spider in capturing food; when an unsuspecting insect wanders close by, the trapdoor suddenly flies open and the insect is soon the victim of the spider's fangs.

—David C. Knight, *The First Book of Deserts* (Franklin Watts, Inc., 1964)

Incidents: The following paragraph is developed by telling an *incident* (brief story). Read the paragraph and observe that the story clearly supports the idea in the topic sentence. Answers for Ex. C, p. 219.

Paragraph • 3

And He spake this parable unto certain which trusted in themselves that they were righteous, and despised others: Two men went up into the temple to pray; the one a Pharisee, and the other a publican. The Pharisee stood and prayed thus with himself. . . "God, I thank thee, that I am not as other men are, extortioners, unjust, adulterers, or even as this publican. I fast twice in the week, I give tithes of all that I possess. . ." And the publican, standing afar off, would not lift up so much as his eyes unto heaven, but smote upon his breast, saying, . . . "God be merciful to me a sinner." I tell you, this man went down to his house justified rather than the other: for every one that exalteth himself shall be abased; and he that humbleth himself shall be exalted.

—Luke 18:9–14

Reasons: **The following paragraph is developed by giving *reasons.* How many reasons are given to support the topic?**

Paragraph • 4

The Spanish-American War was important to America for many reasons. First, by defeating the Spanish navy, America gained recognition as one of the leading sea powers of the world. Next, the war helped to build a lasting alliance between America and England, since Spain had long been an enemy of England. In America, the war helped to bolster patriotism because Northerners and Southerners fought side by side, forgetting the prejudices that had divided them. Last, the war stimulated American industry and brought on a surge of prosperity that carried the nation into the next century.

Exercise A

Select one of the following topics and write a paragraph of approximately 100 words using *examples* to support your topic.

1. Christians are commanded to be the salt of the earth.
2. Some animals make very good pets.
3. I enjoy many sports.
4. There are several things that I really like about my school.

UNIT 13

Exercise B

Select one of the following topics and write a paragraph of approximately 100 words using an *incident* to support your topic.

1. A person who has influenced me in a special way
2. A day I will never forget
3. My first trip to an amusement park (or zoo)
4. The worst storm I ever experienced

Exercise C

Select one of the following topics and write a paragraph of approximately 100 words using *reasons* to support your topic.

1. I like chocolate.
2. I think that the ______?______ will win the next Super Bowl (or World Series).
3. ______?______ is my favorite holiday.
4. Exercise is good for you.

Paragraph Unity

4 *Unity.* **A good paragraph has *unity.*** *Unity* means that every sentence in the paragraph develops the idea stated in the topic sentence. Any sentence that does not support the topic sentence should be removed from the paragraph.

> The movement of water from the sea into the air and then back to the sea is called the water cycle. The water cycle is the mechanism which God has designed to water even those portions of the earth located far from the oceans. The Bible described the water cycle long before man understood the process. In Ecclesiastes 1:7, Solomon wrote, "All the rivers run into the sea; yet the sea is not full; unto the place from where the rivers come, thither they return again."
>
> —*Science: Order and Reality* (Pensacola: A Beka Book, 1993)

Exercise **(1) Put parentheses around the topic sentences in each of the following paragraphs. (2) Cross out any sentences that cause the paragraphs to lack unity.**

1. (On the night of April 14, 1912, the British luxury liner *Titanic* sank in the icy Atlantic Ocean, carrying 1,522 men, women, and children to watery graves). The *Titanic* was one of the largest, fastest, and most opulent ships that had ever been built, and because of her construction, the great *Titanic* was supposed to be unsinkable. ~~I heard that it was a very beautiful ship.~~ But on her first voyage, the *Titanic* suddenly came upon a towering iceberg which scraped her side beneath the waterline, gouging a 300-foot hole in the ship. It quickly became evident that the *Titanic* was indeed sinking. Passengers began to flee in lifeboats, but there were not enough lifeboats for everyone, and many passengers could not leave the ship. Those passengers who did escape in lifeboats watched the *Titanic* sink lower and lower into the water. ~~I imagine that was a dramatic sight.~~ Finally, the huge stern pointed straight up, the great vessel broke in half, and in just two and a half hours, the "unsinkable" *Titanic* slipped beneath the waves. Of the more than 2,200 passengers and crew, only about 700 survived.

2. (Of all the weapons used by the ancients none were so effective as the bow in the hands of the English archer.) Every reader is familiar with romances in which the English bow plays an essential part, and of battles in which it decided the victory. It was brought into England by the Normans, who had obtained it from some of the Norse tribes. Its regulation height was that of the bowman, and the arrow was half the length of the bow, or about three feet, and thus obtained the name of the "cloth-yard shaft." ~~Although they also used spears and clubs, most North American Indians fought their wars armed with~~

~~the bow and arrow~~. Some of the tales which are narrated of the skill with which the bow was handled would prove that even the best of the sharpshooters of modern time, with their weapons of precision, are in no respect superior to the experts who twanged the bow of yew in the days of Robin Hood, and his "merrie archers." To hit a branch a half an inch in thickness, set upright at a distance of three hundred feet, was considered a feat of no extraordinary character. As to penetrating power, it was not an uncommon feat for an English archer to drive a shaft clean through a breastplate of steel, and through the body of the knight behind it.

—F. B. Wilkie, *The Great Inventions*

C Paragraph Coherence

Composition

5 *Coherence.* *Coherence* means that your details are in such good order and the relationships between the details are so clear that the resulting paragraph is *easy to understand.* Following are some things that you can do to make your paragraphs coherent.

a. *Arrange your details* in a definite order.

(1) **Chronological (time) order**

(2) **Space order**

(3) **Order of importance**

b. *Use continuity devices* to help your ideas flow smoothly from one sentence to the next.

(1) **Pronoun reference—**Use pronouns to refer to a noun in a preceding sentence.

(2) **Repetition—**Repeat key words and phrases.

(3) **Transitional expressions** (The following are frequently used transitional expressions.)

again	in addition	on the other hand	across from
also	in fact	otherwise	before me
and, but, yet, nor	in other words	similarly	below
as a result	in short	so	beyond
besides	in the place of	still	here
equally important	likewise	then	in the distance
finally	meanwhile	therefore	nearby
first, second, third	moreover	thus	next to
for example	nevertheless	to sum up	opposite to
for instance	next	whereas	to the left
furthermore	on the contrary	above	to the right

Study the techniques used in the following paragraphs.

UNIT 13

Paragraph Coherence (cont.)

Chronological (Time) Order: This arrangement is useful when the writer must give events in the order they happened. It is used to explain the steps in a process and in writing stories and incidents. Answers for Ex. E, p. 219.

Paragraph • 1

The first step in making cinnamon toast is to preheat the oven to 350 degrees. Then, combine $\frac{1}{4}$ cup sugar with $1\frac{1}{2}$ teaspoons of cinnamon and mix them well. Next, put some slices of bread into a toaster or a preheated oven. After the bread is toasted, spread butter over it while it is still warm. Then generously sprinkle the cinnamon-sugar mixture onto the toast and carefully shake off the excess. Next, cut the toast in strips, or into some other shape. Finally, place the toast into a shallow pan and heat it in an oven until the cinnamon mixture blends with the butter.

Space Order: This arrangement is often used for descriptions. The details of the descriptions may be presented from near to far, from far to near, from top to bottom, from right to left, from center to periphery, and so forth. Regardless of the method you use, details must be presented in a way that makes their location clear. Notice the location of the details in the following paragraph.

Paragraph • 2

The green lay at the extremity of the village, and from it the road branched off in two directions, one leading farther up the hill by the church, and the other winding gently down towards the valley. On the side of the green that led towards the church, the broken line of thatched cottages was continued nearly to the churchyard gate; but on the opposite northwestern side there was nothing to obstruct the view of gently swelling meadow and wooded valley, and dark masses of distant hill.

—George Eliot, *Adam Bede*

Order of Importance: This arrangement is common in paragraphs that are developed by reasons or examples. The writer begins with the least important or least dramatic reason or example and progresses to the most important or most dramatic reason or example. The following paragraph progresses from the least dramatic to the most dramatic. Can you identify the first and the last thing that the Egyptians taught us?

Paragraph • 3

The Egyptians have taught us many things. They were excellent farmers. They knew all about irrigation. They built temples which were afterwards copied by the

Greeks and which served as the earliest models for the churches in which we worship nowadays. They invented a calendar which proved such a useful instrument for the purpose of measuring time that it has survived with a few changes until today. But most important of all, the Egyptians learned how to preserve speech for the benefit of future generations.

—Hendrik van Loon, *The Story of Mankind*

Pronoun Reference: Coherence can be maintained by using pronouns to refer to a noun in a preceding sentence, as is done in the following paragraphs.

Paragraph • 4

The **spirit of liberty** is indeed a bold and fearless spirit; but **it** is also a sharp-sighted spirit; **it** is a cautious, sagacious, discriminating, far-seeing intelligence. **It** is jealous of encroachment, jealous of power, jealous of man; **it** demands checks; **it** seeks for guards; **it** insists on securities; **it** entrenches **itself** behind strong defenses, and fortifies **itself** with all possible care against the assaults of ambition and passion; **it** does not trust the amiable weaknesses of human nature, and therefore **it** will not permit power to overstep **its** prescribed limits. . . .

Neither does **it** satisfy **itself** with flashy and temporary resistance to illegal authority. For otherwise; **it** seeks for duration and permanence; **it** looks before and after, and building on the experience of ages which are past, **it** labors diligently for the benefit of ages to come.

—Daniel Webster

UNIT 13

Repetition: Coherence can be maintained by repeating key words and phrases to remind the reader of the central idea of the paragraph.

Paragraph • 5

While **New France** was still in its infancy, a group of **French** farmers settled in the southern portion of the Maritime provinces and called the region **Acadia.** Unlike their countrymen in the north and west, who came to Canada for the wealth of the fur trade and then returned to **France,** the **Acadians** settled down and made America their home. When the British won control of **Acadia** in 1713, they renamed the colony Nova Scotia, permitting the **Acadians** to remain there under British authority. When war broke out between **France** and England in 1755, the **Acadians** were forced to pledge allegiance to the British crown or leave the colony. Most settled in the thirteen American colonies; some moved as far as Louisiana, near the Mississippi River delta, where they became

(continued)

Paragraph Coherence (cont.)

Paragraph 5, cont.

known as Cajuns. After the American War for Independence, a remnant returned to Canada and settled in New Brunswick, where their descendants carry on **Acadian** culture today. The 19th-century American poet Henry Wadsworth Longfellow described the plight of the **French Acadians** in his poem *Evangeline.*

—*World Geography in Christian Perspective* (Pensacola: A Beka Book, 1998)

Transitional Expressions: Coherence can be maintained by using transitional words and phrases (see page 215). These expressions usually occur at the beginning of a sentence, showing the relationships between sentences.

Paragraph • 6

Moreover, brethren, I declare unto you the gospel which I preached unto you, which also ye have received, and wherein ye stand; by which also ye are saved, if ye keep in memory what I preached unto you, unless ye have believed in vain. **For** I delivered unto you **first of all** that which I also received, how that Christ died for our sins according to the scriptures; and that He was buried, and that He rose again the third day according to the scriptures: and that He was seen of Cephas, **then** of the twelve: **after that,** He was seen of above five hundred brethren at once; of whom the greater part remain unto this present, but some are fallen asleep. **After that,** He was seen of James; **then** of all the apostles. **And last of all** He was seen of me also, as of one born out of due time.

—1 Corinthians 15:1–8

Exercise

Select one of the following topics and write a paragraph of approximately 100 words. Make your paragraph coherent by putting the details in a definite order.

1. Describe how to give a dog a bath, putting the details in *chronological order.*
2. Describe your classroom, putting the details in *space order.*
3. Explain why ___?___ is a good place to visit, putting the details in *order of importance.*

Exercise A **Look again at paragraphs 1–2 on pages 210–211. Can you determine the method of development in each one?** 1. examples 2. reasons

Exercise B **In paragraph 3 on page 212, in the incident given to support the topic sentence, there are two nouns that have a number of pronouns (some are possessive) referring to them. Draw a box around these two nouns. Then circle the pronouns. (These pronouns are used to give coherence.)**

Exercise C **List the key words that are repeated in paragraph 4 on page 213 to give the paragraph coherence.** Spanish, America, War

Exercise D **In paragraph 1 on page 216, circle the time order words that you think give the paragraph coherence.**

Exercise E **(1) Select one of the topics below that can be arranged *chronologically.* (2) Think of an *incident* that you can use to develop a paragraph. (3) Write a paragraph of about 150 words, following the steps of the writing process (see Unit 12) and putting into practice all the things you have studied in this unit.**

Suggested Topics

1. A Christmas that I will never forget
2. My most memorable vacation
3. The day I became a Christian
4. The one time I was really afraid
5. The day I went ___?___ with my Dad
6. The first thing I would do if I were President

Using Proper Outline Form

An outline is an orderly list of the main ideas in an oral or written composition. Outlines are often created to record ideas from lectures and sermons, to record thoughts from one's reading, and to guide one's writing.

In this unit, you will learn how to construct two kinds of outlines: *sentence* and *topical.* In a *sentence* outline, the points are stated as sentences; in a *topical* outline, the points are stated as words or phrases.

1 Make the outline according to the following form.

I. First main idea
  A. Subheading—supports first main idea
    1. Detail—supports subheading A
    2. Detail—supports subheading A
  B. Subheading—supports first main idea
II. Second main idea
  A. Subheading—supports second main idea
  B. Subheading—supports second main idea
    1. Detail—supports subheading B
    2. Detail—supports subheading B

2 Observe the following matters of form.

a. Use Roman numerals for main ideas.
b. Use capital letters for subheadings.
c. Use Arabic numerals for supporting details.
d. Place a period after the numerals and letters that introduce the points in the outline.
e. Begin every point in the outline with a capital letter.
f. Do not put periods after the points if the outline is topical.
g. Indent each level of the outline.
h. If there is an *A,* there must also be a *B.* If there is a *1,* there must also be a *2.*
i. In a topical outline, state the points of each division in parallel form. (Use the same kind of word or phrase.)

3 The following illustrates parallelism in a topical outline.

KINDS OF AIRSHIPS

Not Parallel	Parallel
I. Airships of non-rigid design	I. Non-rigid airships
II. Airships that are semi-rigid	II. Semi-rigid airships
III. Some airships have a rigid design.	III. Rigid airships

Exercise **In the space provided, rewrite the following topical outline, correcting all errors in form. Check it by numbers 2 and 3 on page 220.**

I. Non-green plants
   A. Yeasts.
   B. Molds.
   C. Mushrooms.

II. green plants
   A. Simple plants
   1. algae
   2. Mosses are simple plants.
   B. Vascular plants
      1. spore-forming
      2. Seed-forming

I. Non-green plants
   A. Yeasts
   B. Molds
   C. Mushrooms
II. Green plants
   A. Simple plants
      1. Algae
      2. Mosses
   B. Vascular plants
      1. Spore-forming
      2. Seed-forming

C Steps to Preparing an Outline

Composition

1 **Make a list of ideas that support your subject.** List the ideas as they occur to you. Do not be concerned about the order.

2 **Cross out any unnecessary or unrelated ideas.**

Sample List of Ideas

Early History of Airplanes

Wright brothers
Kitty Hawk, North Carolina
December 17, 1903
~~stunt flying~~
Langley
steam-powered engine
gliders
~~balloons~~
~~dirigibles~~
gasoline-powered engine
propellers
air speed
lift
mail service
turns
rudders
Curtiss
Lilienthal
Chanute
transportation
wind tunnel
Cayley
military
~~hydrogen~~

Note: Some items were crossed out because the writer wanted to limit the topic.

Steps to Preparing an Outline (cont.)

3 **Determine the main headings.** Sometimes you will find these main headings in your list of ideas, but you may have to make up some headings.

4 **Group the remaining ideas under the main headings.**

5 **Decide which points will be subheadings and which points will be supporting details.** You may have to add some subheadings.

6 **Arrange the main points and subpoints in some clear order.**

7 **State the points of each division in parallel form.**

- **a.** If the outline is to be a topical outline, make sure that each point is only a word or phrase.
- **b.** If the outline is to be a sentence outline, make sure that all the points are complete sentences.

8 **Write the final copy.**

Sample Topical Outline

Early History of Airplanes

I. Testing unpowered aircraft
   A. Cayley
   B. Chanute
   C. Lilienthal
      1. Lift experiments
      2. Stability research

II. Developing powered aircraft
   A. Langley
   B. Wright brothers
      1. Wind tunnel
      2. Controls
      3. Gasoline-powered engine
      4. Kitty Hawk, North Carolina
      5. Aviation industry
   C. Curtiss

III. Discovering practical uses for aircraft
   A. Mail service
   B. Military
   C. Transportation

Sample Sentence Outline

Early History of Airplanes

I. Man's experiments with unpowered gliders provided valuable groundwork for later flight developments.
   A. Sir George Cayley, working with the science of aerodynamics, developed the fixed-wing form that is still the basis for modern aircraft design.
   B. Otto Lilienthal did systematic testing with lift and control of gliders and shared his progress results with the Wright brothers.
      1. He built his own hill and tested extensively the principle of lift with both gliders and biplane gliders.
      2. He researched the basics of stability and control, using aerodynamic theory.
   C. Octave Chanute experimented with biplane hang gliders and also shared his results with the Wright brothers.

II. Early in the twentieth century, inventors created the first powered aircraft.
   A. Samuel Langley developed a steam-powered engine and flew successful scale models of his airplane, the Aerodrome, with it.
   B. The Wright brothers made the first successful flight in 1903 and continued to develop and test aircraft.
      1. They used a wind tunnel to test different wing and propeller shapes.
      2. They invented controls that enabled them to make stable turns.
      3. The gasoline-powered engine that they used was built from scratch by their own mechanic.
      4. They made their first successful flight at Kitty Hawk, North Carolina, on December 17, 1903.
      5. They continued to improve the airplane and later began a business of building airplanes and training pilots.
   C. Glenn Curtiss competed with the Wright brothers, building a successful airplane industry, and was successful in interesting the Navy in aviation.

III. After flying safely became a recognized reality, the Americans scrambled to develop practical uses for aircraft.
   A. The U.S. Post Office opened the carrying of airmail to private contractors in 1925.
   B. From the beginning, the United States government was interested in aircraft, especially when they were shown to be able to take off and land on ships.
   C. The introduction of the Douglas DC-3 made air travel, now safe and comfortable, a profitable business.

Exercise A

Insert the following sentences in the outline below. Remember to look for key words when grouping the points of the outline.

- The Vice President presides over the Senate and succeeds the President if the need arises.
- Eight associate justices are also on the Supreme Court.
- The executive departments help the President enforce the law.
- The House of Representatives, or the lower house, is the larger of the two houses.
- Other federal courts have been created to assist the Supreme Court.
- The legislative branch, or Congress, holds the power to make laws.
- The President is the chief executive.
- The Supreme Court is the highest court in the land.
- Both houses of Congress must approve a bill before it can become law.

The United States Government

I. The executive branch sees that the laws of the federal government are enforced.
   A. The President is the chief executive.
   B. The Vice President presides over the Senate and succeeds the President if the need arises.
   C. The Cabinet is composed of the heads of the executive departments.
   D. The executive departments help the President enforce the law.

II. The legislative branch, or Congress, holds the power to make laws.
   A. Congress is composed of two houses.
      1. The House of Representatives, or the lower house, is the larger of the two houses.
      2. The Senate, or the upper house, is the smaller of the two houses.
   B. Both houses of Congress must approve a bill before it can become law.

III. The judicial branch interprets the laws passed by Congress.
   A. The Supreme Court is the highest court in the land.
      1. One chief justice presides over the Supreme Court.
      2. Eight associate justices are also on the Supreme Court.
   B. Other federal courts have been created to assist the Supreme Court.

Exercise B **(1) Use the list at the right to make a topical outline in the space provided. The list includes the main points and subpoints. Title the outline *Basic Mathematics.* (2) On a separate sheet of paper, turn the topical outline into a sentence outline.** For an explanation of arithmetic terms, see your dictionary or *Basic Mathematics I* (A Beka Book). (See *Supplement.*)

Basic Mathematics

I. Addition
  A. Addends
  B. Sum
II. Subtraction
  A. Minuend
  B. Subtrahend
  C. Difference
III. Multiplication
  A. Multiplicand
  B. Multiplier
  C. Product
IV. Division
  A. Dividend
  B. Divisor
  C. Quotient

Multiplication
Quotient
Dividend
Addends
Multiplier
Difference
Product
Subtraction
Multiplicand
Minuend
Divisor
Subtrahend
Addition
Sum
Division

UNIT 14

Exercise C **(1) Select one of the subjects listed below. (2) Make a list of ideas to support your subject. (3) Decide what your main points should be and group the other ideas under them. (4) Prepare the outline according to the proper form. Make sure your points are topics, not complete sentences.**

1. My idea of a perfect school
2. How education will benefit me
3. How to be a friend
4. What is good character?
5. The true gentleman
6. How to recognize a Christian

Exercise D **Make a topical outline of the chapter that you are presently studying in science class.**

Getting to Know Your Library

The library contains a wealth of information about almost any subject. To find information quickly and efficiently, get acquainted with the general arrangement of your library. Locate the on-line catalog or card catalog, the reference section, the indexes to periodical literature, and the book stacks, and become familiar with their content and organization.

1 Dewey Decimal System

One of the first things you need to know about your library is how books are organized on the shelves. Many libraries arrange nonfiction books according to the Dewey Decimal System. This system uses a numbering scheme to indicate the subject matter contained in the various books. The Dewey Decimal System divides the fields of knowledge into ten main classes.

000–099	General works (reference materials)
100–199	Philosophy
200–299	Religion
300–399	Social sciences (economics, law, government, etc.)
400–499	Language
500–599	Pure sciences
600–699	Technology (engineering, aviation, inventions, etc.)
700–799	The arts (includes architecture, music, sports)
800–899	Literature
900–999	History (includes geography, travel books, and biography)

Some libraries using the Dewey Decimal System do not classify books of fiction. Instead, they label these books *F* or *Fic* and place them in a separate section. In this "fiction section" the books are arranged alphabetically by authors' last names. If there is more than one book by the same author, all of those books will be shelved together and alphabetized according to the first word in each title, excluding *a, an,* and *the.*

2 Library of Congress Classification System

Some libraries, especially college libraries and large public ones, use the Library of Congress Classification System. This system uses letters of the alphabet and arabic numerals to provide millions of classification possibilities. A classification number may range in length from a single letter and numeral (such as T1) to two letters, four numerals, one decimal number, and a decimal letter and number combination (such as TH9745.5.F3U6). The Library of Congress Classification System uses the following main classes, identified by a single letter:

A	General works (reference materials)
B	Philosophy; Psychology; Religion
C	Auxiliary Sciences of History (e.g. Archaeology, Biography, etc.)
D	History: General and Old World (Eastern Hemisphere)
E–F	History: America (Western Hemisphere)

G	Geography; Maps; Anthropology; Recreation
H	Social Sciences
J	Political Science
K	Law
L	Education
M	Music
N	Fine Arts
P	Languages and Literature
Q	Science
R	Medicine
S	Agriculture
T	Technology
U	Military Science
V	Naval Science
Z	Bibliography; Library Science

Exercise **Visit your school's library or your city's public library to become familiar with how books are arranged.**

1. Are books arranged by the Dewey Decimal or Library of Congress System?
2. Locate the reference section. You will use this section to complete this chapter.
3. Determine the location of the history and science books. These are the books you will use often in writing reports or research papers.
4. Where are the fiction books located? How are they classified?
5. How are biographies classified? Are they located in a separate section?
6. Does the library use a card catalog or on-line (computer) catalog to index books?

UNIT 15

Composition

C: Using the Catalog

Every library keeps an index or catalog of its holdings to help you locate books on the library shelves. Some libraries store this index on a computer system called an on-line catalog, and some store it on cards in a number of drawers called a card catalog. Both catalogs provide information by author, title, and subject for every book in the library.

The easiest way to find books on your topic is by subject. If you are using a computer, enter the subject to obtain a list of possible sources. If you are using a card catalog, locate the drawer that contains cards on your subject. Each computer entry or card will contain the following information about the book:

1 Author

If a book has more than one author, the other authors will also be listed.

2 Title

Books are indexed alphabetically according to the first word in the title, except for *a, an,* or *the.*

3 Subject

Subject listings are determined by a main word or other key word from your subject. For example, if your subject is "The Presidency of Abraham Lincoln," you would not look for books under the word *the.* Books on this subject would be cataloged under *Abraham Lincoln* or possibly *presidency.*

Some subject cards and computer entries have "see" or "see also" references which list related subject headings in the catalog to which you may refer.

4 Call number

Each book has a classification number (Dewey Decimal or Library of Congress) that helps you find the location of the book on the shelves.

5 Publication date

The date of publication may be important for you to note. For example, a book on Eastern Europe before 1990 would now be obsolete except for historical purposes.

6 Number of pages

The number of pages may indicate the value of a particular book to your research. A book on the Civil War containing only fifty pages might be too limited in its scope.

Exercise

Using the catalog, locate one source for each subject, author, and title listed below. Write down the title, author, classification number, publication date, and number of pages for the book you choose.

Subjects:
1. Engineering
2. the Great Lakes

Authors:
3. C. S. Lewis
4. Daniel Defoe

Titles:
5. *The Adventures of Tom Sawyer*
6. *Pilgrim's Progress*

Using the Reference Section

Your library also has a special room or section where reference works are kept. Reference books are in such great demand that they must be accessible at all times; therefore, they cannot be removed from the reference section.

The reference section is usually the starting point for your research projects. It is there that you can get an overall view of the topic you have selected and can make a list of books (bibliography) that deal with your subject.

Reference books include such works as *encyclopedias, dictionaries, biographical works, atlases, almanacs, books of quotations,* and *yearbooks.* Many reference works are also available on CD-ROM. Get acquainted with the various reference works available in your library.

1 Encyclopedias

Encyclopedias contain summary articles on a wide range of subjects. Sometimes an outline and a bibliography are included with the articles. Therefore, it is usually best to begin any research by consulting an encyclopedia. Following is a list of well-known encyclopedias:

Encyclopaedia Britannica
Encyclopedia Americana
Collier's Encyclopedia
World Book Encyclopedia

2 Dictionaries

Dictionaries contain an alphabetical listing of words in a language, with definitions, pronunciations, etymology, usage labels, and other helpful information. A good dictionary will give guidance concerning the usage of words. Look for usage labels and usage notes to help you determine whether and when a word is correct to use. Some dictionaries, though useful for definitions and general aids, are of no help concerning good usage. *Webster's Third New International Dictionary, Merriam Webster's Collegiate Dictionary* (previously titled *Webster's New Collegiate Dictionary*), and *The Random House Dictionary,* Second Edition Unabridged, fit this category. At this time, the following dictionaries do give guidance concerning usage.

The American Heritage Dictionary of the English Language
Oxford American Dictionary
The Random House College Dictionary
The Random House Dictionary, First Edition Unabridged
Webster's New International Dictionary, Second Edition Unabridged
Webster's New World Dictionary of the American Language

3 Special Dictionaries

When you are searching for an exact word to express your thoughts, refer to *The Synonym Finder* by J. I. Rodale and to *Webster's New Dictionary of Synonyms.* For geographical information, *Webster's New Geographical Dictionary* is a good source. It contains more than 47,000 entries on ancient and modern place names with geographical and historical information. For biographical information, try *Webster's New Biographical Dictionary.* It has concise information about famous persons from the past and present. For more detailed information about the correct usage of words see the following:

The Careful Writer by Theodore M. Bernstein
A Dictionary of the American-English Usage by Margaret Nicholson
A Dictionary of Modern English Usage by H. W. Fowler
Harper Dictionary of Contemporary Usage by William and Mary Morris
Modern American Usage by Wilson Follett

4 Atlases

An atlas is a reference book made up primarily of maps; but it also contains tables, charts, and illustrations that give much additional information about such things as population, principal crops, natural resources, and major industries. Following is a list of useful atlases:

Gold Medallion World Atlas
The Harper Atlas of the Bible
National Geographic Atlas of the World
Rand McNally *Cosmopolitan World Atlas*
Reader's Digest *Atlas of the World*

5 Handbooks of Miscellaneous Information

An almanac is an annual publication that contains an amazing amount of miscellaneous information including census figures; ZIP code listings; election results; information about government, sports, and the arts; advancements in industry, technology, and education; and hundreds of other topics. Since the information in an almanac is not printed in any logical order, you will need to use the index. The two most widely used almanacs are *The World Almanac* and the *Information Please Almanac*. Two other interesting and helpful handbooks of miscellaneous information are *Famous First Facts* by Joseph N. Kane and the *New Century Cyclopedia of Names*.

6 The *Reader's Guide to Periodical Literature*

Frequently, when doing research, you will need to locate the most recent thinking or the most recent developments concerning your subject. You then must turn to the various periodical indexes which serve the same purpose for magazines that the on-line catalog or card catalog does for books. These periodical indexes tell you in which magazines you may locate articles, stories, essays, speeches, and poems that pertain to your subject. Some libraries have a periodical index on-line. If not, most contain a collection of volumes called the *Reader's Guide to Periodical Literature,* a good general index updated once a month. The *Reader's Guide* indexes articles in 180 magazines. The information is indexed by author and by subject. Stories are the only entries indexed by title. In the front of each issue is a listing of the magazines that are indexed and a listing of the abbreviations used in the entries. Study the following excerpt from the *Reader's Guide.*

Sample Reader's Guide Entries

BARTER — Subject entry

Russia (Federation) — Division of subject

Rubles? Who needs rubles? P. Kranz. il *Business Week* no3573 p45–6 Ap 13'98 — Name of author

BARTHELME, PETER — Author entry

Goodbye to all that. por *Newsweek* v131 no15 p16 Ap 13 '98 — Title of magazine

BARTHOLOMEW, ANITA

Herbs that heal. il *Reader's Digest* v151 no908 p152–6 D '97 — Title of article

BARTLESVILLE (OKLA.)

Stores

See also — Cross reference

Keepsake Candles Factory and Country Store

BARTLETT, BRUCE R., 1951–

Tax reform [address, January 28, 1998] *Vital Speeches of the Day* v64 no12 p374–7 Ap 1 '98

BARTLEY, ROBERT L.

The great betrayal [cover story] il pors *National Review* v50 no7 p41–3 Ap 20 '98 — Description of article; Date of magazine

BARTON, BARBARA, D. 1995

about

Barbara's choice. B. Smith. il *Reader's Digest* v151 no908 p143–8 '97 — Volume number; Page numbers

UNIT 15

Using the Reference Section

Exercise A **(1) In an encyclopedia, look up the bibliography (list of books on a subject) for any two of the following subjects. In some encyclopedias the bibliography appears with the article. In others the bibliography is listed in a separate volume. (2) Copy three of the bibliographical entries for each of the subjects you select. Include the author, title, publisher, and publication date.** Answers will vary.

1. Light — ______
2. The War of 1812 — ______
3. Canada's government — ______
4. Franklin, Benjamin — ______
5. Skiing — ______

Exercise B **Using *Roget's International Thesaurus* or *Webster's New Dictionary of Synonyms*, look up the word *examine* and copy three synonyms listed for the word.**

Answers will vary.

______

Exercise C **Use a Bible dictionary and a concordance to complete the following exercise.**

1. What is the definition of *showbread?* Answers will vary.
2. Find the reference of the following: "Behold the Lamb of God, which taketh away the sin of the world." John 1:29
3. List three verses that contain the word *forgiveness.* Answers will vary.
4. Who was the mother of Levi? Leah
5. Finish this verse: For bodily exercise profiteth little: but godliness is profitable unto all things, having promise of the life that now is, and of that which is to come.
(reference 1 Timothy 4:8)

Exercise D **Look up William Jennings Bryan in a biographical reference book. (1) Who was he? (2) How many times was he nominated to run for the U.S. Presidency?**

He was a famous American lawyer and politician. He was nominated to run for the Presidency three times.

Exercise E Using an almanac or an atlas, answer the following questions.

1. What country is west of Egypt? Libya
2. Which U.S. state is largest in population? California
3. What is the address of the U.S. Department of Defense? The Pentagon, Washington, D.C. 20301
4. How long is the Nile River? 4,145 miles or 6,671 kilometers
5. When is President's Day celebrated each year? third Monday in February
6. Who won the 1988 Olympic gold medal in the women's long jump competition? Jackie Joyner-Kersee (United States)
7. What is the capital of Chile? Santiago

Exercise F Using Bartlett's *Familiar Quotations* or Evans's *Dictionary of Quotations*, look up the name of the author who wrote these words: "To be prepared for war is one of the most effectual means of preserving peace."

George Washington

Exercise G Using the *Readers' Guide to Periodical Literature*, find a magazine article for each of the following: (1) Heart Disease (2) the United Nations (3) Tennis. Copy the entire entry, translating the abbreviations into words and identifying the various parts of the entry.

UNIT 15

Writing Summaries

1 A summary is a brief composition that states the main ideas of a longer piece of writing.

2 A summary should be no longer than one third the length of the original.

3 Summaries differ according to their purpose and the type of writing being summarized. Summarize a nonfiction selection according to the following steps:

a. **Read the selection.**
   - Skim the selection rapidly, noticing the main ideas, divisions, and any terms in bold type or italics.
   - Read the entire selection carefully.

b. **Go through the selection again, jotting down the main ideas and important details.**
   - The first and last sentences of each paragraph are usually topic sentences or summarizing sentences.
   - The last paragraph often lists all the main points contained in the preceding paragraphs.
   - Key words or phrases (such as *a primary cause* or *another major reason*) can point you to the main ideas.
   - Omit all examples, illustrations, and minor details.
   - Make sure your ideas are in the same order as in the original selection and that you have not added any ideas of your own.

c. **Write the summary *in your own words.***
   - Put the original selection out of sight.
   - Referring to your list of ideas, write the summary *in your own words.*
   - Do not begin by saying "*This article was about* the theory of evolution." Write as if you are the author of the original article: "The theory of evolution has never been. . . ."

d. **Proofread your summary.**
   - Did you include all the main ideas?
   - Did you omit all examples, illustrations, and minor details?
   - Are your ideas in the same order as the original?
   - Did you write it in your own words?
   - Are there any grammatical or mechanical errors?

4 In a work of fiction, you will not find topic sentences or summarizing sentences as you do in nonfiction. Look instead for the major characters, conflicts, and events in the story.

Exercise A **(1) Read the original selection that follows. (2) Proofread the two summaries according to the points listed under *3.d* on p. 234. Decide which summary is better. List specific reasons why you chose one over the other.** Summary 1 is better. Summary 2 violates all five points listed under 3.d.

Original Selection

Not all ants earn a living by raiding picnics; some ants are "farmers." These peculiar insects do not get food by attacking other animals, but they grow their own food much like a farmer in Kansas or Idaho might. The only difference is that the ants' farms are underground, and their livestock can fit on the end of a finger.

Some ants farm by mistake. Harvester ants collect seeds from nearby plants, separate the kernels from the husks, and toss the husks outside their nests. Sometimes, however, seeds are accidentally thrown out with the husks and sprout into small green plants. The "gardens" beside the harvester ants' nest were never meant to be there.

Other ants carefully tend to their gardens. The leafcutter ant spends most of its time chewing up leaves into a mushy substance which makes a good fertilizer for growing small, underground mushrooms. The mushrooms are eaten by adult and baby ants.

A few ants are "dairy farmers"; their "cows" are beetles, aphids, and caterpillars. The ant "milks" these insects by stroking them with its antennae, causing them to secrete a syrupy substance called "honeydew." In exchange for their "milk," the "cows" are given food and shelter.

God has given ants many different abilities for providing their own food. The farmer ants are but one of the wonders of God's creation. Surely "the firmament showeth His handiwork."

Summary 1

Some ants get their food, not by attacking other animals, but by farming. The harvester ant collects seeds and grows a garden with seeds it accidentally throws away. The leafcutter ant grows mushrooms in a carefully tended garden, fertilized with chewed-up leaves. Some ants use other insects as "cows" to get a syrupy substance called "honeydew." These farmer ants are three examples of the wonders of God's creation.

Summary 2

Not all ants earn a living by raiding picnics; some ants are "farmers." They do just as good a job as a farmer in Kansas or Idaho. Some ants farm by mistake. This is the harvester ant some ants are "dairy farmers" with livestock you can fit on the end of your finger. Some grow mushrooms. It ain't all ants that get food by attacking other animals.

UNIT 16

Exercise B **Write a summary of the following selection. Your summary should be 85 words or less.**

America's desire to be biggest and best in everything has resulted in some very impressive structures. Perhaps the most unusual example is the 630-foot Gateway Arch in St. Louis, Missouri, the largest arch on earth. The stainless steel arch contains an elevator that allows visitors to view St. Louis and the Mississippi River as they have never viewed it before.

Visitors to Chicago can enjoy a unique view of the windy city from the Sears Tower, one of the world's tallest buildings. It surpasses such other notable buildings as the Empire State Building and the World Trade Center in New York. The aluminum-and-glass Sears Tower is 1,454 feet tall. It is an office building that is a dramatic part of Chicago's skyline.

If laid on its side, the Sears Tower would not be half as long as the enormous Verrazano-Narrows Bridge, which measures an incredible 4,260 feet from end to end. Sixty feet longer than the Golden Gate, it is the longest suspension bridge in the world. Strong, slender cables, draped from the two 700-foot towers like a delicate spider web, support a double-decker roadway that connects Staten Island to Brooklyn, New York. It is one of the most beautiful bridges in the world.

It has been said that "What the mind can conceive, the man can achieve." These three structures certainly show what man can do with the mind God has given him. They are all impressive; they are all "made in U.S.A."

Answers will vary. The following sample has been provided:

America's impressive building structures show her desire to be bigger and better than others. The Gateway Arch in Missouri, the largest in the world, provides a spectacular view to visitors who take its elevator ride. The Sears Tower highlights the Chicago skyline and is taller than even New York's skyscrapers. New York's Verrazano-Narrows Bridge is the longest suspension bridge on earth. These wonders "made in U.S.A." show what man can produce with his God-given mind.

Exercise C Summarize the following selection in 65 words or less.

Representatives in the United States Congress generally hold one of two views of representation. Some representatives see their position as that of a *trustee.* In the trustee position, the representative votes according to his personal judgment rather than the views of his constituency. The trustee views his position as one of making the best judgment based upon the information that he has been given. He votes his conscience.

Some representatives take an opposite view and see their position as that of the *delegate.* In the delegate position, the representative votes according to the desires of his constituency rather than his personal judgment. The delegate believes that he must, as closely as possible, represent what the majority of his constituency wants. He votes the will of the people.

However, no representative acts solely as a trustee or a delegate. Those who see themselves mostly as trustees do occasionally vote with the opinion of their constituency while those who see themselves as delegates sometimes vote their conscience. For example, a member of Congress may vote the way his constituency wants on an education bill but may vote his conscience on an issue such as abortion or gun control.

Answers will vary. The following sample has been provided:

United States congressmen usually view their position in one of two ways. Some consider themselves trustees and vote their conscience. Others consider themselves delegates and vote according to the will of their constituency. But none vote strictly one way or the other. Sometimes the way a congressman votes will depend on the issue.

UNIT 16

Exercise D Write a summary of a factual article from a newspaper. The original should be approximately 300 words long. The summary should be one third the length of the original. Clip the article to your summary.

Preparing Written Book Reports

The written book report has three parts: the *introduction*, the *body*, and the *conclusion*. The total length of a written report should be *1 ½ to 2 pages.*

1 The Introduction:

a. **Introduce the title, the author, and the subject or theme of the book in the first sentence.**

> ***Example:*** *Little Women by Louisa May Alcott recounts the girlhood experiences of Jo March and her three sisters.*

b. **Get your readers interested in what you are going to say—perhaps with a striking statement, a quotation, or some background information.** If the book has a setting (time and place), you might include it.

> ***Example:*** *Set in New England around the time of the Civil War, this classic novel provides a glimpse of daily life in a nineteenth-century American household. Though fictional, it reads like a true story because the main characters are fashioned after the author's own family. The character Jo March resembles Louisa herself.*

c. **Close your introductory paragraph with a statement of opinion. Choose one aspect of the book—a moral, a concept, or a principle—that made an impression on you.** Ask yourself, "What did I learn from this book? Would others benefit from it, and if so, how?" You will discuss this statement in the body of your report.

> ***Example:*** *Through the experiences of the March sisters, one can learn to appreciate the family that God has given him.*

2 The Body:

a. **Begin with a short, concise summary (synopsis) of the book, including only the main points or key events. Limit this synopsis to several sentences.**

- **For a fiction book, write a summary of the plot.**

  The plot is the sequence of actions which make up a story. The plot begins with a conflict involving main characters. Sometimes the conflict involves two people. Other times the conflict involves the main character and a variety of people and circumstances. In some stories, conflict may be at work within the main character.

  > ***Example:*** *In the story Little Women, each of the March sisters faces her own conflict with self as she tries to "be good."*

  After you have stated the conflict, recount the events that develop the conflict to the point at which one of the opposing forces is about to prevail over the other. This is called the climax. Following the climax, relate the events that resolve the conflict.

- **For a biography, relate the chief incidents in the subject's life.**
- **For a nonfiction book, write a summary as described in Unit 16.**

b. **In succeeding paragraphs of the body, use incidents, details, and quotations that support the opinion you stated in the introduction. Prove your point.**

Example: *In the opening scene, the March sisters are bemoaning their poverty when Beth gently reminds them how rich they really are: "We've got father and mother and each other." Though lacking in material comforts, the girls gradually learn to appreciate the treasure they have in a loving home. Mother's gentle words and Father's letters from the battlefront remind them of the things that matter in life: relationships, kind words and loving deeds, personal growth and maturity. Meg learns about the emptiness of material wealth when she visits Annie Moffat and tries to fit in with her frivolous and worldly friends. Jo learns to forgive when Amy burns her precious book. Beth teaches them all about selfless giving when she reaches out to help a poor widow and her children and is stricken with a deadly fever. As each girl struggles with her personal weaknesses, she learns to appreciate more fully the family that God has given her and the values they share.*

3 The Conclusion:

a. **Begin the conclusion with a restatement of your opinion. (Avoid the temptation to use the same wording that you used in your introduction.)**

Example: *Of the many lessons to be learned from Little Women, the importance of family relationships is one that no reader should miss. Everyone can learn to appreciate his siblings and parents from the example set by the March sisters.*

b. **Give your thoughts about the book, whether they are favorable or unfavorable.**

Example: *I enjoyed Louisa May Alcott's honest portrayal of family life. Like any ordinary family, the Marches had disagreements and quarrels from time to time, but they remained a close-knit, loving family because they recognized and practiced Scriptural principles of family life: the girls honored their parents, loved each other, and sought to live peaceably together.*

You may comment on the realism of the characters, the charm of the setting, the effectiveness of the imagery, the aptness of the dialogue, or the naturalness of the action. As a Christian, you must also think about the content. How are evil actions presented? Is evil shown in a way that disgusts the reader? Or is it made attractive to the reader? Are the consequences of evil actions shown to be what the Bible says they will be? In this life, good does not always appear to triumph over evil, but the overall import of a book should not make it seem that God's purposes are being overthrown.

In the body of your report, emphasize the moral, the concept, or the principle that impressed you. In the conclusion, evaluate the book according to the criteria above.

Composition

C

Giving Oral Book Reports

1 **The oral book report has two parts: the *written preparation* and the *oral presentation.***

a. **Written Preparation** (50 points)

This preparation should be made as explained on pages 238–239 with one major difference: the *body* should be written in topical outline form.

(1) ***Introduction*** (10 points)
- Write this word for word as you will say it in your oral presentation.
- Attempt to capture the attention of your audience with a striking statement.
- Close your introduction with a statement of opinion about an aspect of the book that you wish to discuss.

(2) ***Body*** (25 points)
- Write this in topical outline form (see page 222).
- Give a summary (synopsis) of the book under your first main point; then discuss your opinion under subsequent points in the outline.

(3) ***Conclusion*** (15 points)
- Write this word for word as you will say it in your oral presentation.
- Begin with a restatement of your opinion.
- End with a brief evaluation of the book, indicating whether you recommend it and why.

Note: The total length of your report should be *1 1/2 to 2 pages.*

b. **Oral Presentation** (50 points)

(1) The time limit is 2 to 3 minutes with a margin of 15 seconds.

(2) You will receive points for the following:
- Posture (10 points)
- Eye contact (10 points)
- Enthusiasm, smoothness, and expression (20 points)
- Poise—going to and from the front of the room (5 points)
- Gestures and mannerisms—not distracting (5 points)

2 **Follow this procedure in preparing an oral book report.**

a. Write the first draft of your oral report.

b. Revise your report.

c. Write your final draft.

d. Make reminder cards (one card for each main point in your outline).

e. Memorize your introduction and conclusion.

f. Practice your report aloud several times. Keep practicing until you can give it smoothly within the time limit.

Study the following example of written preparation for an oral book report.

"Marley was dead: to begin with." This cold, abrupt introduction hardly sounds like the beginning of a heartwarming Christmas story, but anyone who has read A Christmas Carol, by Charles Dickens, knows that the main character, Scrooge, is not a warmhearted creature. This unusual Christmas story set in 19th-century London describes the transformation of a miser named Ebenezer Scrooge from a "covetous old sinner" to a kind, generous benefactor. The moral of A Christmas Carol is as appropriate today as it was one hundred and fifty years ago when Dickens wrote the novel: money is a poor substitute for the love of family and friends.

I. The Plot
  - A. Scrooge, the miser
  - B. Marley's ghost
  - C. The Ghost of Christmas Past
  - D. The Ghost of Christmas Present
  - E. The Ghost of Christmas Yet to Come
  - F. Scrooge, the reformed

II. The Moral
  - A. Scrooge's love of money
    1. His response to the charity collector
    2. His farewell to Belle
  - B. Scrooge's lack of friends
    1. His unfriendly treatment of Fred
    2. His lonely death
  - C. Scrooge's change of heart
    1. His gift to the Cratchits
    2. His visit to Fred's house

In this materialistic world, A Christmas Carol serves to remind us that the people we know and love are far more important than any wealth we might possess. Dickens communicates this valuable lesson to us throurgh characters so apparently real that one expects them to step out of the book at any moment. Scrooge, in particular, provides a vivid illustration of the Scriptural principle that "it is more blessed to give than to receive." Scrooge is miserable and despised when he lives for gain, but when he turns his attention toward others, he discovers joy and acceptance. This profound truth is what gives A Christmas Carol such universal appeal.

UNIT 17

Composition C

Introducing the Research Paper

The research paper is a formal composition written to inform or persuade readers regarding a selected topic. A successful research paper is not only well organized and well written, but is also properly documented. The careful writer *documents,* or records, the source of any information that he gathers in his research. When this information is unique to a particular source, that source is *cited,* or identified, within the research paper.

In this unit, you will learn the steps in preparing and documenting a research paper. These steps are listed chronologically as though each step were to be completed before the next is begun, but sometimes you must work back and forth among the steps. For example, you must do some reading and note taking before you can make a preliminary outline, but you will do most of your reading and note taking afterward. The steps given here follow the writing process presented in Unit 12.

Follow these steps in preparing a research paper:

PLAN

Step 1. Select and limit the subject.
2. Find sources and prepare the working bibliography.
3. Prepare a preliminary outline.
4. Read and take notes.

WRITE

5. Write the first draft.

REWRITE

6. Revise and rewrite the paper.

EDIT

7. Edit the paper.
8. Prepare a list of the works cited.

TYPE

9. Type (or write) the final draft.
10. Proofread the paper and make final corrections.

C Planning Your Paper

Step 1 Select and limit the subject.

a. **Select a subject that interests you.**

b. **Choose a subject that merits attention.**

(1) Does it pose any important questions that you might answer?

(2) Will it be interesting and valuable to your audience (in this case, your teacher and classmates, or perhaps your friends and family)?

c. **Select a subject that has sufficient resource material available.** Check the on-line catalog or card catalog at your local library. Get advice from your librarian.

d. **Limit your subject to one that can be adequately treated within the assigned number of pages.** Subjects such as "The Reformation" or "World War II" are too broad to be covered in a research paper. Think of words or phrases that you can add to your subject to narrow its focus. For example, you might limit the topic "World War II" to "The role of American troops in World War II" or "The impact of World War II on Eastern Europe." (You may have to do some reading on a general subject before you can limit your subject.)

e. **Write out your statement of purpose or thesis statement.** This statement will help you locate pertinent sources and control your reading. The following is a **statement of purpose** for an informative paper: *"I intend to describe the men who gathered at Philadelphia in 1789 to draft the Constitution of the United States."* This sentence simply states the reason you are writing the paper.

If you are writing to prove a point or to persuade your readers to accept an important idea, you must develop a **thesis.** A thesis states an opinion that must be proven. The following is an example of a **thesis statement:** *"The goal of the United Nations is not global peace but global power."* To develop the thesis, you would find full, authoritative evidence to support your claim and arrange the evidence in an effective order.

Exercise A **Choose a general subject for your paper at this time. After you have limited your subject, write out a statement of purpose or a thesis statement for your paper.** TE Note: Suggested topics are listed in the *Supplement,* along with sample statements of purpose and thesis statements. You may wish to develop additional topics for your students.

Exercise B **Make a list of ideas that you think should be included in your research paper. You may have to do some reading on your subject. Look for descriptive details, examples, illustrations, and other significant information relating to your subject; if you are writing a persuasive paper, include arguments supporting (or opposing) your thesis. You will use this list to prepare a preliminary outline.**

Planning Your Paper (cont.)

Step 2 Find sources and prepare the working bibliography.

a. To find sources of information for your paper, check the following references:

(1) Refer to an encyclopedia to get an overall view of your subject. Encyclopedia articles often include a list of related articles and a short bibliography for further reading.

(2) Check the on-line catalog or card catalog in your local library.

(3) Refer to the *Readers' Guide to Periodical Literature* and other periodical indexes at the library.

b. Prepare a bibliography card for every source that looks promising. These cards will serve as your working bibliography. If you do not find enough sources that deal sufficiently with your topic, check with your teacher about changing topics.

c. Make out your cards according to the following instructions.

(1) Use 3 x 5-inch cards.

(2) Use a separate card for each source.

(3) Record all the information necessary for a reader to locate the source. Refer to the sample cards on page 245 and to the Appendix for proper bibliographic form.

Note: The information on your bibliography cards must be accurate in every respect. You will use these cards to prepare your parenthetical citations and your Works Cited page.

(4) For a library book, include the classification number.

(5) If you locate information on the internet, include the complete internet address (URL), as well as the date you accessed the information.

d. Evaluate the sources that you have located.

(1) Is the date of the work significant?

(2) Does the work deal directly with your topic or does it only mention your topic?

(3) Find the major ideas by reading the table of contents and checking the index to see how many pages are listed for your topic.

(4) On the back of each card, write your description and opinion of the work: its strengths and weaknesses and its value to your research.

(5) Lay aside cards for any sources that are definitely inferior or unrelated to your purpose.

Note: To avoid confusing your sources when you begin taking notes, always keep your bibliography cards in alphabetical order.

Sample Bibliography Cards

BOOK

(1) Author's full name (last name first)
(2) Title (underlined)
(3) Editor, if any (may appear in place of author)
(4) Facts of publication:
- City of publication (omit the state)
- Name of publisher
- Year of publication

(5) Library classification number

Griffin, G. Edward. The Fearful Master: A Second Look at the United Nations. Boston: Western Islands, 1964.

JX1977.G745.1964

MAGAZINE or NEWSPAPER

(1) Author's full name, if given (last name first)
(2) Title of article (in quotation marks)
(3) Title of magazine or newspaper (underlined)
(4) Date of publication
(5) Inclusive page numbers of the article
(6) Library classification number

Grigg, William Norman. "Shaping the New World Order." The New American, 17 Apr. 1995, 4–8.

AP2.N373.1995

WORLD WIDE WEB PAGE

(1) Author's full name, if given (last name first)
(2) Title of document (in quotation marks)
(3) Document date (or date of last revision)
(4) Internet address (URL) (enclosed in angle brackets)
(5) Date you accessed the document (enclosed in parentheses)

Schlafly, Phyllis. "The United Nations' American Land Grab." Oct. 1997. <http://www.texaseagle.org/torch/10-97.html> (accessed 3 Mar. 1998)

Note: Publication information may be shortened as follows:
- Except for May, June, July, the names of the months may be abbreviated—Jan., Feb., Mar., Apr., Aug., Sept., Oct., Nov., Dec.
- The names of publishers may be abbreviated. A list of abbreviations for selected publishers is included in the Appendix.

Exercise C **For practice, make bibliography cards for the following sources. (Note: You will need to consult the Appendix for number 4.)** (See *Supplement*.)

1. A book by Norman Rose entitled <u>Churchill: The Unruly Giant</u>, published in 1995 by The Free Press in the city of New York. The classification number is DA566.9.C5.R66.1995.
2. A magazine article entitled "The Maid of New Orléans" on pages 22–30 of <u>Military History</u>. The article was written by Don O'Reilly and appeared in the April 1998 issue.
3. A document entitled "Chapter 5: The Battle of Waterloo" posted on the World Wide Web by A. Libert in 1996. The URL is http://www.ping.be/napoleon.series/100 days/chap5.html. Use today's date for the date accessed.
4. An encyclopedia article entitled "Pima Indians," written by Henry F. Dobyns. The article is in the 1996 edition of <u>The World Book Encyclopedia</u>.

Exercise D **Begin making bibliography cards for your research paper according to the instructions given under Step 2. You will need a minimum of 4 sources. You may use either your history or science textbook as one source.**

Planning Your Paper (cont.)

Step 3 **Prepare a preliminary outline.** (See Unit 14 for detailed outlining instructions.)

a. **Refer to the list of ideas that you made for Exercise B on page 243.**

b. **Look again at your statement of purpose or theses statement and delete from your list any ideas that are not related to that statement.**

c. **Group your ideas under several main headings and make a preliminary outline.**

d. **Your preliminary outline may include only main headings and subheadings.** For a research paper, a **sentence outline** is often better than a **topical outline** because you can more easily see whether your points and your support for those points are connecting well. But sometimes you may have to start with a topical outline and construct a sentence outline after you have completed a first draft of your paper.

e. **When you take notes, make changes in your outline as often as necessary to keep it current with what you are finding in your research.**

Sample Topical Outline

THE UNITED NATIONS: OPPONENT OF FREEDOM

Thesis: The goal of the United Nations is not global peace but global power.

- I. *Political Power*
  - A. *Opposition to national sovereignty*
    - 1. *Statements of UN leaders*
    - 2. *Examples of UN interference in national affairs*
  - B. *Preference for totalitarian government*
    - 1. *Totalitarian philosophy of UN founders and leaders*
    - 2. *Plans for a world army*
- II. *Economic Power*
  - A. *Proposals of global taxes and fees*
  - B. *Regulation of global trade and national economies*
    - 1. *World Trade Organization*
    - 2. *International Monetary Fund*
- III. *Religious Power*
  - A. *Animosity toward Biblical Christianity*
  - B. *Plans for a one-world religion*

Planning Your Paper (cont.)

Sample Sentence Outline

THE UNITED NATIONS: OPPONENT OF FREEDOM

Thesis: The goal of the United Nations is not global peace but global power.

I. The United Nations seeks political power by eroding national sovereignty and promoting global government.
   A. The UN opposes national sovereignty, the freedom of nations to manage their own affairs.
      1. Statements made by UN leaders make clear their opposition to national sovereignty.
      2. The interference of the UN in the internal affairs of various countries illustrates its disregard for national sovereignty.
   B. The UN desires to establish a global government with totalitarian power over all nations.
      1. The totalitarian philosophy of UN founders and leaders over the years has been evident in their approach to people and the environment.
      2. The UN has for many years had plans to disarm national militaries and to build a world army to enforce its policies and programs.

II. The United Nations seeks economic power through taxation and regulation.
   A. The UN wants to levy a variety of global taxes and fees to fund UN functions and operations.
   B. The UN is determined to regulate global trade and national economies.
      1. The World Trade Organization possesses authority to judge in matters of international investment and trade.
      2. The International Monetary Fund uses financial aid to control nations, making them dependent on that aid.

III. The United Nations seeks religious power by uniting the world's religions under one global religion.
   A. The UN views Biblical Christianity as a threat to unity because it teaches only one way of salvation and right living.
   B. The UN envisions a global religion uniting the world's major religions under a single authority.

TE Note: See *Supplement* for sample outlines for suggested thesis statements.

Exercise E **On a separate sheet of paper, prepare a topical outline for your research paper according to the instructions given under Step 3 and in Unit 14. As you take notes, try to expand your topical outline into a sentence outline.**

Planning Your Paper (cont.)

Step 4 Read and take notes.

a. **Use 4 x 6-inch cards.**

b. **Write on only one side of each card.**

c. **At the top left of each card, *identify the source* and page number(s) from which the note is taken: (Landsburg, 145–146).**

   (1) First, locate the source in your alphabetized stack of bibliography cards. If there is no source before or after the one you are using that begins the same way, simply record the first item that appears on the card, usually the author's last name or the title of the work.

   (2) If there are two or more sources that begin the same way, you must distinguish between them on your note cards. For two sources by the same author, include the titles of the works (shortened if possible): (Landsburg, Armchair, 145–146). For two authors with the same last name, include their first names (or initials). (Refer to the Appendix for more examples of in-text citations.)

d. **At the top right of each card, record (from your outline) the topic to which the note pertains.**

   (1) Do not put more than one topic on a card.

   (2) When you need more than one card on the same topic, number the cards to keep them in order.

e. **Three things appear on each card: (a) the identification of the source and page number(s), (b) the topic from your outline, and (c) the note.** (Sometimes teachers may wish to have you identify the kind of note that you have taken—paraphrase, summary, or quotation. If this identification is required, put it at the bottom of the card.)

Sample Note Card

Griffin, 218 *National disarmament (1)*

By the 1960s, the U.S. State Department had devised a program to gradually disarm the U.S. military in accordance with UN plans for national disarmament and a world army to enforce a one-world government.

(paraphrase)

(continued)

Planning Your Paper (cont.)

Step 4, cont.

f. **When taking notes for any paper that includes information from the works of others, you must be careful to avoid plagiarism.** Plagiarism is a form of stealing which consists of taking the opinion, the organization, or the sentence structure of another and presenting it as if it were your own.

To avoid plagiarism, be sure to take notes accurately so that you always give credit for information that is unique to a particular writer.

> **Note:** You must give credit for original ideas and opinions not only when you quote the information but also when you paraphrase or summarize the information. However, you do not need to give credit for factual information (common knowledge or uncontested knowledge) or even for opinions that are widely shared. (See page 259 for a sample plagiarism statement.) If you are not sure whether some information is common or uncontested knowledge, check with your teacher.

g. **Your notes may be paraphrases, summaries, or quotations.** Use paraphrases and summaries when the content of your source is more important than who said it or how it is said. Use quotations when who said it or how it is said is especially important.

h. **Enclose a *quotation* (the exact words of an original) within quotation marks and record it exactly as it is in the original.** Use the exact words, spelling, punctuation, and capitalization. (If the statement was made by someone other than the author, be sure to identify the original source of the quotation on your note card.)

i. **As you take notes, record only what clearly supports a specific point in your outline.** Keep the notes as short as possible.

j. **If while you are taking notes you have a thought of your own, make a note card and record the thought before it slips away. Write "My Own" at the top of the card where you normally put the source.**

Exercise F

(1) Read the following passage carefully.

The root of the UN's failure to oppose the advance of international Communism can be traced to the ideologies of those who founded it. Many of those present at Dumbarton Oaks and San Francisco were socialists, Communists, or even Soviet agents, including Andrei Gromyko [grŭ·mĭk′ô], the head of Communist Russia's delegation, and Alger Hiss, an official at the U.S. State Department later implicated as a spy for the Soviet Union. Hiss served as the secretary-general of the San Francisco Conference. (He was also a close adviser to FDR at the Yalta Conference.) Every secretary-general since the UN's founding has been either an avowed Communist or a socialist.

At the very heart of the United Nations is a collectivist philosophy that opposes the kind of individual freedoms cherished in free nations like the United States. The UN continues to pursue the humanistic, utopian goals of its founders, claiming to seek world peace while laying the foundation for a totalitarian, one-world government. As history has proven time and time again, the real objective of the UN is not world peace but worldwide power.

Thompson, George, and Combee, Jerry. *World History and Cultures.* 2nd ed. Pensacola: A Beka Book, 1997.

Exercise F, cont.

(2) Read the following notes written from the paragraph on page 250. If the note is correct, choose *a* from the list below. If the note is plagiarized or if there is an error in documentation, choose the answer that best explains why. (Remember, you may use the key words of the original without plagiarizing.)

a. no plagiarism
b. exact words of original were used without quotation marks and/or parenthetical citation
c. paraphrase or summary too close to the original (same phrases or sentence structure)
d. paraphrase or summary used without a parenthetical citation

__a__ 1. Although the UN claims to seek world peace, its true goal is worldwide power (Thompson and Combee, 506).
TE Note: Uses key words but different phrasing and sentence structure.

__a__ 2. "At the very heart of the United Nations is a collectivist philosophy that opposes the kind of individual freedoms cherished in free nations like the United States" (Thompson and Combee, 506).
TE Note: Quotation correctly enclosed in quotation marks and properly cited.

__c__ 3. The root of the UN's failure to stop the advance of Communism around the world can be traced to the philosophies of the men and women who founded it (Thompson and Combee, 506). **TE Note:** Phrases and sentence structure plagiarized from the original. Emphasize that changing a word here and there is not a correct way to paraphrase.

__d__ 4. It is no wonder that the UN has failed to stop the expansion of Communism when one considers the philosophies of its founders.
TE Note: Paraphrased correctly but not properly cited.

__b__ 5. Every secretary-general since the UN's founding has been either an avowed Communist or a socialist (Thompson and Combee, 506).
TE Note: Correctly cited but needs quotation marks.

Exercise G

Begin taking notes for your research paper according to the instructions given under Step 4. You will need a minimum of 20 note cards before you begin writing your first draft.

UNIT 18

Writing Your Paper

Step 5 Write the first draft.

a. **Arrange your note cards in order according to the headings in your outline.**

b. **Compare your notes with your outline to make sure that the outline is accurate.**

c. **Write a working introduction.** Start in an interesting way. Then give your readers the background information they need to understand your argument. In the ***last sentence*** of the introduction, **state your thesis** or **purpose.**

d. **Read through the note cards for each level of your outline before you start to write that portion of your paper.**

e. **Write a quick first draft of the body of your paper.**

(1) **Follow the organization of your outline.** The first main point in your outline will be the topic of the first paragraph. Begin a new paragraph for each main point.

(2) **Write on every other line and on only one side of each page.**

(3) **Write the first draft as rapidly as you can.** Do not stop to look up additional information or to correct grammar, mechanics, or sentence structure. Your goal is simply to get your ideas on paper so that you can work with them.

(4) **As you write, identify the sources of all the quotations, summaries, or paraphrases that require documentation.** At the end of the passage to which it refers, record the citation information from your note card: (Nisbet, 96–97). For more information about the placement of parenthetical citations, see the Appendix.

f. **Write the conclusion.**

(1) **Restate your thesis** or **purpose** in the ***first sentence*** of your conclusion. The wording should not be identical to the statement at the end of your introduction, but the key words should be the same, and the statements must not contradict one another.

(2) You may need to summarize your arguments or emphasize the most important ones.

(3) End with a striking fact or quotation, or perhaps a call to action.

Exercise H **Write the first draft for your research paper according to the instructions given under Step 5. You will need 500–600 words in your final paper, with at least two citations.**

Rewriting Your Paper

Step 6 **Revise and rewrite the paper.**

a. **Check the overall *organization* of your paper.**

(1) **Underline the last sentence of your introduction.** This sentence should be your **thesis sentence** or **statement of purpose**.

(2) **Underline the first sentence of your conclusion.** This sentence should be a **reassertion of your thesis sentence** or a **restatement of your purpose.** Compare this statement of your thesis or purpose with the one in your introduction to make sure that they agree.

(3) **Underline the topic sentence of each paragraph.** These sentences should announce the subject of the paragraph, just as the thesis sentence announces the subject of the entire paper. Each topic sentence should not only announce the subject of the paragraph, it should also indicate how the paragraph is connected to the thesis sentence. These sentences should keep the reader informed of "where you are" in the development of your statement of purpose or thesis.

b. **Check your paper for *unity* and *coherence*.**

(1) **Look for the repetition of key words.** Circle the key words in your thesis sentence or statement of purpose. Search the entire paper for these key words or other forms of these words. If these words do not regularly appear throughout the paper, your reasoning will be difficult to follow.

(2) **Check for smooth transitions between paragraphs.** The first sentence of each paragraph should indicate either a **continuation** of an idea from the previous paragraph or a **shift in thought** to a different idea.

(a) Use some **key word or phrase** from the last sentence of the previous paragraph.

(b) Try a **transitional expression** such as *but, yet, besides, another phase, on the other hand, just as, also, again, likewise, in addition, for example, for instance, in short, therefore, finally.*

c. **Check your citations.**

(1) **Have you introduced each citation which is a quotation?** The following are standard ways of introducing quotations.

(a) Introduce the quotation with a colon.

Harland Cleveland, one of the UN's founders, is suggesting a worldwide tax to support the globalists' agenda: "It is high time we looked hard at how to best finance a widening range of international functions that grows more necessary with every passing year" (Grigg, 6).

(b) Introduce the quotation with the word *that.*

According to Grigg, Harland insists that "the UN can and must impose a variety of direct taxes and fees" (6).

(2) **Have you introduced each citation which is a summary or paraphrase?** The following is the usual way of introducing a summary or paraphrase. Note that the essential difference between this introduction and the one above is the absence of quotation marks.

*Harland Cleveland, one of the UN's founders, thinks **that** the UN should exact a worldwide tax to help them carry out their plans to control the world (Grigg, 6).*

(3) **Have you used the best word to introduce each quotation?** Try to use a more specific word in place of the word *said*. Note the different meaning and emphasis of the following introductory words: *admitted, affirmed, agreed, alleged, argued, boasted, claimed, complained, conceded, concluded, continued, denied, disclosed, explained, maintained, objected, proposed, proved, recounted, retorted, suggested, supposed, thought, urged, warned.*

d. Check the mechanical *accuracy* of your citations.

(1) Are all quotations enclosed within quotation marks?

(2) Have you included a citation in parentheses after every piece of information that requires documentation?

e. Revise your introduction.

(1) Is your introduction **interesting?** In the first several sentences, you must make your readers believe that your topic is worth their time to read. You may begin with startling statistics, a brief story, a quotation or proverb, a statement of an unusual opinion, a reference to a historical or current event, or the revelation of a controversy.

(2) Have you provided all the **background information** necessary to help your readers understand the problem that you are posing?

(3) Does the last sentence in your introduction state the **thesis** or **purpose** of your paper? If you are developing a thesis, have you clearly stated the viewpoint or opinion that you intend to prove?

f. Revise your conclusion.

(1) Have you **reasserted your thesis** or **restated your purpose?** Make sure that it does not conflict with anything in your introduction.

(2) Have you **ended in a satisfying way?** Will your readers be left with a clear understanding of your viewpoint? Have you persuaded them to agree with you or to research the subject further?

Exercise **Rewrite your research paper according to the instructions given under Step 6. Continue to write on every other line and on only one side of each page.**

Composition C

Editing Your Paper

Step 7 **Edit the paper.** Refer to the correction symbols in Unit 11.

a. **Check each *paragraph*** for unity and coherence.
   (1) Does every sentence support the topic?
   (2) Are the sentences arranged in the best order?

b. **Check each *sentence*** for clarity and correctness.
   (1) Is each one a complete sentence?
   (2) Do the subjects and verbs agree in number?
   (3) Can you find the antecedent for each pronoun?
   (4) Are all modifiers clearly placed near the words they modify?
   (5) Do any of your modifying phrases dangle?

c. **Check the *words*.**
   (1) Have you used mostly active verbs and concrete nouns?
   (2) Are there any misspelled words?

d. **Check the *capitalization* and *punctuation*.**

Exercise J

Edit your rewritten research paper according to the instructions given under Step 7. Refer to the correction symbols in Unit 11.

UNIT 18

Editing Your Paper (cont.)

Step 8 **Prepare a list of the works cited in your paper.**

a. **Your bibliography cards should be alphabetized by the author's last name or the first word of the title if no author is given.**

b. **Set aside any sources that you did not cite in your paper.**

c. **From the cards that remain, prepare an alphabetized list of works cited.** Refer to the example given below and to the Appendix.

WORKS CITED

Combee, Jerry H. History of the World in Christian Perspective. Pensacola: Beka, 1995.

Griffin, G. Edward. The Fearful Master: A Second Look at the United Nations. Boston: Western Islands, 1964.

Grigg, William Norman. "Shaping the New World Order." The New American, 17 Apr. 1995, 4–8.

Schlafly, Phyllis. "The United Nations' American Land Grab." Oct. 1997. <http://www.texaseagle.org/torch/10-97.html> (accessed Mar. 3, 1998)

Note: The WORKS CITED page lists only those sources actually cited in a paper. If you wish to include some sources that you consulted but did not cite in your paper, you could list these additional sources on a separate page under the heading FOR FURTHER READING.

Exercise K **Prepare the list of works cited for your research paper according to the instructions given under Step 8. (Remember that you need at least two citations, although you may have more.)**

Typing Your Paper

Step 9 **Type (or write) the final draft.**

a. General information.

(1) Use $8\,^1/_2$ x 11-inch white paper.

(2) Use a standard type, such as Courier. Do not use any kind of "script" or other unusual style of type.

(3) Keep the paper neat and clean. Corrections should be few and should be made with such care that they will not be noticeable.

b. Order of pages in the paper.

(1) Title page

(2) Blank page or pledge page

(3) Outline page(s)

(4) Body of the paper

(5) Works Cited page

c. Format of pages in the paper. For detailed instructions and sample pages, refer to pages 258–263.

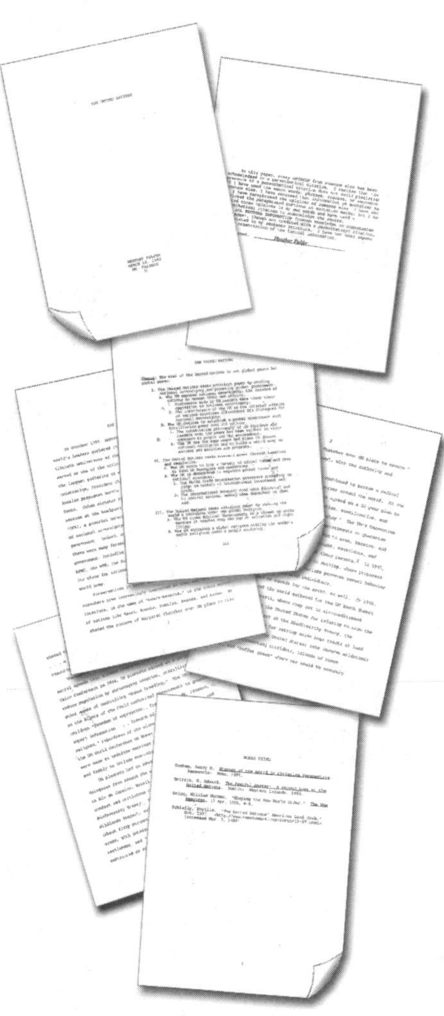

Step 10 **Proofread the paper and make final corrections.**

a. Read the typed copy to make sure that nothing was omitted.

b. Check all the parenthetical references in your paper to be sure that they correspond to the entries in your Works Cited page.

c. Proofread every page, checking the correctness of every letter, every word, and every punctuation mark.

d. Compare your final copy with the sample pages in this textbook to check the margins, indentions, spacing, and other details of format.

Exercise L **Prepare your final research paper according to the instructions given under Steps 9 and 10. (Refer to the sample pages provided on pages 258–263 for typing instructions.)**

Sample Title Page

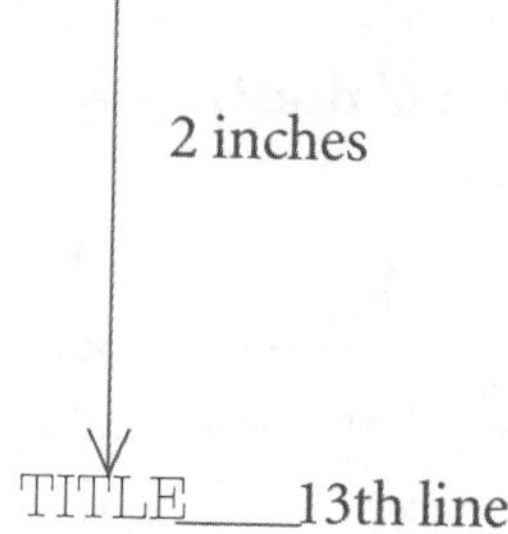

TITLE____13th line

Instructions:

1. Center everything on the page.
2. Maintain a 2-inch margin at the top and bottom of the page and a 1-inch margin at the sides.
3. Type the entire title in upper case letters on the thirteenth line from the top edge of the page.
4. If the title is longer than 48 spaces, type it in two or more double-spaced lines in inverted pyramid style.
5. Follow your teacher's instructions for the placement of your name, the date, and so forth.
6. Although this page is counted in the pagination of the front matter (page i), the page number is *not typed* on the page.

YOUR NAME____51st line
DATE
TEACHER'S NAME
CLASS

2 inches

Sample Pledge Page

1 inch

1 inch

In this paper, every OPINION from someone else has been acknowledged in a parenthetical citation. I realize that the mere presence of a parenthetical citation does not avoid plagiarism. If I have used the exact words, phrases, clauses, or sentences of someone else, I have enclosed that information in quotation marks. If I have paraphrased the opinions of someone else, I have not enclosed the paraphrased portions in quotation marks; but I have stated those opinions in my own words and have used a parenthetical citation to acknowledge the source.

ALL FACTUAL INFORMATION (common knowledge or uncontested knowledge), though not credited with a parenthetical citation, has been stated in my sentence structure. I have not used anyone else's organization of the factual information.

Signed: ____________________________

Instructions:

1. A blank page is sometimes included to prevent the text of the following page from showing through the title page.
2. This page is counted in the pagination of the front matter (page ii), but the page number does not appear.
3. Your teacher may wish to have you sign a pledge stating that you have avoided plagiarism in your paper. Center this pledge on your blank page as shown above.

Sample Outline Page

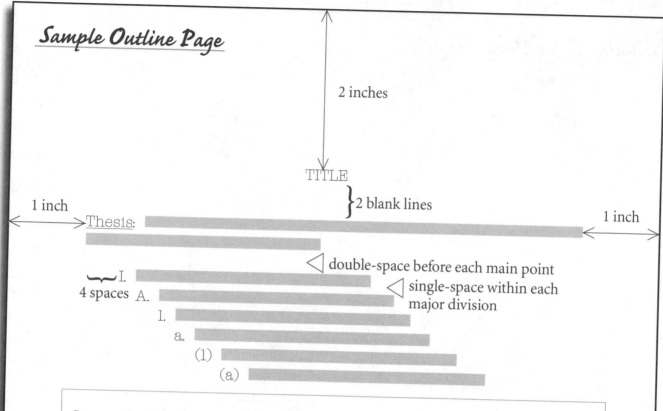

2 inches

TITLE

}2 blank lines

1 inch

Thesis:

1 inch

double-space before each main point

I.

4 spaces A.

single-space within each major division

1.

a.

(1)

(a)

Instructions:

1. Center the title on the thirteenth line (2 inches) from the top edge of the page. Type the title as it appears on your title page.
2. Maintain a 1-inch margin at the sides and bottom of the page.
3. Triple-space (leave two blank lines) after the title.
4. At the left margin, type the word *Thesis* or *Statement of Purpose*. Underline the word and put a colon after it. Strike the space bar once and type your thesis or statement of purpose.
5. Do not include the introduction or conclusion in your outline.
6. Double-space (leave one blank line) before each main point, and single space the lines within each major division.
7. Indent the first Roman numeral four spaces from the left margin. Align succeeding Roman numerals by the periods. Subpoints of the same level should also align.
8. After the period, strike the space bar once and type the first main point. Follow this pattern for each point in your outline.
9. Follow the scheme of notation and indention illustrated above.
10. If your outline requires more than one page, begin typing on the seventh line (1 inch) from the top edge of the second page.
11. Number your outline page(s) with small Roman numerals, beginning with the number iii. Center the page number at the bottom of each page, on the seventh line (1 inch) above the edge. Leave at least one blank line between the last line of text and the page number.

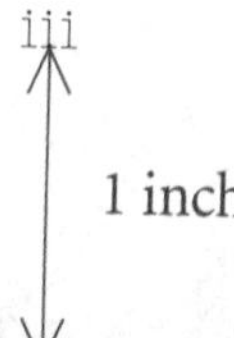

1 inch

Sample Body of Paper

2 inches

TITLE

2 blank lines

1 inch .5-inch indention 1 inch

Instructions for the first page of the body:

1. Center the title on the thirteenth line (2 inches) from the top edge of the page. Type the title as it appears on your title page.
2. Maintain a 1-inch margin at the sides and bottom of the page.
3. Triple-space (leave 2 blank lines) after the title.
4. Indent the first line of each paragraph five spaces (.5 inches).
5. Double-space the text.
6. Center the Arabic numeral 1 at the bottom of the page on the seventh line (1 inch) from the edge.
7. Leave at least one blank line between the last line of text and the page number.

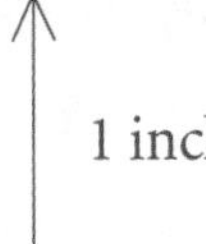

1 inch

UNIT 18

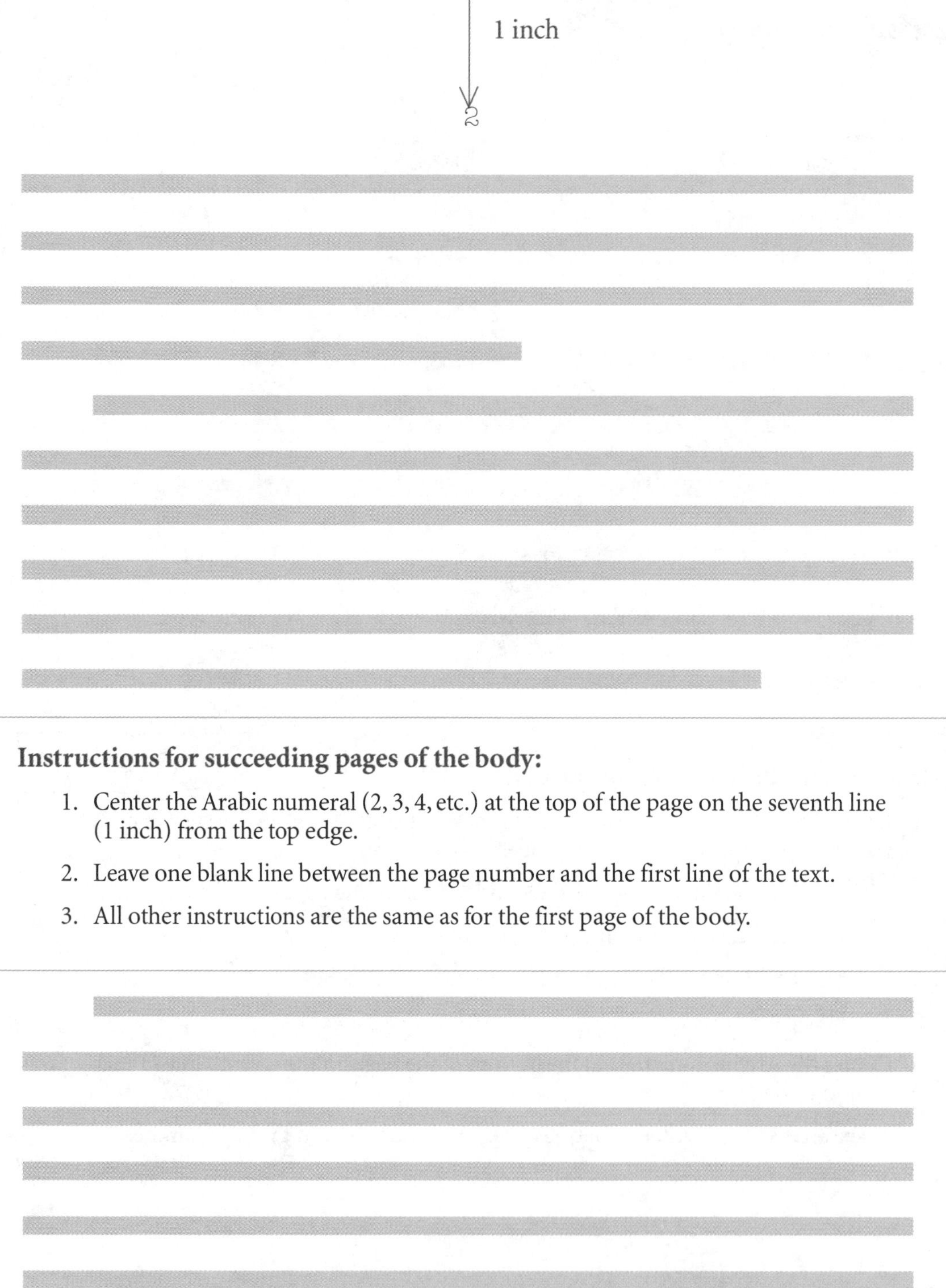

Instructions for succeeding pages of the body:

1. Center the Arabic numeral (2, 3, 4, etc.) at the top of the page on the seventh line (1 inch) from the top edge.
2. Leave one blank line between the page number and the first line of the text.
3. All other instructions are the same as for the first page of the body.

Sample Works Cited Page

2 inches

WORKS CITED

2 blank lines

.5-inch indention

1 inch

1 inch

Instructions:

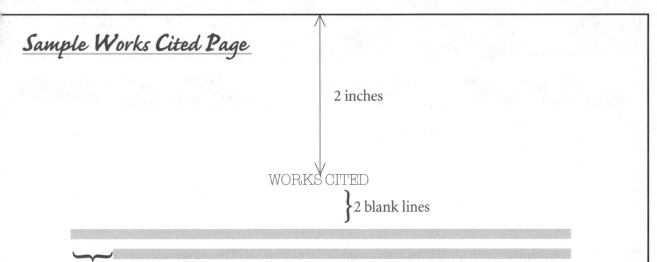

1. The WORKS CITED page contains an alphabetical list of all the sources you used to write the paper.
2. Arrange your bibliography cards in alphabetical order according to the first word that appears on the card. (This is usually the author's last name or the first word of a title.) When alphabetizing your cards, ignore *a*, *an*, or *the* at the beginning of a title.
3. If you prepared your bibliography cards correctly, you can now simply type your list directly from the cards. If you are not sure of any of the information on a card, you must go back to the source and check it.
4. Center the heading WORKS CITED on the thirteenth line (2 inches) from the top edge of the page.
5. Triple-space after the heading.
6. Single-space each entry, but double-space between entries.
7. Begin the first line of each entry at the left margin; indent runover lines five spaces (.5 inches).
8. Center the page number (an Arabic numeral) on the seventh line (1 inch) above the bottom edge of the page. The numbering continues from the preceding pages of the paper.
9. For any succeeding pages, center the page number on the seventh line (1 inch) from the top edge of the page. Leave one blank line between the page number and the first line of the text.

3

1 inch

UNIT 18

Unit 19 *Improving Writing Style*

Composition

C *Correcting a Choppy Style*

A style of writing that consists only of short, simple sentences is not good. There is nothing wrong with simple sentences. Often they are the most effective kind of sentences you could use. However, if all your sentences are simple sentences, you are writing in a choppy, immature manner. This is annoying to the reader. Also you cannot adequately express your thoughts if you use only simple sentences. Study the following ways to correct a choppy style and then put them into practice in your writing.

1 Combine simple sentences into *compound sentences* if the sentences are *closely related* and *equally important.* Use a comma and a coordinating conjunction to join them. (See compound sentence, page 190.)

I cried unto the Lord with my voice. He heard me out of His holy hill. (choppy)
I cried unto the Lord with my voice, and He heard me out of His holy hill. (combined)
Hatred stirreth up strifes. Love covereth all sins. (choppy)
Hatred stirreth up strifes, but love covereth all sins. (combined)

2 Combine simple sentences into *complex sentences* if the sentences are *closely related* but *not equally important.* (See complex sentence, page 193.)

a. You may form a complex sentence that contains an *adjective clause.* Use relative pronouns to introduce the adjective clause.

He shall find good. He keepeth understanding. (choppy)
He *that keepeth understanding* shall find good. (combined)

b. You may form a complex sentence that contains an *adverb clause.* Use subordinating conjunctions to introduce the adverb clause.

Some people are lonely. They have built walls instead of bridges. (choppy)
Some people are lonely *because they have built walls instead of bridges.* (combined)

Exercise A

Combine the following simple sentences into compound sentences. Use a comma and one of the coordinating conjunctions: *and, but, or, nor, for.*

1. David was king of Israel. He never lost his spirit of humility. David was king of Israel, but he never lost his spirit of humility.
2. Abraham obeyed God implicitly. God made of him a great nation. Abraham obeyed God implicitly, and God made of him a great nation.
3. Esther became a national hero of the Jews. She had been the means of preserving her people. Esther became a national hero of the Jews, for she had been the means of preserving her people.
4. Ruth was a stranger in Israel. She set her mind to the task before her. Ruth was a stranger in Israel, but she set her mind to the task before her.
5. Develop a good, sound character. You will become a useful vessel for service. Develop a good, sound character, and you will become a useful vessel for service.

Exercise B

Combine these simple sentences into complex sentences containing *adjective* clauses. Use relative pronouns: *who, whom, whose, which, that.* Use a pair of commas for nonessential clauses. (See Rules 5–6, page 133.) Answers will vary.

1. John Milton wrote the long epic *Paradise Lost.* He was a devoted Christian. John Milton, who wrote the long epic Paradise Lost, was a devoted Christian.

2. *Paradise Lost* is one of the greatest of all epic poems. It describes the fall of man in the Garden of Eden. Paradise Lost, which is one of the greatest of all epic poems, describes the fall of man in the Garden of Eden.

3. Milton was born into a Puritan family. He often wrote pamphlets furthering the Puritan political causes. Milton, who was born into a Puritan family, often wrote pamphlets furthering the Puritan political causes.

4. "When I Consider How My Light Is Spent" is one of Milton's most famous poems. It describes his fear of blindness. "When I Consider How My Light Is Spent," which describes Milton's fear of blindness, is one of his most famous poems.

5. I like his poem "Il Penseroso." It is about a life of quietness and study. I like his poem "Il Penseroso," which is about a life of quietness and study.

Exercise C

Combine these simple sentences into complex sentences containing *adverb* clauses. Use subordinating conjunctions such as *after, although, because, if, since, until, when.* Use a comma after introductory adverb clauses (See Rules 5–6, page 161.) Answers will vary.

1. The city of Amsterdam is connected by a canal to the North Sea. It is a major seaport of Europe.
Since the city of Amsterdam is connected by a canal to the North Sea, it is a major seaport of Europe.

2. Houses in Amsterdam are built on wooden pilings. The ground is very soft and boggy.
Because the ground is very soft and boggy, houses in Amsterdam are built on wooden pilings.

3. Amsterdam was attacked during World War II. The people immediately went to work repairing the damage. After Amsterdam was attacked during World War II, the people immediately went to work repairing the damage.

4. The Netherlands is a crowded country. The Dutch people are still able to find room to grow beautiful fields of tulips. Although The Netherlands is a crowded country, the Dutch people are still able to find room to grow beautiful fields of tulips.

5. Sections of land are recovered from the sea. The area is quickly homesteaded by farmers.
When sections of land are recovered from the sea, the area is quickly homesteaded by farmers.

Composition

C Correcting a Choppy Style (cont.)

3 **When combining two simple sentences into one complex sentence, you must decide which of the two sentences is more important.** One of the sentences may be giving details to accompany a main point in the other sentence. The sentence that contains the main point should remain as it is, and the sentence that contains the details should be made into a dependent clause. This is called *subordination*. You are making the sentence with the details seem of secondary importance, and you are emphasizing the sentence that contains the main point.

Exercise A

Combine these simple sentences into complex sentences that contain adjective clauses. Make the *second sentence* of each pair *subordinate* to the first.

Example: Gerald has been elected president of our class. He is very dependable.
Gerald, **who is very dependable,** has been elected president of our class.

1. The nomads of the Sahara are mostly Moslems. They wander from oasis to oasis. The nomads of the Sahara, who wander from oasis to oasis, are mostly Moslems.
2. Insulin has been isolated as the hormone in the pancreas. It was discovered in 1921. Insulin, which was discovered in 1921, has been isolated as the hormone in the pancreas.
3. David Brainerd died of tuberculosis at the age of 29. Brainerd was a missionary to the Indians of Massachusetts. David Brainerd, who was a missionary to the Indians of Massachusetts, died of tuberculosis at the age of 29.
4. Louis Braille invented the braille system of writing. He was a blind Frenchman. Louis Braille, who was a blind Frenchman, invented the braille system of writing.
5. Herodotus wrote a history of the world up to his time. He was the first Greek historian. Herodotus, who was the first Greek historian, wrote a history of the world up to his time.

Exercise B

Combine these simple sentences into complex sentences that contain adjective clauses. Make the *first sentence* of each pair *subordinate* to the second.

Example: Gerald has been elected president of our class. He is very dependable.
Gerald, **who has been elected president of our class,** is very dependable.

1. The British Library in London has many rare books and manuscripts. It contains approximately 8 million volumes. The British Library in London, which has many rare books and manuscripts, contains approximately 8 million volumes.

2. An ancient library belonged to King Sennacherib of Assyria. It was discovered by British archaeologists in 1850. An ancient library, which belonged to King Sennacherib of Assyria, was discovered by British archaeologists in 1850.

3. Andrew Carnegie made his fortune in the steel industry. Carnegie donated part of his wealth to start libraries across America. Andrew Carnegie, who made his fortune in the steel industry, donated part of his wealth to start libraries across America.

4. The Alexandrian Library was in Alexandria, Egypt. It was the most famous library of the ancient world. The Alexandrian Library, which was in Alexandria, Egypt, was the most famous library of the ancient world.

5. Melvil Dewey was an American librarian. He began the decimal library-classification system. Melvil Dewey, who was an American librarian, began the decimal library-classification system.

Exercise C

The following paragraph contains many short choppy sentences. Rewrite the paragraph, combining sentences as you have been doing in the previous exercises.

Pastor Edward Taylor was perhaps the first great poet produced in America. He was born in England. Taylor came to Massachusetts in 1688. He was suffering persecution in his homeland. He graduated from Harvard. He became a pastor and physician in Westfield, Massachusetts. His poetry was the best produced in the Colonies. It is imaginative and filled with homespun illustrations. Pastor Taylor produced his poetry in the late 1600s. It was not discovered and published until the 1930s. He was not known for many years. He is now considered the best of the Puritan poets. Answers will vary.

Pastor Edward Taylor, who was born in England, was perhaps the first great poet produced in America. Because he was suffering persecution in his homeland, Taylor came to Massachusetts in 1688. After he graduated from Harvard, he became a pastor and physician in Westfield, Massachusetts. His poetry, which is imaginative and filled with homespun illustrations, was the best produced in the Colonies. Pastor Taylor produced his poetry in the late 1600s, but it was not discovered and published until the 1930s. Although he was not known for many years, he is now considered the best of the Puritan poets.

Exercise D

Write a brief paragraph that illustrates all the sentence-combining suggestions listed on page 264. You may use one of the topics listed here.

1. My best friend
2. A person I will never forget
3. A brief sketch of myself
4. A favorite restaurant
5. My room
6. My alarm clock

C Composition

Correcting a Monotonous Style

The majority of our sentences are written with the subject first and then the verb. This is the normal word order of our language. However, if every sentence we write begins with the subject, our style becomes monotonous. To improve this situation, we can move certain modifiers, that usually occur later in the sentence, to the beginning. All sentences cannot and should not be done this way, but if you vary the beginning of some of your sentences, you can greatly improve your writing style.

1 Move an *adverb* to the beginning of the sentence. (Sometimes a comma is needed after the adverb for clarity.)

The principal took care of the situation *immediately*.
Immediately the principal took care of the situation.

2 Move an *adverb phrase* to the beginning of the sentence. (Use a comma after the introductory phrase.)

The race cars were warming up *on the track*.
On the track, the race cars were warming up.

3 Move an *adverb clause* to the beginning of the sentence. (Use a comma after the introductory clause.)

They lived in North Carolina *before they moved here*.
Before they moved here, they lived in North Carolina.

4 Move a *participial phrase* to the beginning of the sentence. (Use a comma after the introductory phrase.)

The hungry dog, *abandoning all caution*, began to eat.
Abandoning all caution, the hungry dog began to eat.

Exercise A **Rewrite each sentence, moving an *adverb* to the beginning.**

1. A loud crashing noise was suddenly heard. Suddenly a loud crashing noise was heard.

2. The mother of the injured child paced the floor nervously. Nervously, the mother of the injured child paced the floor.

3. Susan excitedly shared her plans for summer vacation. Excitedly, Susan shared her plans for summer vacation.

4. Mrs. Ikener worked busily to prepare for the arrival of her guests. Busily, Mrs. Ikener worked to prepare for the arrival of her guests.

5. The boys' furniture will be rearranged later to make room for the new crib and playpen. Later, the boy's furniture will be rearranged to make room for the new crib and playpen.

6. The electricity unexpectedly was disconnected. Unexpectedly, the electricity was discon-nected.

7. He cleverly disguised his voice so as not to be recognized. Cleverly, he disguised his voice so as not to be recognized.

8. The Russian speaker next spoke of his early days in our country. Next, the Russian speaker spoke of his early days in our country.

Exercise B Rewrite each sentence, moving an *adverb phrase* to the beginning.

1. We could view parts of four states from the mountain peak. From the mountain peak, we could view parts of four states.
2. Some unique Indian artifacts are on display in the museum. In the museum, some unique Indian artifacts are on display.
3. Pioneers traveling westward encountered many dangers during their long journey. During their long journey, pioneers traveling westward encountered many dangers.
4. There was often a good sense of camaraderie among the pioneers. Among the pioneers, there was often a good sense of camaraderie.
5. The modern grocery store originated in the early 1900s. In the early 1900s, the modern grocery store originated.

Exercise C Rewrite each sentence, moving an *adverb clause* to the beginning.

1. Jeremiah McAuley lived in Ireland until he was thirteen years old. Until he was thirteen years old, Jeremiah McAuley lived in Ireland.
2. He became involved in crime after he came to live with his sister's family in New York City. After he came to live with his sister's family in New York City, he became involved in crime.
3. The young man got saved, although he had become a drunkard and a criminal. Although he had become a drunkard and a criminal, the young man got saved.
4. McAuley went back to the slums of New York because he wanted to help those like himself. Because he wanted to help those like himself, McAuley went back to the slums of New York.
5. Many of the "down-and-outers" listened to him, since he had once been a derelict himself, and accepted Christ as Savior. Since he had once been a derelict himself, many of the "down-and-outers" listened to him and accepted Christ as Savior.

Correcting a Monotonous Style

Exercise D **Rewrite each sentence, moving a *participial phrase* to the beginning.**

1. America, discovered by Christopher Columbus, was actually named for Amerigo Vespucci. Discovered by Christopher Columbus, America was actually named for Amerigo Vespucci.

2. The captain, sighting some icebergs, immediately changed our course. Sighting some icebergs, the captain immediately changed our course.

3. The principal, peering sternly over his glasses, caused the guilty boys to squirm. Peering sternly over his glasses, the principal caused the guilty boys to squirm.

4. They looked around nervously, smitten by their consciences. Smitten by their consciences, they looked around nervously.

5. Dad officiated the game, watching the action alertly. Watching the action alertly, Dad officiated the game.

Exercise E **Rewrite each sentence, moving an adverb, an adverb phrase, an adverb clause, or a participial phrase to the beginning. Some sentences contain more than one of these modifiers. Move the one that will make the smoothest sentence.**

1. The workers rose early although they were tired. Although they were tired, the workers rose early.

2. That young lady certainly presents a clear example of Christian purity. Certainly that young lady presents a clear example of Christian purity.

3. Crowds of people, hoping to see Jesus, pushed into the house. Hoping to see Jesus, crowds of people pushed into the house.

4. I could not hear him distinctly during the meeting. During the meeting, I could not hear him distinctly.

5. A man, rummaging around in his attic one day, found a box of letters written by Emily Dickinson. Rummaging around in his attic one day, a man found a box of letters written by Emily Dickinson.

6. Our pastor spoke fervently about those who pervert the Scriptures. Fervently our pastor spoke about those who pervert the Scriptures.

7. Paul preached the Gospel of Christ wherever he went. Wherever he went, Paul preached the Gospel of Christ.

8. We had an excellent view of the Statue of Liberty from the ship's deck. From the ship's deck, we had an excellent view of the Statue of Liberty.

9. The scientist mixed the contents of the two test tubes carefully. Carefully the scientist mixed the contents of the two test tubes.

10. The Lord Jesus Christ died on the cross because He loved us. Because He loved us, the Lord Jesus Christ died on the cross.

11. We could feel the ocean breeze from the patio of our vacation condominium. From the patio of our vacation condominium, we could feel the ocean breeze.

12. The Inheritance, written in 1849, was Louisa May Alcott's first novel. Written in 1849, The Inheritance was Louisa May Alcott's first novel.

Exercise F

Write sentences illustrating each of the rules on page 268.

1. Answers will vary.

2.

3.

4.

UNIT 19

Writing Friendly Letters

1 A friendly letter has five parts.

a. **The *heading* gives the complete address of the writer and the date of writing.**

b. **The *salutation* tells to whom the letter is written.** It is followed by a comma.

c. **The *body* is what you have to say.** Each paragraph should be indented.

d. **The *closing* is the farewell.** It is followed by a comma. Use such closings as *Sincerely yours, Your friend, With love*. Do not use *Truly yours, Yours truly,* or *Very truly yours*. These are reserved for formal business letters.

e. **The *signature* is the name of the writer.**

Study the form of the following letter.

Friendly Letter Form

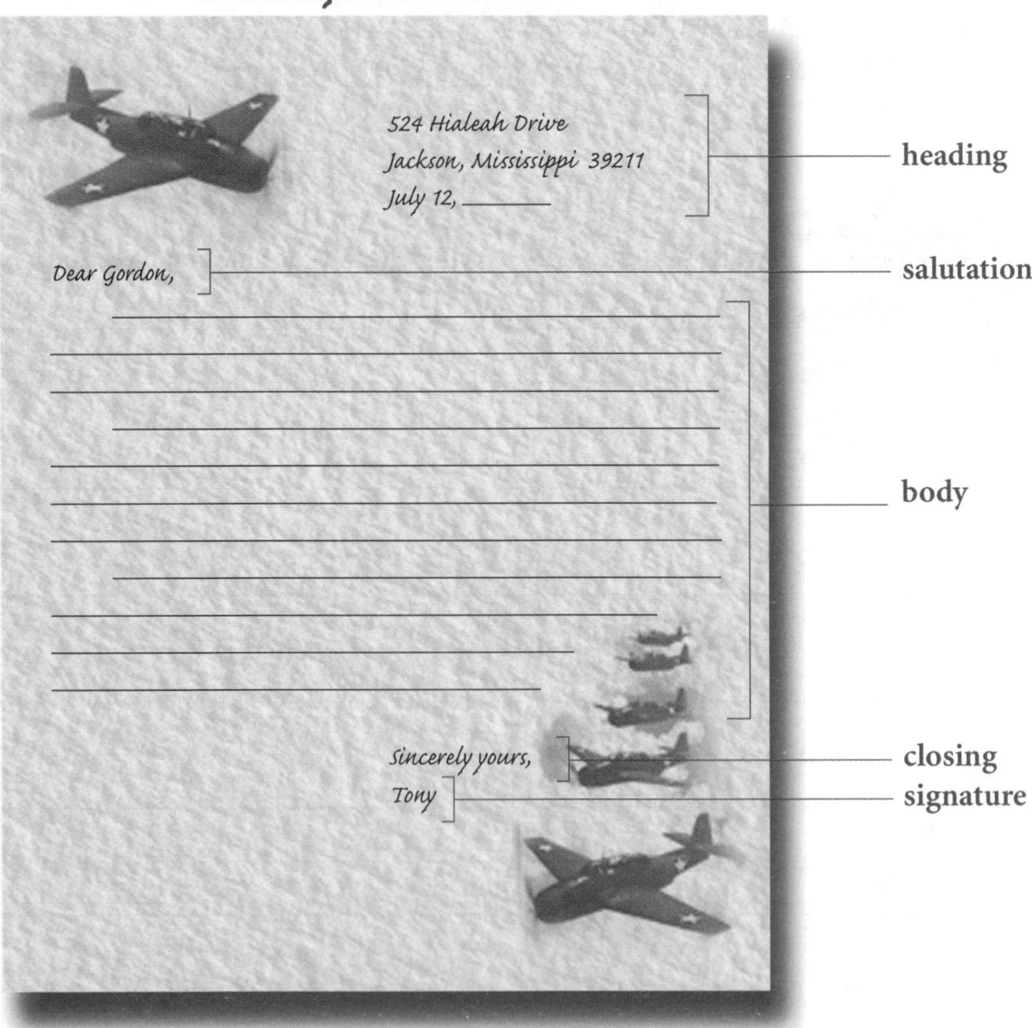

524 Hialeah Drive
Jackson, Mississippi 39211
July 12, ______
heading
Dear Gordon,
salutation
body
Sincerely yours,
closing
Tony
signature

2 **Observe the following suggestions to make your letters appropriate and interesting.**

a. **Use unlined stationery and write with ink.**

b. **Make the letter neat: avoid blots and cross outs; maintain at least half an inch margins at the top, bottom, and sides of the letter.**

c. **Suit your letter to the receiver's interests and to the relationship that exists between you and that person.**
d. **Be sure to answer any question that the other person asked and comment on his letter.**
e. **Do not begin by saying "How are you? I hope you are all right. I am fine."**
f. **Do not close by saying "Well, I can't think of anything else to say, so I guess I'll close for now."**
g. **Do not overuse the word *I*.**
h. **Give interesting details.** The receiver of your letter will enjoy a detailed account of an interesting conversation, the colorful description of a person or place, or the vivid narration of some experience.

Sample Friendly Letter

13 Farmington Avenue
Hammond, Indiana 46320
March 30, ______

Dear Erika,

You came to mind today in English class during a discussion of Poe's short stories. I was reminded of the summer that we "produced and directed" our own version of "The Tell-Tale Heart." You were great as the mad man, but my thumping "heartbeats" made the show, if I do say so myself. We had half the neighborhood kids scared silly!

Things just haven't been the same since your family moved to Indianapolis. But the Lord has helped me as I am sure He has you.

We are having tryouts for the tennis team next Tuesday—pray I'll be able to do my best. Remember that you're invited to Hammond for spring break.

I miss you and think of you often.

Love,
Kaitlin

And until
we meet again
May God hold you
in the palm of His hand.
—Irish Blessing

Writing Friendly Letters (cont.)

Friendly letters that contain a specific message to meet a specific social situation are called *social notes.* Courtesy requires that you write these notes to express your appreciation for a gift, favor, or hospitality.

3 **Two kinds of social notes are the *thank-you note* and the *bread-and-butter note.***
   a. The *thank-you note* should be written to thank someone for a gift or favor.
   b. The *bread-and-butter note* should be written to thank the hostess in the home where you have visited.

4 **Observe the following courtesies when writing social notes.**
   a. Write promptly.
   b. Be brief but sincere.
   c. In a thank-you note give specific reasons for your gratitude.
   d. In a bread-and-butter note mention some of the things that were done for you.
   e. Write about something else as well.

Sample Thank-You Note

847 Wilcox Boulevard
Calhoun, Georgia 30735
May 21, ______

Dear Uncle Charles,

Thank you so much for the $20 that you sent me for the basketball clinic. I had been working on the weekends but still needed money for the registration fee. Your gift was an answer to prayer. I sent in the registration today.

The clinic will last for six weeks this summer. I hope to learn enough to make the basketball team next year. After the clinic the whole family will vacation in Orlando, and we hope to see you then.

With love,
Jordan

Sample Bread-and-Butter Note

5588 North Park Street
Lexington, Massachusetts 02194
August 15, ______

Dear Mrs. Ellis,

Visiting you and Diana last week was the highlight of my summer. I loved the hills of Tennessee, your great cooking, and the special outings you planned for me.

The pictures that I took came out well, especially the ones of the picnic. There is a particularly good one of Diana demonstrating how to eat watermelon!

Thank you for making me feel so welcome. It was an exciting vacation. Tell Diana I will write her soon.

Sincerely,
Maria

Exercise A **Write a friendly letter using one of the following suggestions.**

1. You have just finished your first babysitting job. Some hilarious things happened (though they were not so funny at the time). You know your sister in college would really be amused. Write her a letter describing what happened.
2. You have a pen pal in France who has asked you how your family observes Christmas. Write a description of your family's celebration.
3. Your school basketball team became state champions in a very hard-fought, exciting game last night. Tell your brother in the service all about it.

Exercise B **Write a thank-you note using one of the following suggestions.**

1. Your pastor gave you wise counsel on a personal matter that had been troubling you. His advice proved true and you are grateful. Thank him for his help and encouragement.
2. Just before your parents left you at a friend's house for a two-week vacation, your dad slipped a $20 bill into your hand. Write him a note thanking him and telling him how you spent it.
3. Write a bread-and-butter note. You have spent a weekend at your friend's house. His family showed you all around and treated you grandly.

Writing Business Letters

1 A business letter has six parts.

a. **The *heading* is the same as the heading of a friendly letter.**

b. **The *inside address* is the address of the person or company to whom you are writing.** This is exactly the same as the address on the envelope.

c. **The *salutation* is the greeting.** It is followed by a colon.

- Salutation for a person whose name is used in the inside address.

  Dear Mr. Brown: Dear Miss Smith: Dear Mrs. Green:

- Salutation for a person whose name you do not know, but whose title you do know.

  Dear Sir: Dear Madam:

- Salutation for a group or firm.

  Gentlemen:

d. **The *body* is what you have to say.** Each paragraph should be indented.

e. **The *closing* is the farewell.** It is followed by a comma. The following closings are standard for formal business letters:

  Truly yours, Yours truly, Very truly yours,

f. **The *signature* is the full name of the writer.** If you are typing the letter, you should type your name underneath your signature.

Study the form of the following letter.

Business Letter Form

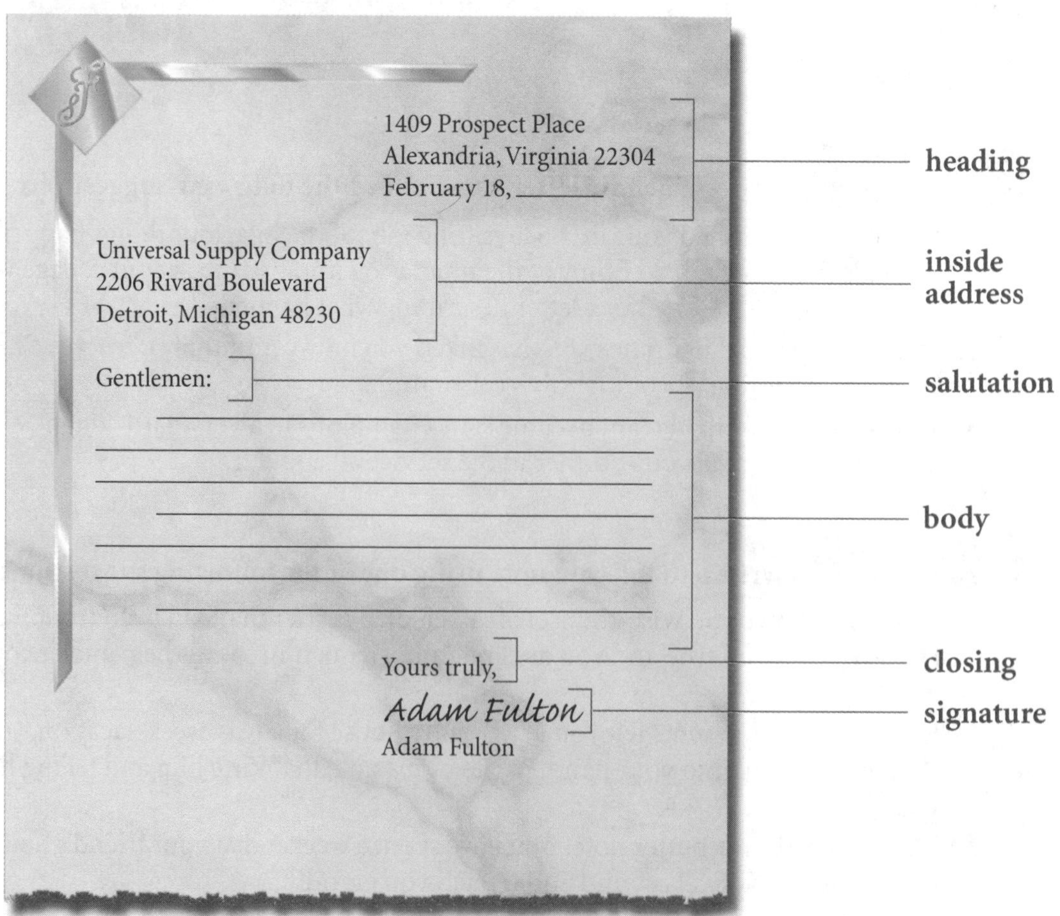
1409 Prospect Place
Alexandria, Virginia 22304
February 18, ______

Universal Supply Company
2206 Rivard Boulevard
Detroit, Michigan 48230

Gentlemen:

Yours truly,
Adam Fulton
Adam Fulton

2 Observe the following suggestions to make your letters appropriate.

a. **Use unlined white paper of standard size: $8^1/_2$ x 11 inches.**

b. **Type the letter or write neatly with blue or black ink.**

c. **Make the letter neat; avoid blots, erasures, and cross outs; maintain at least an inch margin at the top, bottom, and sides of the letter.**

d. **Write only on one side of the page.**

e. **Be brief and to the point. Avoid unnecessary details.**

f. **Be courteous, even when writing to clear up a mistake.**

g. **Avoid using expressions such as *Permit me to state, Please find enclosed,* and *Thanking you in advance.***

3 Two particular kinds of business letters are the *order letter* and the *request letter*.

a. **The *order letter* should include the following information: the description of the item, the quantity, the size, the color, the price, the catalog number, and the place you saw it advertised. Also tell how you are paying: cash, check, money order, or C.O.D.**

b. **The *request letter* should be clear, specific, and courteous.** Avoid vague and general statements. Give only the specific information necessary to fulfill your request, but be careful not to omit anything that is necessary. Routine requests for catalogs and prices may be limited to a one-sentence letter.

Sample Order Letter

312 Ashbrook Street
Dover, Delaware 19901
March 19, ______

Monitor Recordings, Inc.
156 Fifth Avenue
New York, New York 10010

Gentlemen:

Please send me your three-CD set of Bach's 16 Keyboard Concertos, lot number MCS 2149-51 which you advertised for $29.95, including shipping, in your 1999 (no. 4) catalog.

My check for $29.95 is enclosed.

Truly yours,
Fred Silverman
Fred Silverman

UNIT 20

Sample Request Letter

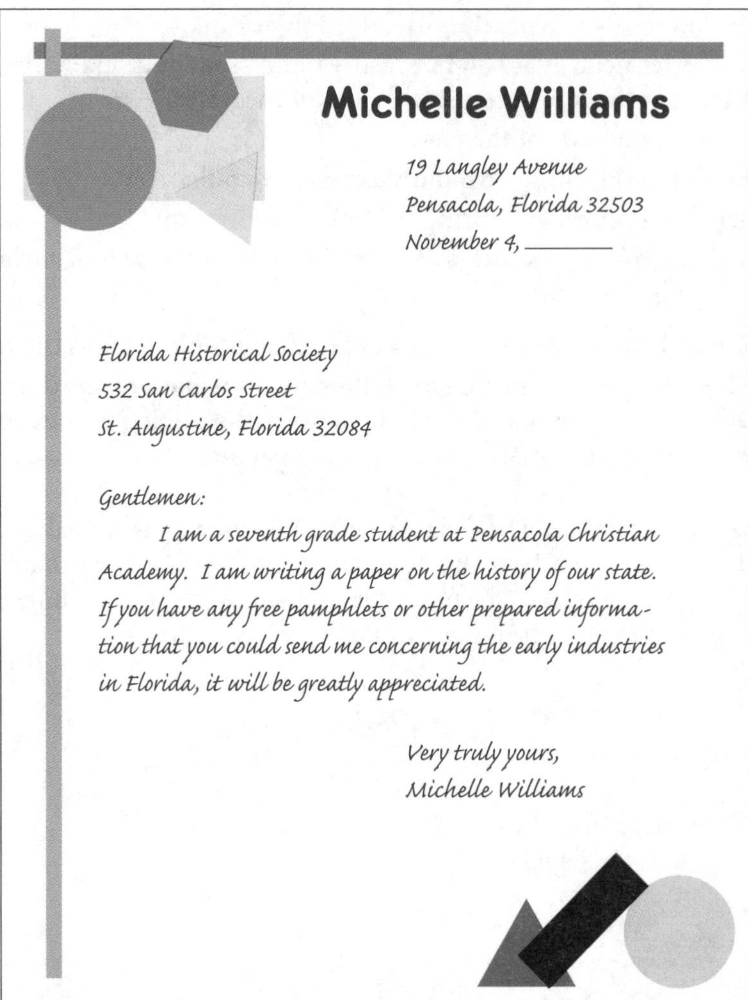

Michelle Williams

19 Langley Avenue
Pensacola, Florida 32503
November 4, ______

Florida Historical Society
532 San Carlos Street
St. Augustine, Florida 32084

Gentlemen:

I am a seventh grade student at Pensacola Christian Academy. I am writing a paper on the history of our state. If you have any free pamphlets or other prepared information that you could send me concerning the early industries in Florida, it will be greatly appreciated.

Very truly yours,
Michelle Williams

Exercise

Write a request letter for any one of the following.

1. You have heard that the Chamber of Commerce is sponsoring an essay contest with a trip to the state capital as first prize. Write for more information.
2. Write a letter to an automobile club requesting tour maps for a trip to some specific area.
3. Write to a travel bureau requesting information about special activities (canoeing, horseback riding, white-water rafting) in an area you would like to visit.

Exercise A

Capitalization and Punctuation. (1) Draw a line through each incorrect small letter. Write a capital above it. (2) Add all necessary punctuation.

1. wasn't general william booth the founder of the salvation army in england, john?
2. his book entitled in darkest england pointed out the poverty of many people.
3. according to the war cry, the salvation army's magazine, the international headquarters is located at 101 queen victoria street in london.
4. the salvation army volunteers are "soldiers"; at present there are four hundred fifty thousand (450,000) of these volunteers in the united states alone.
5. in luke 14:21, our lord said, "go out quickly into the streets and lanes of the city, and bring in hither the poor and the maimed."

Exercise B

Subjects, Verbs, Complements, and Participles. (1) Draw two lines under each verb. (2) Draw one line under each subject. (3) Box any complements. (4) Circle any participles.

1. The little reed, bending to the force of the wind, stood upright again when the storm had passed over.
2. (You) Please all, and you will please none.
3. Dad repaired my brother's broken bicycle.
4. The blizzard brought freezing snow and biting wind, but inside the house we were warm and safe.
5. We would often be sorry if our wishes were gratified.
6. We could not see the delivery man's van hidden by the garage.
7. Mr. Jackson gave each of the volunteers a free pass to the football game.
8. Because Wade was such a good runner, he won first prize in the marathon.
9. Sixteen years have passed, and we are finally free.
10. Wondering about the future, Jared asked his father for advice.

Exercise C

The Sentence. In the blank before the number, write *s.* for sentences, *frag.* for fragments, or *r.o.* for run-ons.

frag. 1. Born in 1863 to Christian parents in England.

r.o. 2. G. Campbell Morgan became an eminent Bible scholar, he taught many of the converts of D. L. Moody.

frag. 3. As he preached to thousands in Westminster Chapel in London.

s. 4. From 1919 to 1933, he conducted an itinerant ministry in America.

frag. 5. The many commentaries, books, articles which he authored.

Exercise D

Parts of Speech. In the blanks below the paragraph, identify the parts of speech of the italicized words. Write *n.* for nouns, *pro.* for pronouns, *adj.* for adjectives, *v.* for verbs, *adv.* for adverbs, *prep.* for prepositions, *conj.* for conjunctions, and *interj.* for interjections.

At the *bottom*[1] of the world *lies*[2] a wasteland of ice and rock called Antarctica. Towering mountains, *treacherous*[3] glaciers, and temperatures *that*[4] drop 100 degrees below zero make Antarctica a *challenge*[5] to explorers and scientists. *Although*[6] it was discovered in 1820, no *widespread*[7] *exploration*[8] *of*[9] Antarctica was attempted until after 1900. The *struggle*[10] to reach the South Pole *turned*[11] into a race *between*[12] an *expedition*[13] from Norway and *one*[14] from *Britain*[15]. Roald Amundsen, the leader of the *Norwegian*[16] group, *took*[17] *extreme*[18] measures to reach the South Pole first. Dogs that *grew*[19] *ill*[20] were shot and used as *food*[21] *for*[22] the men *and*[23] for the dogs *that*[24] were *still*[25] pulling the sleds. Both groups *struggled*[26] closer and *closer*[27] to the Pole. On January 18, 1912, Robert Scott, the leader of the British crew, *triumphantly*[28] announced to his men that they had reached their goal. *Alas!*[29] Triumph gave way to disappointment *when*[30] Scott found a flag flying above the barren terrain. It was Amundsen's flag: his expedition had arrived *at*[31] the Pole on December 14, 1911. The *Norwegians*[32] had won the race. Weak, *discouraged,*[33] and low *on*[34] *supplies,*[35] the *Britons*[36] *began*[37] their *return*[38] journey. Tragically, *they*[39] *died*[40] less than *eleven*[41] miles *from*[42] an *emergency*[43] relief *station.*[44] *Today,*[45] the *research*[46] center at the South Pole *bears*[47] the names of the two men *whose*[48] race for the Pole solved *many*[49] of the mysteries of the *frozen*[50] land at the bottom of the world.

1. n.	11. v.	21. n.	31. prep.	41. adj.
2. v.	12. prep.	22. prep.	32. n.	42. prep.
3. adj.	13. n.	23. conj.	33. adj.	43. adj.
4. pro.	14. pro.	24. pro.	34. prep.	44. n.
5. n.	15. n.	25. adv.	35. n.	45. adv.
6. conj.	16. adj.	26. v.	36. n.	46. adj.
7. adj.	17. v.	27. adv.	37. v.	47. v.
8. n.	18. adj.	28. adv.	38. adj.	48. adj.
9. prep.	19. v.	29. interj.	39. pro.	49. pro.
10. n.	20. adj.	30. conj.	40. v.	50. adj.

Exercise E

Using Nouns. Above each italicized word write its use. Abbreviate as follows: *s.* (subject), *p.n.* (predicate nominative), *d.o.* (direct object), *i.o.* (indirect object), *ap.* (appositive), *d.a.* (direct address), and *o.p.* (object of a preposition).

d.o. o.p.
1. We should always pay our *debts* on *time.*

ap. p.n.
2. William H. McGuffey, *editor* of the famous McGuffey Readers, was an early American *educator.*

d.a. s. ap.
3. *Dana,* wasn't *Monrovia,* the *capital* of Liberia, named after President James Monroe?

i.o. d.o. o.p.
4. America paid *Russia* seven million *dollars* for the territory of *Alaska.*

s. p.n.
5. A *promise* made is a *debt* unpaid.

Exercise F

Recognizing Adjectives, Adverbs, and Prepositions. Identify each italicized word as either an adjective, an adverb, or a preposition by writing *adj.*, *adv.*, or *prep.* above it.

adv. adv. adv.
1. The toddler fell *down* several times, but each time he got back *up* and tried *again.*

adj. adv. adv.
2. That *silly* person *evidently* does *not* perceive the gravity of her decisions.

prep. adv. adj.
3. We went *to* bed *early* last night so we would be ready to go fishing *this* morning.

prep. adj.
4. The church *in* that village was built in the *early* part of the twelfth century.

prep. adv. adv.
5. A breeze blew *through* the valley and carried our kite *up higher.*

Exercise G

Using Adjectives and Adverbs. (1) Cross out any incorrect words and make corrections where necessary. (2) Circle any misplaced modifiers and draw arrows to where they should be.

1. (Hanging on a nail in the broom closet,) Mrs. Nelson found her dusting rags.

or those
2. Father told me (on Saturday) he would take me to see ~~them~~ horses.

good quickly badly
3. It is ~~well~~ that you left ~~quick~~; it stormed ~~bad~~ after you left.

other weak
4. Solomon was ~~more~~ wiser than any ^ man in the Bible, yet even he was ~~weakly~~ when confronted by temptation.

surely well
5. You ~~sure~~ did act ~~good~~ today, Tom; I'm proud of you.

else
6. The slave Joseph was nobler than anyone ^ in Egypt, because he was a servant of Jehovah.

Those bitter
7. ~~Them~~ pomegranates taste ~~bitterly~~; in fact, they are the ~~most~~ bitterest fruit I have ever eaten.

worst
8. Of the many kings of Israel, Ahab was perhaps the ~~baddest~~.

or
9. I read about a mother who had quadruplets (in today's newspaper.)

less
10. It would be ~~more~~ better to use a fertilizer with ~~fewer~~ potassium.

Exercise H

Recognizing Participial Phrases and Prepositional Phrases. Identify each italicized phrase as either a participial phrase or a prepositional phrase. For each participial phrase write *part.* in the blank. For each prepositional phrase write *prep.* in the blank.

part. 1. *Showing her love for Christ,* Dorcas spent her life helping others.

prep. 2. The owner *of this house* was the inventor of the cotton gin.

part. 3. A girl *hidden in the bushes* overheard the princess's predicament.

prep. 4. *After the toil and the heat of the day,* we can always go to God for rest.

part. 5. We could see a hummingbird *flitting from flower to flower.*

part. 6. *Sheltered in the arms of God,* we Christians should not worry.

part. 7. The privilege of every person *forgiven by Christ* is the hope of the resurrection.

prep. 8. *Throughout the world tonight,* many people will go to bed hungry.

Exercise I

Complements. Each of the following sentences contains at least one complement. Underline each complement and above it write *d.o.* (direct object), *i.o.* (indirect object), *p.n.* (predicate nominative), or *p.a.* (predicate adjective).

1. John Huss was a forerunner (p.n.) of the Protestant Reformation.
2. It did not seem strange (p.a.) to him that a man should give his life (d.o.) for Christ.
3. He read many (d.o.) of the writings of John Wycliffe, the English reformer.
4. Huss became a heretic (p.n.) in the eyes of the Church because Huss opposed the Pope's power (d.o.).
5. The Pope gave Huss (i.o.) a promise (d.o.) of safe passage to a Church council.
6. The Pope had given Huss (i.o.) his word (d.o.), but he did not keep his promise (d.o.).
7. John Huss was brave (p.a.) and gave the Church (i.o.) an excellent example (d.o.) of a consecrated saint.

Exercise J

Sentence Structure. Identify each sentence according to structure. In the blank write *S* (simple), *Cd* (compound), *Cx* (complex), or *CdCx* (compound-complex).

Cx 1. When I cry unto Thee, then shall mine enemies turn back.

Cd 2. The transgressors shall be destroyed together; the end of the wicked shall be cut off.

S 3. With my voice unto the Lord did I make my supplication.

Cd 4. Purge me with hyssop, and I shall be clean.

Cx 5. O God, to whom vengeance belongeth, shew Thyself.

S 6. Better is a little with righteousness than great revenues without right.

CdCx 7. Though he fall, he shall not be utterly cast down, for the Lord upholdeth him with His hands.

Cx 8. As the hart panteth after the water brooks, so panteth my soul after Thee, O Lord.

Exercise K Diagraming. On a separate sheet of paper diagram each sentence.

(See *Supplement*)

1. Alexander conquered the world of his day, yet he never conquered his own passions.
2. If wishes were horses, beggars would ride. —*English Proverb*
3. Remember not the sins of my youth nor my transgressions.
4. He that winneth souls is wise.
5. Walking along the mountain trail, I could see the small cabin in the distance.
6. The desire of the righteous is only good, but the expectation of the wicked is wrath.
7. The Lord turned the captivity of Job, when he prayed for his friends.
8. The printing press is one lever which moves the mind of the world.
9. They that trust in the Lord shall be as Mount Zion which cannot be moved.
10. Thy word is a lamp unto my feet and a light unto my path.

Exercise L Subject and Verb Agreement. Cross out the incorrect verb form in parentheses.

1. "Missions" (was, ~~were~~) the topic of our pastor's sermon today.
2. There (~~is~~, are) many people who are not obeying God's command to witness.
3. A few dollars (is, ~~are~~) not much to give to help send missionaries to the field.
4. Each of us (gives, ~~give~~) according to our love for Christ.
5. One of the things which God hates(is, ~~are~~) a proud look.
6. Everyone (~~answer~~, answers) to God for his own sins.
7. Neither Fred nor the Smiths (~~is~~, are) going to sing in church tonight.
8. The adornment of a child of God (is, ~~are~~) a meek and quiet spirit.
9. The church (was, ~~were~~) agreed that the erring brother should be disciplined.
10. "Sinners in the Hands of an Angry God" (is, ~~are~~) being read to our class.

Exercise M Using Verbs. Cross out all incorrect verb forms and make the necessary corrections.

1. While crossing the river, several horses were ~~drug~~ dragged downstream by the fierce current and ~~drownded~~ drowned.
2. The monkeys ~~clumb~~ climbed down out of the trees and ~~attackted~~ attacked with vigor the food left for them.
3. I ^had better clean up this room; someone has ~~lain~~ laid things all over it.
4. Because Betty has ~~taken sick~~ become ill you ^had better call the doctor.
5. ~~Ain't~~ Isn't Pastor Hertzler the one who ~~brung~~ brought the message from 1 Corinthians 11?
6. ~~Leave~~ Let him ~~rise~~ raise the window; we need some fresh air.
7. I want ^to get off this old bridge, Myron; I believe its supports are ~~busted~~ broken.
8. While the Trojans ~~laid~~ lay in bed asleep, the Greeks ~~snuck~~ sneaked out of the huge, wooden horse.

Exercise N

All Usage. Make whatever changes necessary to correct all usage problems in the following sentences.

1. We couldn't see ~~nothing~~ anything ~~beside~~ besides the darkness as we ~~snuck~~ sneaked down the staircase.
2. If you had ~~of~~ listened ~~good~~ well, you would ~~of~~ have known where to carry the books ~~to~~.
3. Neither our Lord nor His disciples ~~was~~ were welcome inside ~~of~~ Nazareth.
4. Everything ~~accept~~ except the kippered herring was ~~aten~~ eaten; the total amounted ~~up~~ to a tremendous bill.
5. The Prayer Warriors ~~are~~ is an organization at our school; ~~us~~ we students meet and pray for men and women who are serving the Lord in other nations.
6. ~~Bring~~ Take this notice to Mr. Dettweiler's office, Joseph, and ~~lie~~ lay it on his desk.
7. Shelley ~~took sick at about~~ became ill or noon, and ~~us~~ we girls took her ~~in~~ into town to a doctor.
8. Our grocery bills, ~~beside~~ besides extras, amounted ~~up~~ to $250.
9. ~~Can~~ May Douglas and ~~me~~ I ~~sit~~ set these packages where they belong ~~at~~?
10. *Parallel Lives of Noble Greeks and Romans,* the best~~est~~ authority on ancient times, ~~were~~ was the basis for much of Shakespeare's writing.
11. Be sure ~~and~~ to add yeast so that the dough will ~~raise~~ rise.
12. We should ~~learn~~ teach ourselves not to want ^to get out of a situation merely because it is unpleasant.
13. I ^had better ~~sit~~ set this safety flare ~~besides~~ beside the road.
14. There ~~is~~ are not many excuses for not doing homework, but I would ~~of~~ have done mine if I hadn't ~~took sick at about~~ become ill or five o'clock.
15. The bowls of soup ~~was~~ were steaming on the table when we entered.
16. I'm doing ~~good~~ well on my science project, ~~aren't I~~ am I not?
17. The monkey ~~throwed~~ threw the peeling on the ground after he had ~~et~~ eaten all the banana.
18. ~~Between~~ Among Harry, Tom, and Dave, Tom is the ~~goodest~~ best kite flyer.
19. There ~~is less~~ are fewer parts in this clock than I realized.
20. I used to ~~could~~ be able to take ~~real~~ really good pictures with this camera until it got ~~busted~~ broken.
21. Mrs. Baker ~~snuck~~ sneaked in the back door after the concert had ~~began~~ begun.
22. ~~Them~~ Those students who didn't take good notes did ~~poor~~ poorly on this last exam.
23. Ben and ~~me~~ I ~~was~~ were jumping off ~~of~~ a stump into the lake when a thunderstorm came up.
24. I've ~~et~~ eaten more food than any ^other member of my family, but I haven't ~~growed~~ grown very much.

Capitalization

A. Capitalize *proper nouns* and words formed from proper nouns. (p. 2)

1. **Capitalize names of *particular persons.*** (p. 2)
   William Jennings Bryan, U.S. Grant

2. **Capitalize names of *particular places.*** (p. 2)
   a. Continents—Europe, North America
   b. Countries—Venezuela, Germany
   c. Sections of the country—the West, the Northeast (Do not capitalize these words when they refer only to a direction: east of the river, driving north.)
   d. States—Texas, Nebraska
   e. Cities—Scranton, Little Rock
   f. Islands—Isle of Wright, Catalina Island
   g. Bodies of water—Lake Huron, Salton Sea
   h. Streets, highways—Fifth Avenue, Pennsylvania Avenue, Twenty-second Street (The second part of a hyphenated number is not capitalized.)
   i. Mountains—Rocky Mountains, Mount McKinley
   j. Parks—Everglades National Park, Big Bend National Park

3. **Capitalize names of *particular things.*** (p. 2)
   a. Special organizations—United Nations, Philharmonic Society of New York
   b. Calendar items and special events—January, Ash Wednesday (Do not capitalize the seasons: spring, summer, fall, winter.)
   c. Historical events and periods—Romantic Period, the Reformation
   d. Nationalities, races, and religions—Czech, Caucasian, Shintoism
   e. Languages and particular courses—Spanish, Home Economics 101, Algebra II (The number following the subject indicates that it is a particular course.)
   f. Brand names of business products—Braun camera, Conn trumpet (Do not capitalize the common noun following the brand name.)
   g. Monuments, bridges, planets, documents, and any other particular things—Badlands National Monument, Saturn, Atlantic Charter

4. **Capitalize words referring to the *Deity* and *Holy Scripture.*** (p. 2)
   Holy Spirit, Revelation, His will (Do not capitalize the word *god* when referring to pagan deities.)

5. **Capitalize words formed from *proper nouns.*** (p. 2)
   a. Proper adjectives—North American, Parisian
   b. Abbreviations of proper nouns—**FBI** (Federal Bureau of Investigation), **FDIC** (Federal Deposit Insurance Corporation)

   Note: Sometimes proper names and words formed from proper names lose their original meaning through frequent usage and are not capitalized: china dishes, morocco leather. When you are in doubt about a word, refer to your dictionary.

6. **Capitalize a common noun or adjective only when it is a *part of a proper name.*** (p. 2)
   Brooklyn Bridge, a bridge; Salt Lake City, a city

   Note: The phrase *Sunday school* is not a proper noun. Sunday is capitalized because it is a day of the week, but school is not capitalized.

Capitalization (cont.)

B. Capitalize *titles of persons.*

1. **Capitalize titles when they are used *before a person's name,* as part of the name.** (p. 7)

   President Roosevelt, Secretary of Defense Melvin Laird, Governor Aiken, Mayor Holmes, King David, Captain Bligh, Dr. R. D. Byrd, Mrs. Jones

2. **Titles *following a name* or *used alone in place of a name* are not usually capitalized unless used in direct address.** (p. 7)

   Exception: *President* is usually capitalized when it refers to the President of the United States of America.

   Theodore Roosevelt, President of the United States; the President of the United States; Melvin Laird, secretary of defense; Patrick Henry, the governor of Virginia; Frank Holmes, the mayor; David, the king of Israel; the senator; the congressman; the pastor; the archbishop of Canterbury; "Good morning, Governor, Senator, Congressman, etc."

3. **Capitalize *family-relationship words* when they are used *before a person's name* and when used *alone in place of the name.*** (p. 7)

   We visited Uncle Paul and Aunt Kathleen on vacation.
   What shall we buy Mother for Christmas?
   Her father died at the age of ninety-two.
   Several cousins have come to visit.
   Yes, Dad, we will be glad to help.

   Note: Do not capitalize these words when they are preceded by a possessive unless the title is considered part of the name.

   my Uncle Robert, my Aunt Emma (*Uncle* and *Aunt* are considered part of the name.)
   my cousin Brooke, his brother Bill (*Cousin* and *brother* are not part of the name.)

C. Capitalize the *titles of works.*

Capitalize the first and last words and all important words in the titles of *books, magazines, newspapers, poems, stories, plays,* and *works of art.* (Unimportant words are coordinating conjunctions, prepositions, and the articles *a, an,* and *the.*) (p. 7)

Far from the Madding Crowd (book)
"The Reaper and the Flowers" (poem)
Charioteer of Delphi (sculpture)

Exception: The article *the* is not capitalized before the title of a magazine or a newspaper (even when the article is part of the title) when the title is written within a sentence.

The name of the newspaper is the *Indianapolis Star.*

D. Capitalize the *first word of every sentence* (including quoted sentences). (p. 7)

The fool hath said in his heart, "There is no God."

E. Capitalize the pronoun *I* and the interjection *O.* (p. 7)

In Thee, O Lord, do I put my trust.

F. Capitalize the *first word in every line of poetry,* whether or not the word begins a sentence. (p. 7)

Let us, then, be up and doing,
With a heart for any fate;
Still achieving, still pursuing,
Learn to labor and to wait.

—*Longfellow*

Punctuation

A. End Marks

1. A *declarative sentence* ends with a *period.* (A declarative sentence is one that makes a statement.) (p. 12)

Important principles may and must be held inflexible. —*Lincoln*

2. An *imperative sentence* ends with a *period* or an *exclamation point.* (An imperative sentence is one that gives a command or makes a request.) (p. 12)

Don't give up the ship. Look out below!

3. An *interrogative sentence* ends with a *question mark.* (An interrogative sentence is one that asks a question.) (p. 12)

Will Jesus find us watching?

4. An *exclamatory sentence* ends with an *exclamation point.* (An exclamatory sentence is one that shows sudden or strong feeling.) (p. 12)

Religion! What treasure untold
Resides in that heavenly word! —*Cowper*

5. An abbreviation ends with a period. (p. 12)

Mr. Mrs. adj. Dr. U.S.

Exception: It is now general practice to omit periods for abbreviations of organizations.

CBS FBI YMCA

B. Commas

1. Use a *comma and a coordinating conjunction* *(and, but, or, nor, for, yet)* **to join two simple sentences.** (, and) (p. 13)

Foolishness is bound in the heart of a child, **but** the rod of correction shall drive it far from him.

2. Use a *single comma* to indicate that a word or words have been omitted, or to avoid a possible misreading. (,) (p. 13)

a. Use single commas to separate three or more *items in a series.*

Mercury, Venus, and Mars are planets in our solar system. (The comma after *Mercury* is there because the word *and* has been omitted. The comma after *Venus* is there to avoid a possible misreading.)

b. Use single commas to separate *two or more adjectives preceding a noun.* (Do not put a comma between the last adjective and the noun it modifies.)

A hungry, pleading look was in his eyes. (The single comma is placed after the word *hungry* because the word *and* has been omitted.)

If the last adjective is so closely related to the noun it modifies that the two words seem to form one expression, do not use the comma to separate that adjective from other adjectives.

Hamlet is a famous Shakespearian tragedy. *(Shakespearian tragedy forms one expression; no comma is needed after famous.)*

c. Use a single comma any time *to avoid misreading.*

While mowing, Bill discovered a snake.

3. Use a *pair of commas* to indicate a *nonessential element* in a sentence. (,—,) (p. 16)

Note: The *pair of commas* is *one* mark of punctuation composed of two symbols, but these symbols are not to be thought of as two *single commas.* Also, if the nonessential elements come first or last in a sentence, you see only one half of the pair of commas.

Punctuation (cont.)

a. Use a pair of commas to set off *nonessential appositives* and *appositive phrases.*

Anton Bruckner, *an Austrian composer,* was also a noted organist.

Note: If the appositive is short and closely connected to the noun it follows, omit the commas.

Ethelred the Unready

b. Use commas to set off *nonessential participial phrases, nonessential adjective clauses,* and *nonessential adverb clauses.*

My father, *who will emcee the program,* was well acquainted with Mr. Henry.

Note: Introductory adverb clauses are set off by commas. Adverb clauses at the end of a sentence do not require commas unless nonessential.

When He giveth quietness, who then can make trouble?
I will give you an A *if your average is 94.5 or above.*
I will give everyone the discount, *whether they have a coupon or not.*

c. Use a pair of commas to set off words used in *direct address.*

Samuel, did you feed the cat? (Here you see only one half of the pair of commas. The part before the word *Samuel* is unnecessary.)

d. Use a pair of commas to set off the words *well, yes, no,* or *why* when they are nonessential. When these words come at the beginning of a sentence, you use only the second half of the pair of commas. The part before the word is unnecessary.

Yes, Abraham was buried in the cave of Machpelah.

e. Use a pair of commas to set off *parenthetical expressions.*

This exam was, *I believe,* more difficult than the last one.

4. **Use a single comma to set off *introductory modifying phrases.*** (Do not use a comma after an introductory adverb phrase that comes immediately before the verb it modifies.) (p. 16)

In 1998, the Chicago Bulls won the NBA championship. (short adverb phrase)
After many hours of hard work, the meal was finally ready. (long adverb phrase)
Growing in the garden are three kinds of melons. (The introductory phrase comes immediately before the verb it modifies.)

5. **Use commas to separate the parts of *dates and addresses* within sentences.** Use a comma after the last part if it does not end the sentence. (Do not use a comma between the month and the day or between the state and the ZIP code.) (p. 19)

On August 15, 1998, we moved to 112 Madison Avenue, Boise, Idaho 83702.

6. **Use a comma after the *salutation of a friendly letter;* use a comma after the *closing of all letters.*** (p. 19)

Dear Joan,   Yours truly,

C. Semicolons

1. **Use a *semicolon* between independent clauses *if you do not choose to use a comma and a coordinating conjunction.*** (The coordinating conjunctions are *and, but, or, nor, for, yet.*) (p. 21)

I will not leave you comfortless; I will come to you.

2. **Use a *semicolon* before transitional words such as *accordingly, besides, consequently, however, nevertheless, then, therefore, thus.*** (These words are not equivalent to coordinating conjunctions.) (p. 21)

Good works are important; however, only faith will save a sinner.

3. **A *semicolon* may be necessary between independent clauses even with a coordinating conjunction *to make it obvious where the first clause ends.*** (This semicolon is usually needed when there are commas in the first clause or when the clauses are long.) (p. 21)

   Cakes, pies, and cookies make good desserts; but fruits are more healthful.

D. Colons

1. **Use a *colon* before listed items introduced by such words as *as follows* or *the following.* Do not use a colon to introduce a list that is the complement of a verb or the object of a preposition.** (p. 21)

   On our vacation, we traveled to: Carlsbad, Albuquerque, and Santa Fe. (incorrect—colon separates the preposition from its object)

   We visited the following places on our vacation: Carlsbad, Albuquerque, and Santa Fe. (correct)

2. **Use a *colon* between the *chapter and verse* of a Biblical reference.** (p. 21)

   Deuteronomy 29:29 is one of my favorite verses.

3. **Use a *colon* between the *hour and the minute* of a time reference.** (p. 21)

   12:00 P.M. 6:15 A.M. 7:20 P.M.

4. **Use a *colon* after the *salutation of a business letter.*** (p. 21)

   Dear Mrs. Patterson: Dear Sir:

E. Italics and Hyphens

1. **Underline** (italicize) **the *titles* of *books, magazines, newspapers, plays, works of art,* and the names of *ships, trains, aircraft,* and *spacecraft.*** (Underlining indicates those words that would be italicized if your sentences were set in type by a typesetter.) (p. 24)

   Wiley Post flew around the world in eight days in the Winnie Mae.

   Our history book contains a picture of Saint Mark Rescuing a Slave, a painting by Tintoretto.

   Note: The articles *a, an,* and *the* at the beginning of a title are italicized only when they are a part of the title.

   Exception: The article *the* is not italicized before the title of a magazine or a newspaper (even when the article is part of the title) when the title is written within a sentence.

2. **Use a hyphen if you must *divide a word at the end of a line.*** (p. 24)
   - **a.** Do not divide a one-syllable word. *(food,* not *fo-od)*
   - **b.** Divide only between syllables. *(wis-dom,* not *wi-sdom)*
   - **c.** Do not divide after a single letter. *(able,* not *a-ble)*
   - **d.** Do not carry over a two-letter syllable. *(money,* not *mon-ey)*
   - **e.** Divide words with prefixes after the prefix. *(Anti-Christ,* not *An-tichrist)*

3. **Use a hyphen in *compound numbers* from *twenty-one* through *ninety-nine.*** (p. 24)

   Rembrandt painted self-portraits when he was *twenty-three* and when he was *fifty-two.*

4. **Use a hyphen in *fractions* used as *adjectives.*** (p. 24)

   A *two-thirds* majority is needed to pass this bill.

Punctuation (cont.)

F. Quotation Marks

1. **Use quotation marks to enclose the *exact words* of a speaker (a direct quotation).** Do not use quotation marks for an indirect quotation, which is a rewording of the person's statement. (p. 26)

   Benjamin Franklin said, "Little strokes fell great oaks." (direct quotation)

   Benjamin Franklin said that little strokes fell great oaks. (indirect quotation)

2. **Capitalize the *first word* of a direct quotation.** If the quotation is interrupted by other words, the second part should not begin with a capital letter unless the second part is the beginning of a new sentence or is a word that would be capitalized anyway. (p. 26)

   "The best prize that life offers," said Theodore Roosevelt, "is the chance to work hard at work worth doing."

3. **The exact words of a speaker should be *set off* from the rest of the sentence by using a *comma,* a *question mark,* or an *exclamation point.*** (p. 26)

   "Have you read this story yet?" asked Bob.

   "What a good story this is!" exclaimed Bob.

   "I think I've read this story before," said Bob.

4. ***Commas* and *periods* always go *inside* the closing quotation marks.** (p. 26)

   "Gold is the most useless thing in the world," wrote Henry Ford.

   Henry Ford said, "Gold is the most useless thing in the world."

5. ***Colons* and *semicolons* always go *outside* the closing quotation marks.** (p. 26)

   Please note the following things as you read "Rikki-Tikki-Tavi": setting, plot, and character development.

   One of my favorite poems is William Wordsworth's "Daffodils"; Wordsworth also wrote other poems about nature.

6. ***Question marks* and *exclamation points* go *inside* the closing quotation marks when they apply to the quoted matter only. They go *outside* when they refer to the whole sentence.** (p. 27)

   Who was it that said, "Haste makes waste"? (The question mark applies to the entire sentence.)

   Mr. Parker asked, "Does haste really make waste?" (The question mark applies to the quoted words only.)

7. **In quoting *more than one sentence,* use quotation marks only at the beginning and at the end of the whole quotation. Do not put quotation marks around each sentence.** (p. 27)

   Someone once said, "Sloth makes everything difficult. Industry makes everything easy."

8. **In writing conversation, begin a new paragraph each time the speaker changes.** (p. 27)

   Then said Evangelist pointing with his finger over a very wide field, "Do you see yonder wicket gate?"

   The man said, "No."

   Then said the other, "Do you see yonder shining light?"

   He said, "I think I do."

9. **Use quotation marks to enclose titles of *short stories, short poems, songs, chapters, articles,* and other *parts* of books or magazines.** (p. 27)

   "The Raven"   "Jesus, the Very Thought of Thee"   "Trees"

10. **Use single quotation marks for an element within a quotation that also requires quotation marks.** (p. 27)

    Miss Anderson asked, "How many of you have memorized 'Columbus' by Joaquin Miller?"

G. Apostrophes

1. **Use an apostrophe to form the *possessive case* of nouns.** (p. 30)
   a. To form the possessive case of a *singular noun,* first write the *singular form* of the word. Then add an *apostrophe and s.* **('s)** (See exceptions on p. 30.)

      spider*'s* web

   b. To form the possessive case of a *plural noun that does not end in s,* first write the *plural form* of the word. Then add an *apostrophe and s.* **('s)**

      children*'s* games

   c. To form the possessive case of a *plural noun that ends in s,* first write the *plural form* of the word. Then add an *apostrophe.* **(')**

      cats' tails

2. **Use an apostrophe to show that letters have been *omitted* from a word. Such words are called contractions. Contractions should be avoided in formal writing.** (p. 30)

   there's = there is   don't = do not

   Several words require a slight change in spelling.

   will not = won't   shall not = shan't   cannot = can't

   Note: Possessive pronouns do *not* use apostrophes to show possession—*its, hers, theirs,* etc.

3. **Use an *apostrophe and s* to form the *plurals of letters, numbers, signs,* and *words used as words.*** (p. 30)

   His *e*'s are very similar to his *3*'s.

   Note: The plurals of years written as numerals may be formed by adding *s* alone.

   1920s   1860s

The Sentence

A. There are four kinds of sentences classified according to their purpose.

1. **A *declarative sentence* makes a statement.** It ends with a period. (p. 36)

   The wages of sin is death.

2. **An *imperative sentence* gives a command or makes a request.** It ends with a period or an exclamation point. The subject of an imperative sentence is the word *you,* understood but not expressed. (p. 36)

   Give me liberty or give me death!

   Please pass the potatoes.

The Sentence (cont.)

3. **An *interrogative sentence* asks a question.** It ends with a question mark. (p. 36)
   Is there a man who is wiser than God?
4. **An *exclamatory sentence* shows sudden or strong feeling.** It ends with an exclamation point. (p. 36)
   How precious is the word of God!

B. Learn these parts of a sentence.

1. **The *complete subject* of a sentence is that part about which something is said.** (complete subject = simple subject plus its modifiers) (p. 37)
   The **judgments** of the Lord are true and righteous altogether.
2. **The *simple subject* is the main word or group of words in the complete subject.** (simple subject = complex subject minus its modifiers) (p. 37)
   The **judgments** of the Lord are true and righteous altogether.
3. **The *complete predicate* of a sentence is the part that says something about the subject.** (complete predicate = simple predicate [verb] plus its modifiers and words that complete the verb) (p. 37)
   The judgments of the Lord **are** true and righteous altogether.
4. **The *simple predicate (verb)* is the main word or group of words in the complete predicate.** (simple predicate [verb] = complete predicate minus its modifiers or words that complete the verb) (p. 37)
   The judgments of the Lord **are** true and righteous altogether.
5. **A *verb phrase* is a main verb and its helping verbs.** (p. 37)
   I know whom I *have believed*.
6. **A *compound subject* consists of two or more subjects connected by *and, or,* or *nor*. These subjects are used with the same verb.** (p. 42)
   Joy **and** happiness accompany the saints.
7. **A *compound verb* consists of two or more verbs connected by *and, or, nor,* or *but*. These verbs are used with the same subject.** (p. 42)
   The chauffeur washed **and** waxed the Rolls-Royce.
8. **A *complement* is sometimes needed to complete the meaning started by the subject and predicate. In general you may locate a complement by asking *who, whom,* or *what* after the verb.** (p. 46)
   Mr. Adams is sick this morning. (sick = complement)
   Note: Complements cannot be within prepositional phrases.

C. A *sentence* is a group of words that expresses a complete thought. It always has a subject and a predicate. (p. 47)

There are no gains without pains.

D. A *fragment* is a separated sentence part that does *not* express a complete thought. (p. 47)

Ascending into Heaven. (fragment)
Ascending into Heaven, Christ disappeared into the clouds. (sentence)

E. **A *run-on sentence* is two or more sentences written incorrectly as one sentence.** (Sentences cannot be correctly written with *only* a comma between the sentences or with *no punctuation* between.) (p. 49)

Run-on — William Howard Taft was a large President he was six feet tall and he weighed over 300 pounds.

Corrected — William Howard Taft was a large President. He was six feet tall, and he weighed over 300 pounds.

Definitions of the Parts of Speech

A. **A *verb* is a word that *shows action, links* a word to the subject, *helps* another verb, or merely *indicates existence.*** (pp. 56, 57)

B. **A *noun* is a word that names a person, place, thing, or idea.** (pp. 56, 80)

C. **A *pronoun* is a word that takes the place of a noun.** (pp. 56, 106)

D. **An *adjective* is a word that modifies a noun or a pronoun. It answers the questions *what kind, which one, how many, how much,* or *whose.*** (pp. 56, 122)

E. **An *adverb* is a word that modifies a verb, an adjective, or another adverb. It answers the questions *where, when, how, how often,* or *to what extent.*** (pp. 56, 156)

F. **A *preposition* is a word that shows how a noun or a pronoun is *related* to some other word in the sentence.** (pp. 56, 174)

G. **A *conjunction* is a word that *joins* words or groups of words.** (pp. 56, 181)

H. **An *interjection* is an *exclamatory word* that is not related to the other words in a sentence.** (pp. 56, 182)

Verbs

A. **A *verb* is a word that *shows action, links* another word to the subject, *helps* another verb, or merely *indicates existence.*** (p. 57)

1. **An *action verb* expresses *physical or mental action.*** (p. 57)
   sink, swim, scream, shuffle (physical action verbs)
   think, see, realize, decide (mental action verbs)
2. **A *linking verb* does not express action. It *links* a word in the predicate to the subject.** (p. 58)
   Judas *was* the betrayer of Jesus.

Verbs (cont.)

Linking Verbs	
am were is be are being was been (May also be used as helping verbs)	taste look grow feel appear remain smell become stay sound seem (May also be used as action verbs)

3. **A *helping verb helps* the main verb to make a statement.** (p. 60)

   I ***will*** *bless* the Lord at all times. (***Will*** helps *bless* show action.)

   The Lord ***is*** *become* my salvation. (***Is*** helps *become* link *salvation* to *Lord.*)

   We ***will*** *be* there today. (***Will*** helps *be* indicate existence.)

Helping Verbs		
am were is be are being was been (May also be used as linking verbs)	have do has does had did (May also be used as action verbs)	shall may will might should must would can could (Always helping verbs)

4. **A *verb phrase* is a main verb and its helping verbs.** (p. 60)
5. **A *verb phrase* is sometimes *interrupted* by adverbs.** The adverb *not* is a common interrupter. (p. 60)

   He *should* **easily** *complete* the test in time.

   I *have* **not** *seen* the righteous forsaken.
6. **The *subject* of an interrogative sentence usually interrupts the verb phrase.** (p. 60)

   Have **you** *seen* the righteous forsaken?

B. **A *verbal* is a verb form used as a noun, adjective, or adverb.** (p. 62)

C. **A *participle* is a verbal used as an *adjective* to modify a *noun* or a *pronoun.*** A participle has an ending similar to a verb (*-ing, -d, -ed, -t,* or *-en*), but functions as an adjective in the sentence. (p. 63)

Looking through the old book, I made an exciting discovery. (*Made* is the verb. *Looking* is a participle modifying the pronoun *I.*)

Whistling loudly, Harold walked into the room. (*Walked* is the verb. *Whistling* is a participle modifying the noun *Harold.*)

D. Verbs have four *principal parts:* the *present,* the *present participle,* the *past,* and the *past participle.* Some special rules apply when using the principal parts. (p. 64)

1. **All verbs may be classified as *regular* or *irregular* verbs, depending on the way that the past and past participle are formed.**
2. ***Regular verbs* form the past and past participle by adding *-d* or *-ed* to the *present.*** (p. 64)

   walk, walk***ed,*** (have) walk***ed***
3. ***Irregular verbs* form the past and past participle in other ways.** (See page 65 for forms of irregular verbs.)

   know, knew, (have) known
4. **Both regular and irregular verbs form the *present participle* by adding *-ing* to the *present.*** (p. 64)

   see (present), see***ing*** (present participle)
5. **Sometimes *spelling changes* must be made when forming the *past,* the *past participle,* and the *present participle.*** (p. 64)
   - **a.** For verbs ending in *y* preceded by a consonant, change the *y* to *i* before adding *-ed.*

     cr***y,*** cr***ied***
   - **b.** For verbs ending in a single consonant preceded by a single vowel, usually double the final consonant before adding *-ed* or *-ing.*

     sto***p,*** sto***pp***ing, stop***ped***
6. **Do not confuse the past with the past participle. Never use a helping verb to form the *past.* Always use a helping verb, such as *have* or *had,* to form the *past participle.*** (p. 64)

   He *ate* (not *had ate*) the pie yesterday. (No helping verb is used with the past.)

   He *had eaten* (not *eaten*) several pies. (A helping verb must be used with the past participle.)
7. **Do not use such incorrect forms as the following: *attackted, brung, busted, clumb, drownded, drug* (for *dragged*), *et, aten, growed, snuck, stoled, throwed, thunk.*** (p. 66)

   The balloon burst (not *busted*).

E. **The *tense* of a verb *indicates* the *time* expressed by the verb.** (*Tense* means *time.*) A verb tells when things happen: past, present, or future. The verb changes form to express six different tenses. (p. 68)

Present tense: I *go.* (He *goes.*)

Past tense: I *went.*

Future tense: I *shall* (or *will*) *go.*

Present Perfect tense: I *have gone.* (He *has gone.*)

Past Perfect tense: I *had gone.*

Future Perfect tense: I *shall* (or *will*) *have gone.*

Note: When you are writing, select one tense and do not change to a different tense without good reason. If you begin writing in the past tense, do not switch to the present. If you begin with the present, do not switch to the past.

Verbs (cont.)

F. **The following verbs are especially troublesome.**

1. **The verb *sit* means "to be seated." Its principal parts are *sit, sitting, sat, (have) sat.*** (The verb *sit* rarely requires an object.) (p. 70)

   I *sat* on a stump.

2. **The verb *set* means "to put or place something." Its principal parts are *set, setting, set, (have) set.*** (The verb *set* usually requires an object.) (p. 70)

   Obj.
   Larry *set* his **books** on his desk.

3. **The verb *rise* means "to go up" or "to get up." Its principal parts are *rise, rising, rose, (have) risen.*** (The verb *rise* never requires an object.) (p. 71)

   The kite *rose* in the wind.

4. **The verb *raise* means "to lift something" or "to push up something." Its principal parts are *raise, raising, raised, (have) raised.*** (The verb *raise* usually requires an object.) (p. 71)

   Obj.
   The scout *raised* the **flag** while the bugle played.

5. **The verb *lie* means "to recline." Its principal parts are *lie, lying, lay, (have) lain.*** (The verb *lie* never requires an object.) (p. 72)

   A dog *was lying* on the porch.

6. **The verb *lay* means "to put or place something." Its principal parts are *lay, laying, laid, (have) laid.*** (The verb *lay* usually requires an object.) (p. 72)

   Obj.
   I *laid* the **pencil** on her desk.

G. **Be careful to use the following verbs correctly.**

1. ***Bring* or *take*? *Bring* indicates movement toward you. *Take* indicates movement away from you.** (p. 73)

   Bring me that newspaper. *Take* these pots into the kitchen.

2. ***Can* or *may*? *Can* refers to ability. *May* refers to permission.** (p. 73)

   I *can* swim well. *May* I go swimming tomorrow?

3. ***Learn* or *teach*? *Learn* means "to obtain knowledge." *Teach* means "to give instruction."** (p. 73)

   Have you *learned* to study effectively?
   Mr. Calbert *taught* us good study habits.

4. ***Let* or *leave*? *Let* means "to allow." *Leave* means "to go away from" or "to cause to remain."** (p. 73)

   When will you *let* Christ come into your heart?
   When will we *leave* for home?

H. **Avoid these common errors in verb usage.**

1. **Do not use *ain't* and *aren't I*.** (p. 74)

   My books *ain't* here. (incorrect) I am the owner, *aren't I?* (incorrect)
   My books *aren't* here. (correct) I am the owner, *am I not?* (correct)

2. **Do not use *better* for *had better.*** (p. 74)
   I *better* apologize for my rudeness. (incorrect)
   I *had better* apologize for my rudeness. (correct)

3. **Do not use *didn't go to* for *didn't mean to* or *didn't intend to.*** (p. 74)
   Harry *didn't go to* tear the page. (incorrect)
   Harry *didn't mean to* tear the page. (correct)

4. **Do not use *took sick* for *became ill.*** (p. 74)
   Ann Judson *took sick* in Burma and died. (incorrect)
   Ann Judson *became ill* in Burma and died. (correct)

5. **Do not use *used to could* for *used to be able to.*** (p. 74)
   I *used to could* work long hours without tiring. (incorrect)
   I *used to be able to* work long hours without tiring. (correct)

6. **Do not use *want in, want on, want off,* or *want through.*** (p. 74)
   Anna wants *off.* (incorrect) We want *in.* (incorrect)
   Anna wants *to get off.* (correct) We want *to join.* (correct)

A. A *noun* is a word that names a person, place, thing, or idea. (p. 80)
persons—*O. Henry, sailor, nephew*
places—*county, plaza, Paradise*
things—*lamp, train, flower*
ideas—*freedom, friendliness, love*

B. A *compound noun* is two or more words used as a single noun. (p. 80)
Nancy Hanks great-aunt barnyard madman

C. A *collective noun* names a group and is singular in form. (p. 80)
congregation assembly flock herd

D. A *common noun* names a person, place, thing, or idea, but does not say which particular one. (p. 81)

man city book gentleness

E. A *proper noun* names a *particular* person, place, or thing and always begins with a capital letter. (p. 81)
C. I. Scofield Lisbon *Roget's Thesaurus*

F. Verbs must agree in number with noun subjects. (p. 82)

1. ***Singular subjects* take *singular verbs; plural subjects* take *plural verbs. Nouns* ending in *s* are usually plural; *verbs* ending in *s* are usually singular.** (p. 82)
   Cowboys ride the prairie.
   The prairie offers exciting adventure.

Nouns (cont.)

2. **The number of a subject is not affected by phrases between the subject and the verb.** (p. 82) (For exceptions, see p. 84, rule 7.)
   Many words in the report were misspelled.
3. ***Compound subjects* joined by *and* take a plural verb.** (p. 83)
   A workbook and a pencil are needed for tonight's homework.

   Note: Sometimes subjects joined by *and* refer to one person or are considered as one thing. Use a *singular* verb in this situation.

   Macaroni and cheese makes a tasty side dish. (Macaroni and cheese is only *one* dish.)
4. **When a *compound subject* is joined by *or* or *nor,* the verb agrees with the nearer subject.** (p. 83)
   Either the class president or the other officers are supposed to plan a program.
   Neither the students nor the teacher has seen a tornado.
5. ***Collective nouns* may be either singular or plural.** A collective noun is a noun that is singular in form but refers to a group. (For example: *jury, team, class, family*) When the collective noun acts as a *unit,* it is *singular;* but when the members of the group act *individually,* the collective noun is *plural.* (p. 84)
   Our team is playing in a tournament this week. (singular)
   Our team are discussing new uniforms. (plural)
6. **The words *there* and *here* are rarely used as subjects.** When a sentence begins with *there* or *here,* you must look carefully to find the subject. (p. 84)
   There is no substitute for hard work.
7. ***Amounts* are usually singular.** (p. 84)
   Fifty cents is the price of this pen.
8. ***Titles* of literary works, works of art, organizations, and countries are usually singular even if they are plural in form.** (p. 84)
   The Acts of the Apostles was written by Luke.
9. ***Doesn't, isn't,* and *wasn't* are *singular* and must be used with singular subjects. *Don't, aren't,* and *weren't* are *plural* and must be used with plural subjects.** (p. 84)
   The Bible isn't an ordinary book.
   The books of the Bible aren't ordinary books.
10. **A few words, although plural in form, take singular verbs. *Mathematics, civics, rickets, measles, mumps,* and *news* are examples of such words.** (p. 84)
    The news was encouraging.

G. Nouns may be used as *predicate nominatives.*

1. **A *predicate nominative* is a noun (or a pronoun) that follows a *linking verb* and *renames* or *explains* the subject.** This noun (or pronoun) means the same thing or person as the subject. (p. 86)
   David was the *son* of Jesse. (*Son* renames the subject *David.*)
2. **In a sentence containing a predicate nominative, you can always replace the verb with the word *equals.*** (p. 86)
   David *was* a king. (David *equals* a king.)

3. **Predicate nominatives can *never* be *in prepositional phrases.*** (p. 86)

   Jonathan was the *son* of Saul. (*Son* is the predicate nominative, not *Saul,* because *Saul* is in a prepositional phrase.)

4. **Predicate nominatives *may be compound.*** (p. 86)

   William Blake was a *poet* and an *artist.*

5. **Predicate nominatives are sometimes called *subject complements.* Subject complements always follow linking verbs.** (p. 86)

H. Nouns may be used as *direct objects.*

1. **A *direct object* is a noun (or a pronoun) that follows an action verb and receives the action from that verb. It answers the questions *whom* or *what* after the verb.** (p. 89)

   Mr. Hall painted his *house.*

2. **If no word answers the questions *whom* or *what* after the action verb, the sentence does not have a direct object.** (p. 89)

   Mr. Hall paints during the afternoon.

3. **Direct objects can *never* be in *prepositional phrases.*** (p. 89)

   Pat drank a *glass* of water. (*Glass* is the direct object, not *water,* because *water* is in a prepositional phrase.)

4. **Direct objects *may be compound.*** (p. 89)

   The Lord translated *Enoch* and *Elijah.*

I. Nouns may be used as *indirect objects.*

1. **An *indirect object* is a noun or a pronoun (not in the possessive case) that precedes the direct object and tells *to whom,* or *for whom,* or *to what,* or *for what* the action of the verb is done.** (p. 92)

   Uncle Remus told the *children* a story. (*Story* is the direct object; *children* is the indirect object.)

2. **An indirect object can *never* be *in a prepositional phrase.*** (p. 92)

   I wrote my *Congressman* a letter. (*Letter* is the direct object; *Congressman* is the indirect object.)

   I wrote a letter to my Congressman. (*Letter* is the direct object; *Congressman* is the object of the preposition *to.*)

3. **Indirect objects *may be compound.*** (p. 92)

   The pilot gave the *passengers* and the *crew* special instructions for the crash landing.

4. **Always *look for the direct object first,* then the indirect object. If there is no direct object, there can be no indirect object.** (p. 92)

J. Nouns may be used as *objects of prepositions.* (Refer to page 174 for a list of prepositions.)

1. **A *phrase* is a group of related words that *does not contain a verb or a subject.*** (p. 95)

Nouns (cont.)

2. **A *prepositional phrase* consists of a preposition, its noun** (or pronoun) **object, and any modifiers of the object.** (See p. 174 for a list of commonly used prepositions.) (p. 95)

   Prep. N. Obj.

   Bob took a picture *of the antique Ford*. (*Of* is the preposition; *Ford* is the object.)

3. **A prepositional phrase *may have a compound object.*** (p. 95)

   This concerto is written *for* ***piano*** *and* ***orchestra.***

4. **You can tell the difference between an indirect object and an object of a preposition by noting the location of the noun to be identified.** An indirect object is always *between* the verb and the direct object; an object of a preposition comes *after* a preposition. (p. 95)

K. Nouns may be used as *appositives* and as nouns of *direct address.*

1. **An *appositive* is a word that follows a noun and explains or identifies that noun.** (p. 96)

   Robert Boyle, the "*Father* of Chemistry," was a faithful Christian.

2. **An appositive *may be compound.*** (p. 96)

   Two scientists, *Pierre and Marie Curie,* discovered radium.

3. **An *appositive phrase* is an appositive with all its modifiers.** (p. 96)

   James and John, *my cousins from the Netherlands,* were able to come to the reunion.

4. **A nonessential appositive phrase is *set off by commas* because it is not closely related to the word it follows.** An appositive which is closely related to the word it follows is *essential* and should not be set off by commas. (p. 96)

   Joanna, my friend from Kansas City, is visiting me this week.

   My brother *Mike* helped me clean out the garage.

   Note: Appositives that follow proper nouns are usually nonessential.

5. **A *noun of direct address* is the name of the person to whom a sentence is directed. It is set off by commas.** (p. 96)

   Did you say, *Mr. Whitfield,* that shirts are on sale this week?

6. **Nouns of direct address *may be compound.*** (p. 96)

   Charles and Roy, please sit down immediately.

Pronouns

A. A *pronoun* is a word that takes the place of a noun. (p. 106)

Mr. Baxter leaves early so that *he* can avoid rush-hour traffic. (The pronoun *he* takes the place of the noun *Mr. Baxter.*)

B. An *antecedent* is the word for which a pronoun stands. (p. 106)

Mr. Baxter leaves early so that he can avoid rush-hour traffic. (*Mr. Baxter* is the antecedent of the pronoun *he.*)

C. **There are various kinds of pronouns.**

1. ***Personal pronouns*** **refer to** ***the speaker (I, me, we, us, my, mine, our, ours);*** **the** ***person spoken to (you, your, yours);*** **and** ***the person spoken about (he, she, it, they, him, her, them, his, hers, its, their, theirs).*** (p. 106)
2. ***Interrogative pronouns*** **are used to ask a question** ***(who, whom, whose, which, what).*** (p. 106)
3. ***Demonstrative pronouns*** **point out the person or thing referred to** ***(this, that, these, those).*** (p. 106)
4. ***Indefinite pronouns*** **point out indefinite persons or things (*****each, either, one, anybody, some, more, all,*** **etc.)** (p. 106)
5. ***Compound pronouns*** **are pronouns combined with** ***self*** **or** ***selves (myself, ourselves, yourself, yourselves, himself, herself, itself, oneself, themselves).*** (p. 106)
6. ***Relative pronouns*** **are used to introduce dependent clauses** ***(who, whom, whose, which, that).*** (p. 106)

D. **Verbs must agree in number with pronoun subjects.**

1. **These** ***indefinite pronouns*** **are** ***singular*** **and take a singular verb:** ***each, either, neither, one, everyone, everybody, no one, nobody, anyone, anybody, someone, somebody.*** (p. 107)

   Everyone in the audience *was delighted* with the play.
2. **These** ***indefinite pronouns*** **are** ***plural*** **and take a plural verb:** ***both, few, several, many.*** (p. 107)

   Many of John Adam's descendants *were involved* in politics.
3. **These** ***indefinite pronouns*** **may be either** ***singular*** **or** ***plural*****:** ***some, any, none, all, most.*** **To determine the number of these words, look at the context of the sentence.** (p. 107)

   Some of the *pieces* to this puzzle are missing. (*Some* refers to *pieces,* which is plural.)
   Some of the *pie* is gone. (*Some* refers to *pie,* which is singular.)
4. ***Doesn't, isn't,*** **and** ***wasn't*** **are** ***singular*** **and must be used with singular subjects.** ***Don't, aren't,*** **and** ***weren't*** **are** ***plural*** **and must be used with plural subjects. (Exception: Use** ***don't*** **with the pronouns** ***I*** **and** ***you.*****)** (p. 108)

   Incorrect: He *don't* scare me.
   Correct: He *doesn't* scare me.
   Correct: They *don't* scare me.
5. **The verb agrees with the subject, not the predicate nominative.** (p. 108)

   One of the sources of government funds *is* income taxes. (The predicate nominative *taxes* is plural, but that has no effect on the subject-verb agreement.)

E. **Pronouns may be used as** ***subjects*** **and as** ***predicate nominatives.*** (Predicate nominatives follow linking verbs and rename the subject. Predicate nominatives *may be compound.*) (pp. 109–110)

Pronouns (cont.)

1. **Only nominative case pronouns may be used as subjects or predicate nominatives.** (pp. 109–110)
   They are going with us. (*They* is the subject.)
   The winner of the contest was *she*. (*She* is the predicate nominative.)

Nominative Case Pronouns	
Singular	**Plural**
I	we
(you)	(you)
he, she, (it)	they

Note: The pronouns in parentheses are also objective case pronouns (see pp. 111–112).

2. **Most problems occur when subjects or predicate nominatives are *compound*. It is helpful to try the pronoun alone in the sentence.** (pp. 109–110)
   Cheri and (me, I) bought some stationery.
   Me bought some stationery. (incorrect)
   I bought some stationery. (correct)
   Cheri and *I* bought some stationery.
3. **Sometimes the subject is *followed by an appositive*. It is helpful to try the pronoun apart from the appositive.** (p. 109)
   (Us, We) students did well on the exam.
   Us did well on the exam. (incorrect)
   We did well on the exam. (correct)
   We students did well on the exam.
4. **The expression *It is me* or *It's me* is now commonly used in everyday conversation. However, in formal writing follow the rule and write *It is I*.** (p. 110)

F. **Pronouns may be used as *direct objects, indirect objects,* and as *objects of prepositions.*** (p. 111)

1. **Pronouns used as *direct objects, indirect objects,* and *objects of propositions* must be objective case pronouns.** (pp. 111–112)
   God gave *us* His only begotten Son. (indirect object)

Objective Case Pronouns	
Singular	**Plural**
me	us
(you)	(you)
him, her, (it)	them

Note: The pronouns in parentheses are also nominative case pronouns (see pp. 109–110).

2. **Most problems occur when the objects are *compound*. It is helpful to try each pronoun alone in the sentence.** (pp. 111–112)

    Mrs. Peters gave Frank and (I, me) our report cards. (compound indirect object)
    Mrs. Peters gave *I* our report cards. (incorrect)
    Mrs. Peters gave *me* our report cards. (correct)
    Mrs. Peters gave Frank and *me* our report cards.

3. **Sometimes the object is *followed by an appositive*. It is helpful to try the pronoun apart from the appositive.** (pp. 111–112)

    The photographer took pictures of (we, us) students.
    The photographer took pictures of *we*. (incorrect)
    The photographer took pictures of *us*. (correct)
    The photographer took pictures of *us* students.

G. ***Possessive case pronouns* show ownership or relationship.** The underlined words in the list below are *used as adjectives* (p. 113). Some authorities refer to them as possessive adjectives. *His* and *its* may be used as pronouns or as adjectives.

My book is on *his* desk.

Possessive Case Pronouns	
Singular	**Plural**
my, mine	our, ours
your, yours	your, yours
his, her, hers, its	their, theirs

Note: Possessive case pronouns do not use apostrophes to show possession. The possessive form of the pronoun *it* is written *its*. The contraction of the words *it is* is written *it's*.

Adjectives

A. **An *adjective* is a word that modifies a noun or a pronoun. It answers the questions *what kind, which one, how many, how much, or whose*.** (A *modifier* makes the meaning of another word more specific by describing or limiting that word.) (p. 122)

topic outline (what kind)

that tree (which one)

eight dollars (how many)

enough milk (how much)

his trunk (whose)

1. **Most adjectives come before the words they modify as in the examples above. In some sentences adjectives come after the words they modify.** (p. 122)

    The bill was *enormous*.

2. **Several adjectives may modify the same word.** (p. 122)

    The huge red apples rested in a bowl on the table.

Adjectives (cont.)

3. **The words *a, an,* and *the* are always adjectives. They are called *articles.*** (Do not confuse *an* with *and. And* is a conjunction; *an* is an adjective.) (p. 122)
4. **Possessive nouns and certain possessive pronouns are usually called adjectives.** (p. 122)

   Amy's most prized possession is *her* Bible.
5. **A *participle* is a verb form used as an adjective. A participle will have an ending similar to a verb *(-ing, -d, -ed, -t,* or *-en),* but will function as an adjective to modify a noun or pronoun.** (pp. 63,122)

   A *growing* boy needs a lot of protein.

   The small puppy *found* by my neighbor was quickly returned to its home.

B. A *proper adjective* is a word formed from a proper noun and, like a proper noun, begins with a capital letter. (p. 124)

Proper nouns	**Proper adjectives**
Spenser	*Spenserian* stanza
Paul	*Pauline* epistles
Rome	*Roman* emperor

C. A *predicate adjective* is an adjective that follows a *linking verb* and *modifies* the subject. (p. 127)

The rice pudding was *delicious.* (*Delicious* is a predicate adjective modifying the subject *pudding.*)

1. **Predicate adjectives *may be compound.*** (p. 127)

   The clouds were *dark* and *ominous.*
2. **Predicate adjectives are sometimes called *subject complements.*** Subject complements always follow linking verbs. (p. 127)
3. **To find a predicate adjective, first locate the verb. Then ask the questions *what* or *how* after the verb.** (pp. 127 and 143)

D. Prepositional phrases may be used as adjectives. (p. 130)

1. **A prepositional phrase that modifies a noun or a pronoun is called an *adjective phrase.*** (p. 130)
2. **An adjective phrase answers the questions *what kind, which one, how many, how much,* or *whose.*** (p. 130)

E. Participial phrases may be used as adjectives. A *participial phrase* consists of the participle together with its modifiers or complements. The modifiers may be single adverbs or prepositional phrases. (p. 131)

Adv. Part. D.O.
Busily doing his homework, Aaron did not wish to play baseball with the gang.

F. **Dependent clauses may be used as adjectives.** (p. 133)

1. **A *clause* is a group of words that contains both a subject and a verb. It is used as a part of a sentence.** (p. 133)
2. **An *independent clause* expresses a complete thought and can stand alone as a sentence.** (p. 133)

   The Bible was written by forty men who were inspired by the Holy Spirit.
3. **A *dependent*** (subordinate) ***clause* does not express a complete thought and cannot stand alone as a sentence.** (p. 133)

   The Bible was written by forty men *who were inspired by the Holy Spirit.*
4. **A dependent clause that modifies a noun or pronoun is called an *adjective clause.*** (p. 133)

   Blessed is the man *that endureth temptation.*
5. **Adjective clauses are introduced by words called *relatives. Who, whom, which,* and *that* are relative pronouns. *Whose* is a relative adjective.**
6. **A relative serves two purposes: (1) It introduces the clause. (2) It serves a grammatical function within the clause.** (p. 133)

   He is the boy ***who*** *called us.* (***Who*** is the subject of *called.)*

   He is the boy ***whom*** *we elected.* (***Whom*** is the object of *elected.)*

G. **Adjective modifiers must be placed and punctuated correctly.** (p. 136)

1. **Make sure to place adjective modifiers so they sensibly modify the noun or pronoun that you intend.** (p. 136)
2. **Adjective phrases and adjective clauses should come immediately after the words they modify.** (p. 136)

   The man was in a wheelchair *with a broken leg.* (misplaced phrase)
   The man *with a broken leg* was in a wheelchair. (corrected)
3. **Participial phrases may come immediately after the words they modify or they may be at the beginning of the sentence.** If a participial phrase comes at the beginning of a sentence, it must modify the subject of the sentence that follows it. Otherwise the sentence will have a *dangling participle.* (p. 136)

   The pitcher threw a curve ball *wearing a red cap.* (misplaced)
   The pitcher *wearing a red cap* threw a curve ball. (corrected)
   Neatly pressed and starched, the maid hung the suit up in the closet. (dangling)
   Neatly pressed and starched, the suit was hung in the closet by the maid.
4. **Nonessential adjective clauses and nonessential participial phrases should be set off by commas.** The adjective clause or participial phrase is nonessential if it can be removed from the sentence without changing the meaning of the independent clause. (p. 136)

   Fish, which are coldblooded creatures, are a good source of food. (nonessential clause)
   The fish that are on sale this week are red snappers. (essential clause)
   Note: Participial phrases at the beginning of a sentence are always set off by commas.

Adjectives (cont.)

H. Adjectives have three degrees of comparison: *positive, comparative,* and *superlative.* (p. 138)

1. **The *positive* degree is used when no comparison is expressed.** (p. 138)
   This book is *old.*
2. **The *comparative* degree is used when *two people or things* are being compared.** (p. 138)
   This book is *older* than my grandfather.
   - **a.** Most *one-syllable* and some *two-syllable* adjectives form the comparative by adding *-er* to the positive.
   - **b.** Most adjectives of *two syllables* form the comparative degree by using the word *more.*
   - **c.** All adjectives of *three or more syllables* form the superlative degree by using the word *more.*
3. **The *superlative* degree is used when *three or more things* are being compared.** (p. 138)
   This book is the *oldest* one in the library.
   - **a.** Most *one-syllable* and some *two-syllable* adjectives form the superlative degree by adding *-est* to the positive.
   - **b.** Most adjectives of *two syllables* form the superlative degree by using the word *most.*
   - **c.** All adjectives of *three or more syllables* form the superlative degree by using the word *most.*
4. **The comparative and superlative degrees of a few adjectives are formed *irregularly.*** (p. 138)

Positive	Comparative	Superlative
good	better	best
well	better	best
bad	worse	worst
ill	worse	worst
many	more	most
much	more	most

I. Be careful to use adjectives correctly.

1. **Avoid the *double comparison.* Never use *-er* and *more* together or *-est* and *most* together. Only one form is needed.** (p. 140)
   This jam is *more sweeter* than that jelly. (incorrect)
   This jam is *sweeter* than that jelly. (correct)
2. **When comparing a person with a group of which that person is a member, use *other* or *else* with the comparative.** (p. 140)
   Jim is smarter than any boy in the room. (incorrect)
   Jim is smarter than any *other* boy in the room. (correct)

3. **Use *fewer* with items that can be counted; use *less* with a quantity of a substance.** (p. 140)

    This recipe requires *fewer* eggs than that one does.
    This recipe requires *less* milk than that one does.

4. ***Them* is never used as an adjective; use *those* instead.** (p. 140)

    Them french fries were delicious. (incorrect)
    Those french fries were delicious. (correct)

Procedure for Finding & Identifying Complements

A. *Find the verb* in the sentence.

B. Ask *who* or *what* before the verb to *find the subject.*

C. Ask yourself if the verb is an *action verb* or if it is a *linking verb.*

D. If the verb is an *action verb,* look for a noun or a pronoun that answers *whom* or *what* after the verb. (Say the verb. Say *whom* or *what.*) If there is a word that answers one of those questions, it is the *direct object.*

E. Say the *subject, verb,* and *direct object* together to see if you have chosen sensible answers.

F. If the sentence does have a direct object, look for a noun or a pronoun between the action verb and the direct object that answers *to whom* or *for whom,* or *to what* or *for what* after the verb. If there is a word that answers one of those questions, it is the *indirect object.* (If a sentence does not have a direct object, it cannot have an indirect object.)

G. Say the *subject, verb, indirect object,* and *direct object* together to see if you have chosen sensible answers.

H. If the verb is a *linking verb* (see page 58), look for a noun or a pronoun that follows the verb and renames the subject. If there is one, it is the *predicate nominative.*

I. If there is no predicate nominative, look for an adjective that follows the *linking verb* and describes the subject. If there is one, it is the *predicate adjective.*

J. Not all verbs need a complement, but look for one just in case.

Adverbs

A. An *adverb* is a word that modifies a verb, an adjective, or another adverb. It answers the questions *where, when, how, how often,* or *to what extent.* (p. 152)

went *away* (where) arrived *today* (when) laughed *loudly* (how)

seldom speaks (how often) *unbelievably* large (to what extent)

Adverbs (cont.)

1. **The word *not* or its contraction *n't* is always an adverb and usually modifies a verb.** (p. 152)
2. **Adverbs modify *verbs* most of the time. An adverb that modifies a verb may be *before or after* the verb it modifies. It may be *in the middle of a verb phrase* that it modifies. Or it may be *at the beginning of the sentence,* nowhere near the verb it modifies.** (p. 152)

   I *occasionally* go to the opera.

   The tenor sang *beautifully*.

   I have *never* heard such a beautiful aria.

   Sometimes this opera is sung in English.
3. **Adverbs also modify *adjectives.* When adverbs modify adjectives, they are located *immediately before* those adjectives and usually tell *how* or *to what extent.*** (p. 152)

   I am *somewhat* unsure about my answer.
4. **Adverbs occasionally modify *other adverbs.* When adverbs modify other adverbs, they are located *immediately before* those adverbs and usually tell *how.*** (p. 152)

   He arrived at the meeting *rather* late.

B. **Adverbs must be distinguished from adjectives.**

1. **Use *adjectives* to modify *nouns* or *pronouns.* Use *adverbs* to modify *verbs, adjectives,* or *adverbs.*** (p. 156)

   The band was *loud.* (adjective) The band played *loudly.* (adverb)
2. **Use a predicate adjective after linking verbs.** (p. 156)

   Sam looks *happy.* (not *happily*)
3. **Distinguish between *good* and *well.* Always use the word *good* as an adjective. *Well* is an *adverb* when it modifies a verb; *well* is an *adjective* when it refers to a person's health.** (p. 156)

   The meal tasted *good.* (adjective)

   The response to the survey was *good.* (adjective)

   Corn grows *well* in this soil. (adverb modifying the verb)

   I do not feel *well.* (adjective referring to the person's health)
4. ***Sure, real,* and *bad* are not usually used as adverbs.** (p. 156)

   I was *surely* tired after mowing the lawn. (not *sure*)
   Jill plays tennis *really* well. (not *real*)
   I wanted to go very *badly.* (not *bad*)

C. Prepositional phrases may be used as adverbs. (p. 157)

1. **A prepositional phrase that modifies a verb, an adjective, or an adverb is called an *adverb phrase*. An adverb phrase usually answers the questions *where, when, how,* or *why*.** (See p. 174 for a list of commonly used prepositions.) (p. 157)

   The concert started *with an overture*. (The adverb phrase modifies the verb *started*, telling *how*.)

   I am safe *in the Lord's hands*. (The adverb phrase modifies the adjective *safe*, telling *where*.)

   Early *in the morning* our song shall rise to Thee. (The adverb phrase modifies the adverb *early*, telling *when*.)

2. **Adverb phrases modify verbs more often than they modify adjectives or adverbs.** (p. 157)

D. Dependent clauses may be used as adverbs. (p. 161)

1. **A dependent clause that modifies a verb, adjective, or adverb is called an *adverb clause*. Adverb clauses usually answer the questions *where, when, how, why, to what extent,* or *under what condition*.** (p. 161)

   We built a new school *after the old one burned down*. (modifies the verb *built*)

   My room looks neater *than Amy's does*. (modifies the adjective *neater*)

   The beans sprouted sooner *than I had expected*. (modifies the adverb *sooner*)

2. **Adverb clauses are introduced by *subordinating conjunctions: after, although, as, as if, as much as, as long as, as soon as, because, before, if, in order that, since, so that, than, though, unless, until, when, whenever, where, wherever, while.*** (Some of these words may also be used as *other* parts of speech.) (p. 161)

3. **Introductory adverb clauses are set off by commas. Adverb clauses at the end of a sentence do not usually require commas.** (p. 161)

   Before you arrive, please call. Please call *before you arrive*.

E. Be careful to place adverbs correctly. (p. 164)

1. **An adverb phrase or clause that modifies a verb may be placed *before or after* the verb it modifies, but *not between* two verbs that it might modify.** (p. 164)

   Mr. Wilmington said *on Saturday* he would be leaving. (modifier between two verbs that it might modify—incorrect)

   On Saturday Mr. Wilmington said he would be leaving. (corrected)

   Mr. Wilmington said he would be leaving *on Saturday*. (corrected)

2. **An adverb phrase or clause that modifies an adjective or an adverb is usually placed immediately *after* the word it modifies.** (p. 164)

   The boy felt happy *in his heart*. (modifies adjective)

   I can jump higher *than you can*. (modifies adverb)

Adverbs (cont.)

3. **Place adverb modifiers as close as possible to the words they modify.** (p. 164)
   As the boat drifted peacefully, the old sea captain rested his eyes *on the surface of the water*. (misplaced)
   As the boat drifted peacefully *on the surface of the water,* the old sea captain rested his eyes. (better)
   We could watch the sun rising *from our campsite* every morning. (misplaced)
   From our campsite, we could watch the sun rising every morning. (better)

F. Adverbs have three degrees of comparison: *positive, comparative,* and *superlative.* (p. 165)

1. ***Most adverbs*** **form the comparative and superlative degrees by using *more* and *most*.** (p. 165)
   skillfully *more* skillfully *most* skillfully
2. **A few adverbs form the comparative and superlative degrees by adding *-er* and *-est*.** (p. 165)
   fast fast***er*** fast***est***
3. **A few adverbs are *irregular* in form.** (p. 165)

Positive	Comparative	Superlative
well	better	best
much	more	most
badly	worse	worst
little	less	least
far	farther	farthest

4. **Remember to use the *comparative* degree when *only two* things are being compared.** (p. 165)

G. Be careful to use adverbs correctly. (p. 166)

1. **Avoid the *double comparison*. Never use *-er* and *more* together or *-est* and *most* together. Only one form is needed.** (p. 166)
   Jason can run *more faster* than Trevor. (incorrect)
   Jason can run *faster* than Trevor. (correct)
2. **Use the *comparative* degree when comparing *two* persons or things. Use the *superlative* degree when comparing *three or more* persons or things.** (p. 166)
   Of the two coats, the wool one has lasted *longer*. (not *longest*)
   Of all the buildings in town, the city hall was built *best*. (not *better*)
3. **Avoid the *double negative*. The following words are called negatives: *no, not* (or *n't*), *none, never, no one, nothing, hardly, scarcely*. Do not use two negative words in the same statement.** (p. 166)
   I hadn't *scarcely* noticed the time. (incorrect)
   I had *scarcely* noticed the time. (correct)

Prepositions

A. **A *preposition* is a word that shows how a noun or a pronoun is related to some other word in the sentence.** (p. 174)

Preposition List					
aboard	among	between	from	over	underneath
about	around	beyond	in	past	until
above	at	but	into	since	unto
across	before	by	like	through	up
after	behind	down	near	throughout	upon
against	below	during	of	to	with
along	beneath	except	off	toward	within
amid	beside	for	on	under	without

B. **A *prepositional phrase* consists of a preposition, its noun or pronoun object, and any modifiers of the object.** (p. 174)

A mist hung *over the pond.*

C. **The *object of a preposition* is the noun or pronoun that completes a prepositional phrase. A preposition must always have an object.** (p. 174)

Prep. (beyond) **Obj.** (horizon)
Lightning flashed beyond the *horizon.*

D. **A preposition may have a *compound object.*** (p. 174)

Prep. (between) **Obj.** (Lazarus) **Obj.** (man)
A great gulf was fixed between *Lazarus* and the rich *man.*

E. **The object of a preposition may have modifiers.** (p. 174)

Prep. (on) **Obj.** (train)
I arrived on the afternoon *train.*

F. **Be careful to use the following prepositions correctly.**

1. ***(beside, besides) Beside* means "by the side of"; *besides* means "in addition to."** (p. 177)

   I sat *beside* a visitor.

   The library has many more new books *besides* these.

2. ***(between, among)* Use *between* in referring to two people or things; use *among* in referring to more than two.** (p. 177)

   A fence ran *between* two houses.

   Great harmony exists *among* the club members.

3. ***(except, accept) Except,* as a preposition, means "excluding." *Accept* is a verb and means "to receive" or "to agree to."** (p. 177)

   Everyone voted *except* Roger.

   Ben *accepted* the nomination.

4. ***(in, into)* Use *in* for location within; use *into* for motion from outside to inside.** (p. 177)

   Dr. Johnson stood *in* the rain.

   Dr. Livingstone went *into* the jungles of Africa.

Prepositions (cont.)

5. ***(of, have)* *Of* is a preposition and should not be used for the helping verb *have.*** (p. 177)

   You should *of* been there. (incorrect)

   You should *have* been there. (correct)

6. ***(to, and)* Do not use the conjunction *and* after the words *try* and *sure.* Use the word *to* instead.** (p. 177)

   Be sure *and* come on time. (incorrect)

   Be sure *to* come on time. (correct)

G. **Avoid using unnecessary prepositions.**

1. ***(amounts up to)* Omit the preposition *up*.** (p. 179)

   The tax on your purchase *amounts up to* $1.25. (incorrect)

   The tax on your purchase *amounts to* $1.25. (correct)

2. ***(at about)* Omit one of the prepositions.** (p. 179)

   The tornado touched down *at about* 7:30 A.M. (incorrect)

   The tornado touched down *at* 7:30 A.M. (correct)

   The tornado touched down *about* 7:30 A.M. (correct)

3. ***(had of)* Omit the preposition *of.*** (p. 179)

   If he *had of* been here, he would have been angry. (incorrect)

   If he *had* been here, he would have been angry. (correct)

4. ***(inside of* or *outside of)* Omit the preposition *of.*** (p. 179)

   He planted the tree *outside of* the fence. (incorrect)

   He planted the tree *outside* the fence. (correct)

5. ***(Where . . . to)* Omit the preposition *to.*** (p. 179)

   Where did you go *to* on vacation? (incorrect)

   Where did you go on vacation? (correct)

6. ***(Where . . . at)* Omit the preposition *at.*** (p. 179)

   Where did he stop *at* to eat? (incorrect)

   Where did he stop to eat? (correct)

Conjunctions

A. **A *conjunction* is a word that joins words or groups of words.** (p. 181)

B. **The following conjunctions are called *coordinating conjunctions: and, but, or, nor, for, yet.*** (p. 181)

   Meat **and** *fish* are high in protein.

C. **There are some other coordinating conjunctions that go in pairs: *either—or, neither—nor, both—and, not only—but also.*** (These conjunctions are called *correlative conjunctions.*) (p. 181)

   Either *he* **or** *I* will win the election.

   Both *Bob* **and** *Sue* have read this book before.

D. ***Subordinating conjunctions*** **are used to introduce adverb clauses:** ***after, although, as, as if, as much as, as long as, as soon as, because, before, if, in order that, since, so that, than, though, unless, until, when, whenever, where, wherever, while.*** (Some of these words may also be used as prepositions or as other parts of speech.) (p. 181)

Look **before** *you leap*.

Interjections

A. **An** ***interjection*** **is an exclamatory word that is not related to the other words in a sentence.** (p. 182)

B. **An exclamation point is usually used after an interjection, but a comma may be used after a mild interjection.** (p. 182)

Wow! Jack just hit a home run!
Oh, I didn't know that.

Sentence Structure

A. Sentences are made up of *clauses.*

1. **A** ***clause*** **is a group of words that contains both a subject and a verb.** It is used as a part of a sentence. (p. 190)
2. **An** ***independent clause*** **expresses a complete thought and could stand alone as a sentence.** (p. 190)
3. **A** ***dependent (subordinate) clause*** **does not express a complete thought and cannot stand alone as a sentence.** (p. 190)

B. A *simple sentence* contains one independent clause and no dependent (subordinate) clauses. Both subject and verb may be compound. (p. 190)

C. A *compound sentence* contains two or more independent clauses but no dependent (subordinate) clauses. Compound sentences may be joined by (1) a comma and coordinating conjunction or (2) a semicolon. (*And, but, or, nor, for* are the most commonly used conjunctions; however, any of the coordinating conjunctions listed on page 184 may be used.) (p. 190)

In my distress I cried unto the Lord, and He heard me. (SV, and SV)

I will not leave you comfortless; I will come to you. (SV; SV)

Sentence Structure (cont.)

D. **A *complex sentence* contains one independent clause and one or more dependent (subordinate) clauses. Dependent clauses always have introductory words (sometimes understood) that join them to an independent clause (*who, whom, which, that, whose, after, although, as, as if, because, since, when,* etc.)** (p. 193)

He [that regardeth reproof] shall be honored. (one independent clause and one dependent clause = complex sentence)

E. **A *compound-complex sentence* contains two or more independent clauses and one or more dependent (subordinate) clauses.** (p. 195)

He [that walketh with wise men] shall be wise, but a companion of fools shall be destroyed. (two independent clauses and one dependent clause = compound-complex sentence)

Documentation for Research Papers

1. **To give proper credit for a quotation, paraphrase, or summary that requires documentation, you may cite the source in parentheses within the text of your paper. This method of documentation is called *parenthetical citation.***

   a. If possible, identify the source in the context of a sentence and simply cite the page number in parentheses at the end of the sentence.

   > **Marvin Lubenow,** who has studied the human fossil record for twenty-five years, believes that Joachim Neander, after whom the Neanderthal was named, would have totally rejected human evolution **(77).**

   b. If you do not identify the source in the text, you must include the name of the source with the page number in parentheses. This kind of citation may consist of the author's name only—as in this example—but if you have two different sources written by the same author, a title is also necessary.

   > Joachim Neander, after whom the Neanderthal was named, would have totally rejected human evolution **(Lubenow, 77).**

   c. Both of the citations above tell the reader that the cited information came from **page 77** of a work written by an **author** whose last name is **Lubenow**. If the reader wants to know the name of the work and the publication information, he can refer to the "works cited" list at the end of the paper. There in the alphabetical list of sources the reader would find the following information:

   > Lubenow, Marvin L. *Bones of Contention: A Creationist Assessment of Human Fossils.* Grand Rapids: Baker, 1992.

   The idea is to include in a citation the information necessary for the reader to locate the source in the accompanying list of works cited.

   > **Note:** After the first citation of a source, subsequent citations of the same source can be simply a page number in parentheses—as long as there is no intervening citation of another source. If you cite another source and then return to the first source, you must identify the first source again in one of the ways mentioned above.

2. **Prepare your citations according to a standard form.** (For sample citations of different sources, see pages 318–323.)

   a. Name of the author.

   (1) Give only the last name of an author unless the bibliography lists more than one author with the same last name, in which case you should add the first initial of each author.

   (2) If authorship cannot be determined, begin the entry with the title of the work: (*Chicago Manual,* 441)

b. Title of the work.

(1) Omit the title of a work if only one work by the author is cited.

(2) When there are two or more sources by the same author in the list of works cited, add the title of the book. Put a comma between the author's name and the title and another between the title and the page number:

(Gilbert, *Blood Pressure*, 19)

(3) Shorten titles as much as possible. For example, the following title

Heritage of Freedom: United States History in Christian Perspective

could be shortened to

Heritage of Freedom.

c. Page references.

(1) Refer to page(s) by number alone, without the word *page(s)* or the abbreviations *p.* or *pp.* Simply type a comma after the author's name, space once, and type the page number:

(Phillips, 51)

TE Note: For more information on how to type inclusive numbers, see Turabian's *Manual* section 2.67 or the *Chicago Manual* sections 8.69–70.

(2) Refer to more than one page like this:

(Phillips, 132-33)

3. Place the citation where it will offer the least hindrance to the flow of thought and still be as close to the material documented as possible.

a. The parenthetical citation should precede the punctuation mark that ends a sentence, clause, or phrase.

Treadwell thinks that the results are very often noticeably different from what the critics think (165). Others, like Trager and Smith (367-73), have never attempted to form an opinion on this matter.

b. When a parenthetical citation falls at the end of a direct quotation, put the citation after the closing quotation mark.

Smith and Hall thought the suggestion "absurd" (452), but Krasky thought it "deserving of attention" (539).

c. If a quotation ends with a question mark or an exclamation point, retain the question mark or exclamation point and add a period after the parenthetical reference.

In Stansky's strange novel *The Subterranean Life*, the main character wonders, "Where did I come from, and where am I going?" (57).

Sample abbreviations for names of publishers

The names of publishers may be abbreviated in your works cited entries. Listed below are some of the abbreviations that you would find in *Books in Print* published by the R. R. Bowker Company.

Publisher's name	Abbreviation
A Beka Book Publications	Beka
American Library Association	Amer. Lib. Assn.
Baker Book House	Baker
Basic Books	Basic
Cambridge University Press	Cambridge U Pr
Clarendon Press	Clarendon Pr
Educational Resources Information Center	ERIC
Farrar, Straus and Giroux, Inc.	Farrar
Gale Research, Inc.	Gale
Harcourt Brace Jovanovich	Harcourt
HarperCollins Publishers, Inc.	HarpC
Harvard Law Review Association	Harvard Law Rev. Assn.
Houghton Mifflin Co.	Houghton
Little, Brown and Company, Inc.	Little
Macmillan Publishing Co., Inc.	Macmillan
McGraw-Hill, Inc.	McGraw
The MIT Press	MIT Pr
The Modern Language Association of America	MLA
Mott Media	Mott Media
The National Council of Teachers of English	NCTE
W. W. Norton and Co., Inc.	Norton
Oxford University Press	Oxford U Pr
Prentice Hall Press	Prentice
Random House, Inc.	Random
Regnery Publishing, Inc.	Regnery
Charles Scribner's Sons	Scribner
Simon & Schuster, Inc.	Simon
The University of Chicago Press	U of Chicago Pr
University Press of Mississippi	U Pr of Mississippi
U.S. Government Printing Office	USGPO
Yale University Press	Yale U Pr

Sample parenthetical citations (PC) and corresponding works cited entries (WC) for several common sources (See pages 319–323 for additional samples.)

(1) BOOK with one author

PC (Hughes, 127)

WC Hughes, Jonathan. *American Economic History.* Glenview: Scott, 1983.

with editor, compiler, or translator as author

PC (Gage, 32)

WC Gage, John, ed. and trans. *Goethe on Art.* Berkeley: U of California P, 1980.

with institution, association, or the like as author

PC (American Council on Education, 12-13)

WC American Council on Education. *American Universities and Colleges.* 9th ed. Washington, D.C.: Amer. Council on Educ., 1964.

with no author given

PC (*Chicago Manual*, 441)

WC *The Chicago Manual of Style.* 14th ed. Chicago: U of Chicago Pr, 1993.

(2) GENERAL MAGAZINES

PC (Gilder, 23-24)

WC Gilder, George. "What Ronald Reagan Doesn't Know about His Own Achievements." *National Review,* 29 June 1984, 22-25.

(3) ENCYCLOPEDIA (**Note:** For unsigned articles, simply omit name and begin with title.)

PC (Kistiakowsky)

WC Kistiakowsky, Vera. "Nuclear energy." *The World Book Encyclopedia,* 1992 ed.

(4) ENCYCLOPEDIA ON CD-ROM

PC ("Depression")

WC "Depression of the 1930s." *New Grolier's Encyclopedia,* 1993 ed. CD-ROM. Grolier Electronic, Oct. 1993.

(5) WORLD WIDE WEB (WWW) PAGE (**Note:** For unsigned articles, simply omit name and begin with title.)

PC (Miller)

WC Miller, Thomas A. "Chlorinated Hydrocarbons." 5 Nov. 1996. <http://entmuseum9.ucr.edu/ent128/chlorine.html> (accessed 4 May 1998)

Sample parenthetical citations (PC) and corresponding works cited entries (WC) for other types of sources

SINGLE-VOLUME BOOKS

Two authors

PC (Hoebel and Frost, 325-26)

WC Hoebel, E. Adamson, and Everett L. Frost. *Cultural and Social Anthropology.* New York: McGraw, 1976.

Three authors

PC (Anderson, Fox, and Twomey, 537)

WC Anderson, Ronald A., Ivan Fox, and David P. Twomey. *Business Law.* 12th ed. Cincinnati: South-Western, 1984.

More than three authors

PC (Wilcox et al., 113)

WC Wilcox, Clair, Willis D. Weatherford, Jr., Holland Hunter, and Morton S. Baratz. *Economies of the World Today.* 3d ed. New York: Harcourt, 1976.

Editor, compiler, or translator with an author

PC (Locke, 35)

WC Locke, John. *An Essay Concerning Human Understanding.* Edited by Peter H. Nidditch. Oxford: Clarendon Pr, 1975.

Anthology (article, essay, or other component part by one author in a work edited by another)

PC (Webster, 48)

WC Webster, Noah. "On the Education of Youth in America." In *Essays on Education in the Early Republic,* ed. Frederick Rudolf, 41-77. Cambridge: Harvard U Pr, Belknap, 1965.

Book in a series

PC (Gwynn, 85)

WC Gwynn, Aubrey. *Roman Education from Cicero to Quintilian.* Classics in Education, no. 29. New York: Teachers Coll. Pr, 1926.

Edition other than the first

PC (Machlis, 65)

WC Machlis, Joseph. *The Enjoyment of Music: An Introduction to Perceptive Listening.* 3d ed. New York: Norton, 1970.

A reprint edition (republished book)

PC (Machen, 43)

WC Machen, J. Gresham. *The Virgin Birth of Christ.* New York: Harper, 1930. Reprint, Grand Rapids: Baker, 1965.

Pamphlets (same as books)

PC (Emery, 12)

WC Emery, Donald W. *Sentence Analysis.* New York: Holt, 1961.

MULTIVOLUME BOOKS

A multivolume work (when referring to two or more of the volumes)

If you are using two or more volumes of a work, identify the specific volume in the citation. Cite the total number of volumes in the works cited entry directly before the publication information.

PC (Newman, 2:809)

WC Newman, James R. *The World of Mathematics.* 4 vols. New York: Simon, 1956.

A multivolume work (when using only one of the volumes)

If you are using only one volume of a work, you may omit the volume number from your citation, but you must include in your works cited entry the volume number and the publication information for that particular volume.

PC (Newman, 809)

WC Newman, James. *The World of Mathematics.* Vol. 2. New York: Simon, 1956.

If you are using only one volume of a work that has separate titles, you may cite the work as if it were an ordinary book, omitting the details concerning volumes.

PC (Churchill, 37)

WC Churchill, Winston S. *The Birth of Britain.* New York: Dodd, 1956.

Or you may include the details, as in the following example:

PC (Churchill, 37)

WC Churchill, Winston S. *The Birth of Britain.* New York: Dodd, 1956. Vol. 1 of *A History of the English-Speaking Peoples.* 4 vols. 1956-58.

PERIODICALS

Newspapers

PC (Herndon, 1)

WC Herndon, Keith. "Farms Down to a Record Low in State." *Atlanta Constitution,* 23 May 1984, B1.

CD-ROM

For a source published on CD-ROM, the citation should contain either the author's name or the title of the work (or portion of the work) cited. The works cited entry is much the same as it is for printed material, except that the publication information for the CD-ROM is listed at the end. This additional information usually includes the title of the CD-ROM, the publication medium (CD-ROM), the name of the publisher (or vendor), and the date of electronic publication.

Book

PC (Harrison)

WC Harrison, William. *Description of Elizabethan England* (1577). *World Literary Heritage.* CD-ROM. Irvine: Softbilt, 1994.

Magazine

PC (Lane)

WC Lane, Charles. "Picked Pocket." *New Republic,* 19 Dec. 1994, 12-14. *MAS Full Text Elite,* Disc 1 CD-ROM. EBSCO, 1995.

Newspaper

PC (Toner)

WC Toner, Robin. "Senate Approves Welfare Plan That Would End Aid Guarantee." *New York Times,* 20 Sept. 1995, national ed., A1. *New York Times Ondisc.* CD-ROM. UMI-Proquest, Dec. 1995.

Essay

PC (Sainte-Beuve)

WC Sainte-Beuve, Charles Augustin. "What Is a Classic?" Translated by E. Lee. 1837. *World Literary Heritage.* CD-ROM. Irvine: Softbilt, Aug. 1994.

No written source available

PC (Pixel)

WC Pixel Multimedia (Tel Aviv) and Aaron Witkin Associates (London). *The Dead Sea Scrolls Revealed,* interactive ed. CD-ROM. Logos Research, Jan. 1994.

Note: Other types of portable electronic publications (diskettes, magnetic tapes, and so forth) are documented in the same manner as CD-ROMs.

ON-LINE SERVICES

For a source obtained from an on-line service, the citation should contain either the author's name or the title of the work (or portion of the work) cited. The works cited entry includes the author's name (if known); the title of the document; the document date or date of last revision (if known); the Internet address (URL), enclosed in angle brackets (<>); and the date you accessed the document. Note that no hyphen is used if the URL must be divided at the end of a line.

World Wide Web (WWW) page—no author or date given

PC ("Airborne Laser System")

WC "Airborne Laser System." <http://www.boeing.com/defense-space/military/abl/> (accessed 5 May 1998)

World Wide Web (WWW) page—part of larger online work

PC (Graham)

WC Graham, John F. "Chapter 19: The Space Shuttle." *Space Exploration: From Talisman of the Past to Gateway for the Future.* 1995. <http://www.space.edu/projects/book/chapter19.html> (accessed 4 May 1998)

Document obtained via File Transfer Protocol (FTP)

PC (*Federal Firearms Regulations Reference Guide*)

WC *Federal Firearms Regulations Reference Guide.* 18 Aug. 1997. <ftp://ftp.atf/treas.gov/atfnet/firearms/pubs/atfp5300.4tx> (accessed 4 May 1998)

SPECIAL FORMS

The Bible

Neither the Bible nor its individual books are underlined or put in quotation marks. Always identify the version being quoted or cited.

PC (1 Cor. 13:1-13 KJV)

WC The Bible (King James Version).

Note: Except in specialized works, the Bible is not usually listed in a bibliography. A textual reference is sufficient.

Sermons

PC (Schettler)

WC Schettler, Jim. "Three Steps to Knowing God's Will." Sermon. Campus Church, 25 July 1993, Pensacola.

Interviews (personal)

PC (Hopkins)

WC Hopkins, E. W., Jr., First Mutual Savings Association. Interview by author, 20 Sept. 1995, Pensacola.

Lectures

PC (Reese)

WC Reese, John. "The Philosophical Roots and Fruits of Communism." Class lecture. Pensacola Christian Coll., 7 Mar. 1994, Pensacola.

Tape recordings

PC (Dickinson)

WC Dickinson, Emily. *Emily Dickinson: A Self-Portrait.* Read by Julie Harris. Caedmon SWC 2026. Audiocassette.

Videotapes

PC (Hugo)

WC Hugo, Victor. *Les Miserables.* Directed by Glenn Jordan. 123 min. ITC Entertainment, 1978. Videocassette.

Television programs

PC *(Rejoice in the Lord)*

WC *Rejoice in the Lord.* Television broadcast. WPMI, Pensacola. 8 July 1994.

Radio programs

PC *(Radio Bible Class)*

WC *Radio Bible Class.* Radio broadcast. WPCS, Pensacola. 4 May 1994.

Index

C

Index

R

S

T

U

V

Teacher Supplement

for Grammar *and* Composition I

Contents

Beka Book® Language Series

Grammar and Composition I Teacher Key
Fourth Edition

Editors: Jean Spitsbergen, Heather Fulfer

A Beka Book, a Christian textbook ministry of Pensacola Christian College, is designed to meet the need for Christian textbooks and teaching aids. The purpose of this publishing ministry is to help Christian schools reach children and young people for the Lord and train them in the Christian way of life.

Photo on page 335 by Corel.

English Grammar in Christian Perspective

The *A Beka Book* Philosophy of English Grammar

Language: A Gift from God

The *A Beka Book* Grammar and Composition Series is written from the Christian perspective that *language is a gift from God* to man. Language sets mankind apart from all other living things. With this wonderful gift, man can think, reason, and speak; he can study God's Word and learn of His ways; and he can share the gospel with others.

Modern linguists reject the truth of Creation and embrace the evolutionary philosophy that language, like man, *evolved*. They try to explain speech as a chance discovery made by primitive man and developed over the centuries from crude grunts and gibberish into the myriad of complex languages spoken around the world today. Yet to speak, one must think, and to think, one must have language. So which came first, language or speech?

The Christian perspective of language does not have this problem of logic. **The Biblical account of Creation explains the origin of man and language** with four simple words—*"In the beginning, God. . . ."* God created language when He breathed into man the breath of life. Adam could name all the animals, and communicate with Eve, his wife, using the gift of language created by God in the beginning.

Grammar Instruction

This grammar and composition program has a **twofold purpose: to emphasize the orderly structure of our language and to train students to use the English language effectively.** The injunction to *"let all things be done decently and in order"* can be readily applied to language. Modern linguists believe that language remains in a constant state of evolution and that those who teach a standard of correct grammar are hindering the "evolutionary process" of language development.

Theirs is a "transformational" grammar that is constantly changing as it is carelessly used in speech and in writing. They insist that language should be free from rules and restraints since there is no *correct* way to order a sentence, to use a word, or even to spell. In this way, the philosophy of *relativism* has infiltrated the English language classroom and eroded the ability of many students to communicate effectively. **The Christian perspective calls for standards of correct grammar, usage, and spelling** to preserve our language from deteriorating into utter confusion.

Skills for Effective Communication

The goal of the *A Beka Book* Grammar and Composition Series is to equip students with the tools they need to become effective communicators both in speaking and in writing. The carefully devised lessons, exercises, and writing assignments in each work-text teach students to recognize the different parts of speech, to fit these parts of speech together to form sentences, to join sentences together to make paragraphs, and to organize paragraphs into compositions. Students are taught to develop complete and orderly thoughts and to communicate those thoughts in language that is clear and concise.

In a day of poor and lazy language skills, ***A Beka Book* teaches students the essentials of correct grammar and standard usage and prepares them to use God's gift of language effectively** in years to come.

General Information

Grammar and Composition I correlates with the English 7 Curriculum, which includes daily plans for the school year for this grammar text as well as for literature, composition, vocabulary, spelling, and poetry. The English 7 Curriculum plans the course of study for the year, freeing you to concentrate on the other details of teaching. *Grammar and Composition I* may also be used independently of the other materials in the program.

Special Features of the Text

Grammar and Composition I provides

- clear, concise instruction in the use of standard English
- an abundance of exercises
- sentence diagraming
- cumulative reviews
- composition exercises related to the grammatical point being studied
- the writing process and the steps of writing a research paper
- a compact handbook of rules and definitions

The cumulative reviews and the handbook of rules and definitions deserve special mention. **Cumulative reviews** have been conveniently placed throughout this textbook. The value of systematic review can hardly be overemphasized. Because a single exposure to new material rarely yields permanent results, new material must be reviewed repeatedly over an extended period of time. If you assign all of the reviews, you will be immensely pleased with the results by the end of the year. (These reviews are already worked into the English 7 Curriculum daily plans.) The **handbook of rules and definitions** is especially valuable for reviewing for tests because all of the rules and examples are brought together there without any intervening exercises. For example, when reviewing for the first mid-semester examination, instead of having to leaf through fifty-five pages of text, one can turn to the handbook and find all of the rules together on only nine pages. In the **composition unit,** students are introduced to the writing process and the steps of writing a research paper, as well as to writing paragraphs, summaries, book reports, and letters.

Suggestions for Using This Textbook

1. For maximum effectiveness, teach the grammar and mechanics units in the order they are given in the book. It is not wise to try to teach the grammar units in a different sequence. The grammar exercises are carefully planned to contain only work the students have studied up to that point. If you rearrange the units, the exercise sentences will contain material your students have not studied yet.
2. Use the cumulative reviews at the end of each unit to help prepare the students for their tests, which come approximately every three weeks. The nine-weeks reviews are called master reviews.
3. Realize that there is no perfect sequence for teaching grammar. Sometimes when teaching one grammatical point, you will notice that other grammatical elements seem to crowd around calling for attention. For example, in unit 3 when teaching how to locate the subject of a sentence, you will warn the students that the subject cannot be in a prepositional phrase. When you mention a prepositional phrase, several other grammatical questions may arise: What is a phrase? A preposition? The object of a preposition? A noun? A pronoun? In such situations you must improvise. In this instance, you may direct the students to page 174 and briefly explain rules 1 and 2.
4. Have the students memorize certain lists of words. These lists, if memorized, will greatly facilitate the understanding and application of English grammar. You should make it your goal to have every student in your class memorize these lists:
   - **a.** The thirty-four verbs on page 37.
   - **b.** The sixty prepositions on page 174.
   - **c.** The three lists of indefinite pronouns on page 107.
   - **d.** The nominative and objective case pronouns on pages 109 and 111.
   - **e.** The coordinating conjunctions on page 181.

By following the suggestions given here, you can make effective use of this textbook, knowing that at the year's end you will have taught grammar, mechanics, and usage in a clear, coherent manner and that you will have helped the students develop basic composition skills.

Supplement

Page 44, Ex. A (Ex. C., Page 43)

1. The visiting orphans ate and drank heartily.

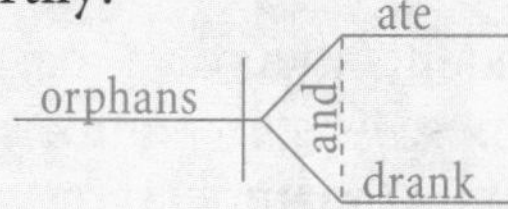

2. James and John were called the Sons of Thunder.

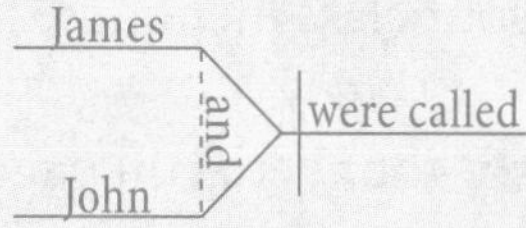

3. Tennis and golf are popular sports and can be played by young or old.

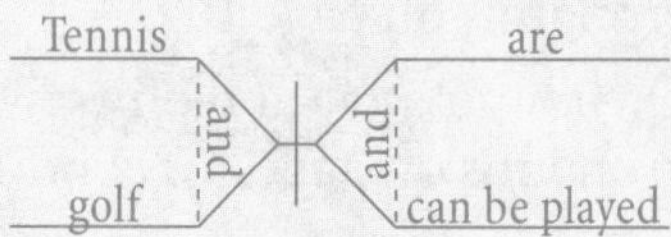

4. Apples and oranges are picked by hand and put into a pail or bag.

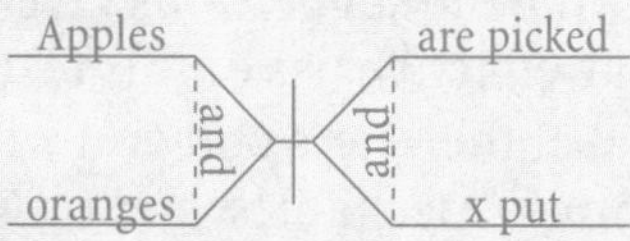

5. Flying squirrels and flying lemurs stretch their webbed legs and glide from tree to tree.

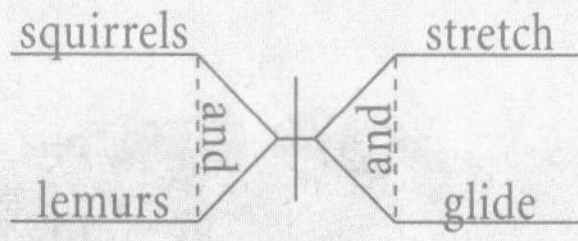

6. Spain and France are separated by the Pyrenees Mountains.

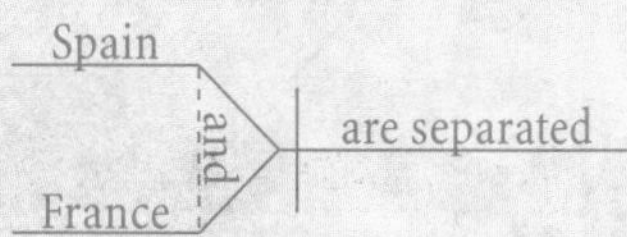

7. Many Canadians and New Englanders hunt and fish for a living.

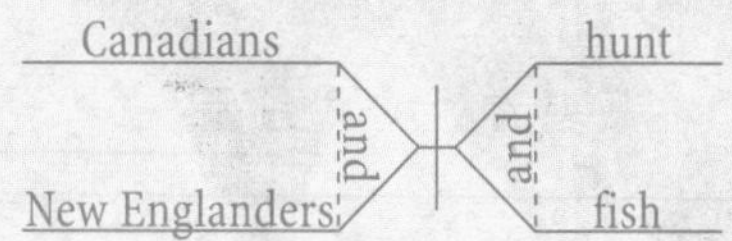

8. The father forgave the Prodigal Son and prepared a feast.

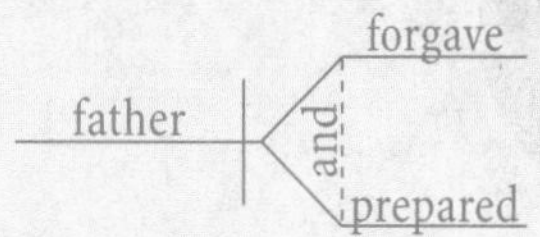

9. Heatstroke and heat exhaustion can overcome a person and cause real suffering.

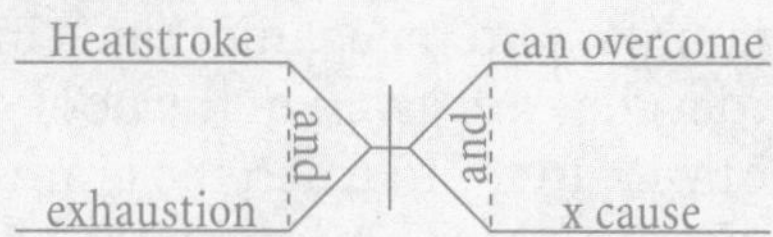

10. During World War II, Anne Frank and her family were betrayed and taken to concentration camps.

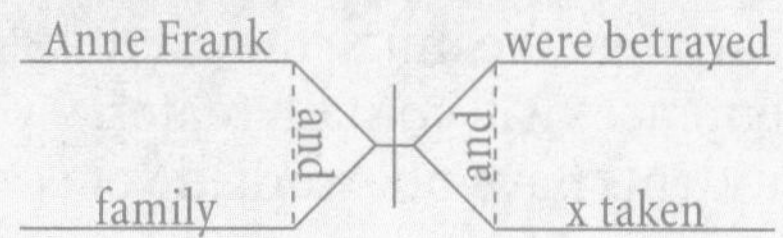

Page 44, Ex. B

1. In ancient times, Celts and other peoples lived in France.

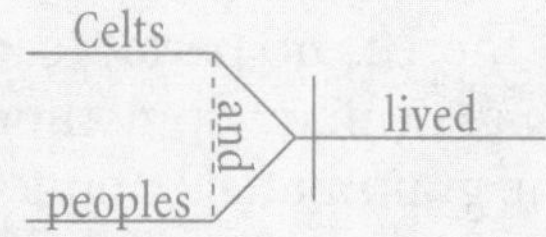

2. Acetone and charcoal are two products of the forest.

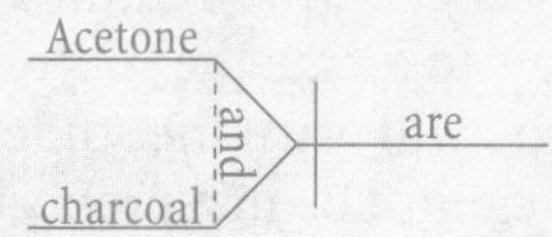

3. California and Florida have large citrus industries.

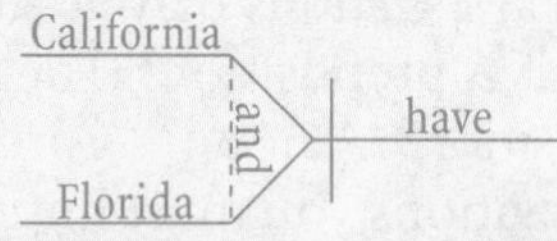

4. John Smith and William Bradford wrote descriptions of colonial life.

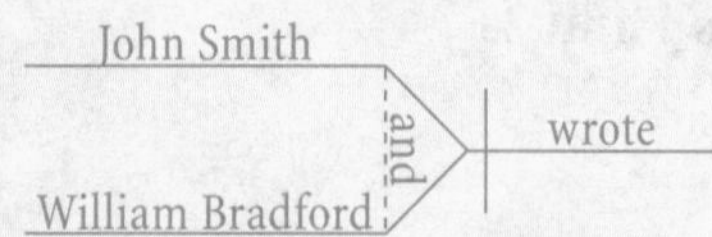

5. Apples and pears can be severely damaged by the caterpillars of the codling moth.

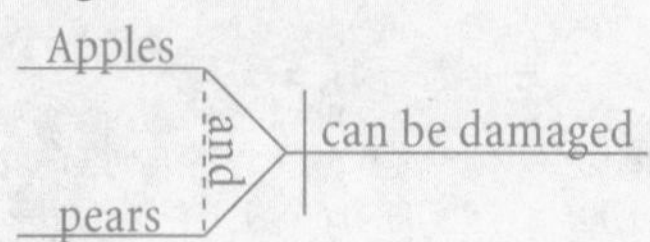

6. Grant and Lee rank among the finest soldiers in U.S. history.

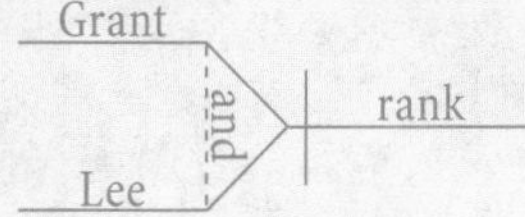

Page 45, Ex. C

1. Spare moments of time may be discovered and used effectively.

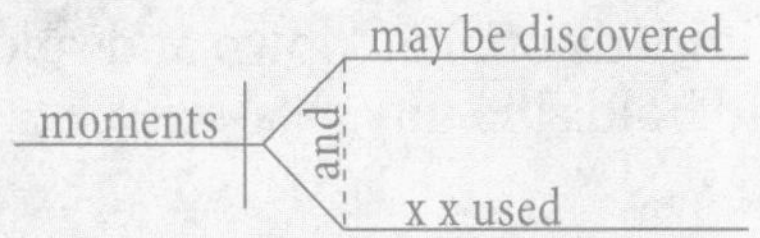

2. One doctor translated a Latin work and rode his rounds at the same time.

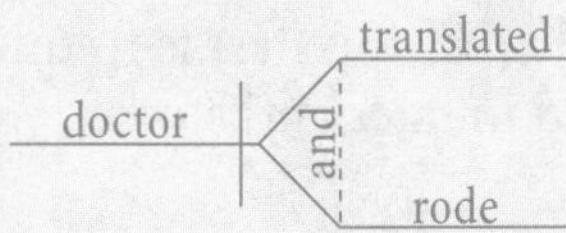

3. Melanchthon, the reformer, noted every idle minute and redeemed it in good labor.

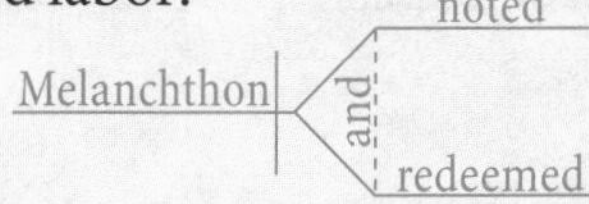

4. Sir Walter Scott was injured and confined to his bed.

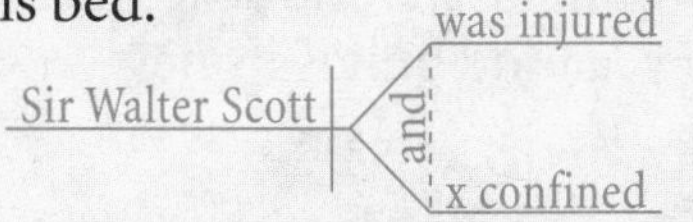

5. He used his time and began his great poem "The Lay of the Last Minstrel."

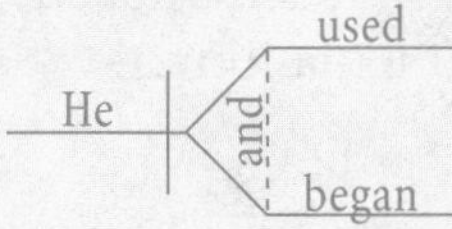

6. The mayfly lives as an adult only a few hours but accomplishes its purpose in life in those moments.

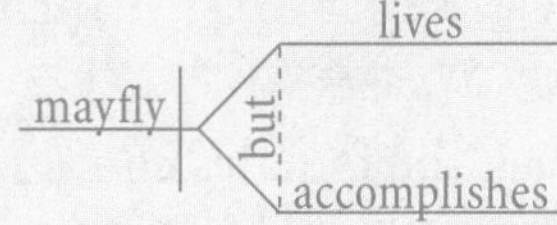

Page 45, Ex. D

1. Cottonseed and soybeans are used as protein supplements for cattle.

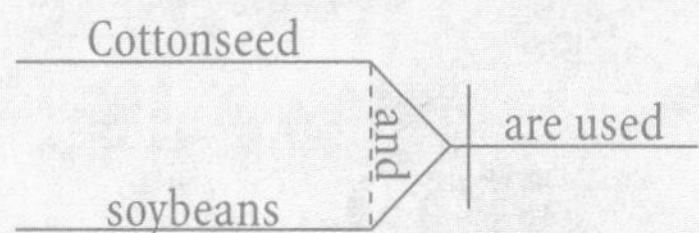

2. Diesel engines burn cheap fuel and can perform heavy-duty work.

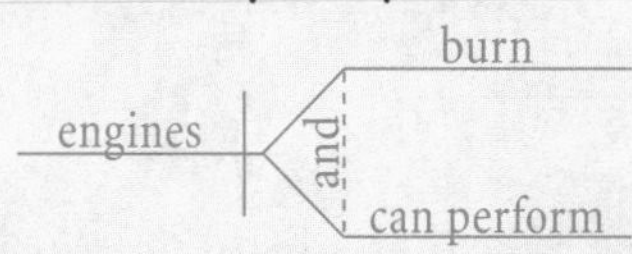

3. Electronic equipment and aircraft parts are manufactured in Dallas, Texas, a major center for such production.

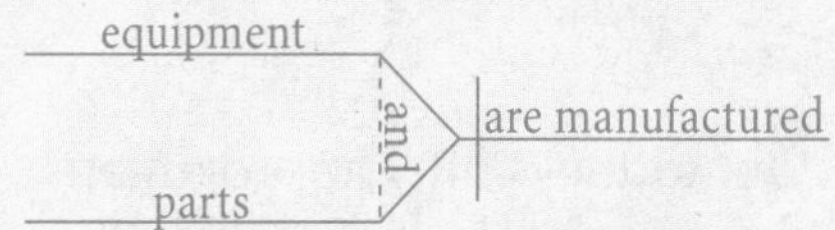

4. Reservoirs and lakes often provide recreational areas for boating and swimming.

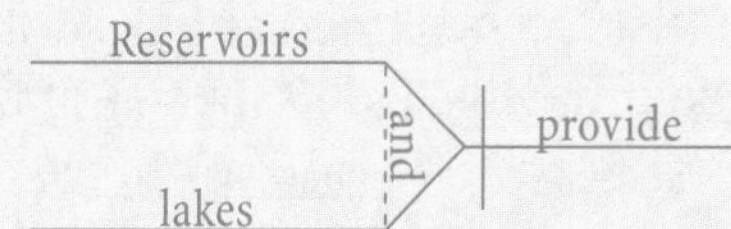

5. Operating from underwater laboratories, divers can live and work for weeks without surfacing.

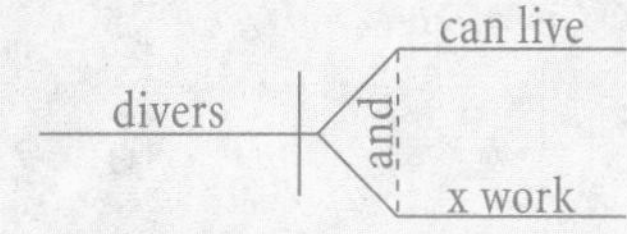

6. Cranes and derricks lift and move heavy loads.

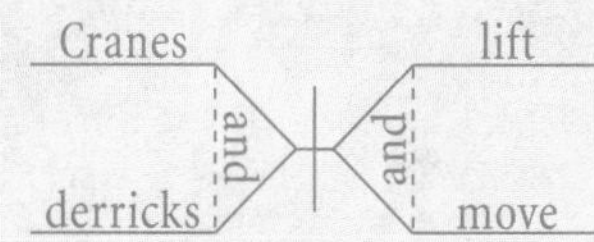

7. Most viruses can be seen only by means of a powerful electron microscope.

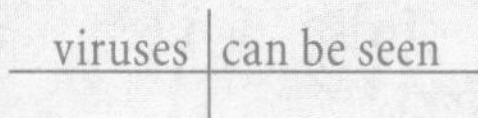

8. Computers on a space shuttle control the launch process and navigate the shuttle.

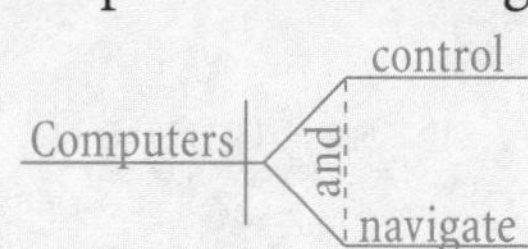

Supplement

Page 45, Ex. D, cont.

9. Both clams and oysters are classified as mollusks.

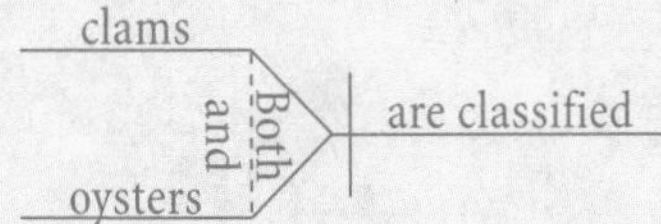

10. Iron reacts with oxygen in the air and forms rust.

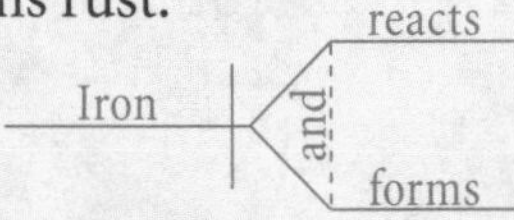

11. Mercury becomes a liquid at room temperature and flows easily and rapidly.

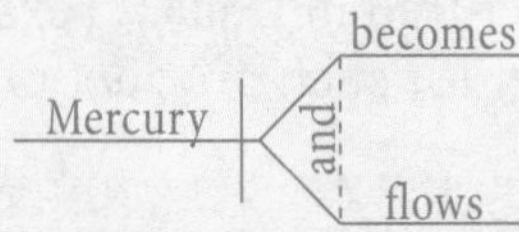

12. Our kidneys filter approximately forty-five gallons of blood daily.

kidneys | filter

13. Scientists have named and described approximately 22,000 species of fish.

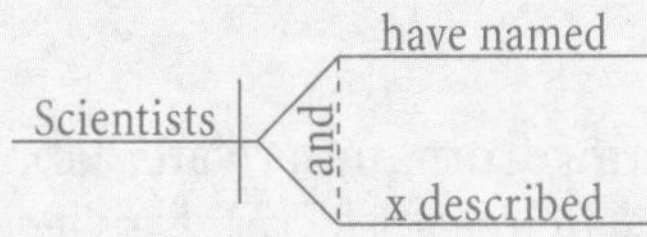

14. Miners may use several different methods in the extraction of salt.

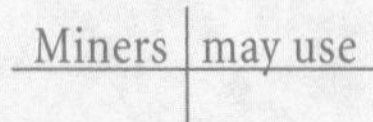

15. Farmers feed salt to livestock and use it as a preservative for hay in storage.

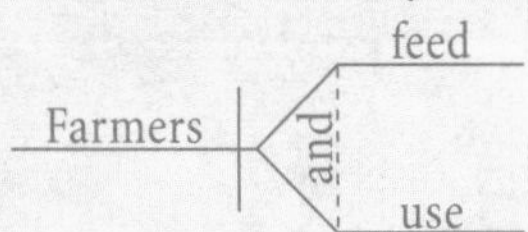

Page 55, Ex. E

1. Owls and cowbirds will often steal nests from other birds.

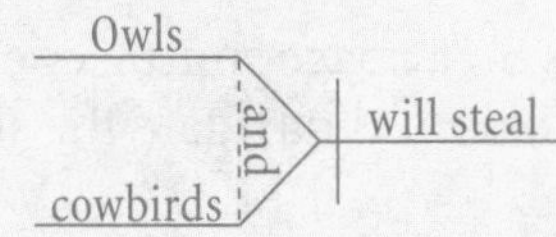

2. Flamingos scrape mud together and build a conelike nest.

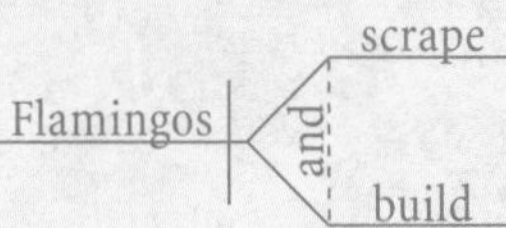

3. The hummingbird's nest is the size of a golf ball.

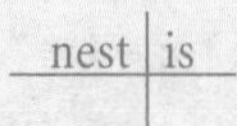

4. It is made of plant down and spider webs and holds the tiny, pea-sized eggs.

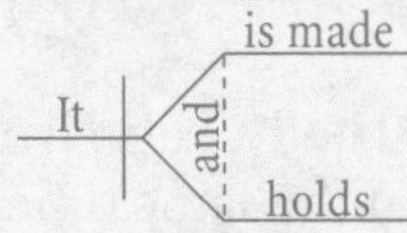

5. The eagle's cliff-top nest is frequently mentioned in tales and stories.

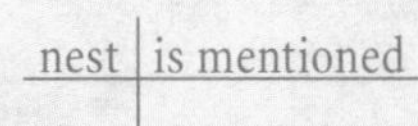

6. Grasses and plant fibers compose the oriole's saclike nest.

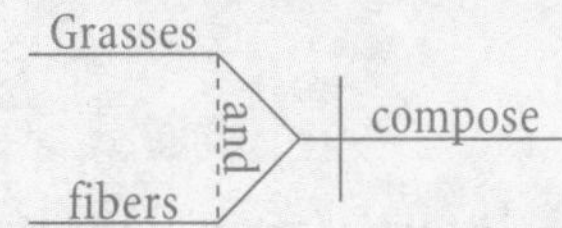

7. The robin often returns to the same spot each year and builds its nest.

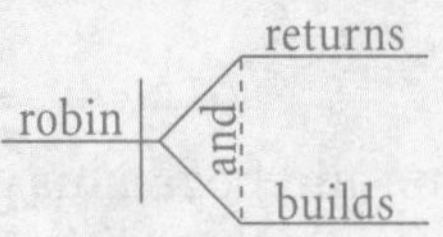

8. Wrens will nest in such unusual places as an old hat or a mailbox.

Wrens | will nest

9. Martins send out scouts for good houses.

Martins | send

10. Upon arrival, the females can immediately settle into their new homes.

females | can settle

Page 88, Ex. B (Ex. A, Page 86)

1. Edison was the inventor of the phonograph.

   Edison | was \ inventor

2. One of the smallest countries is San Marino.

   One | is \ San Marino

3. Peter became a great preacher after Pentecost.

   Peter | became \ preacher

4. The Amalekites were Israel's enemies.

   Amalekites | were \ enemies

5. Charles Dickens remains a well-known novelist.

   Charles Dickens | remains \ novelist

6. Walter Mondale was our Vice President.

   Walter Mondale | was \ Vice President

7. Jesus is the resurrection and the life.

   Jesus | is \ resurrection and life

8. I am the way, the truth, and the life.

   I | am \ way x truth and life

9. The Lord is my light and my salvation.

   Lord | is \ light and salvation

10. Ye are My witnesses.

    Ye | are \ witnesses

Page 88, Ex. B, cont. (Ex. B, Page 87)

1. Dwight L. Moody was a great American evangelist.

   Dwight L. Moody | was \ evangelist

2. Presbyterian missionaries were the first white settlers in Hawaii.

   missionaries | were \ settlers

3. Jeremiah was the weeping prophet of Israel.

   Jeremiah | was \ prophet

4. none

5. The Copperheads were Northerners opposed to President Lincoln's policies.

   Copperheads | were \ Northerners

6. France is a country with many tourist attractions.

   France | is \ country

7. none

8. David was a man after God's own heart.

   David | was \ man

9. The Lord Jesus is the Shepherd and Bishop of our souls.

   Lord Jesus | is \ Shepherd and Bishop

10. Michael is an archangel of the Lord.

    Michael | is \ archangel

11. Adoniram and Ann Judson became pioneer missionaries to Burma.

    Adoniram x and Ann Judson | became \ missionaries

Supplement

Page 88, Ex. B, cont.

12. none

13. none

14. Wasn't Clara Barton the founder of the American Red Cross?

Clara Barton | Was \ founder

15. Methodist circuit riders became carriers of the Gospel to frontier communities.

riders | became \ carriers

Page 91, Ex. B (Ex. A, Page 89)

1. Alone, Captain Joshua Slocum sailed his sloop around the world.

Captain Joshua Slocum | sailed | sloop

2. Nathaniel Bowditch published a famous book on the subject of navigation.

Nathaniel Bowditch | published | book

3. Captain Robert Gray inaugurated the Northwest coast-Hawaii-China trade.

Captain Robert Gray | inaugurated | trade

4. Captain Gray named the Columbia River after his ship, the *Columbia*.

Captain Gray | named | Columbia River

5. American shipwrights and fishermen perfected the schooner.

shipwrights
and
fishermen
perfected | schooner

6. Frederic Tudor, a Boston merchant, sold ice, tea, and spices.

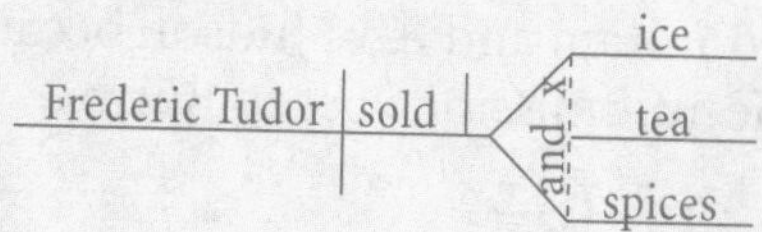

7. Whaling brought large profits during the 1700s and 1800s.

Whaling | brought | profits

8. The head of a sperm whale provided pure oil and spermaceti.

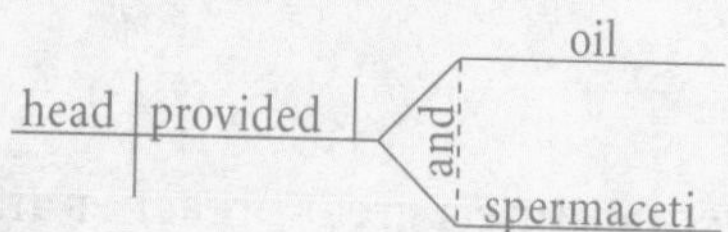

9. Until the introduction of kerosene in 1860, whale oil lamps gave the best light.

lamps | gave | light

10. David Bushnell built the first American underwater craft.

David Bushnell | built | craft

11. Jacques Piccard designed the *Trieste* for underwater research.

Jacques Piccard | designed | *Trieste*

12. At 35,820 feet, the *Trieste* touched the bottom of the ocean.

Trieste | touched | bottom

13. The submarine U.S.S. *Tennessee* can launch missiles without surfacing.

submarine | can launch | missiles

14. The Navy did not use airplanes and aircraft carriers extensively until World War II.

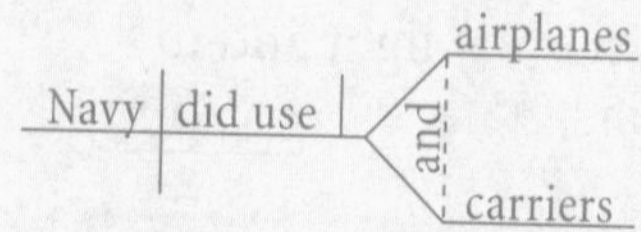

Page 91, Ex. B, cont. (Ex. B, Pages 89–90)

1. Frogmen can destroy underwater mines and beach obstacles.

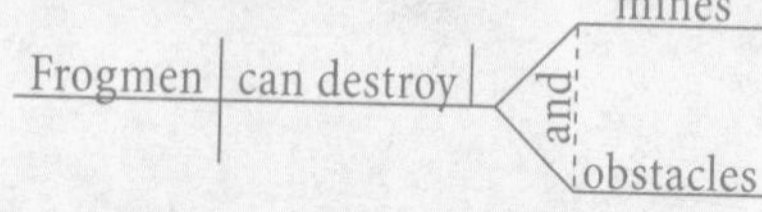

2. Planes from aircraft carriers can destroy enemy shipping and disrupt communications.

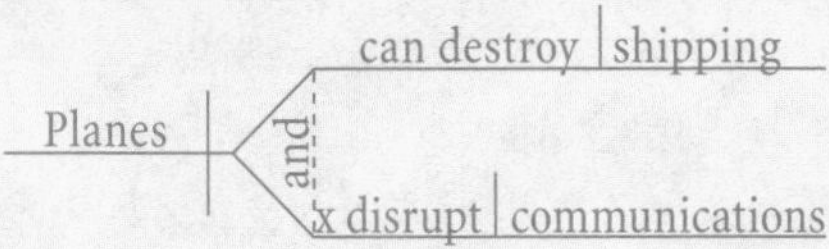

3. Paratroopers drop behind enemy lines and demolish bridges and cut supply lines.

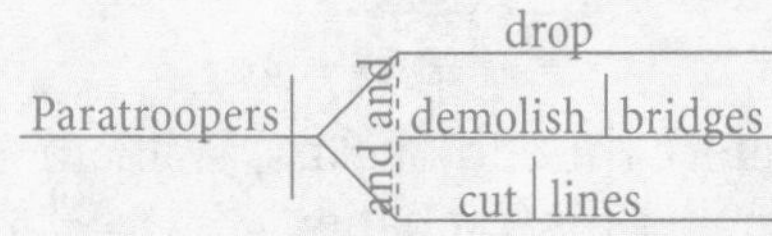

4. Armored vests protect combat flyers and soldiers during wartime.

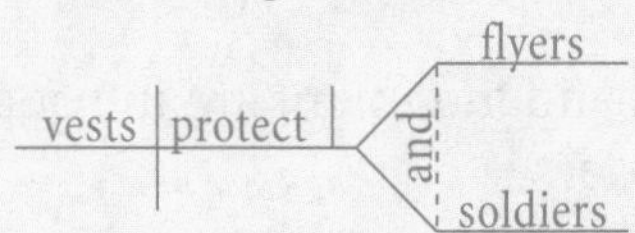

5. Logistic units provide cold weather clothing, boots for arctic wear, and uniforms for use in temperate climates.

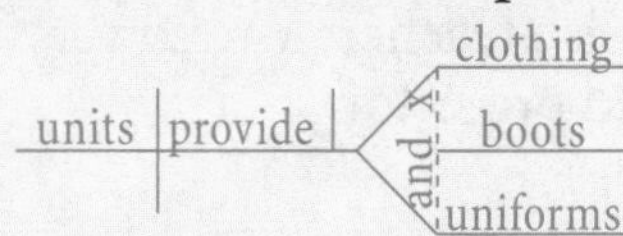

6. Infantrymen must throw grenades and fire various weapons.

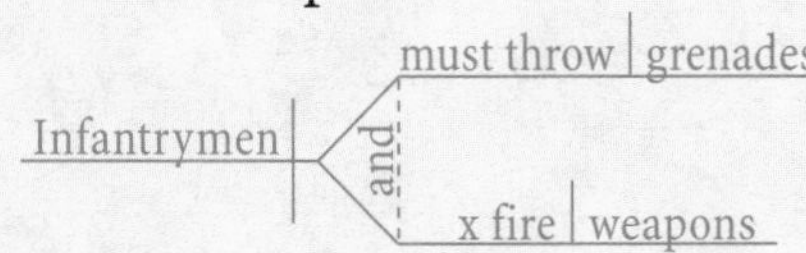

7. The artillery protects the troops and neutralizes the enemy's fire.

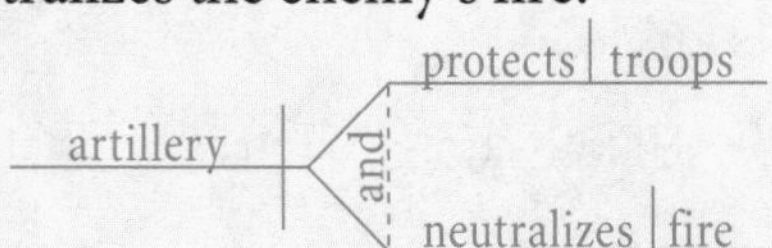

8. Rockets also provide support for troops in the field.

Rockets | provide | support

9. The U.S. Army Infantry Center at Fort Benning, Georgia, conducts airborne and Ranger training courses.

U.S. Army Infantry Center | conducts | courses

10. Army aircraft can spot enemy targets for the artillery and can provide rapid transportation to and from the front line.

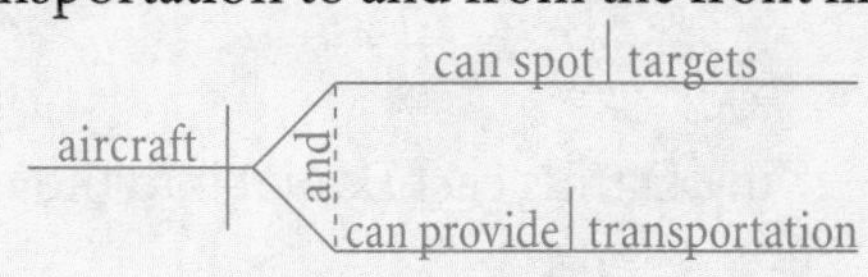

11. The U.S. Army Airborne Center at Fort Rucker, Alabama, trains pilots and maintenance men for various aircraft.

12. Soldiers use gas masks and airtight clothing as protection from chemical warfare.

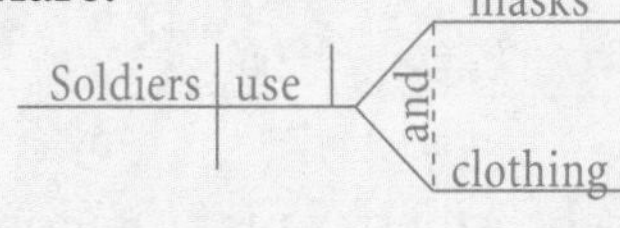

13. The men in the Special Forces infiltrate enemy positions and train local people in guerrilla warfare.

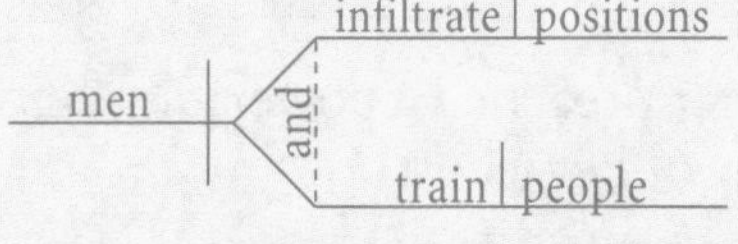

14. Engineers repair roads, build bridges, and construct landing strips.

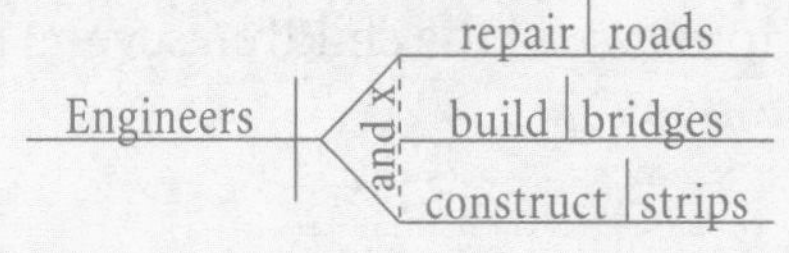

Page 93, Ex. B (**Ex. A, Page 92**)

1. I gave Dad a watch for Father's Day.

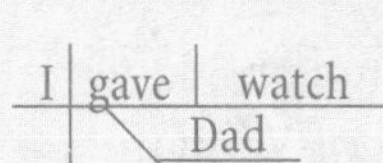

2. Miss Wilson's class took a history test last Friday.

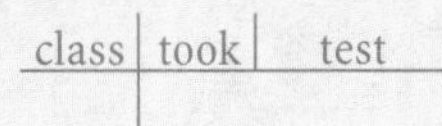

3. Eric sent his family a postcard from Arizona.

Eric | sent | postcard
family

Supplement

Page 93, Ex. B, cont.

4. Paul wrote the Corinthian church two letters.

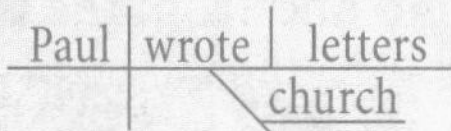

5. King Darius cast Daniel into the lion's den.

King Darius | cast | Daniel

6. God sent the Israelites manna every morning.

God | sent | manna
Israelites

7. Samuel anointed David for the throne of Israel.

Samuel | anointed | David

8. Arabia sells America many gallons of oil each day.

Arabia | sells | gallons
America

9. Peter preached a powerful sermon on the day of Pentecost.

Peter | preached | sermon

10. Mother read the children several bedtime stories.

Mother | read | stories
children

Page 105, Ex. I (Ex. H, Page 105)

1. Ben Jonson, an English playwright and poet, was a friend of William Shakespeare.

Ben Jonson (playwright and poet) | was \ friend

2. Mrs. Wilson made chocolate chip cookies and purchased soft drinks for our class party.

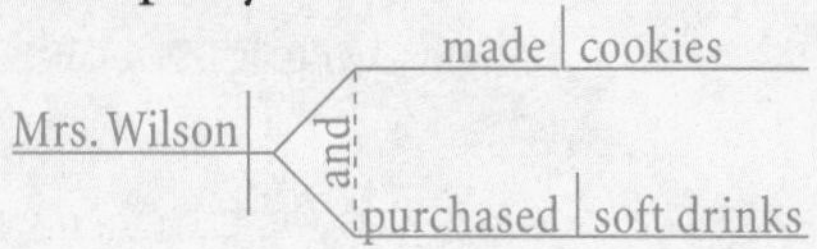

3. Deanna gave her brother a striped tie on his birthday.

Deanna | gave | tie
brother

4. Before the end of class, William gave the teacher his test paper.

William | gave | paper
teacher

5. Reason and judgment are the qualities of a leader.

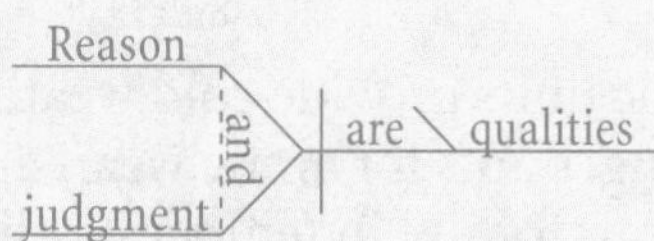

6. My English teacher, Mr. Lowery, used an overhead projector.

teacher (Mr. Lowery) | used | projector

7. Kristen and Sarah were class officers this fall.

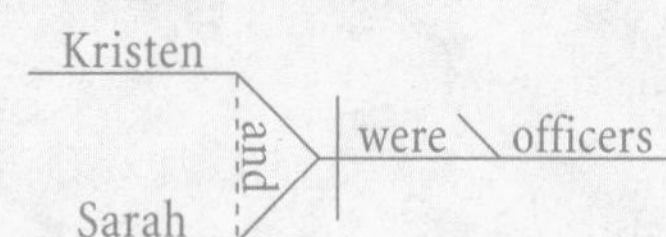

8. Mike, our starting center, has sprained his ankle.

Mike (center) | has sprained | ankle

Page 129, Ex.

1. That ancient Ming porcelain had a slight crack.

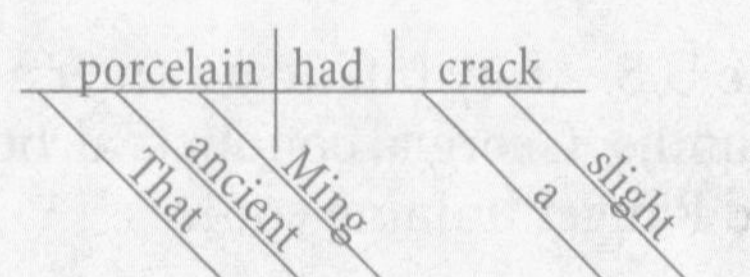

2. The mad rushing waters overflowed the pioneer's tiny boat.

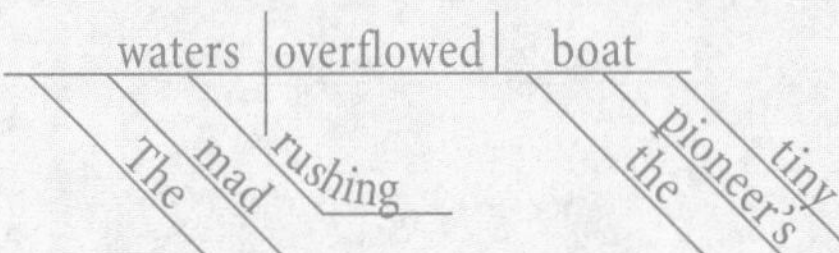

3. The persecuted Christians were joyful and courageous.

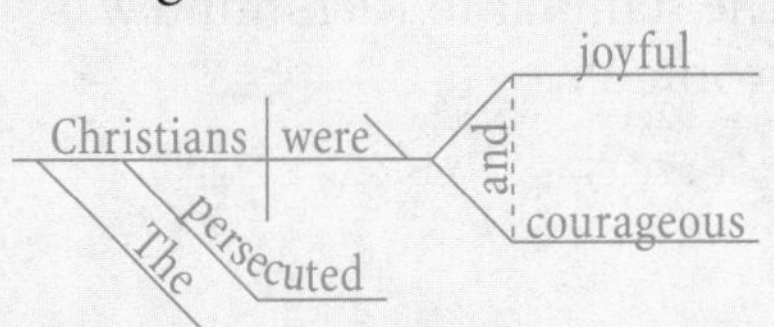

4. Cowardly Shimei hurled several awful curses.

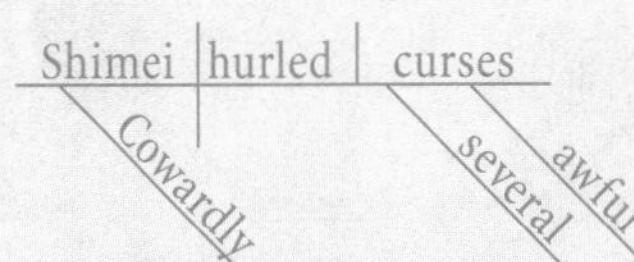

5. One great storm destroyed the invincible Armada.

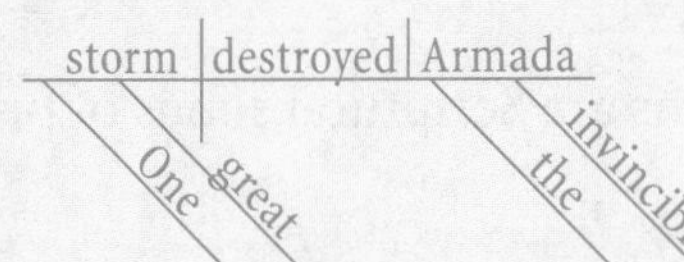

6. New England maple trees produce magnificent orange and red leaves.

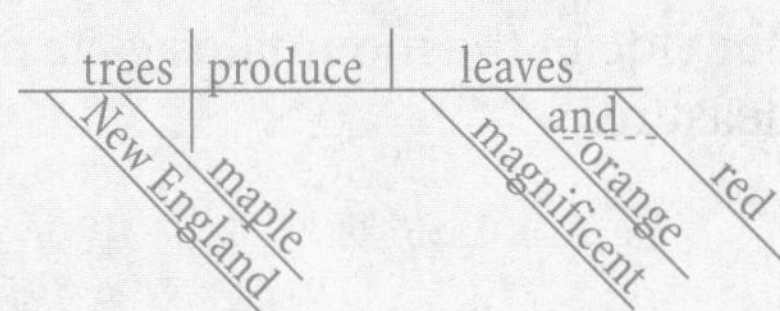

7. The Jewish Holy Place contained a tall golden candlestick.

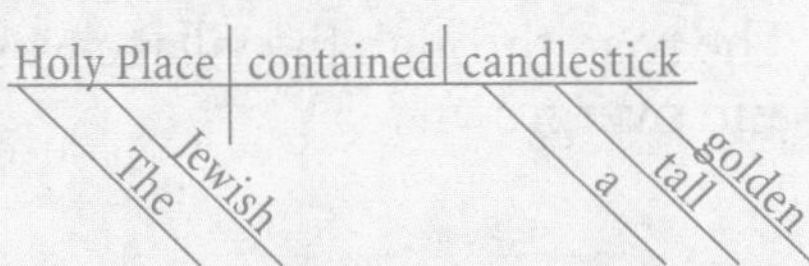

8. The guilty sinners were miserable.

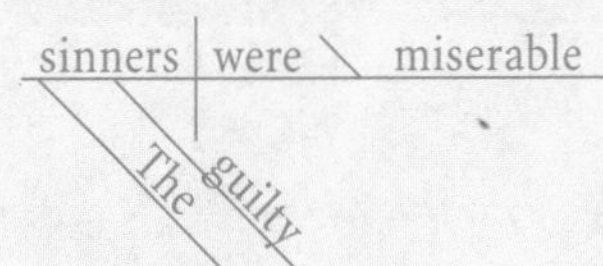

9. A noble Hebrew woman saved her entire race.

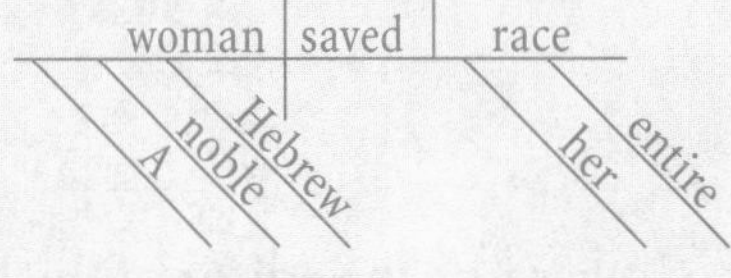

10. The wandering tribes were victorious.

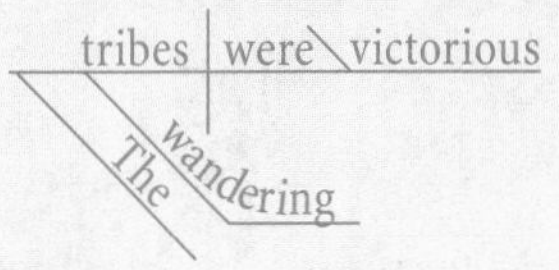

Page 132, Ex. A

1. The mirror in the golden frame sparkled.

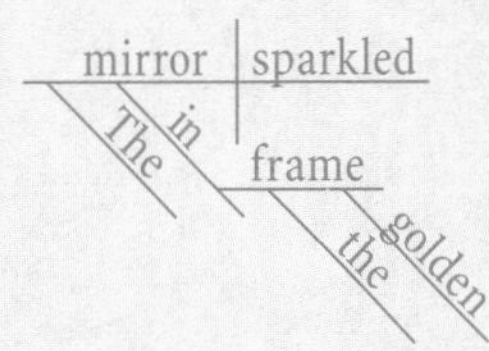

2. John Alden married the Pilgrim girl with golden hair and blue eyes.

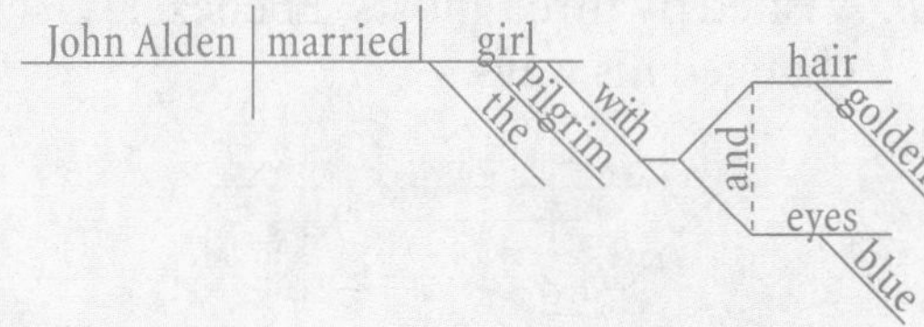

3. Sneezing loudly during the service, Ralph disturbed the entire congregation.

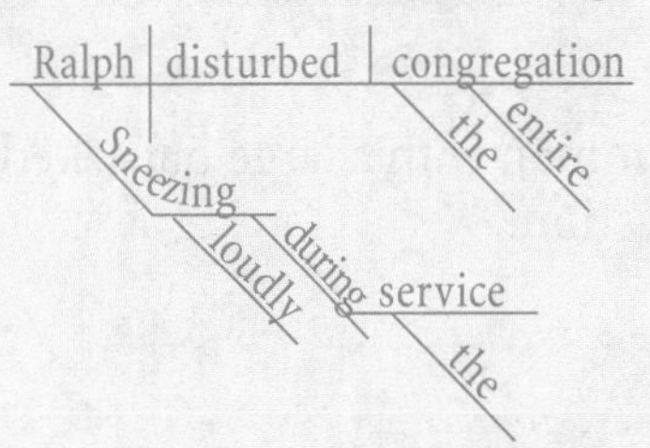

4. Sweeping the kitchen floor, Mom whistled a tune.

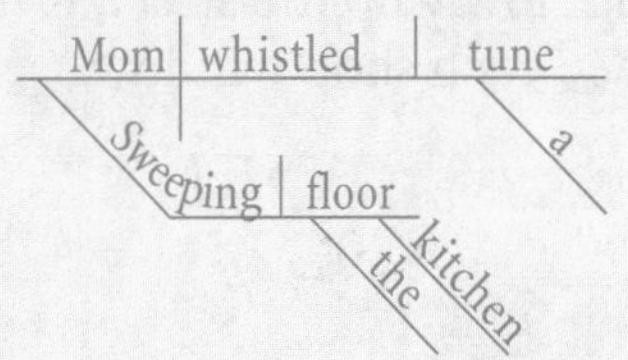

Supplement

Page 132, Ex. A, cont.

5. Our God is Ruler of heaven and earth.

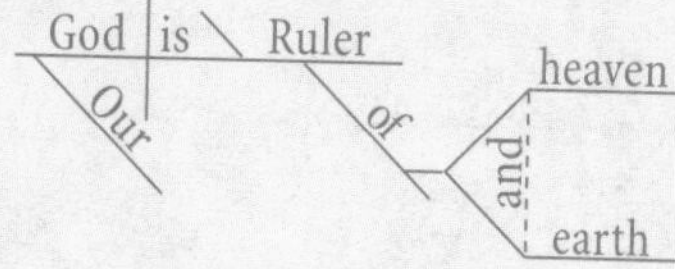

6. Mr. Gower was the editor of the local newspaper.

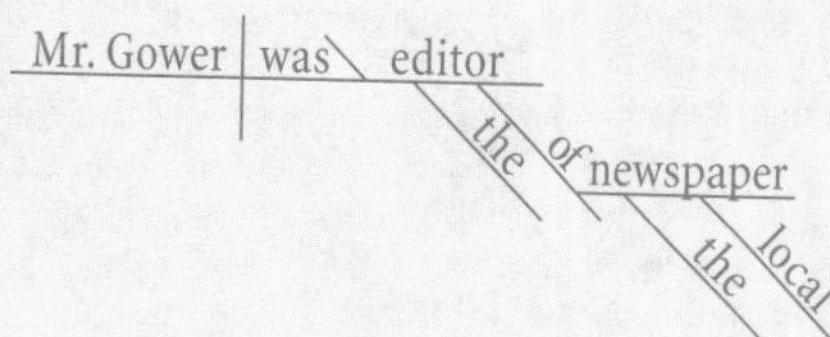

7. Giving his clerk little pay, Scrooge expected long hours of work.

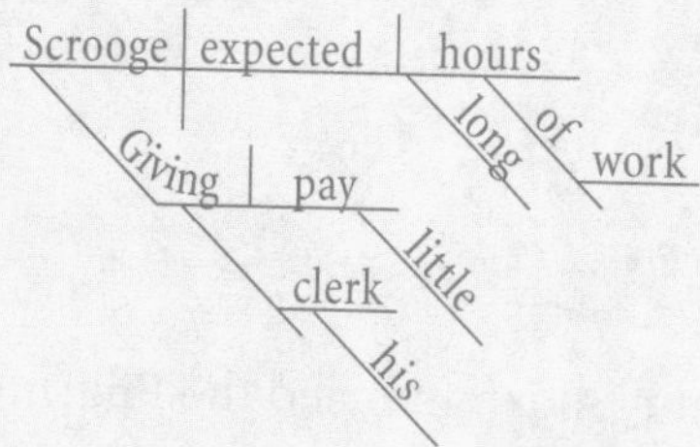

8. Visited by three ghosts, Ebenezer changed his ways.

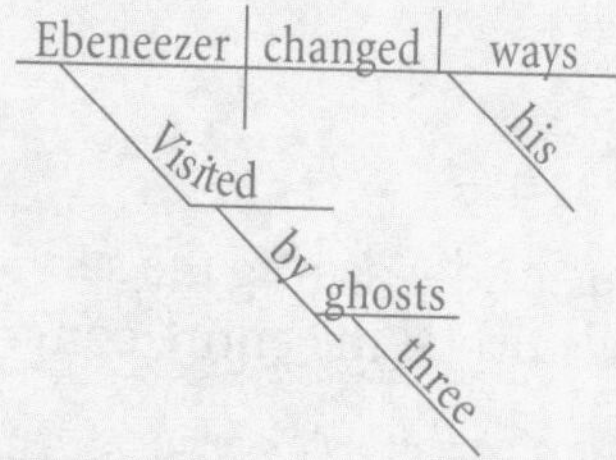

9. A woman with a large hat asked me a question.

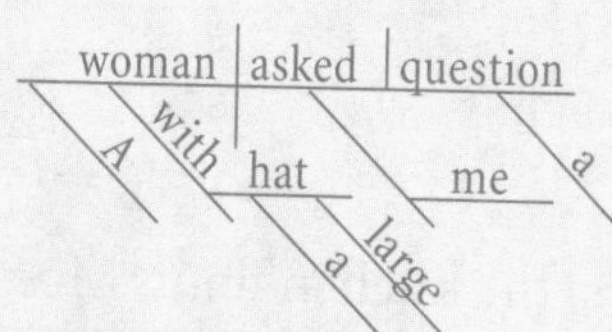

10. Walking slowly up the street, Kyle examined each shop window.

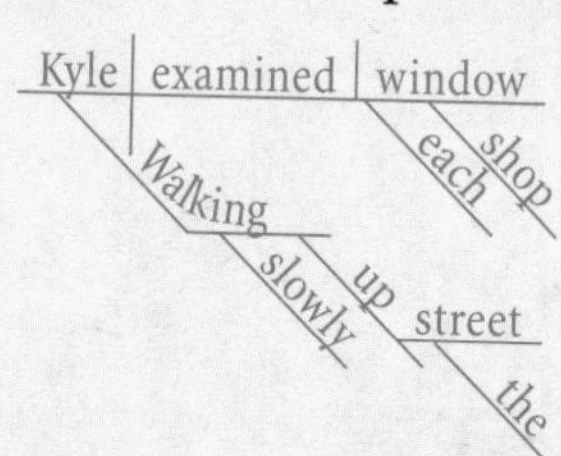

Page 132, Ex. B (Ex. A, Page 130)

1. David was a descendant of the noble Ruth.

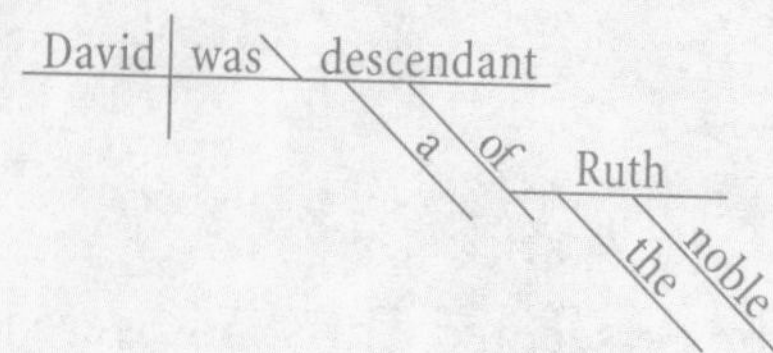

2. The seminar in Richmond was profitable.

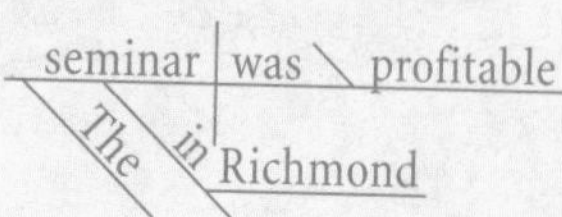

3. My horse is the chestnut mare with the white star on its forehead.

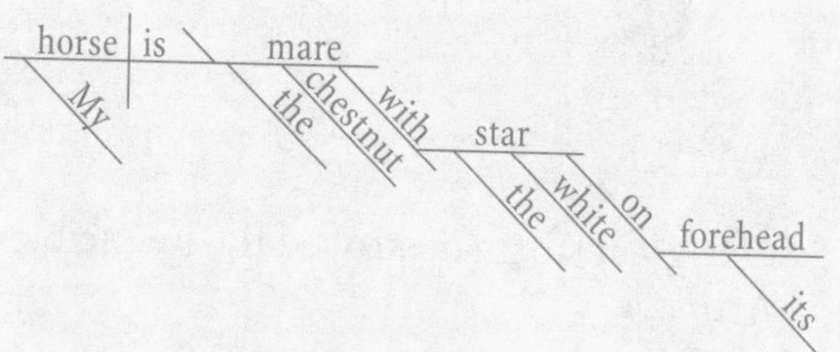

4. Hymns are Scriptural songs of praise.

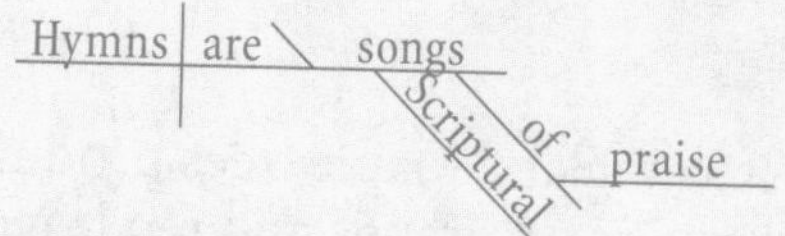

5. Our ride in the mountains gave me great pleasure.

ride | gave | pleasure
Our
in
mountains
the
me
great

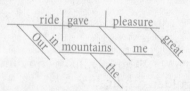

6. The road through the village was rutted and overgrown.

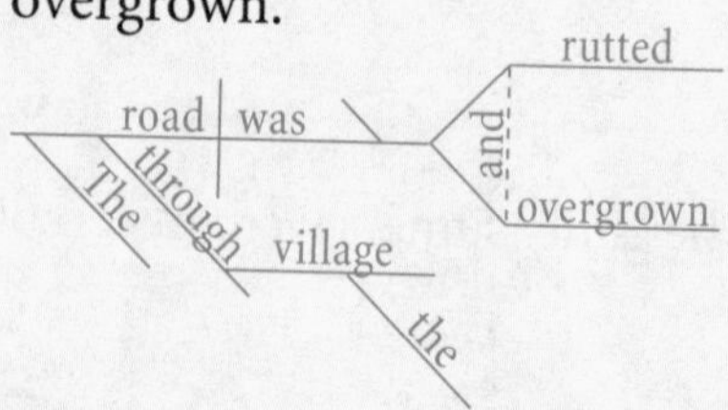

7. A speaker from Washington addressed our local farm board.

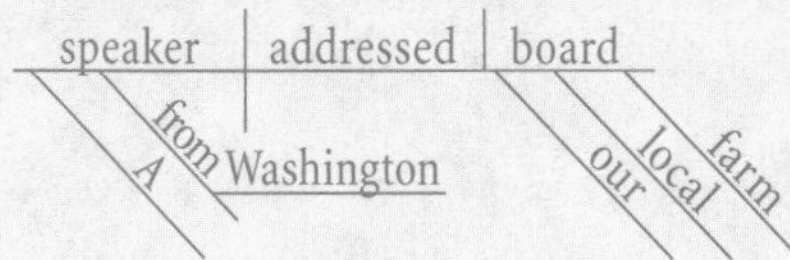

8. Our new neighbor is that fellow in the green jacket.

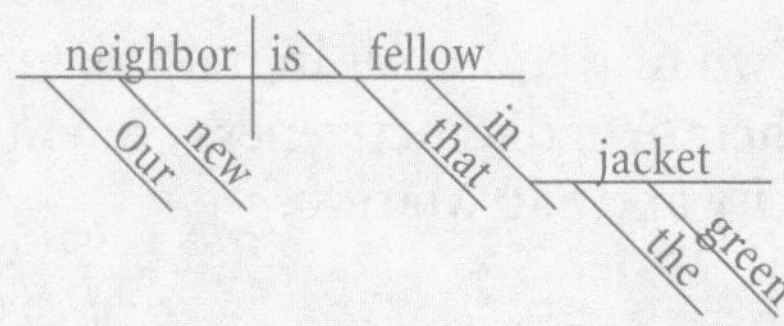

9. Acreage around the lake is marshy and uninhabitable.

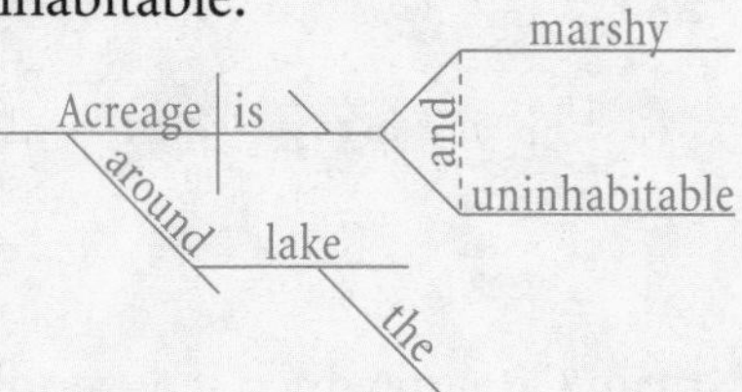

10. Only one of the healed lepers was thankful.

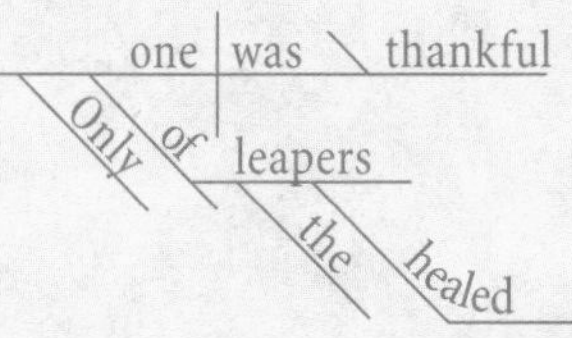

Page 132, Ex. B, cont. (Ex. A, Page 131)

1. The lad holding the horse's reins was small.

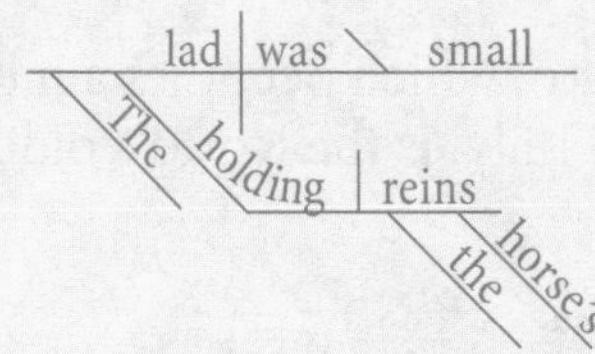

2. Cowering to a maid, Peter denied his Lord.

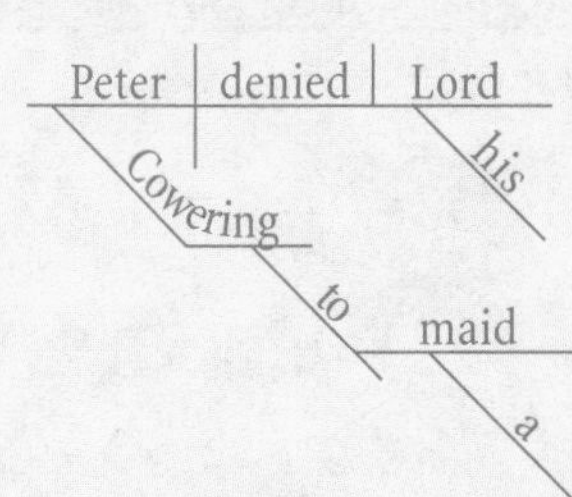

3. Workers skilled in metallurgy were imported from Tyre.

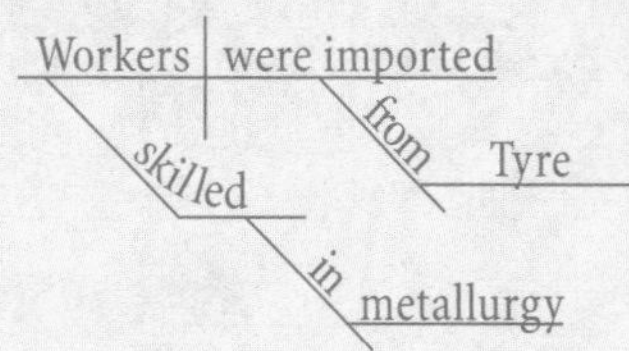

4. Pleased with the news, the old gentleman smiled.

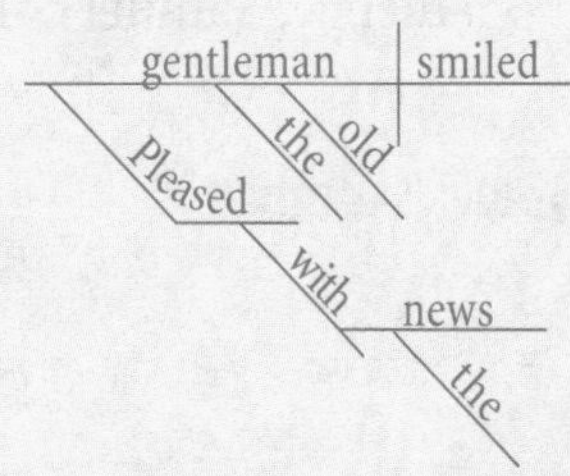

5. The saints tread upon a road paved with pure gold.

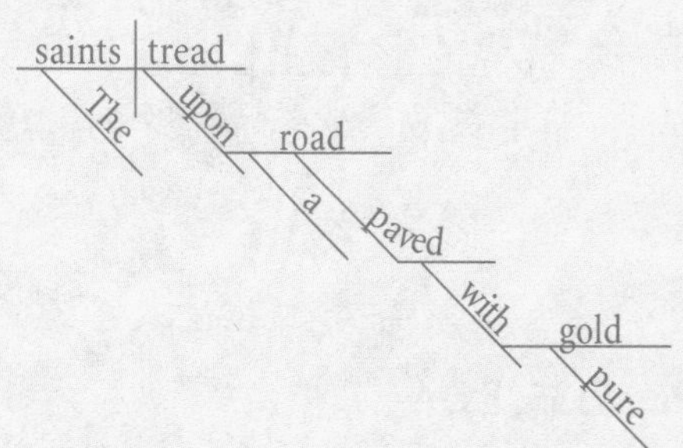

6. Daniel, thrown into the lions' den, still trusted God.

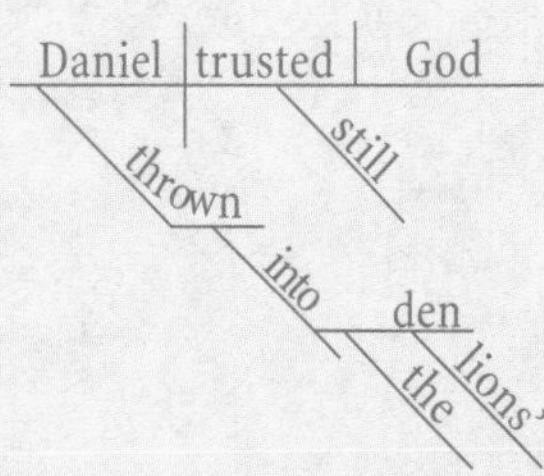

7. Blown over during the storm, the ancient oak destroyed a small home.

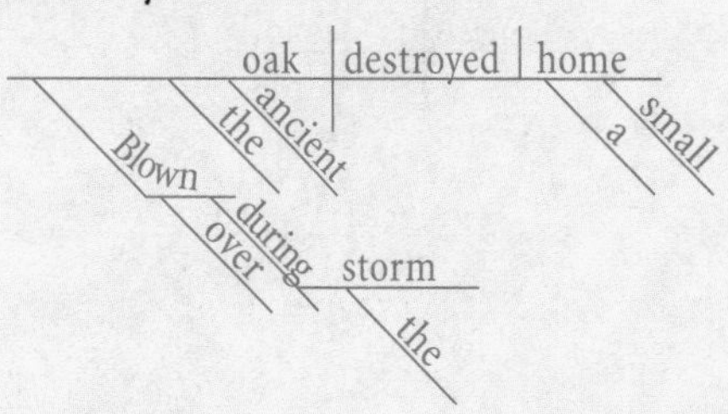

Supplement

Page 132, Ex. B, cont.

8. Waving at the ship, the children stood at the dock.

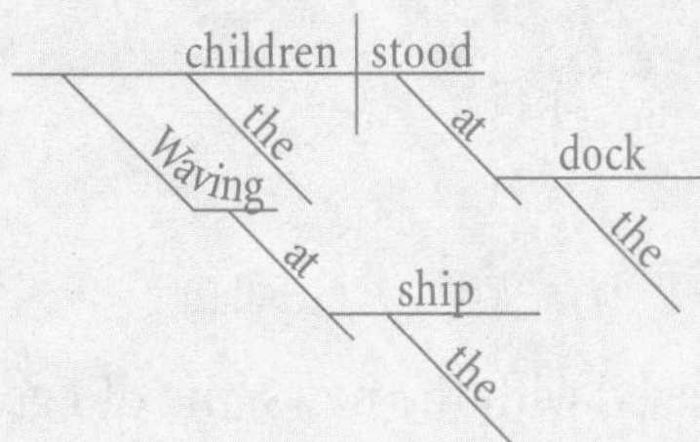

9. Trained in obedience, Samuel could be trusted.

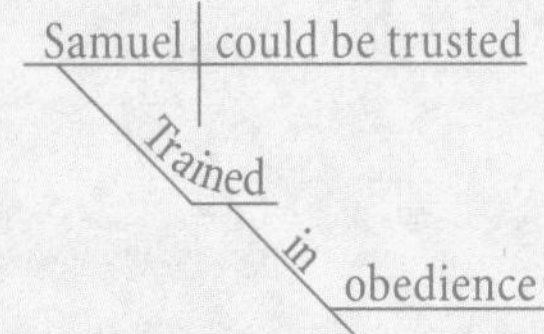

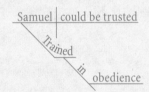

10. Crying quietly, the little girl sat on the street curb.

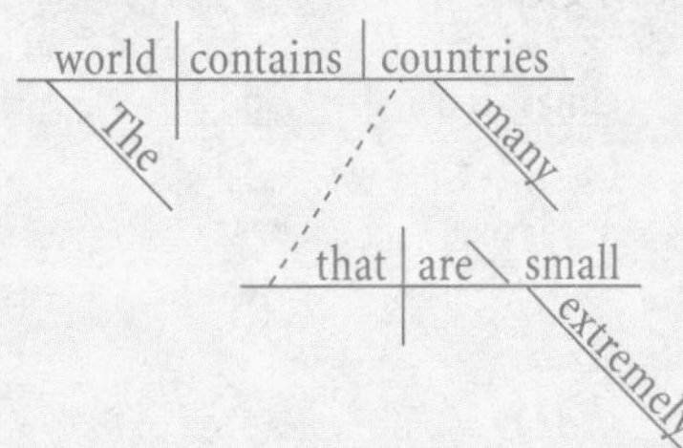

Page 135, Ex. A

1. The world contains many countries that are extremely small.

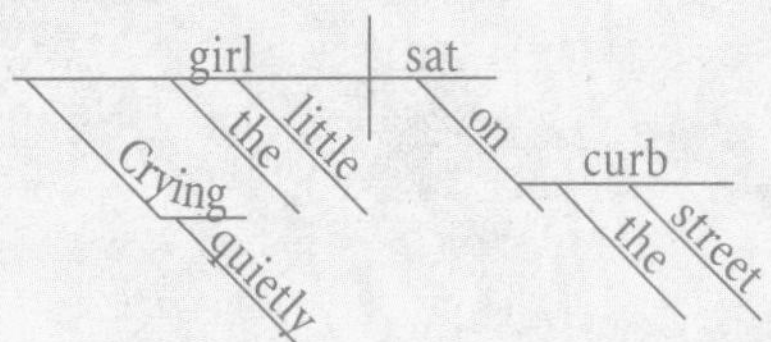

2. Monaco is a small country whose ruler is a prince.

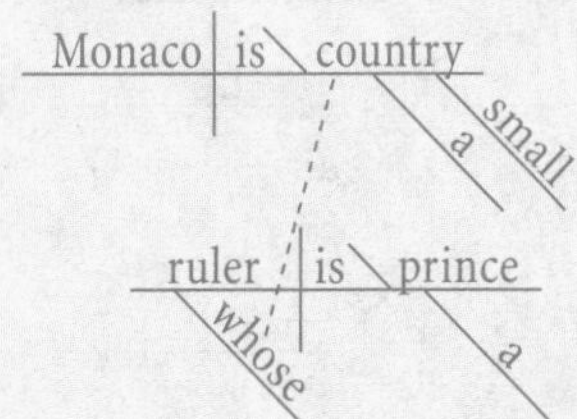

3. Monte Carlo, which is the capital of Monaco, is a famous tourist resort.

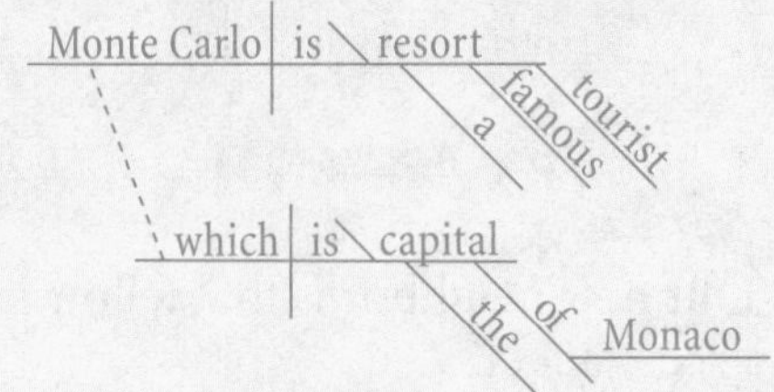

4. Two tiny countries in Italy that maintain their own distinctiveness are Vatican City and San Marino.

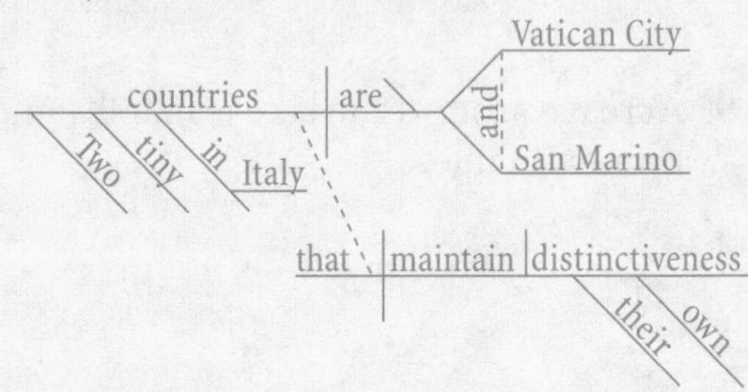

5. Vatican City, in which few people live, is the world's smallest independent state.

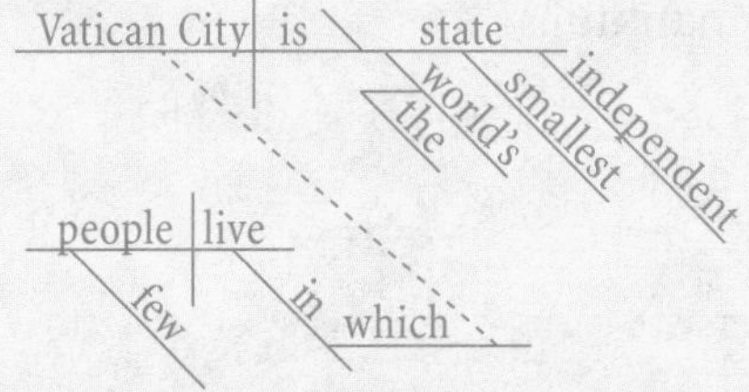

Note: In sentences 5, 6, and 7, the article *the* modifies a noun being used as a possessive adjective. Although functioning as adjectives, these nouns retain their noun properties and can be modified by adjectives.

6. San Marino, which occupies a mountain in central Italy, is the world's oldest republic.

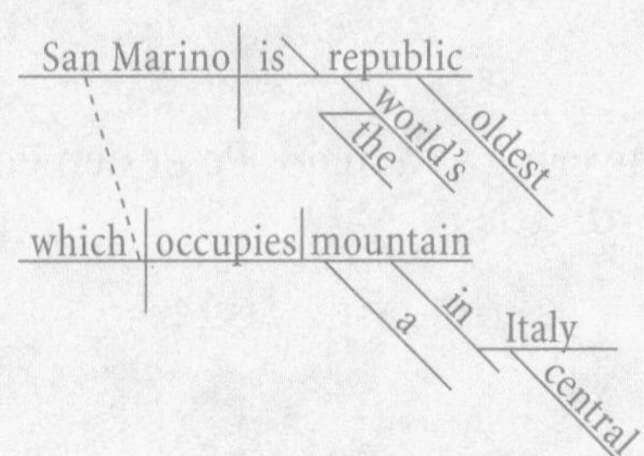

7. El Salvador is the Western Hemisphere's smallest country that is not an island.

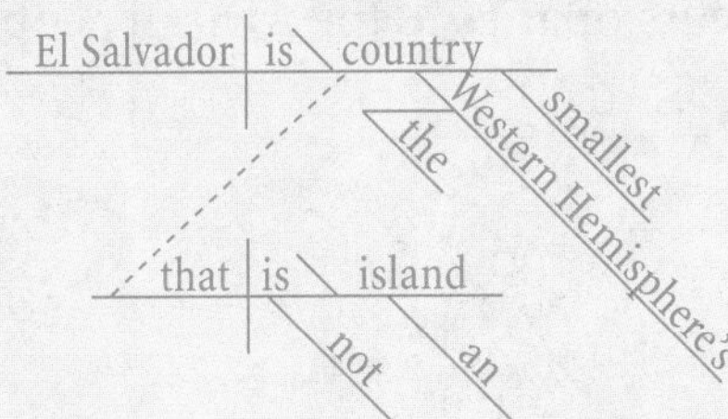

8. The Bahamas, whose economy depends largely on tourism, comprises a chain of small islands near Cuba.

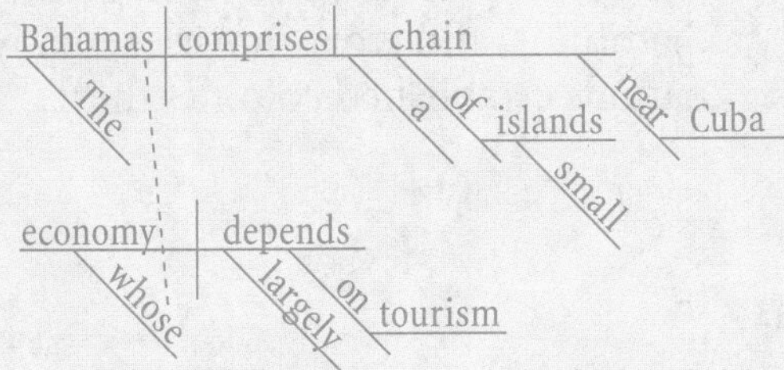

Page 135, Ex. B (Ex. A, 1–6, Page 133)

1. Arthur was the only one that could pull the sword from the stone.

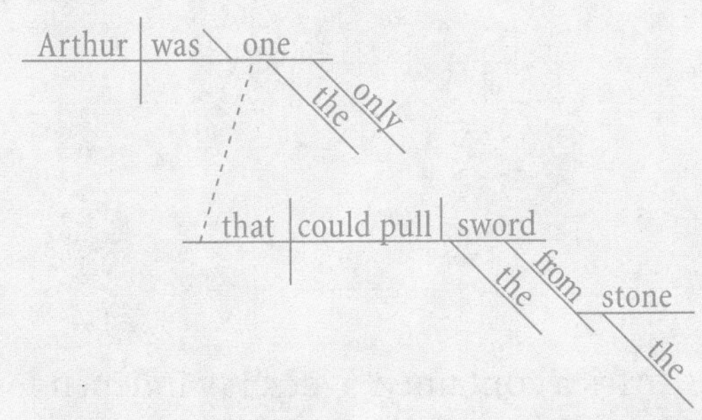

2. The person who is elected to this office will represent our class at the council meeting.

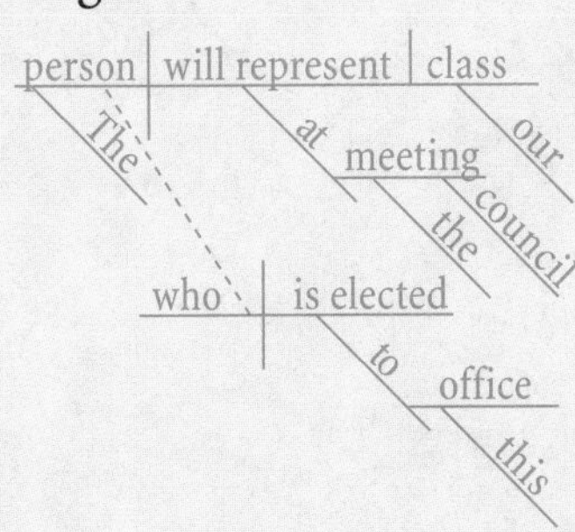

3. Andrew Jackson is the President whom we studied today.

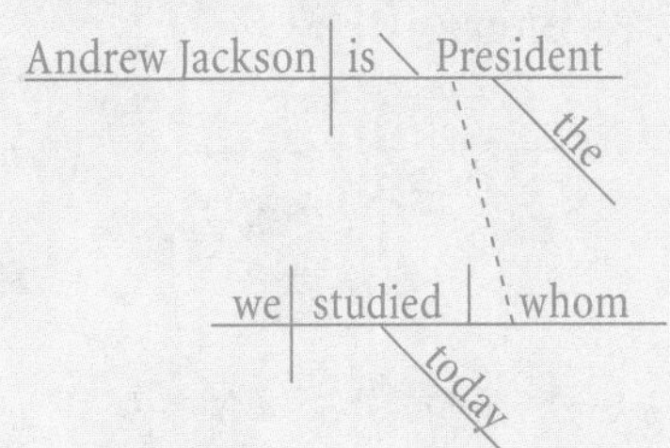

4. The incandescent light bulb is an invention that revolutionized our nation.

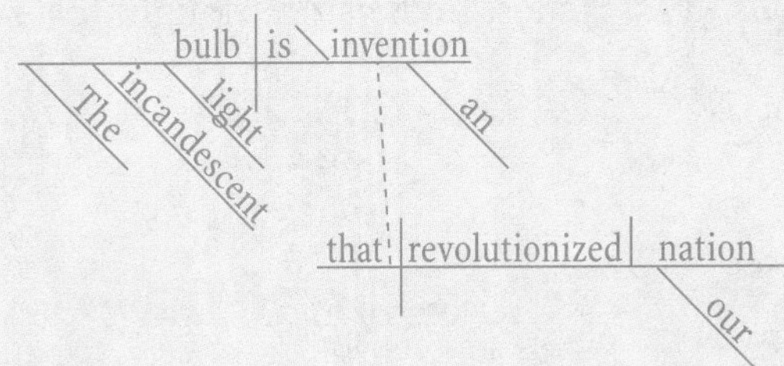

5. South Carolina was the first state which seceded from the Union.

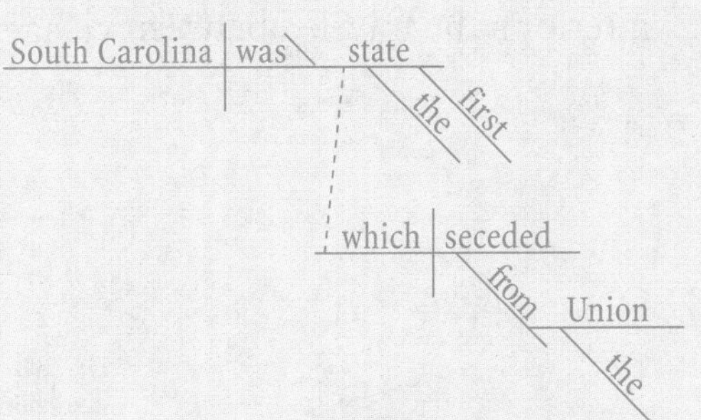

6. Mr. Foxhall is the gentleman with whom we made the agreement.

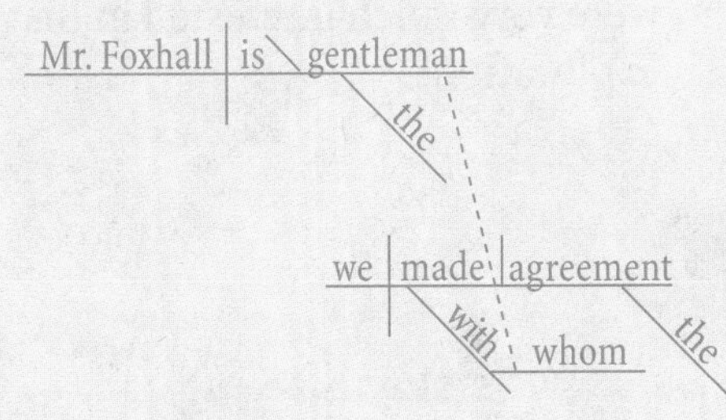

Supplement

Page 163, Ex. A

1. When David Livingstone went to Africa in 1841, few Europeans had penetrated Africa's interior.

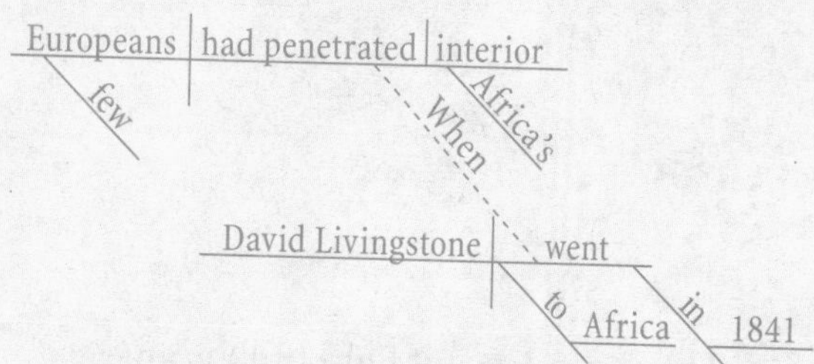

2. While many Europeans desired Africa's vast riches, Livingstone sought lost souls.

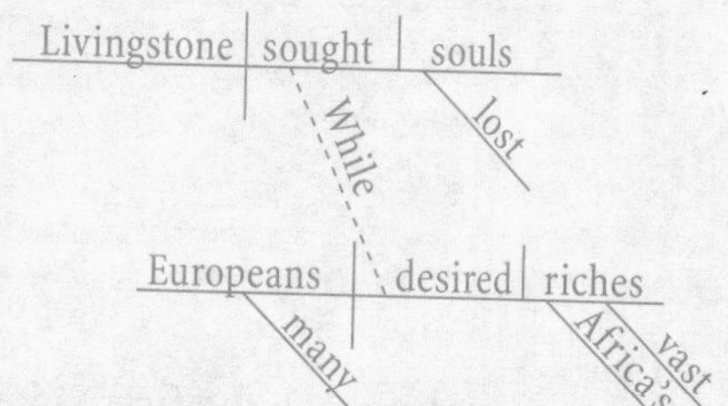

3. Livingstone thoroughly explored Africa's interior as he traveled between villages.

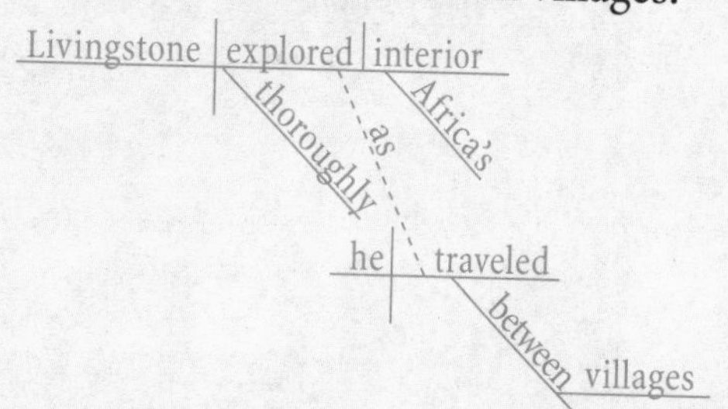

4. Many newspapers wrote stories about Livingstone's travels because Europeans were very much interested in his explorations.

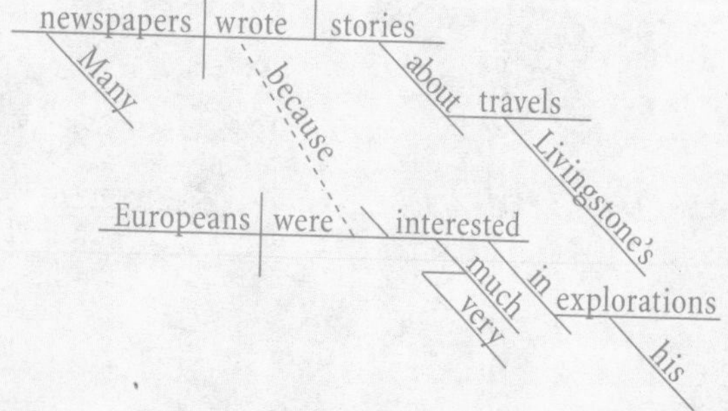

5. Soon many Europeans went to Africa for wealth, although others became missionaries to the African people.

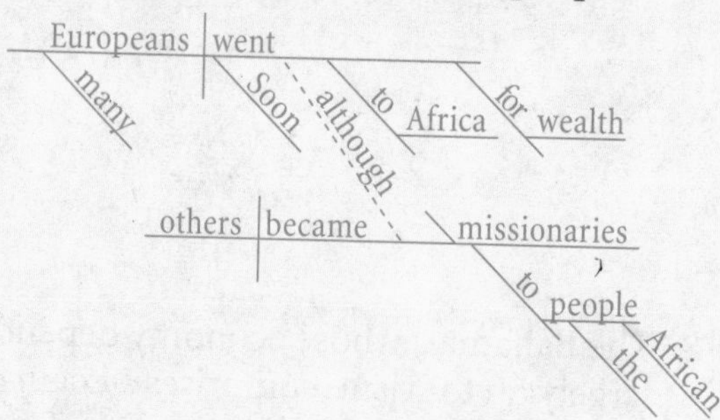

6. Because explorers discovered gold, diamonds, and ivory in Africa, many nations established colonies there.

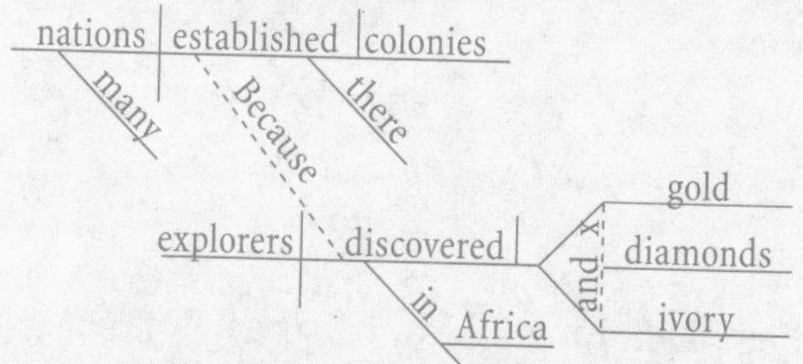

7. After World War II ended, many of these colonies became independent nations.

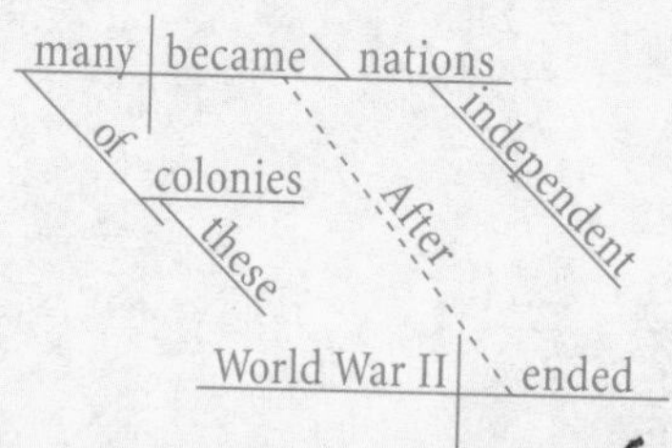

8. Africa contained over sixty independent countries before the twentieth century closed.

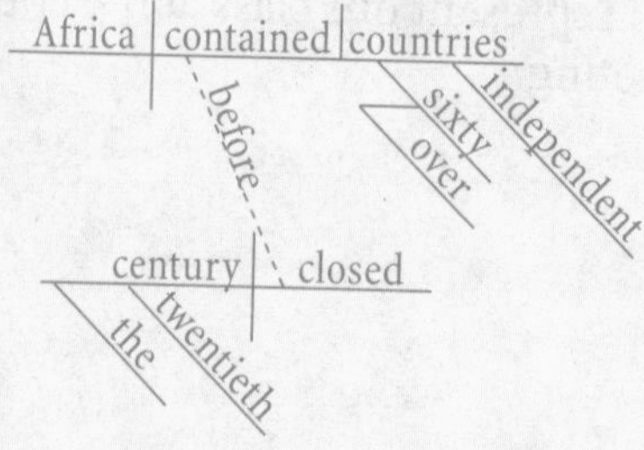

Page 163, Ex. B (Ex. B, 1–6, Page 162)

1. Although everything seemed calm, we were actually in the eye of a hurricane.

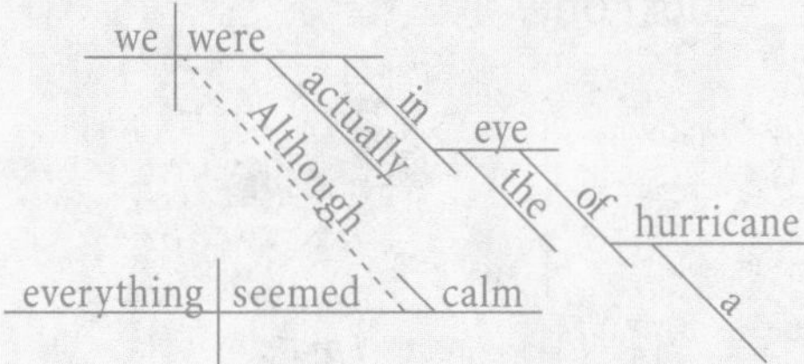

2. Moses could not enter the Promised Land because he had disobeyed God.

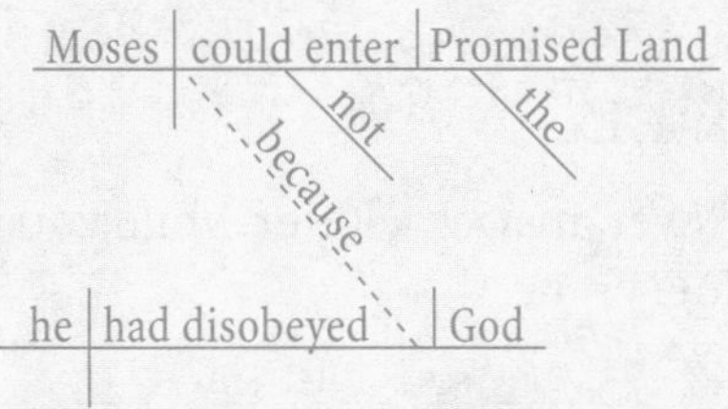

3. The teacher, when he had received the homework, resumed his lecture.

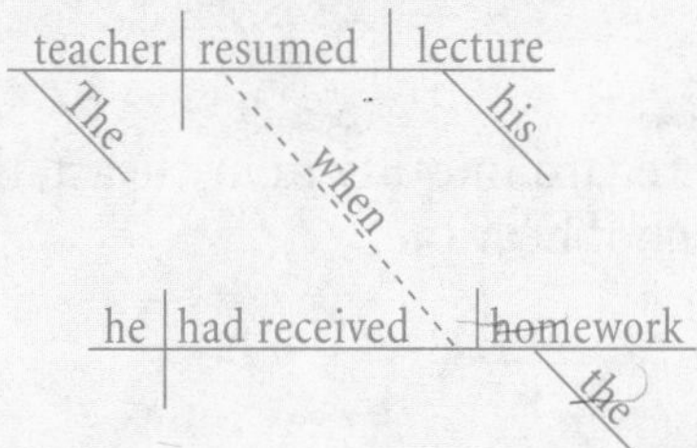

4. Because it has no outlet, the Dead Sea has a large concentration of salt.

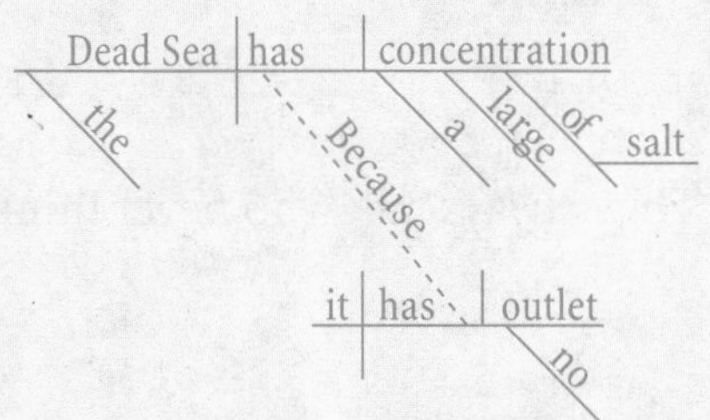

5. The nation expressed deep sorrow when President Lincoln died.

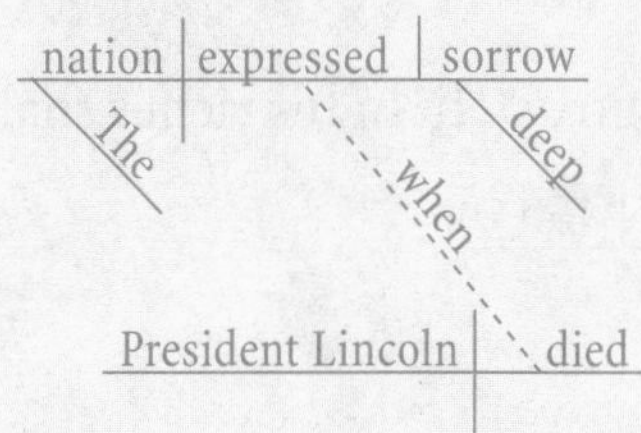

6. Katherine was working so that she could go to college.

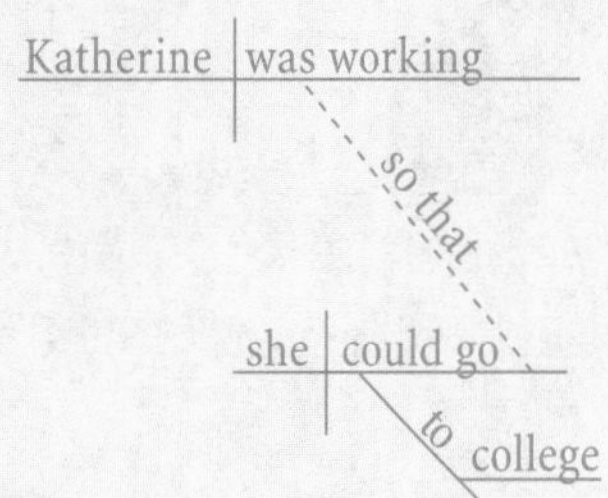

Page 192, Ex.

1. Jules Verne wrote novels, but he did not write poetry.

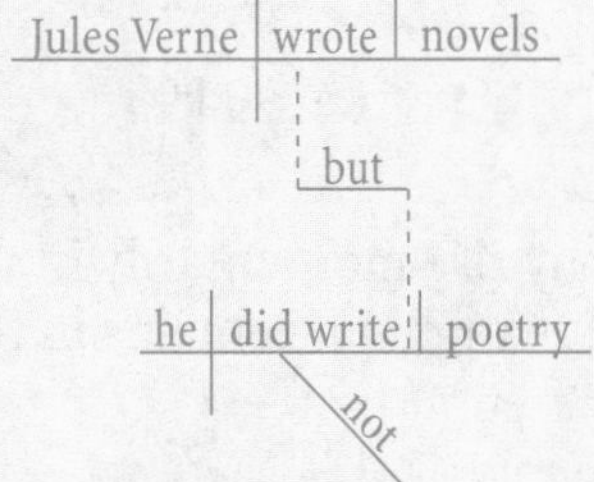

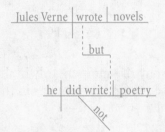

2. Schubert was a German composer; Goethe was a German writer.

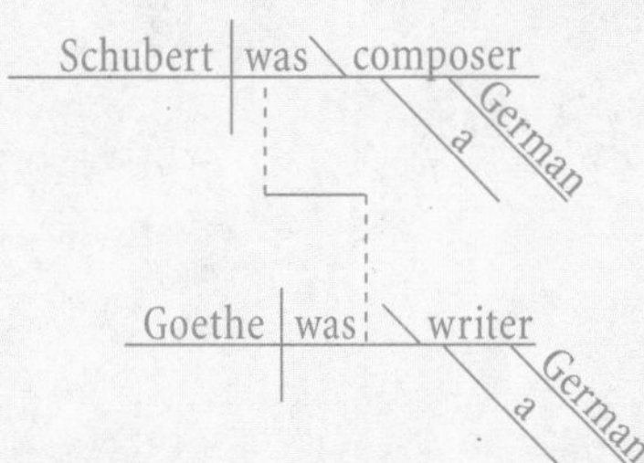

3. The eyes of the Lord preserve knowledge, and He overthroweth the words of the transgressor.

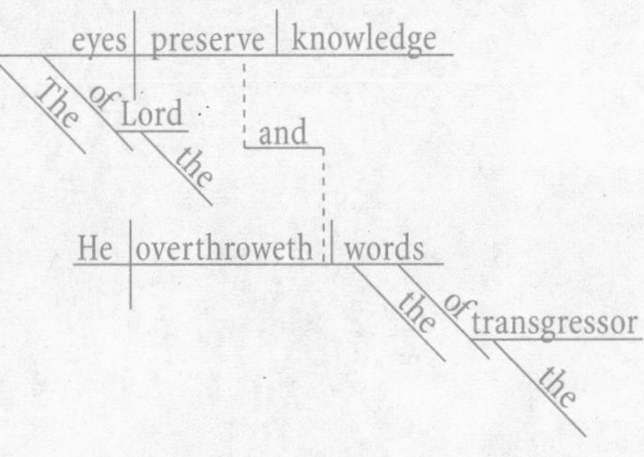

Page 192, Ex. cont.

4. People ask you for criticism, but they only want praise.

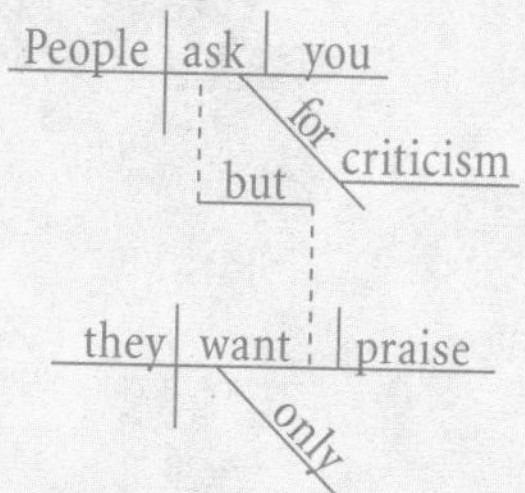

5. Idleness is death; activity is life.

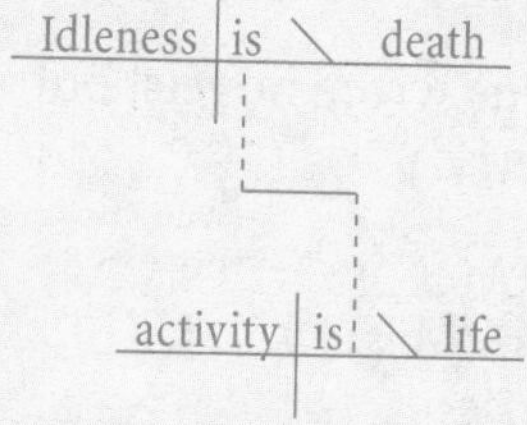

6. Anger may rise momentarily in the heart of a wise man, but it remains in the heart of a fool.

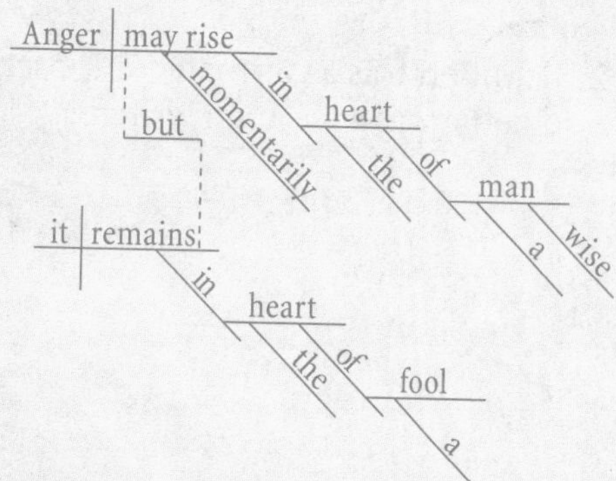

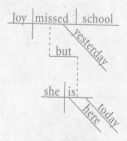

7. Joy missed school yesterday, but she is here today.

Joy
missed
school
yesterday
but
she
is
here
today

8. I read *Little Women* for my last book report, and I may read *Little Men* for my next one.

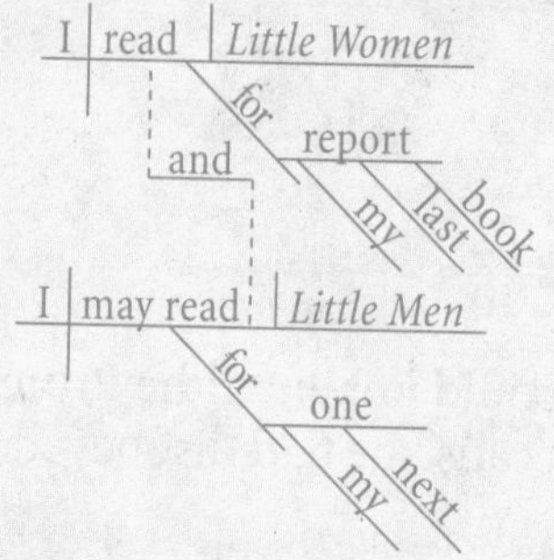

Page 194, Ex.

1. Never answer a letter while you are angry.

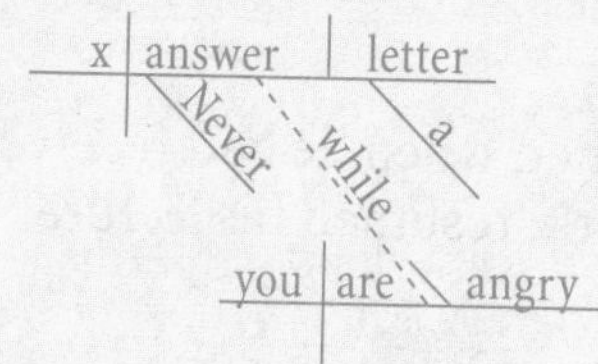

2. If I regard iniquity in my heart, the Lord will not hear me.

Lord
will hear
me
the
not
If
I
regard
iniquity
in
heart
my

3. They always talk who never think.

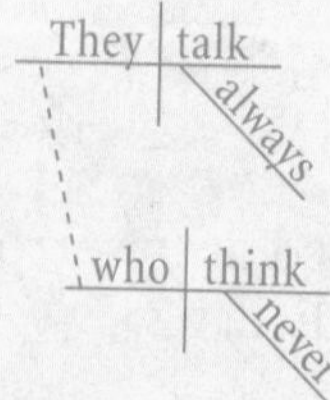

4. He that trusteth in his riches shall fall.

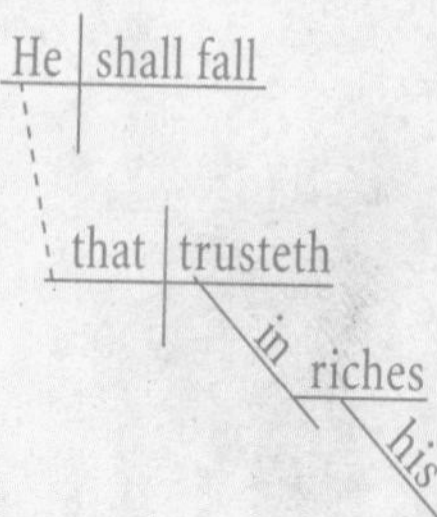

5. If a man love Me, he will keep My words.

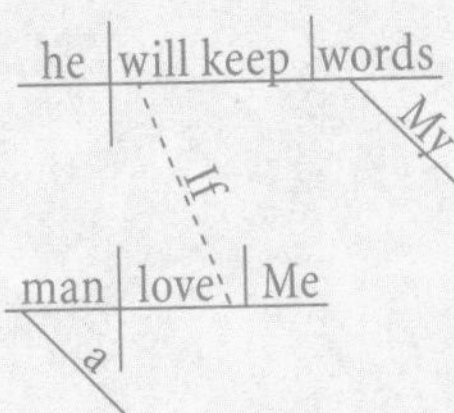

6. They that sow in tears shall reap in joy.

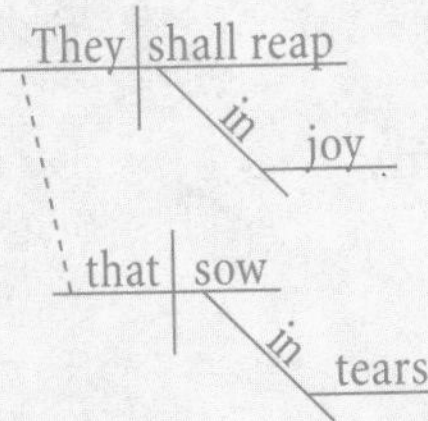

7. Happy is that people whose God is the Lord.

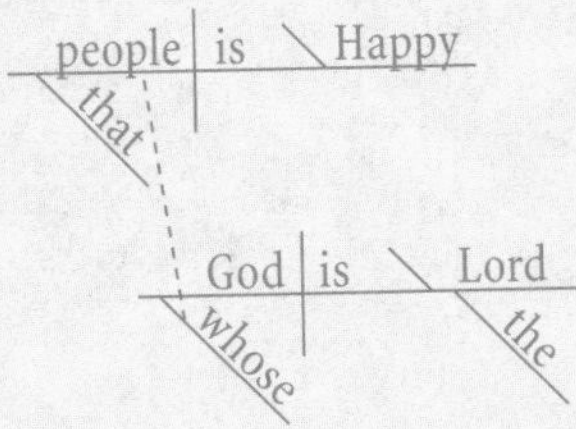

8. He who would be famous must be a hard worker while he is obscure.

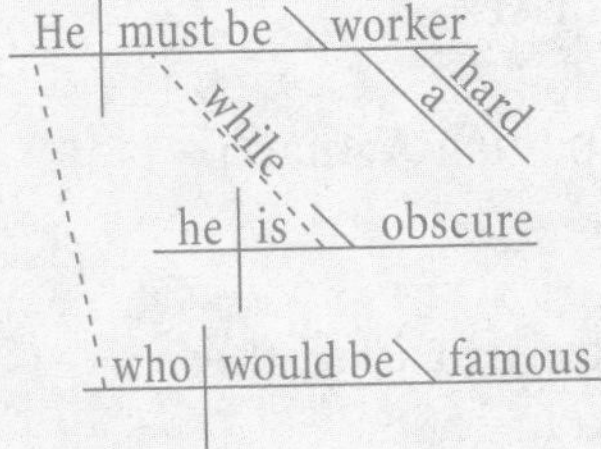

Page 196, Ex.

1. The auditorium was empty when the first guests arrived; after a few minutes, the auditorium became full.

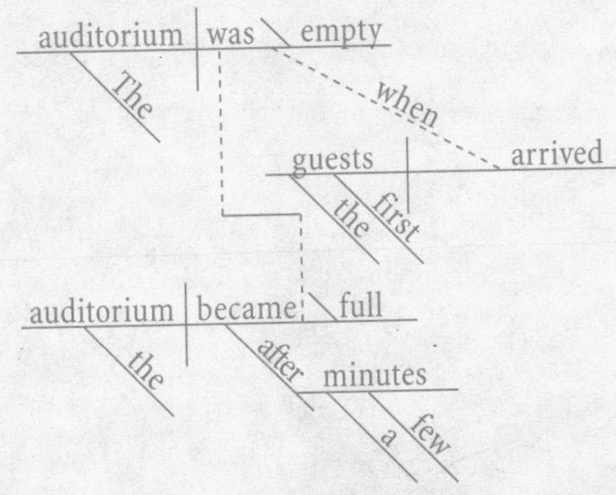

2. Everyone that asketh receiveth, and he that seeketh findeth.

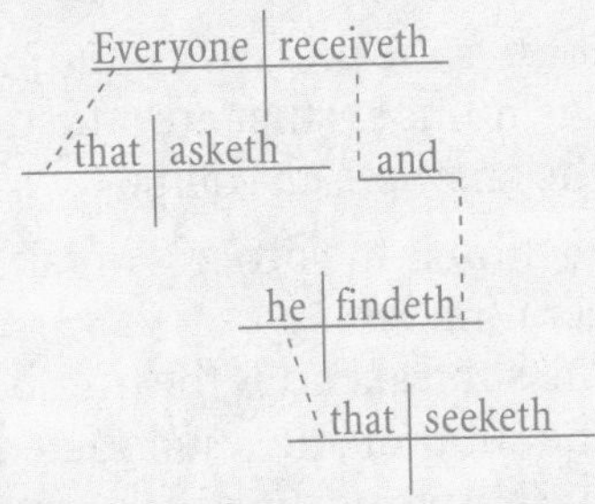

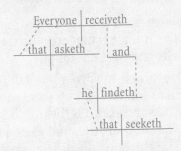

3. The crepe myrtles which bloom in Florida in June are lovely, but the spring azaleas are my favorite.

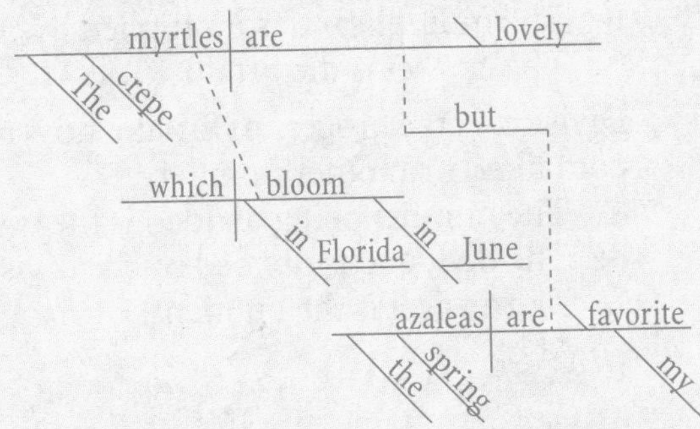

4. Our house was the right size for our family when my father built it, but now we must move to a larger home.

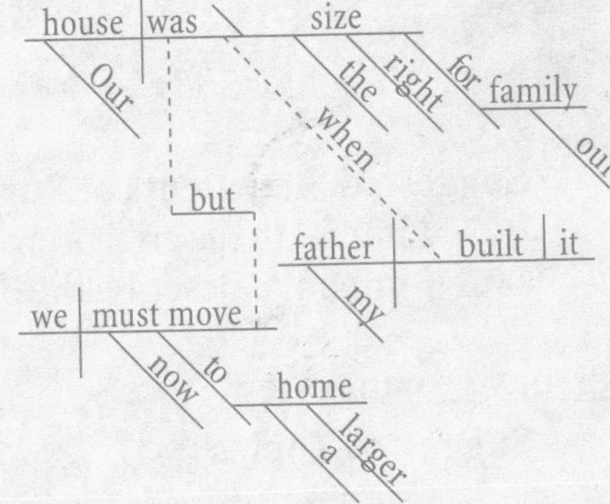

Supplement

Page 225, Ex. B

Sentence Outline

Basic Mathematics

I. Addition is the process of putting like numbers together.
   A. The numbers that are added together are called addends.
   B. The answer is the sum.

II. Subtraction is the process of taking a smaller number away from a larger number.
   A. The subtrahend is the number being subtracted.
   B. The subtrahend is subtracted from the minuend.
   C. The answer is the difference.

III. Multiplication is the process of adding one number to itself as many times as there are units in another.
   A. The number being multiplied is the multiplicand.
   B. The multiplicand is multiplied by the multiplier.
   C. The answer is the product.

IV. Division is the process of finding how many times one number is contained in another number.
   A. The number being divided is the dividend.
   B. The dividend is divided by the divisor.
   C. The answer is the quotient.

Page 243, Ex. A

Informative paper

•Suggested Topics

1. Storms
2. Ants
3. A Healthy Body
4. The Birth of Christ
5. Martin Luther
6. Defeat of the Spanish Armada

• Suggested Statements of Purpose

1. I intend to describe four major kinds of storms and the causes of them.
2. I intend to describe the defeat of the Spanish Armada in 1588.

Persuasive paper

• Suggested Topics

1. Communism
2. Evolution
3. Nuclear Defenses
4. Home Schooling
5. Global Warming
6. Seatbelt Use

• **Suggested Thesis Statements and Outlines**

1. Thesis: Communism still poses a threat to the free world.
   I. Communism is alive and well in many countries.
      A. Red China remains a powerful foe of freedom in Asia.
      B. South Africa and other African nations continue to struggle with Communism.
      C. Russia and Eastern Europe are still under the influence of Communists.
   II. The long-term goal of Communism is still a worldwide Communist revolution.
      A. Communist leaders admit that the ultimate goal of Communism is to dominate the world.
      B. Communists continue their diligent work of subverting free nations in order to spread the revolution.

2. Thesis: Evolution is a matter of faith not science.
   I. Science deals with conditions that can be observed, tested, and repeated (the scientific method).
      A. Science is the study of God's creation and of the God-ordained laws that govern it.
      B. Observation and experimentation are possible in truly scientific fields.
   II. Evolution is not based on true science.
      A. The claims of evolutionists are not verifiable.
      B. Much scientific evidence contradicts evolution.
   III. Evolution is based on faith.
      A. Evolutionists put their faith in materialism.
      B. Evolutionists choose to believe in evolution because the alternative is to believe in Creation.

Page 246, Ex. C

1. *Rose, Norman. Churchill: The Unruly Giant. New York: The Free Press, 1995.*

   DA 566.9.C5.R66.1995.

2. *O'Reilly, Don. "The Maid of New Orleans." Military History, Apr. 1998, 22-30.*

3. *Libert, A. "Chapter 5: The Battle of Waterloo." 1996. <http://www.ping.be/napolean.series/100 days/chap 5.ntml> (accessed today's date).*

4. *Dobyns, Henry F. "Pima Indians." The World Book Encyclopedia, 1996 ed.*

Page 283, Ex. K

1. Alexander conquered the world of his day, yet he never conquered his own passions.

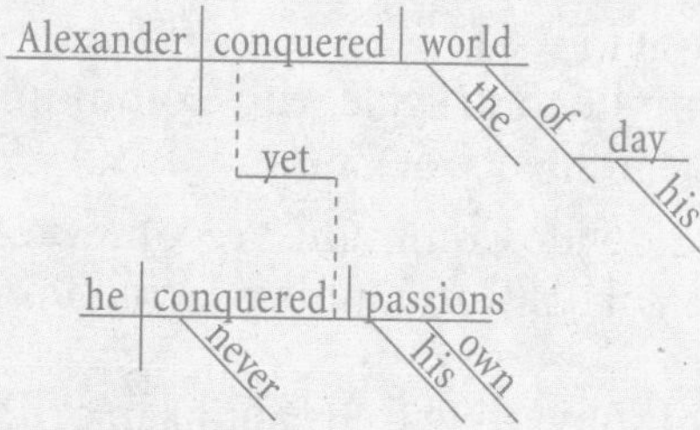

2. If wishes were horses, beggars would ride.

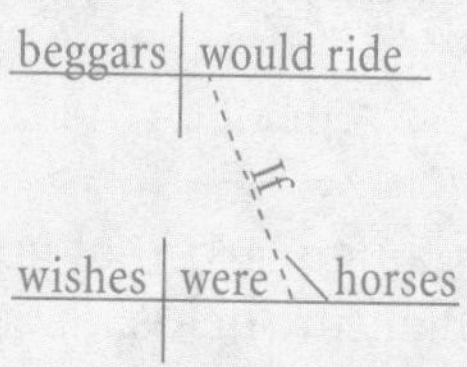

3. Remember not the sins of my youth nor my transgressions.

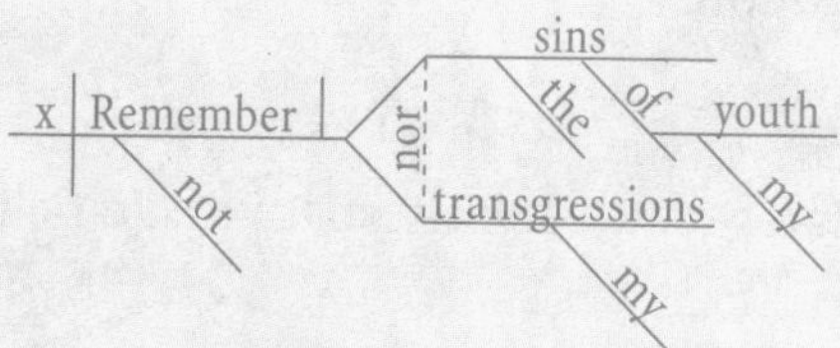

4. He that winneth souls is wise.

He | is \ wise

that | winneth | souls

5. Walking along the mountain trail, I could see the small cabin in the distance.

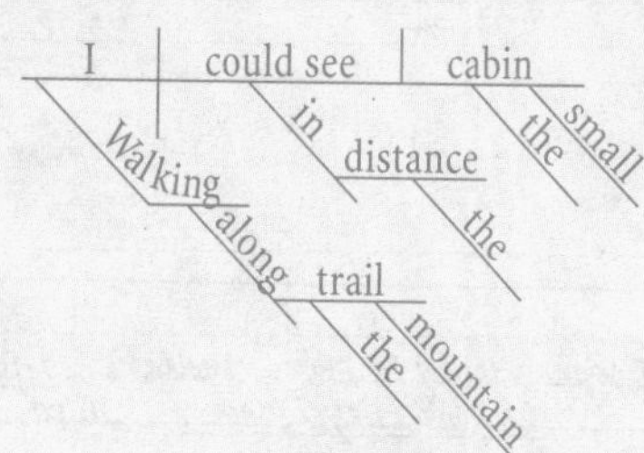

6. The desire of the righteous is only good, but the expectation of the wicked is wrath.

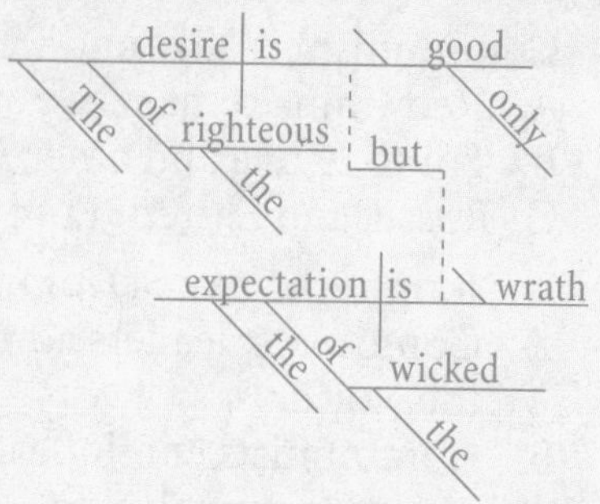

7. The Lord turned the captivity of Job, when he prayed for his friends.

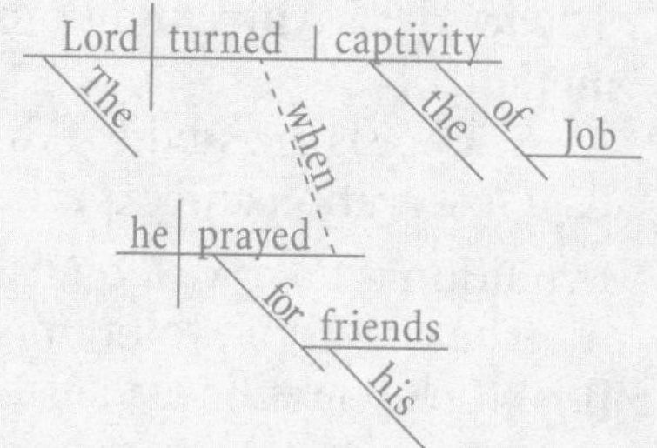

8. The printing press is one lever which moves the mind of the world.

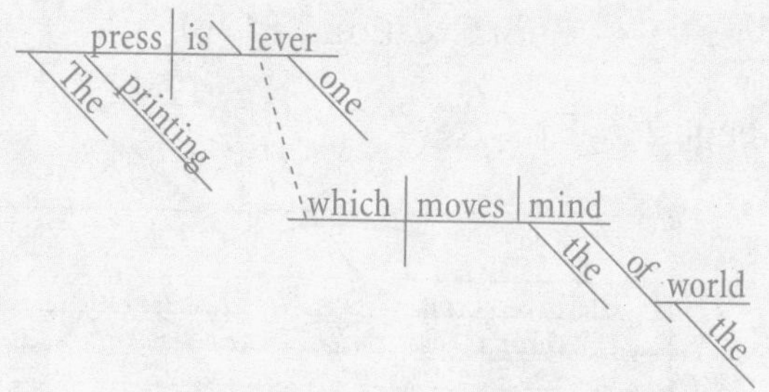

9. They that trust in the Lord shall be as Mount Zion which cannot be moved.

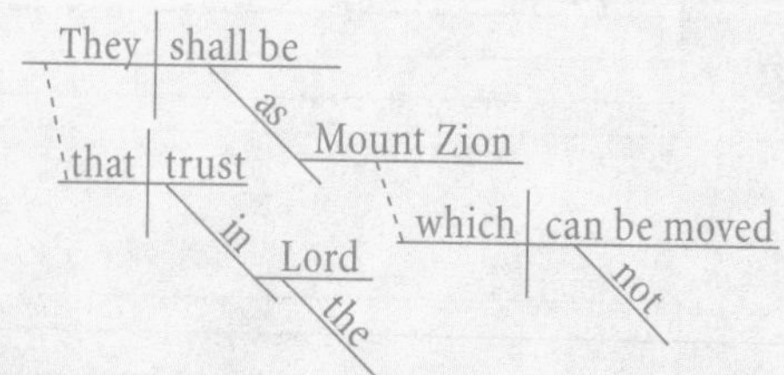

10. Thy word is a lamp unto my feet and a light unto my path.

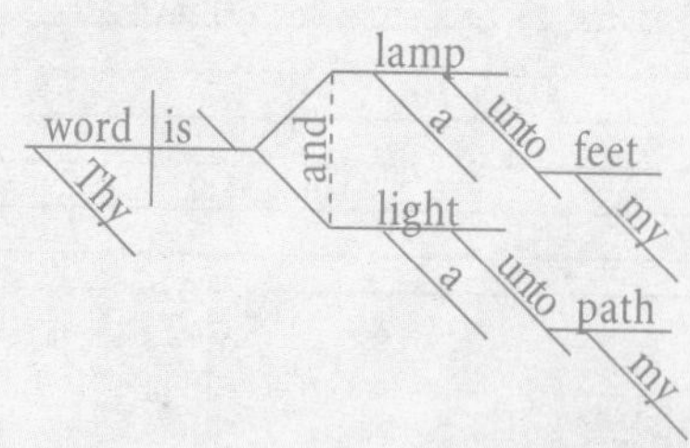